W9-BEP-127

THE
IRISH
EXPERIENCE

ATLANTIC
OCEAN

North Channel

Lough Foyle

(London-
Derry derry)
LONDONDERRY

Lifford

DONEGAL

ULSTER

Strabane

ANTRIM

*Donegal
Bay*

TYRONE

*Lough
Neagh*

Belfast

FERMANAGH

ARMAGH

DOWN

Sligo

LEITRIM

MONAGHAN

SLIGO

CAVAN

Dundalk

Irish

MAYO

Carrick

LONGFORD

LOUTH

Sea

Westport

CONNAUGHT

ROSCOMMON

WESTMEATH

MEATH

Drogheda

GALWAY

Galway

OFFALY

KILDARE

DUBLIN

Dublin

ARAN IS.

R. Shannon

LEINSTER

Wicklow

CLARE

LAOIGHIS

WICKLOW

Shannon

TIPPERARY

KILKENNY

CARLOW

Limerick

Kilkenny

LIMERICK

Tipperary

WEXFORD

Tralee

KERRY

Killarney

WATERFORD

Wexford

Dingle Bay

MUNSTER

CORK

Cork

Waterford

Youghal

St. George's Channel

Cobh

Bantry Bay

IRELAND

| 0 | 25 | 50 | 75 | 100 |

MILES

—— NORTHERN IRELAND (U.K.)
···········
—— REPUBLIC OF IRELAND

SCOTLAND

IRELAND

ENGLAND

WALES

FRANCE

THE
IRISH
EXPERIENCE

A Concise History

Thomas E. Hachey, Joseph M. Hernon, Jr.,
and Lawrence J. McCaffrey

Revised Edition

M.E. Sharpe
Armonk, New York
London, England

Library of Congress Cataloging-in-Publication Data

Hachey, Thomas E.
The Irish experience : a concise history / Thomas E. Hachey, Joseph M. Hernon, Jr.,
and Lawrence J. McCaffrey.—Rev. ed.
p.   cm.
Includes bibliographical references and index.
ISBN 1-56324-791-7 (hardcover : alk. paper).—
ISBN 1-56324-792-5 (pbk. : alk. paper)
1. Ireland—History.
I. Hernon, Joseph M.
II. McCaffrey, Lawrence John, 1925–
III. Title.
DA910.H33   1996
941.5—dc20
96-7644
CIP

Printed in the United States of America

The paper used in this publication meets the minimum requirements of the
American National Standard for Information Sciences—
Permanence of Paper for Printed Library Materials,
ANSI Z 39.48-1984.

QP (c)   10   9   8   7   6   5   4   3   2   1
QP (p)   10   9   8   7   6

TO OUR STUDENTS AND COLLEAGUES
IN IRISH STUDIES

Contents

Preface

"Some nations, like the Irish, are *too* historically minded, in the sense that they cannot get out of the past at all," observed the twentieth-century English historian G. M. Trevelyan. But his friend and countryman, G. M. Young, in his now classic *Victorian England: Portrait of an Age* (1936), called English policy in Ireland "the one irreparable disaster of [English] history" and concluded that what England "could never remember, Ireland could never forget." And how true both statements are for the "losers" and "winners" in various stages of history, for the diverse array of small nations and the domineering great powers, for the pessimists and the optimists in history. One can view Irish history from the perspective of the Anglo-Irish stage as the beginning and the end of English colonialism. But *The Irish Experience* is much broader than that and ultimately and ironically a microcosm of the human experience.

Indeed, the reader will discover that it is very difficult over the centuries to define an "Irishman" in an ethnic, racial, or religious sense. And it is equally difficult to ponder "the Irish question" for, as various wits have noted, every time one gets the answer, the Irish change the question. At various times the answer has been religious, economic, political, geographic, and even psychological.

While reflecting on Irish history, one must confess, as did James Joyce in *Ulysses*: "History is a nightmare from which I am trying to awake." And so much of Irish history reads like a Greek tragedy that the reader must also agree with Joyce in *Portrait of the Artist as a Young Man*: "Ireland is the old sow that eats her farrow." Moreover, it is difficult to view much of Irish history after the Anglo-Norman Conquest other than, in Joyce's words, through "the cracked looking glass of a servant."

Nevertheless, the authors of this text will attempt the impossible: to paint an artistic and insightful portrait of a broad expanse of Irish history. We confess our limitations with Oscar Wilde's remark: "Anybody can make history. Only a great man can write it." But we also accept our professional obligations with Wilde's irreverent but subtly sophisticated observation, "The one duty we owe to history is to re-write it."

We hope that our historical hindsight merits a high rating, but we know that our historical looking glasses have their own imperfections. We can only hope that to some small degree in *The Irish Experience* we approach the ideal of the artist-historian about whom Joyce wrote in *Portrait*: "The artist, like the God of the creation, remains within or behind or beyond or above his handiwork, invisible, refined out of existence, indifferent, paring his fingernails."

Finally, for the second edition of *The Irish Experience,* we have brought the narrative forward from 1988 to 1996. Moreover, pertinent studies that have been published during that eight-year time frame have been included in an expanded "Recommended Readings" section. We wish to thank Dr. Catherine Flanagan for her timely and welcome assistance in the preparation of this new edition. Most particularly, we want to express our appreciation to those who have bought and used the book since it was first published in 1989. Your comments and suggestions, always most welcome, will be our guide in the preparation of yet the next edition.

AUTHORS' NOTE

Since this volume is a synthesis of Irish studies scholarship as well as an interpretation of the Irish historical experience and precludes the use of footnotes, we would like to acknowledge our debt to those whose work made our effort possible. We have tried to credit their contributions in the Recommended Reading section. It is as much a long footnote as it is a bibliography.

Thomas E. Hachey
Joseph M. Hernon, Jr.
Lawrence J. McCaffrey

The Irish
Experience

PART I   *From Cuchulain to*
     O'Connell, 200 B.C.–A.D. *1800*
by Joseph M. Hernon, Jr.

CHAPTER 1

Celtic, Christian, and Scandinavian Ireland, 200 B.C.–A.D. 1170

"Lord, how quickly doth that country alter one's nature!" wrote the Elizabethan poet Edmund Spenser about his life in Ireland as one of the "New English" adventurers of the sixteenth century. And the physical geography of the "Emerald Isle" for thousands of years has helped to shape human affairs throughout Ireland. Despite its exquisite compactness of almost 33,000 square miles, the island is characterized by great geological and topographical diversity. Its geography, like its history, cannot be easily simplified and mystifies the outsider.

THE ROLE OF GEOGRAPHY IN IRISH HISTORY

Ireland's geography helps to explain why it has never been completely conquered and why "divide and rule" has often been the only way to govern the island. Though generally saucer-shaped with mountainous uplands around the rim, this ring of uplands is broken in many places, often ending in spectacular sea-cliffs. Though it has a large, flat heartland, the multiplicity of lakes and bogs has hindered movement there and prevented central Ireland from becoming a center of political power.

Indeed, if would-be conquerors and writers have found Ireland an intellectual cul-de-sac, the island is geographically and politically a series of cul-de-sacs, each with its separate uplands and lowlands and its individually distinctive culture. The fragmented geography of Ireland helps to explain its cultural diversity as it has discouraged political unity over the centuries.

One area that receives less rain and contains less bog and fewer mountains has played a conspicuous role in Irish history. It is the "Eastern Triangle," its base extending from the Wicklow Mountains just south of Dublin Bay, north a little over 50 miles to the town and port of Dundalk. The sides of the rough isosceles triangle then go inland to Lough Owel, near present-day Mullingar, County Westmeath. This triangle of territory, largely "Royal Meath," is one of the most vulnerable to outside invaders because of a long break in the chain of mountains and the rivers Liffey and Boyne leading inland. But more than any other area it has dominated the rest of the island. It contains Dublin, the capital; Newgrange, the prehistoric site; Tara, seat of the high kings and later associated with the "Croppies" of 1798 and O'Connell in 1843; the site of the *Book of Kells;* Maynooth, seat of the earls of Kildare; and the site of the decisive Battle of the Boyne.

This triangle contains some of the earliest settlements in Ireland. The burial chambers at Newgrange, Knowth, and Dowth in the Boyne valley date from the third millennium B.C. The tomb at Newgrange is built with an opening over the entrance that permits the rising sun on a midwinter's day to shine through a 60-foot passage on a stone at the end of the burial chamber. We can only speculate how this structure relates to the religious beliefs of the builders, who lived perhaps as much as a thousand years before Stonehenge.

THE IMPORTANCE OF CELTIC MYTH

One of the most famous early Celtic sites is Emain Macha in County Armagh. This pagan capital of Ulster is the setting for some of the episodes in the Irish *Iliad,* the Gaelic epic known as *Tain Bo Cuailnge* (The Cattle Raid at Cooley). The Ulster saga features its great hero, Cuchulain, known for his savage strength. Cuchulain killed one opponent as his sword "struck down through the crown of his head and split him to the navel." Patrick Pearse, leader of the Easter Rising of 1916, would later transform the dying Cuchulain into a Christian martyr using the hero's words to inspire the boys at Pearse's St. Enda's school: "Though I live but a year and a day, I will live so that my name goes sounding down the ages." This saga and the Fenian epics would inspire modern Irish nationalism.

Yet these mythological stories have a basis in fact in early Celtic society. Emain Macha is identified as the city of Isamnion on a map of Ireland drafted by Ptolemy of Alexandria in the second century A.D. According to folk tales, this royal site of Queen Macha—a Celtic goddess—was founded in the third century B.C. and was reportedly abandoned following its destruction by men from Connacht (such as the soldiers of Queen Maeve in the *Tain*) in A.D. 332. But recent archaeological research suggests the first use of the site in the seventh century B.C. and destruction and abandonment as early as the second century B.C.

This speculative analysis does, however, offer insights into the blending together of the prehistoric and pre-Celtic with early Celtic and Christian history. Perhaps there were substantial Celtic settlements in Ireland earlier than is generally thought. But one fact is clear. The enduring fame of Emain Macha as late as the time of Saint Patrick led him about A.D. 444 to choose Armagh (literally Ard Mhacha, or Macha's Height), a twin hill barely 2 miles from the ancient ruins, as the site for his principal church in Ireland. So Armagh, the primatial see of Christianity in Ireland, commemorates the memory of the Celtic goddess Macha.

THE CELTICIZATION OF IRELAND

Speculative is the only word to describe the process of the Celticization of Ireland. Indeed, the population over thousands of years can be playfully compared to one huge Irish stew, slowly stirred, with new ingredients added every few centuries according to no known recipe. Elements of Celtic civilization can be dated from the third century B.C., when the Celts fled the conquering Romans, whose empire spread as far as England. But it is difficult to assert that a Celtic type of language flourished throughout Ireland even by the first century A.D.

Celtic society was organized along tribal lines with as many as 150 *tuatha* or tribes in early historic Ireland. Each *tuath* was headed by a *ri* ("king" or "chief"), but there was no larger organization except loose and volatile alliances negotiated by the individual kings. Occasionally, claims to be Ard-Ri ("high king") were asserted by various kings, usually to little effect, though some were crowned in sacred rites at Tara, the traditional seat of the Ard-Ri.

Each *tuath* was organized along communal lines. There were also *tuatha* who were not free who lived in a depressed state as slaves of the upper class of a dominant *tuath*. Individual rights were protected only in relation to the joint family or the common interests of the *tuath*. Wealth, as in the epic *Tain,* was generally determined by the possession of cattle. Capital punishment was rare; arbitration and fines were stressed, and it was up to the *tuath* to avenge the murder of one of its own. Though the Celtic *tuatha* had druids (priests) and brehons (jurists to interpret the law), it was the *fili* (poet) who was of special significance, particularly the *ollamh* (the highest level of poet). These poets played the roles of sage, prophet, and historian for the *tuath*. The *ollamh* had the legal status of a *ri*. He could glorify heroes, or his satirical verse could humiliate individuals and even depose kings. It was no accident that poets, poetry, and satire would play such an important role in later Irish history.

THE COMING OF CHRISTIANITY TO IRELAND

Celtic society, however, would soon be transformed by the arrival of Christianity. It would liberate people in the lower orders of the *tuatha* and afford them upward mobility through education and by overriding class restrictions. The Irish celebrate the beginning of Christianity with the arrival of Saint Patrick in A.D. 432, though a chronicle reports that the pope sent Palladius in 431 to be the "first bishop of the Irish Christians." Another document, the *Confession* of Saint Patrick, describes how he baptized many thousands. The son of a Roman official in Britain, as a teenager he was taken captive in an Irish raid and for six years was a slave-herdsman in Ireland. During his captivity, he became a Christian convert and resolved to devote his life to God's service. After escaping, he returned to Ireland years later as a bishop to ordain and baptize. The process of conversion spread gradually and incorporated many pagan Celtic practices into Christianity.

For example, the cult of Saint Brigid, the Mary of the Gael, is built on one of the important Celtic goddesses with the same name, meaning "the high one." She was the patron of poetry, music, and especially fertility. Saint Brigid's *Life* is the oldest account of an Irish saint, written in the middle of the seventh century by Cogitosus of Kildare (Brigid's city), where the Church of Saint Brigid was a double monastery with one section for nuns and another for monks. The monastery may have been ruled by a female bishop who later became an abbess with a male coadjutor bishop as her assistant. Saint Brigid's feast day was celebrated on February 1, the old Celtic feast of Imbolc, which, stressing fertility, marked the "beginning of the lactation of the ewes."

Other Celtic festivals were incorporated into the Christian calendar such as Samhain, on November 1, the festival of the dead near the beginning of winter with the rituals of Halloween. It became All Saints' Day, followed by All Souls' Day on November 2.

Christian monasticism began to flourish in Ireland in the sixth century, largely in its harsher Middle Eastern, as opposed to laxer Continental, form. It stressed an ascetic life with extreme mortification of the flesh and individual sanctity. But evangelism would soon become a major trademark of Irish monasticism as Irish missionaries established religious houses in Britain and throughout Europe.

THE FIRST MISSIONARIES FROM IRELAND

Saint Columba, the first important missionary to leave Ireland, sailed in 563 with twelve disciples to found a monastery on the small island of Iona off the west coast of Scotland. Today the religious center of the world's Presbyterians, Iona became the mother of monasteries in Scotland and the traditional burial site of her kings, including Duncan and Macbeth. And one of Columba's disciples, Saint Aidan, founded the great English monastery at Lindesfarne, Northumberland, where the Venerable Bede wrote his *Ecclesiastical History*.

Though Saint Brendan of Clonfert, who died in 578, reached North America according to medieval legend, it was the far-flung mission of Saint Columbanus, begun about 590, that had the most lasting results. Coming from a monastery at Bangor on the south shore of Belfast Lough, he founded a great monastery at Luxeuil in France and one at Bobbio in northern Italy, where he lies buried. In themes that would be echoed many centuries later, he boasted that among the

"Irish, living at the edge of the world, followers of Saints Peter and Paul—there has never been a heretic or a schismatic." He warned one pope not to allow "the head of the church to be turned into its tail . . . for in Ireland it is not a man's position but his principles that count."

The most famous disciple of Columbanus was Saint Gall, who carried the Gospel to Switzerland. Irish monasteries and religious houses were especially evident in the Low Countries and northeastern France and were also established in Cologne, Würzburg, Regensburg, Vienna, and Lucca. In the eighth century, Saint Vergilius preached in Salzburg; and as late as 1049, the Irish monk known as Aaron of Cologne was consecrated archbishop of Cracow.

THE GOLDEN AGE OF IRISH MONASTICISM

In addition, the Isle of Saints had become known as the Isle of Scholars. The English monk Alcuin of York had studied at an Irish monastery (believed to be Clonmacnoise) and became master of the Palace School at the court of Emperor Charlemagne. Many of the leading scholars of the Carolingian renaissance of the ninth century were Irish, such as Sedulius Scotus, an expert on Cicero, who taught at Liège, Metz, and Cologne; and John Scotus Eriugena, the intellectual giant of the age, who joined the Royal School at Laon in the court of Charles the Bald in 845. A superb Latin and Greek scholar but principally a master dialectician, Eriugena was a major influence in the development of medieval mystical thought whose chief work would centuries later be condemned by a pope and a Vatican commission.

During the so-called Dark Ages on the European continent, the words *Scotus* (Irishman) and *scholar* became virtually synonymous. And the great Irish monastic settlements, such as Clonmacnoise on the banks of the Shannon and Glendalough in the Wicklow Mountains south of Dublin, were the equivalent of great university cities, the repositories of the classics of Western civilization. And they would attract many students from Britain and the continent.

This Golden Age of seventh- and eighth-century Irish monasticism is especially remembered for its artwork, particularly its illuminated manuscripts. The most famous is the *Book of Kells*. Now on display in the library of Trinity College, Dublin, the *Book* is a hand-decorated folio manuscript of the four Gospels, with portraits of Christ and the four evangelists, among others, dating from 750 to 800. Originally drawn at the monastery of Iona or possibly Lindisfarne, it was sent to the Monastery of Kells, it is believed, for protection from the Viking raids of the ninth century. With its intricate spiral designs, its Coptic-Egyptian symbols, its intriguing and varied flights of fantasy from page to page and monk-artist to monk-artist, the *Book of Kells* has a unique and unrivaled beauty.

Metalwork also flourished during the eighth century, as evidenced by the Ardagh Chalice, with its curvilinear Celtic designs and masterful interlacing of gold filigree and beautiful engraving and enameling. Perfection in carving displaying an equal amount of whimsy was extended in the early ninth century to stone sculpture, particularly the large Celtic crosses known for their astonishing workmanship.

The best-preserved Celtic cross dates from the early tenth century: Muiredach's Cross at Monasterboice, County Louth. It is massive and nearly 18 feet tall, with the Crucifixion and scenes from the life of Christ on the east face and the Last Judgment and scenes from the Old Testament on the west. As in the *Book of Kells,* there are Coptic echoes in the Osirian appearance of Christ; but Viking-type swords can be seen on the panel portraying the arrest of Christ.

ARRIVAL OF THE VIKINGS

The Vikings first attacked Ireland in A.D. 795, on the isle of Lambay, off Dublin Bay. The early Vikings came from the fjord country of western Norway (later from Denmark and settlements in the Hebrides) and were initially interested in plundering the treasures of the monasteries. But gradually, through the ninth and tenth centuries, the coastal settlements the Vikings established at Dublin, Waterford, Cork, and Limerick became major trading centers with ports in Britain and on the continent. The Dublin Vikings minted the first Irish silver coinage, and the Viking influence came to be seen not only in place names but throughout Irish culture and art.

The first reaction of the monks to the Viking raids can be seen in the more than sixty "round towers" that survive on Irish monastic sites. These tapered bell towers, built of mortared stone, vary in height from 70 to 120 feet. They contained four or five stories and a doorway 10 to 15 feet above the ground that required a ladder to reach. During the raids, the monks hid themselves and their riches in these towers.

From A.D. 900 to 1000 the Vikings began forming alliances with various Irish kings, intermarrying with the Irish, and blending into Irish society. They succeeded in focusing the center of political gravity on the east coast ports, and by the end of the eleventh century, a majority of the Norse-Irish, or Ostmen as they were called, had become Christians with close ties to Canterbury in England.

A FIRST HIGH KING

At the beginning of the eleventh century, Ireland appeared to have found a high king who was truly king of Ireland, Brian Boru. Though he has been romantically portrayed as turning the tide of Scandinavian fury, his rise to power was more complicated. After fighting his way to become king of Munster in 978, by the year 1000 he had conquered Leinster and captured Dublin. He married Gormlaith, mother of Sitric, king of the Dublin Ostmen; and in 1002, Brian was recognized as high king of Ireland, by Malachy, king of Tara, who had been nominal high king since 980. In 1005, Brian Boru visited Armagh, where he confirmed its ecclesiastical supremacy over the Irish church, and his secretary recorded this decision in Latin in the ninth-century *Book of Armagh:* "in conspectu Briani imperatoris Scotorum" (in the presence of Brian, emperor of the Irish).

In 1013 widespread rebellion broke out against Brian throughout Leinster, aided by Gormlaith and Sitric. In the Battle of Clontarf on Good Friday, April 23, 1014, Brian defeated an alliance of Gaelic Leinstermen, Dublin Ostmen, and Norsemen from the Isle of Man and the Orkneys. Though the battle was the final blow to Viking hopes of dominating Ireland, Brian Boru was killed, along with his oldest son, and Ireland was soon back to its infighting and political instability. Until the coming of the Anglo-Normans, most of the remaining high kings would be recorded by chroniclers as "king with opposition."

THE IRISH CHURCH

Nor would the church structure be unified. Even as early as the sixth century, monasteries headed by abbots assumed greater importance than the traditional Roman dioceses governed by bishops appointed by the pope. Over the next few centuries, the monasteries grew in wealth and political power. Some were city-states with their own armies, and some had virtually hereditary abbots, the position passing to nephews or, occasionally, illegitimate sons. Many had lay governors directing the secular side of the monasteries, and most became integrated in local dynastic politics. In any case, from an administrative viewpoint, the structure of the church, like the political structure in Ireland, was chaotic.

The Christian Ostmen, however, living in the coastal towns, increasingly sought an ecclesiastical system of bishoprics similar to that of western Europe and England. Perhaps because Scandinavia was converted to Christianity by English missionaries, the Ostmen looked to the archbishop of Canterbury for direction and for the consecration of their bishops.

Irish ecclesiastical culture had been at odds with Roman church culture and its desire for order at least since the Synod of Whitby in 664. At that time, the Irish had a different method of calculating the date for celebrating the feast of Easter, while the Roman style, reintroduced by Saint Augustine of Canterbury, prevailed in England. With reports, probably from urban Norse-Irish converts, about the lax conditions among rural Gaelic Christians, such as improper marriages and ordinations, Rome desired reform. But the papacy through most of the twelfth century—often driven from Rome by mob anarchy and competing with rival antipopes—was in no position to enforce discipline on the Irish church.

Self-discipline, however, was moving the Irish church closer to Rome throughout the first half of the twelfth century. The culmination came at the Synod of Kells in 1152, which, in the presence of a papal legate, completed the reorganization of the Irish church along diocesan lines, with four metropolitan archdioceses: Armagh, Dublin, Cashel, and Tuam.

It was, then, with providential irony that an Englishman was elected pope in 1154, and the imperial arm of a reform-minded papacy would extend to Ireland. The papacy would acknowledge the new king of England as "lord of Ireland" in order "to proclaim the truths of the Christian religion to a rude and ignorant people, and to root out the growth of vice from the field of the Lord."

CHAPTER 2

The Anglo-Norman Conquest, A.D. 1170–1700

THE PALE AND GAELIC IRELAND, 1170–1485:

ARRIVAL OF THE ANGLO-NORMANS

Hanging in the National Gallery of Ireland is an extravagant Victorian painting entitled *The Marriage of Strongbow and Eva.* Painted by Daniel Maclise in 1854, this melodramatic portrayal depicts Strongbow's victorious foot resting on a Celtic cross as his suppliant bride Eva, daughter of Dermot MacMurrough, accepts her fate, surrounded by a writhing mass of fallen Celtic warriors.

But the beginning of the Anglo-Norman conquest of Ireland cannot be so simply portrayed. The beginning of the 800-year tragedy of Anglo-Irish relations was casual, if not comic—fitting for the plot of a modern soap opera. But like so much of later British imperialism, it started in a "fit of absence of mind." Perhaps it was inevitable that the descendants of William the Conqueror should at least expand their power and influence from Wales to the Irish coast in order to control the Irish

Sea. An unruly Celtic frontier would remain a natural strategic concern for the Norman conquerors of England.

For over a century and one-half after the death of Brian Boru in 1014, there was little national unity in Ireland and periods when the chroniclers even failed to name a high king. By the decade of the 1150s, Irish history would take a fateful turn in the personal struggle between two warrior kings: Dermot MacMurrough, king of Leinster, and Tiernan O'Rourke, king of Breifne (present-day County Leitrim). Both were allies of opposing kings in the war for supremacy in Ireland, and in 1152 MacMurrough committed the unpardonable act, in the eyes of O'Rourke, of abducting O'Rourke's wife Dervorgilla; according to one account, she "wept and screamed in pretence, as if Dermot were carrying her off by force." They were hardly Romeo and Juliet—he was 42, she, 44. Though O'Rourke recaptured her the following year, he was bent on revenge against MacMurrough, and the opportunity came when in 1166, with various allies, O'Rourke destroyed MacMurrough's palace at Ferns, County Wexford. Dermot then fled Ireland, first to Bristol and then on to France to seek the aid of Henry II, king of England.

Dermot found Henry in Aquitaine, part of the Norman-French-speaking king's far-flung Angevin Empire. Henry II (1154–1189), great-grandson of William the Conqueror, was the direct ruler of more than one-third of France and all of England. Like his great-grandfather, he was a descendant of the Vikings or Norsemen who had conquered the section of northeastern France that became Normandy. Ironically, out of a desire for royal control, Henry II created a centralized but effective legal and administrative system throughout England, as the laws and customs of the Angles and the Saxons were "trodden under foot, only to be trodden into shape." But Henry's venture into Ireland would hardly be as successful.

Shortly after becoming king of England, in 1155 Henry II sought and received permission through the papal bull, *Laudabiliter,* granted by Pope Adrian IV (Nicholas Brakespeare, the only English pope in history), to become "lord of Ireland." The pope was concerned about effective Roman control over the "ignorant and rude" Christians in Ireland, especially the yearly contribution of Peter's pence to Rome. Of course, Henry II desired to stabilize the "Celtic fringe" of his empire.

But Henry had many other concerns and was not especially interested in Dermot MacMurrough's invitation a decade later. On his way back to Ireland, however, Dermot visited a powerful Anglo-Norman knight out of favor with Henry II, Richard FitzGilbert de Clare, nicknamed "Strongbow," earl of Pembrokeshire—located barely 60 miles across the Irish Sea from Dermot's kingdom. Strongbow agreed to lead an army to Ireland to restore Dermot to power provided that Dermot give Strongbow his eldest daughter, Eva, in marriage and designate him his heir as king of Leinster.

Dermot returned to Ferns in Wexford in 1167, accompanied or joined later by Norman-Welsh knights whose names would become famous in Irish history: FitzHenry, Carew, FitzGerald, and Barry. He was also aided by a colony of Flemish knights settled in Wales with such names as Prendergast, Fleming, Roche, and Synott. But Strongbow took his time in coming, landing near Waterford on August 23, 1170, with about 200 knights and 1000 soldiers.

Strongbow quickly captured the town of Waterford and then married Eva. On September 21, Dublin fell to Strongbow and his Normans, and its Norse-Irish king, Hasculf, and his followers fled to the Hebrides. When Dermot MacMurrough died in the spring of 1171, Strongbow inherited the kingdom of Leinster but still had to defeat a return attack on Dublin by the Norse, kill Hasculf, and break up a joint Gaelic-Irish siege of Dublin. But the greatest threat to Strongbow's power came from his own feudal lord, Henry II of England.

On October 17, 1171, Henry II, with a well-equipped army of 500 knights, foot soldiers, and over 3000 archers, landed near Waterford. His motives were mixed. In his struggle in England over church-state relations, the previous Christmastide his henchmen had assassinated "that troublesome priest," Thomas Becket, archbishop of Canterbury. Fearful of papal interdict, Henry launched his invasion of Ireland, perhaps to assuage the papacy by implementing *Laudabiliter*. In Ireland he would do penance for Becket's murder and check the growing power of Strongbow.

Henry II made a triumphal procession to Dublin as the Normans, Gaelic-Irish, and Norse-Irish all paid homage to him. And at the urging of Pope Alexander III, the Irish bishops—including Saint Lawrence O'Toole, archbishop of Dublin—pledged their fealty. Henry also gave the kingdom of Meath to Hugh de Lacy as a counterbalance to Strongbow's influence, and later, by the Treaty of Windsor of October 6, 1175, in return for recognition as his overlord, Henry acknowledged Rory O'Connor as high king of the unconquered areas.

Herein lay the great tragedy of the Anglo-Norman invasion of Ireland: the half-conquest of Ireland. Henry and his successors could not control their Norman barons as they seized more Irish lands, despite the Treaty of Windsor, but in a haphazard fashion. By the mid-thirteenth century, the Norman conquest of Ireland began to slow down for lack of any organized plan and because the Norman kings of England were waging wars in Scotland, Wales, and on the continent. So the Gaelic-Irish kings began to reassert their power and in 1263 even offered the high kingship to Haakon IV, King of Norway, in return for his support in expelling the "English" (the Anglo-Irish or English-speaking descendants of the Anglo-Normans) from Ireland. Though Haakon died before he could act, the invitation is the first instance of a pattern for the next 700 years of Ireland's seeking help from other European powers against the English.

In this context, by the end of the thirteenth century, the Anglo-Irish would distinguish between *terra pacis* and *terra guerre,* the land of peace and the land of war. Despite a century of castle building, including Dublin Castle, and the establishment of new inland towns, the Anglo-Irish grip was weakening, and various Gaelic chiefs were regaining their kingdoms and even expanding them. This tug-of-war between the Anglo-Irish ascendancy and Gaelic Ireland would continue back and forth for over two centuries. Divisions in each side (whether civil war in England or rivalries among the Gaelic lords) would often give momentum to the other side.

THE ANGLO-NORMAN LEGACY

Yet the permanent legacy of the Anglo-Normans, later Anglo-Irish, was substantial. In addition to their castles and towns, they built most of the medieval cathedrals such as St. Patrick's in Dublin and St. Canice's in Kilkenny and rebuilt Christ Church Cathedral, Dublin, where Strongbow is buried. They also brought with them new religious orders dedicated to popularizing the Gospels: Dominicans, Franciscans, Augustinians, and Carmelites.

Perhaps most significant in terms of the history of Ireland as a nation is the legal system the Anglo-Normans transplanted to Ireland. They brought with them the jury system, the beginning of county organization, and a kind of civil service with a method of accounting, a state budget, and a presiding treasurer. In addition, within the Anglo-Irish community there gradually developed a representative assembly known as a parliament (from the French for "talk" or "discuss").

Historians generally date the beginning of Parliament in England from the "model parliament" of 1295 summoned by King Edward I. Likewise, the first Irish Parliament was the 1297 assembly at Dublin, representing, of course, the descendants of the Anglo-Normans. As in England, the Irish Parliament gradually evolved over the next century into a more representative body as delegates from the counties (usually knights) and towns—the so-called commons—established their right to be present in a House of Commons, while the noblemen (barons, viscounts, earls, and so on) and spiritual lords (the bishops) met in the House of Lords. But for centuries the Irish Parliament would do little more than rubber-stamp Crown policies.

THE SCOTTISH INVASION, THE BLACK DEATH, AND THE SHRINKING PALE

During the early fourteenth century, the Gaelic kings managed to unite and invite Edward Bruce, brother of Robert, king of Scotland, to become high king of Ireland. In 1314 the Scots under Robert repulsed an English invasion of Scotland, commanded by Edward II, at the Battle of Bannockburn, and in 1315 Edward Bruce landed at Larne, County Antrim. In 1316 in Dundalk he was recognized as high king by an alliance of Irish chiefs, mainly from Ulster and Connacht. Aided by famine, Robert Bruce wreaked havoc with raids from his base in Ulster on Anglo-Irish towns in the midlands, but he failed to unite the Gaelic Irish. When he was defeated and killed at Faughart, County Louth, in 1318, the Gaelic lords returned to their squabbling.

More than quarreling was going on in England as Edward II was forced to abdicate in 1327. Then Edward III propelled England into the on-again, off-again Hundred Years War against France. But the plague that hit England in 1348 also weakened its control of Ireland.

Starting in the southwest English ports in 1348, having spread from the continent, the Black Death swept away over one-third of the population of England within a year. The bubonic plague also hit the Irish ports, and the winter of 1348–1349 killed about one-third of the population of the towns, who were principally Anglo-Irish. The Gaelic lordships were not as hard hit.

With few immigrants from England and decimated by the Black Death, the Anglo-Irish community after 1350 was increasingly on the defensive. In a Parliament at Kilkenny in 1366, the English settlers enacted the notorious Statutes of Kilkenny—which some historians have suggested were an early form of apartheid for Ireland. The laws attempted to protect the Anglo-Irish settlers from becoming "degenerate" by legislating that they should speak English in their community and should not wear Irish dress. They also banned "the games which men call 'hurlings' with great clubs at ball upon the ground, from which great evils and maims have arisen to the weakening of the defence of the said land." The statutes officially forbade Anglo-Irish intermarriage with "the Irish enemy" and the acceptance of Celtic Irishmen into English religious orders. Furthermore, the Anglo-Irish born in Ireland were to be treated equally with the English born in England but living in Ireland.

Yet the Statutes of Kilkenny were more symbolic of the weakening position of the Anglo-Irish as they lost ground to local Gaelic chiefs and often had to pay them protection money. Increasingly, from the end of the fourteenth century, the "English pale" or the "land of peace" was shrinking to little more than Dublin and an area of perhaps 30 square miles north and inland, plus some isolated patches and walled towns. And many of the Anglo-Irish, of necessity, were becoming Gaelicized.

THE HUNDRED YEARS WAR AND THE GAELIC RESURGENCE

During a lull in the Hundred Years and Scottish wars, King Richard II landed in 1394—the first English king to visit Ireland since King John in 1210. Richard's policy of conciliation with the Gaelic lords alienated the Anglo-Irish, and no sooner had he left than the agreement broke down. Richard was forced to return in 1399, but shortly after arriving he heard of the rebellion at home of Henry Bolingbroke, heir of John of Gaunt, duke of Lancaster. When Richard returned to England, he was deposed in favor of "Henry IV" and killed. Richard II was the first of many English monarchs and politicians to find involvement in Ireland disastrous for their fortunes in England.

During the first half of the fifteenth century, the resurgence of Gaelic influence continued, as the Lancastrians—Henry IV (1399–1413), Henry V (1413–1422), and Henry VI (1422–1461)—were too busy continuing to fight the Hundred Years War against France. Though winning the major battles, England finally lost the war, losing all of its French territories except the port of Calais. But two years after the end of the war, the bitter dynastic civil war known as the War of the Roses broke out, and Ireland was caught up in the struggle between the Red Rose of the House of Lancaster and the White Rose of the House of York.

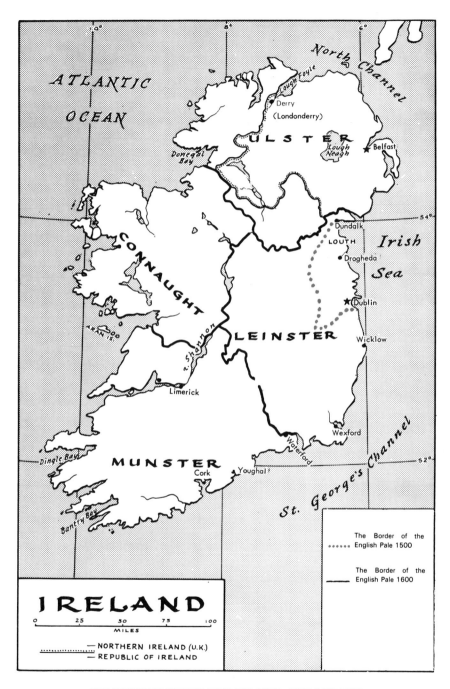

THE BORDERS OF THE ENGLISH PALE, 1500 AND 1600

THE WAR OF THE ROSES

In 1460 the Irish pawn checkmated the English king, Henry VI of Lancaster, when the Irish Parliament at Drogheda, summoned by his rival to the throne, Richard, duke of York, made it treason to question his authority as lord lieutenant of Ireland and asserted that Ireland was bound only by laws passed or accepted by the Irish Parliament. Though the duke of York was defeated and killed back in England, the Yorkist cause triumphed in 1461 when his son was crowned Edward IV (1461–1483).

The 30-year War of the Roses was a tragedy of ruthless, personal ambitions, based on confusing dynastic claims, in which the Anglo-Irish participated. Edward IV had his fractious brother, the duke of Clarence, lord lieutenant of Ireland, drowned in a butt of his favorite wine; and Richard III (1483–1485), made famous as the evil hunchback in Shakespeare's play, probably had his two nephews— Edward V and his younger brother, Richard, duke of York, the sons of Edward IV—killed in the Tower of London. Likewise, Irish lord deputies, such as the earl of Desmond, executed by Sir John Tiptoft, and later Tiptoft himself, lost their heads in the vicious power struggle. By the 1470s the three great earls, who had dominated Ireland throughout the fifteenth century—Ormond, who had sided with the losing Lancastrians; Desmond, who was too Gaelicized for the Anglo-Irish; and Kildare—were now reduced to one, the Fitzgerald, earls of Kildare, to whom the government of Ireland was virtually abandoned.

THE TUDOR REVOLUTION, 1485–1603:

HENRY VII AND THE KILDARE SUPREMACY

The English pale of government in Ireland had shrunk almost to disappearance when Henry Tudor defeated Richard III at the Battle of Bosworth Field in 1485. Henry was immediately crowned Henry VII of England but still faced chaos, if not opposition, in Ireland.

In 1487 an imposter named Lambert Simnel, the young son of an obscure Oxford tradesman who claimed to be Edward, earl of Warwick, son of the duke of Clarence, was crowned Edward VI, king of England, in Christ Church Cathedral, Dublin. He was enthusiastically accepted by the Anglo-Irish, including the earl of Kildare. But the plot failed when an Irish army led by the earl of Kildare's brother, accompanied by 2000 German mercenaries, invaded England and was defeated at Stoke.

Again in 1491 another imposter, a youth named Perkin Warbeck, landed in Cork and claimed to be Richard, second son of Edward IV (one of the princes now believed killed by Richard III in 1483). Though the plot fizzled and Warbeck was eventually executed, the earl of Kildare, who had been pardoned by Henry VII for his support of Simnel and then appointed lord deputy of Ireland, remained uncomfortably neutral, from Henry VII's viewpoint, in this latest Yorkist plot and was arrested by his replacement as deputy, Sir Edward Poynings, and sent as a prisoner to England.

Henry had sent Poynings to Ireland as lord deputy to convene a "packed" Parliament, which adopted in 1494 the notorious law bearing his name that would hamstring every Anglo-Irish Parliament until 1782. Poynings' Law provided that no Parliament could be convened in Ireland without the approval of the king of England and that his privy council had first to approve any legislation being considered by the Irish Parliament. But Poynings' Law would not become important until the seventeenth and eighteenth centuries.

To buttress Poynings' Law, Henry decided on a temporizing policy, returning Kildare in 1496 to his position as lord deputy once Warbeck was no longer a threat. In Henry's presence, Kildare was confronted by an enemy, the bishop of Meath, who warned the king: "You see the sort of man he is; all Ireland cannot rule him." To which Henry is supposed to have replied: "No? Then he must be the man to rule all Ireland."

Garret Mór (the Great) Fitzgerald (1478–1513), eighth earl of Kildare, through a series of marriages of sons and daughters, formed a network of alliances with the great Gaelic and Anglo-Irish families and became virtual ruler of Ireland. With these alliances the Kildare power continued into the reign of the next king of England, as the "Kildare Rental," begun in 1518, made Garret Óg (the Young), the ninth earl, a kind of "godfather" of Ireland, collecting protection money from the Gaelic lords as long as he served as lord deputy. But a great revolution in church and state in England would eclipse the power of the House of Kildare in Ireland.

HENRY VIII'S REVOLUTION AND THE REFORMATION

It was the son and heir of Henry VII who permanently altered the course of Irish history. Crowned king of England in 1509, Henry VIII, who reigned until 1547, was the very incarnation of Machiavelli's prince, with his elastic conscience, desire for efficiency, and iron will. When he failed to win papal approval of a divorce from his wife, Catherine of Aragon, he forced the English Parliament to appoint him "supreme head" of the Church of England and substitute his authority for that of the pope. To be a good Englishman, one had to be a communicant of the Church of England (the Anglican church). Likewise, the English, state-controlled Church of Ireland came into existence in 1537 and the kingdom of Ireland in 1541—both with the authority of the English Parliament, not the papal grant of *Laudabiliter*. The separate kingdom of Ireland would last until the Act of Union in 1801. The "protestant" Church of Ireland would become the religion of most of the "New English" caste minority ruling Ireland, and the Celtic majority and most of the "Old English" remained "Catholics" loyal to the pope. For over two centuries, in the official English view, Irish Catholicism was a subversive movement tantamount to treason.

To implement the Tudor Revolution in religion and government in Ireland, Henry VIII developed a "New English" bureaucracy there that ended the rule of the Kildares as unofficial kings of Ireland. An uprising led by Thomas, Lord Offaly, son of the ninth earl of Kildare, broke out when the earl was imprisoned and rumored executed in the Tower of London. "Silken Thomas," Lord Offaly, left in charge of the Irish Council of State, rode into Dublin on June 11, 1534, with a band of 140 horsemen wearing silk fringes on their helmets. Offaly flung his sword of state down before the council, declaring that he was no longer Henry's deputy but his enemy. Lord Offaly hoped for the assistance of Emperor Charles V and associated the Kildare cause with that of the papacy. But Silken Thomas—by that time the tenth earl of Kildare due to the death of his father—was defeated in 1535 in the Kildare's Maynooth Castle by the new lord deputy, Sir William Skeffington, who granted the infamous "Maynooth pardon"—the entire garrison was executed. Silken Thomas, who surrendered later, and his five uncles were hanged, drawn, and quartered as common criminals at Tyburn in London, and Henry VIII became de facto as well as de jure king of Ireland with the same ruthlessness shown to Thomas More, who also asserted traditional values against the "modern," authoritarian statecraft of Henry.

It was in the interest of Tudor absolutism that Irish religious practices were made to conform with English practice. As in England, the dissolution of the monasteries and friaries was decreed. Under Edward VI (1547–1553), Protestant theology and liturgy were officially established in Ireland. The Mass was prohibited, and the *Book of Common Prayer* promulgated in English. But only among palesmen—not in Gaelic-speaking areas—was there any religious conformity.

THE PLANTATIONS AND ELIZABETHAN IRELAND

Though Catholicism was restored briefly during the reign of the daughter of Catherine of Aragon and Henry VIII, Mary Tudor (1553–1558)—the notorious Bloody Mary of Foxe's *Book of Martyrs* who executed hundreds of Protestant heretics—in Ireland Queen Mary was an authoritarian Tudor who introduced the idea of "plantation." The project involved driving out the native Celtic population from a particular area and replacing it with loyal "English" settlers. The counties of Leix and Offaly were to be the site of the first such plantation. The Irish Parliament enacted legislation "that Leix should become Queen's County and Offaly King's County, that the whole territory should be confiscated, and that the English system of local organization and law enforcement should be established." Two-thirds of the land was to be planted with Englishmen born in England or Ireland.

The Tudor effort to Anglicize Ireland was intensified during the long reign of Elizabeth I (1558–1603). New efforts were made to transform Ireland in religion, culture, and politics. The Reformation widened the gulf between the two islands as politics and religious ideology became inseparable. Queen Elizabeth—the daughter of Henry VIII and Anne Boleyn—was proclaimed illegitimate in a papal bull, and

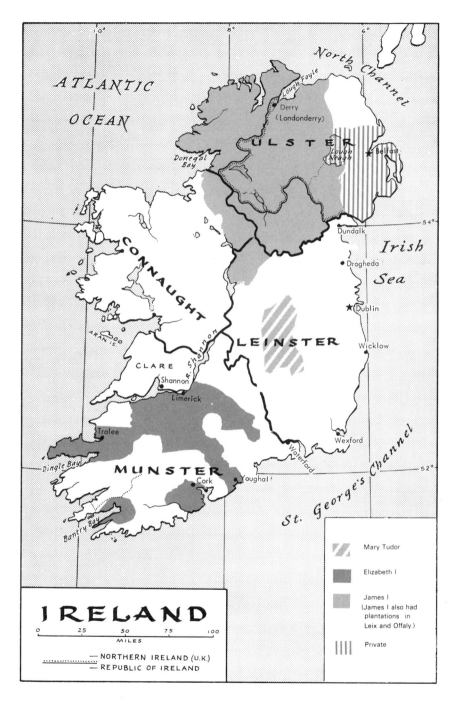

PLANTATIONS

the papacy gave its blessing to the revolt of the Desmonds in Munster (1579–1583). The Desmond Revolt was brutally crushed, Sir Walter Raleigh leading the massacre at Smerwick in Kerry. The earl of Desmond's head was sent to Elizabeth to adorn London Bridge, and the New English adventurers were rewarded.

Elizabeth began the plantation of Munster in 1584 when 500,000 acres of fertile land was confiscated by the Crown. The most famous of the "undertakers," who pledged to bring English settlers to farm the land, were Sir Walter Raleigh— later founder of the "lost colony" in North Carolina—who was given 12,000 acres, mainly in County Cork, and Edmund Spenser, author of the epic poem of tribute to Elizabeth, "The Faerie Queen." Spenser would complain that the "Old English," the descendants of the Anglo-Normans, were "much more lawless and licentious than the very wild Irish. . . . The most part of them were degenerated and growen allmost meere Irish, yea and more malicious to the English than the very Irish themselves." But the New English would fail to pacify Munster for many of the reasons the Anglo-Normans had failed. It was too difficult to attract sufficient numbers of English yeoman farmers to stabilize the Celtic frontier. And future generations of the New English, like so many in the past, would eventually become "more Irish than the Irish."

The Elizabethan Reformation in Ireland was also responsible for the establishment of the first Irish university when Trinity College, Dublin, was founded in 1592. Its purpose was, of course, to Anglicize the Irish and convert them to Protestantism in the form of the Church of Ireland, with the English monarch as its head. It was at first little more than a Protestant seminary under the leadership of its first great professor, James Ussher, regius professor of divinity. And it was still considered more safely Puritan than Oxford and Cambridge during the 1650s, when Increase Mather, who would become the first important president of Harvard, and his brother Samuel studied there. But even Trinity College, not much more than a century after its foundation, became a seedbed of Irish nationalism, albeit of a Protestant variety to begin with.

The close of Elizabeth's reign featured another Irish rebellion. This time she sent her young lover, the earl of Essex, to defeat The O'Neill and The O'Donnell of Ulster. He failed miserably and lost his head as well as his heart to Elizabeth. She replaced him with her ablest general, Lord Mountjoy, who as lord deputy overwhelmed a Spanish and Irish army at Kinsale in 1601.

THE ENGLISH, THE WILD IRISH, AND THE WILD INDIANS

The saying in the New World that the only good Indian is a dead Indian originated in the doctrine that the only good "wild Irishman" is a dead wild Irishman. During the Elizabethan plantations, English colonists railed against the "wild Irish." In 1598 Chief Justice Sir William Saxey wrote that Irish rebels seized English infants "from the nurse's breasts" and had the babies' "brains dashed against the walls." He also claimed that the Irish cut out the tongues and cut off the noses of their English prisoners. Of course, this all occurred at a time when the "civilized"

English were drawing and quartering prisoners. In 1637 Roger Williams warned John Winthrop that if the New England Indians were not treated kindly, they might "turne wild Irish themselves."

The character of Irish warfare anticipated that of the American Indians. For English colonists, the native Irish invented the ambush. One English account in 1618 described how the wild Irish

> will plash down whole trees over the passes, and so intricately wind them, or lay them, that they shall be a strong barricade, and then lurk *in ambush* amongst the standing wood, playing upon all comers as they intend to go along. On the bog they likewise presume with a naked celerity to come as near our foot and horse is possible, and then fly off again, knowing we cannot or indeed dare not follow them.

One such contested area was "the shillelagh," a heavily wooded section of Wicklow where the native Irish hid in wait, armed with clubs, later known as shillelaghs.

PLANTATION, CIVIL WAR, AND REVOLUTION, 1603–1700:

THE LONDONDERRY PLANTATION AND THE ULSTER SCOTS

James I's reign (1603–1625) was most significant for the Stuart dynasty's continuation of the plantation policy of the Tudors. James (Stuart) VI of Scotland became James I of England, thus uniting the two kingdoms in his person upon the death of Elizabeth. Among the 2 million Irish acres to be planted were the entire county and town of Derry, which were given to the city of London, to be divided among the twelve city companies. And so the town was renamed Londonderry—perhaps the most troubled part of Northern Ireland today.

The famed Flight of the Earls in 1607 robbed Ulster of its natural aristocracy when Hugh O'Neill, earl of Tyrone, and Rory O'Donnell, earl of Tyrconnell, fled to the continent to avoid arrest, cherishing, perhaps, the hope of returning to Ireland with a Spanish army. They both died in exile in Rome, and buried with them in the Holy City were the last hopes of an independent Gaelic Ireland. Their flight gave the Anglo-Irish government in Dublin the opportunity to expropriate their lands, and thousands of Scots and English were settled on the confiscated territory.

The new Scottish settlers would play an important role in history. As Ulster Scots, they helped shape a distinctive Ulster regionalism different from the rest of Ireland. These combative Scottish Presbyterians were toughened by their experiences on the Celtic frontier. Though they were protected by the Ulster custom of tenant right, their native Irish neighbors lived without any security of tenure and could be evicted at any time. These Scottish Calvinists, like their Boer counterparts in South Africa, would develop a toughness of spirit that the course of history would make constantly tougher.

When the penal laws of the eighteenth century excluded Presbyterians from public employment, many thousands of the descendants of these Ulster Scots emigrated to the North American colonies, settling along the Appalachian frontier. These so-called Scotch-Irish were the great Indian fighters of the colonial period of American history, adapting their experience of fighting the wild Irish for generations. The Scotch-Irish were the backbone of George Washington's Revolutionary army, and Ulster Scots were the ancestors of many famous Americans, including Andrew Jackson, John C. Calhoun, and Woodrow Wilson.

PLANTING MUNSTER

Under James I, Munster was becoming a Protestant province—at the time even more so than Ulster. This resulted largely from the efforts of one man, the penniless "carpetbagger" Richard Boyle, who arrived in 1588. He soon grew wealthy as he bought up Raleigh's vast estate for 1000 pounds and also purchased some of the earl of Desmond's confiscated estates as well as abbey lands. He built several towns, among them Bandon, where he introduced the iron-smelting and linen-weaving industries and imported English settlers. He was created earl of Cork in 1620 and had four sons who were peers and another, Robert, who enunciated the famous Boyle's law that the volume of a gas varies inversely to the pressure. The great earl was a new kind of magnate whose wealth and political importance infuriated the old landed peers.

ENGLISH OPPOSITION TO THE STUART MONARCHS

But the Irish scene, as so often, was a mere sideshow to the great drama on the English stage. The chief actors were the Stuart monarchs James I and Charles I and the Parliaments, mainly the House of Commons, dominated by the Puritan "rising gentry" and their Protestant allies, the town merchants. The wily Queen Elizabeth was succeeded by James I, the comic offspring of the executed Mary, Queen of Scots, and Lord Darnley. The pedantic James, with his slobbering Scottish accent, was all that a king should not be, especially one who preached the political dogma of divine hereditary right. Though wise in book learning, he was a poor judge of men. And he passed on to his son, the ill-fated Charles I (1625–1649) the inept, swashbuckling favorite George Villiers, duke of Buckingham, whose warlike expeditions against Spain and France virtually bankrupted the monarchy. These escapades lowered the prestige of Charles I because Buckingham's wars had led to unparliamentary taxation, arbitrary imprisonment, and martial law over civilians, all of which were defined as illegal in the famed Petition of Right, which Charles conceded to his Parliament in 1628 in exchange for their vote of revenues for his use.

But the Petition of Right was just the beginning of the struggle. The House of Commons grew increasingly jealous of the taxing power and fearful of an army it could not control. When Buckingham was assassinated by a Puritan fanatic in 1628, Charles, though abandoning foreign adventures, became increasingly alienated from the Puritan-dominated House of Commons, whose members held the speaker down in his chair and passed resolutions against "Popery and Arminianism" (the toleration of Catholic beliefs in the Church of England) and "Tonage and Poundage" (taxes). Charles then dismissed Parliament and ruled on his own from 1629 to 1640, not only dispensing with Parliaments but also packing the judiciary.

THE ELEVEN YEARS TYRANNY

The Eleven Years Tyranny increasingly alienated the Puritan middle class and stiffened its opposition to the monarch's arbitrary power. But Charles did win one new ally who would prove to be a major force in Ireland and, too late, in England, Thomas Wentworth, later earl of Strafford.

"Black Tom" had been an active member of the House of Commons in opposition to Buckingham, but this supporter of the Petition of Right would cross over to the king's side and subvert its principles for the rest of his life. In 1632 Wentworth was appointed lord deputy of Ireland, and the purpose of his policy of "thorough" was to make Ireland the second jewel in the Crown with a budget surplus for the king, who was reigning without Parliament. Wentworth maintained relative tolerance for Catholics and realized that the real enemies of the Church and the Crown were the stubborn Presbyterians of the North. When he got the charter of the London companies forfeited in Ulster, he made a fatal enemy in the city of London and its members of Parliament.

After the Scots Presbyterians revolted against Charles and signed their Covenant with God in 1638, Wentworth, now earl of Strafford, raised an Irish army of 9000 men. But he was soon recalled to England by Charles as the king summoned Parliament to raise taxes to fight the Scots. Strafford advised the king to summon his first Parliament in eleven years, but the "Short Parliament" in the spring of 1640 refused to provide money to subdue Scotland and focused instead on grievances against the king's and Strafford's "tyranny." After the Parliament was quickly dismissed, Strafford, in his single-handedly brave but autocratic fashion, attempted to raise an army in his own Yorkshire to counter the Scottish army that had crossed the river Tweed, occupied northeastern England, and demanded, as the price for evacuation, their own terms and money. Charles I was forced, then, to call another Parliament in the autumn of 1640.

THE CIVIL WAR, THE REBELLION OF 1641, AND CROMWELL

The so-called Long Parliament, greeted by an enthusiastic populace in London, was a turning point in English history that precipitated civil war between Cavaliers (supporters of the king) and Roundheads (parliamentarians), led by their general,

Oliver Cromwell. But first, the desperate and politically inept king sacrificed his ablest supporter, the earl of Strafford, to mob rule, as Parliament, through a bill of attainder, legislated his execution. Charles signed the bill, and on May 12, 1641, the ex-parliamentarian Strafford went to the scaffold uttering the immortal line, "Put not thy trust in princes."

The removal from the Irish government of Strafford's iron grip created a chaotic situation to which an adage that echoed down centuries of Anglo-Irish history would apply: "England's difficulty is Ireland's opportunity." Consequently, the Catholic clergy organized a rebellion to break out simultaneously in several parts of Ireland on October 23, 1641. But the Rebellion of 1641 is most famous for the Catholic "atrocities" against Protestants in Ulster. In fact the memory of 1641 aroused anti-Catholic feelings among Ulster Protestants that have lasted for centuries. Angry, dispossessed Catholic peasants took revenge upon the Protestant settlers, looting and burning their towns and killing thousands, among them a hundred Protestants who drowned in the river Bann at Portadown.

When news reached England of the massacres, contemporary accounts exaggerated the number of Protestant victims, (approximately 4000) to as much as 300,000, as recorded by Sir John Temple in his *History of the Rebellion* (1646). These accounts further fanned the flames of anti-Catholic feeling in England fed annually by the celebration of Guy (Guido) Fawkes Day commemorating the discovery of the "gunpowder plot" on November 5, 1605, planned by Jesuits and English supporters of the papacy to blow up the king and the entire Parliament. No wonder, then, that the Puritan Roundheads and Oliver Cromwell were bent on revenge against Catholics in their Irish campaign.

The Protestant Reformation flourished in England, as on the continent, where there was a sizable middle class, especially among merchants in large towns. In Ireland there was no such native class, and the Celtic peasants viewed Protestantism as an English import, alien to their cultural as well as religious beliefs. These Gaelic peasants still lived in the Middle Ages and shared the values of those times, including a natural allegiance to lord, king, and pope. The Puritans' "New Model Army" was financed by the moneyed merchant interests of London and by the new gentry outraged at the economic and political depredations of the king and the old aristocracy. So at every twist and turn of events during the civil war in both England and Ireland, one is confronted with the politics of religion.

The course of the civil war in Ireland from 1641 to 1652 was shaped by the complexity of shifting interests: royalist versus parliamentarian, Catholic versus Protestant, Episcopalian Protestant versus Presbyterian Protestant, Old Irish and Old English versus New English, and Old Irish versus Old English. The Old Irish provided perhaps the best of the Catholic armies, the army of Ulster, under the legendary Owen Roe O'Neill. But they were often at odds with the Old English, who dominated the government and parliament of the Catholic Confederation located in Kilkenny. Even the Confederation of Kilkenny was split between supporters of the papal nuncio, Giovanni Battista Cardinal Rinuccini, who wanted an independent Ireland, and Charles I's lord deputy, the Episcopalian earl of Ormond,

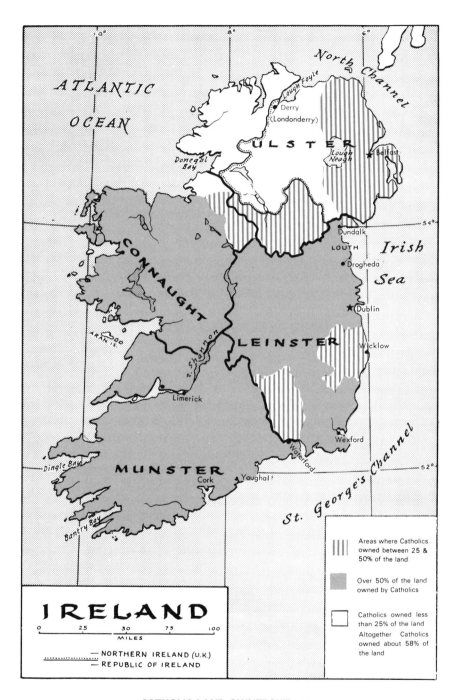

CATHOLIC LAND OWNERSHIP, 1641

of the ruling Butler family of Kilkenny Castle, who had regained power with the demise of the Kildares under Henry VIII's Reformation. Ormond wanted to make Ireland a stronghold of the English Crown in its struggle with the Parliament at Westminster. The mini–civil war or lack of cooperation between Old Irish and Old English meant that Ireland was easy prey for Cromwell's Ironsides regiment once they had won in England and Charles I had been executed.

Cromwell's campaign in Ireland shaped Irish history in two ways: memories of the Drogheda Massacre and resettlement of the Old Irish west of the river Shannon, described as "To Hell or Connacht." Cromwell and his 3000 Ironsides landed in Ireland in August 1649 and stayed until May 1650. With about 30,000 men under his command, he secured Dublin and then laid seige to the royalist garrison at Drogheda, which he sacked, giving no quarter to the entire garrison of Anglo-Irish royalists, mostly Episcopalian, and such recusant clergy (Catholic priests) as he could find. Though the slaughter of several thousand soldiers and priests is possible, nationalist historians have perhaps embellished the account to include all women and children. Cromwell, in his retribution for the Rebellion of 1641, would give the Catholic side historical ammunition for centuries of debate between Catholic and Protestant apologists over atrocities.

After Wexford suffered a fate similar to Drogheda's as a warning, Cromwell left his son-in-law, General Henry Ireton, to do the mopping up, and over 30,000 Irish and Anglo-Irish soldiers were permitted to flee to the continent. But it would be the Cromwellian plantation that would perpetuate the "curse of Cromwell" in Gaelic folklore.

Under the Act of Settlement of 1652, virtually the entire Old Irish population would have their land confiscated and be forced into the infertile, rock-strewn province of Connacht and present-day County Clare—parts of which bear greater resemblance to the landscape of the moon than the rest of Ireland. But the act could not be entirely enforced for the same reasons that forced settlements had failed earlier. Yet the process of creating a dominant Protestant ascendancy loyal to England continued, even with the end of Cromwell's protectorate and the restoration of the monarchy in 1660 under Charles II.

THE STUART RESTORATION

After a decade of harsh Cromwellian dictatorship, much of England wanted to celebrate Christmas again and end Puritan excesses. And the memory of the unfair trial and execution of Charles I "did not wash the balm from kingship, but gave it a new anointing." With a firm desire to die on the throne and not on the block like his father, Charles II (1660–1685) was the shrewdest of the Stuart monarchs, best remembered for his many mistresses and for siring the illegitimate ancestors of a sizable portion of the current English aristocracy. He had come to the throne with the aid of middle-of-the-road Irish Protestant aristocrats and was forced to renege on a promise to restore loyal Catholics to their lands. Indeed, the Cromwellian land settlement was largely legitimized with an official Protestant Ireland governing a dispossessed, disenfranchised Catholic population. And Dublin became a predominantly Protestant capital. But as early as the Navigation Act of 1663, which banned Irish exports to the American colonies and established prohibitive tariffs on the importation of Irish cattle into England, the Irish Protestant establishment was on a collision course with English economic interests.

The quarter-century reign of Charles II was, beneath its happy-go-lucky, gay foppery, a dress rehearsal for the Glorious Revolution of 1688–1689, the final act in the struggle between Parliament and the Stuart dynasty. And this time the final scene would be set in Ireland.

Though Charles had secretly negotiated the Treaty of Dover of 1670 with France, agreeing to help Louis XIV attack Holland and also to convert himself and the English nation to Catholicism, he was forced to back away from both agreements. His brother, James, duke of York, did become a Catholic convert; but Parliament confronted the king with the Test Act of 1673, which excluded from all civil and military offices anyone who refused to take Communion according to the Church of England.

While Charles and his brother and heir, James, were flirting with Catholic absolutism, antipopery feeling intensified during the famous 1678 conspiracy of Titus Oates, who claimed to know of a "popish plot," organized by Jesuits, to assassinate Charles, make the Catholic duke of York king, and massacre all Protestants who refused to become Catholics. All this was to be accomplished with the aid of Irish and French troops. Oates became a popular hero of the London mob.

In the controversy swirling around Oates's perjured testimony, the English party system began, with the Whig (liberal "country") members of Parliament opposed to the Tory (conservative, royalist-Anglican "court") members. *Tory* and *Whig* were slang terms used by critics to describe the political parties: A Tory was an Irish Catholic bandit who attacked English settlers, and a Whig was a rebel Scottish Presbyterian whose Covenant advocated murdering bishops. The Whigs appealed to the electorate on a platform calling for Protestantism, toleration of all but Catholics, liberty of the subject, commercial advantages for the middle class, and parliamentary supremacy. The Tories' platform urged support for the Church of England, opposition to complete toleration of any other faith, and a preference for royal supremacy over Parliament. As the Whigs tried to exclude James from succeeding his brother to the throne, Charles, depending on a French subsidy, reigned for his last four years without calling a Parliament and died a Catholic in 1685.

THE GLORIOUS REVOLUTION

James, the Catholic-convert brother so feared by the Protestant Whigs, succeeded Charles as James II, an even stupider version of his grandfather James I. Crowned in 1685, he looked for inspiration and help to the absolutist French regime of Louis XIV, who that very year revoked the Edict of Nantes and began persecuting the

Protestant Huguenots. (Ironically, thousands of Huguenots settled in Ireland, especially Ulster, where they applied their skills to the linen trade.) And so when James II dispensed with laws against Catholics and Protestant dissenters, his motives appeared questionable to the majority of Englishmen who were Anglican communicants. Furthermore, in uncompromising fashion, he appointed a Catholic, the earl of Tyrconnell, lord deputy of Ireland, and a Jesuit, Father Petre, a member of his privy council. But when his Italian-Catholic wife, Mary of Modena, gave birth to a son in 1688, a match was put to the religious powderkeg, as the future Catholic James III (the ''Old Pretender'') would inherit the throne before his Protestant half-sisters, Mary, consort of William of Orange, and Princess Anne. Even moderate Anglicans joined dissident Whigs in opposition to the reestablishment of ''Catholic absolutism,'' and the political situation in the summer and autumn of 1688 quickly became ''thy head or my head.''

The Glorious Revolution was actually more of a *coup d'état* than a revolution. William of Orange, stadholder of Holland, was a cautious man, and he insisted on a formal invitation signed by seven Whig and Tory aristocrats to become, along with his wife, Mary, daughter of James II and his Protestant first wife, Anne Hyde, king and queen of England. But it was the defection to the Williamite side of the English army, especially its commander, Sir John Churchill, later duke of Marlborough, that made the Revolution Settlement possible after James II fled to France. And so a ''convention Parliament'' declared the throne vacant because James II, ''having endeavored to subvert the constitution of the kingdom by breaking the original contract between king and people,'' had ''abdicated the government,'' and agreed that William III and Mary II should be joint sovereigns of England.

The Glorious Revolution in England dealt a deathblow to the so-called divine right of kings and created a constitutional monarchy dependent on Parliament. And the new regularized Parliament would enact a bill of rights that guaranteed for itself frequent sessions, free elections, and freedom of debate and also made illegal, without parliamentary approval, suspension of the laws, levying of taxes, and maintenance of a standing army. Also, the Revolution Settlement brought to England an independent judiciary with tenure, determined by Parliament, and habeas corpus.

UNPACIFIED IRELAND, THE BATTLE OF THE BOYNE, AND THE SIEGE OF LONDONDERRY

But if the Revolution were glorious for England, in unpacified Ireland it was gloomy and bloody, ushering in the notorious penal times. Even during Charles II's reign in 1681, the popular Catholic archbishop of Armagh, Oliver Plunkett, was executed for treason (only to be canonized as a Catholic saint by Pope Paul VI in 1975). And Ireland became the battleground between the opposing armies of William (English, Dutch, Danish, Ulster Scots, and French Huguenots) and James (Irish and French Catholic).

CATHOLIC LAND OWNERSHIP, 1688

Shortly after William and Mary became joint monarchs of England, in March 1689, James II landed in Ireland. The Irish Parliament, now almost entirely Roman Catholic of the Old English, not Gaelic, variety, removed all civil disabilities imposed because of religion and repealed the earlier acts of settlement in order to expropriate the confiscated property belonging to almost all the Protestant land-owners in Ireland. This "patriot Parliament" would have repealed Poynings' Law were it not for James's opposition.

But the outcome would be decided on the battlefield. James II decided to make a stand about 30 miles from Dublin at the river Boyne, "the old Rubicon of the pale," against William's army, which had landed in Ulster. On July 1, 1690, James's ill-trained and poorly led Irish infantry proved to be no match for William's superior troops. And the Battle of the Boyne proved to be the most decisive battle of modern Irish history. James would leave for France and William for England, and their respective armies were led by the French general, the marquis de St. Ruth, and the Dutchman Godbert de Ginkel. Unfortunately for the Irish cause, St. Ruth and Tyrconnell, James's lord deputy, were jealous of each other, and both disliked the most popular Irish general, Patrick Sarsfield, earl of Lucan. The final battle was fought on July 12, 1691, near Ballinasloe, at Aughrim Hill, where the Jacobites, disheartened at the death of their commander, St. Ruth, were defeated as they retreated to their garrison at Limerick. Their remaining leader, Sarsfield, negotiated on October 3, 1691, the so-called Treaty of Limerick, which permitted some 11,000 soldiers to sail to France and promised some measure of toleration for Roman Catholics such as they had under Charles II. But the Irish Protestant ascendancy that dominated the new Irish Parliament in Dublin would break the treaty on the issue of toleration for Catholics, in retaliation for the 1688 (Catholic) Parliament's con-fiscation of their lands, and with the vivid memory of that other great event in the minds of Protestants, the fifteen-week siege of Londonderry in 1690.

In fact, the siege mentality of Ulster Protestants today is often traced back to the events of 1690 in Londonderry. For 105 days, about 30,000 Protestants crowded into the walled city of Londonderry and withstood the siege of James II's forces until they were relieved by William's fleet on July 28 and the Jacobite army retreated. During the long siege, thousands within the walls died of starvation, and Lord Macaulay, writing a century and a half later his *History of England,* would attempt to do for Londonderry "what Thucydides had done for Plataea."

Macaulay's 1849 words might well be written today: "Still the wall of Lond-onderry is to the Protestants of Ulster what the trophy of Marathon was to the Athenians." He noted that at the most vulnerable point in the wall, the Protestants of Londonderry erected a pillar with a statue on top of the man who rallied the Protestant defenders, the Rev. George Walker, which stood (until blown up in the recent "troubles") with a Bible in one hand and the other pointing down the river to William's relief fleet in the bay. Yet even a sympathetic Macaulay, who considered his account of the siege some of his best writing, wrote that the virtues of the Protestant heroes would become the vices of their tyrannical Protestant heirs, as "unhappily the animosities of her brave champions have descended with their glory." These siege sentiments would be nourished by the Orange Order, of 1795.

THE FAILURE OF THE GLORIOUS REVOLUTION IN IRELAND

Perhaps actions of the Jacobites justified a siege mentality among the Irish Protestant ascendancy in the 1690s—so recently threatened with the loss of life and property—who proceeded with a vengeance to break the Treaty of Limerick. But

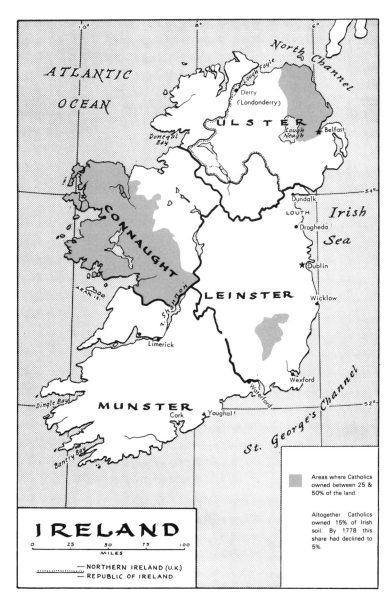

CATHOLIC LAND OWNERSHIP, 1703

their fears pursued in the name of "freedom, religion, and law" unleashed nearly a century of persecution, barbarism, and tyranny upon the Catholic majority. The liberties associated with the Glorious Revolution in England such as habeas corpus (1679) and an independent judiciary (1701) would not be enacted in Ireland until 1782 in the aftermath of the American Revolution. In the mid-eighteenth century, John Bowes, lord chancellor of Ireland, would write: "The law does not suppose any such person to exist as an Irish Roman Catholic."

Alas, these poor, dispossessed Irish children of the pope would even be abandoned by the Holy Father in their moment of need. Pope Innocent XI had supported William of Orange's wars against the power-hungry Louis XIV to restore the balance of power on the continent and check an independent Gallican church. He even approved William's accession to the thrones of England and Ireland. And so when news of the Protestant victory at the Boyne over the Irish Catholic allies of the king of France reached Rome, the Vatican ordered a solemn *Te Deum* to celebrate the event.

CHAPTER 3
The Age of Swift, 1700–1750

Though the reign of Queen Anne from 1701 to 1714 might be considered an Augustan age in England, Alexander Pope would ironically write regarding "John Bull's other island": "Let Ireland tell, how Wit upheld her cause." That wit, of course, belonged to Jonathan Swift, who lived from 1667 to 1745. Forged by personal disappointment and human sensitivity, Swift's "fierce indignation" spotlighted English intolerance and cruelty in Ireland.

SWIFT'S EARLY CAREER

Born in Dublin of a royalist Anglo-Irish background, Swift was educated at Kilkenny School, where the playwright William Congreve was also studying, and then Trinity College, Dublin. From 1689 until 1713, Swift held a variety of positions, many of them as an Anglican priest, in England and Ireland. In London he was a friend of Pope, Addison, and Steele and was known for his satirical essays. After angling for a high position, possibly a bishopric, in the Church of England, while

JONATHAN SWIFT
(1667–1745)

(Irish Tourist Board)

Tory friends of his controlled the government during Queen Anne's reign, Swift suffered a cruel disappointment when the Tory ministry appointed him dean of St. Patrick's Cathedral, Dublin. And he wrote English friends that he was condemned to lifelong exile in "wretched Dublin, in miserable Ireland." Swift's tenure as dean would last until his death as he lost all hope of promotion, since the Whigs were in power from George I's accession to the throne until 1760. After a quarter of a century as dean of St. Patrick's, he was still protesting his accident of birth in Ireland: "I happened to be dropped here."

Yet in one of the darkest periods in Ireland's history, the Irish people found a champion because, as he wrote, "what I did for this Country was from perfect Hatred of Tyranny and Oppression." Ironically, this crotchety Anglican dean, "contemptuous of the opinion of his fellows," who hid his virtues and paraded his faults, when he walked through the streets of Dublin received "a thousand hats and blessings."

SWIFT AND THE PENAL LAWS

Swift must have been quickly appalled at what he saw from St. Patrick's deanery. Most of the penal laws against Catholics were harsh, if not grotesque. They could not practice law, hold Crown offices, purchase land, or take a lease for longer than thirty-one years. All Catholic education was outlawed, and Catholics lost the right to vote and be elected to Parliament. A Catholic could not own a horse worth more than 5 pounds; otherwise, any Protestant could buy it for that sum.

One extreme measure almost enacted in 1719 provided that all unregistered priests who were first offenders be branded on the cheek "with a large P." The bill passed the Irish House of Commons but was amended by the Irish privy council to substitute castration for branding. But Poynings' Law was at least once put to good use when the English privy council rejected the substituted penalty in favor of branding. Finally the bill lost in the Irish House of Lords, not for humanitarian reasons but because of a technicality involving Catholic leases.

Church of Ireland Protestants and the Ulster Presbyterians were united in oppression of the Catholics but in all else were divided. The Toleration Act of 1719 freed Protestant dissenters from the obligation of attending Church of Ireland services. But while the dissenters were still banned, along with Catholics, from civil and military posts, the Ulster Presbyterians generally accepted this test act in order to suppress the Catholics. And so English exploitation during the Protestant ascendancy of the first half of the eighteenth century was made easier by the Presbyterian fear of Catholics, as the English privy council practiced a policy of "divide and rule" in Ireland.

SWIFT AND PROTESTANT PATRIOTISM

During the height of this English exploitation, however, the Protestant ascendancy, goaded by Jonathan Swift's satire, developed an identity separate from that of their English governors. This Protestant "patriotism" especially intensified after the Declaratory Act of 1720, passed by the British Parliament, went beyond Poynings' Law in formally asserting the right to legislate directly for Ireland without the approval of the Irish Lords and Commons—which it had already been doing for some time.

This Protestant sense of independence had been increasing with every new bit of mercantilist legislation originating in London, such as the "Cattle" Act of 1663. And this point of view was first expressed by a friend of John Locke's, William Molyneux, who published *The Case of Ireland's Being Bound by Acts of Parliament in England Stated* in 1699. Influenced by Locke's theories on the consent of the governed which were associated with the Glorious Revolution, Molyneux argued: "If . . . it be concluded that the Parliament of *England* may bind *Ireland;* it must also be allowed that the People of *Ireland* ought to have their *Representatives* in the Parliament of *England.*" And in views on taxation without representation adopted later by the American revolutionaries, he declared: "To tax me without Consent, is little better, if at all, than down-right Robbing me."

It was, then, in the spirit of Molyneux that Swift in 1720 anonymously published *A Proposal for the Universal Use of Irish Manufacture; . . . Utterly Rejecting and Renouncing Everything Wearable That Comes from England.* So Swift became spokesman of the Irish Protestant merchants as he attacked the English ban on the export of Irish woolen manufactures. That "the Irish should burn everything English but the people and the coals" would become his best-known maxim—later adopted by Arthur Griffith as the economic policy for *Sinn Fein.**

Jonathan Swift would joke during this period of "pure English" administration of Ireland that the Whig government in London appointed good Englishmen to run the Irish government but on their way to Dublin they were murdered and their assassins donned their robes to assume office. And the "Wood's halfpence" crisis of 1722–1723 would dramatically pit the Irish Protestant ascendancy and their Parliament against the English executive governing Ireland.

THE DRAPIER'S LETTERS

The Whig government of Sir Robert Walpole granted a patent to George I's German mistress, the duchess of Kendal, to mint a large quantity of copper halfpence for Ireland. She in turn offered the monopoly, for a bribe of 10,000 pounds, to William Wood, a Wolverhampton ironmaster. When the coins began to appear in Ireland, there was widespread refusal to accept them, and the Irish Parliament, stung by the lack of consultation, was in an uproar of opposition. But it was Swift's intervention that raised this squabble over currency to a clear assertion of Irish national rights.

Though absorbed in writing *Gulliver's Travels* and disappointed at his failure to arouse public opinion with the *Proposal* of 1720, Swift rose to the occasion in 1724. Under the pseudonym M. B., Drapier, he published a series of letters excoriating the English government in Ireland. In *The Drapier's Letters* he used the device of turning accepted Whig principles espoused by Locke and Molyneux against the Whig government of Robert Walpole. Because he said he got his political education from liberal Whig philosophers, the drapier wrote sarcastically that he based his attack on Wood's halfpence on the wrong premises: "I foolishly disdained to have Recourse to *Whining, Lamenting,* and *Crying for Mercy,* but rather chose to *appeal* to *Law* and *Liberty* and *the common Rights of Mankind,* without considering the *Climate* I was in."

The Drapier's Letters were devastatingly effective because they were based on self-interest. In fact the "virtual unanimity" of Irish opposition to the halfpence was not created by anything so abstract as Irish nationalism but by specific economic grievances. The Drapier wrote in his fourth letter: "Money, the great *Divider*

---

*Swift attributed this maxim to John Vesey, "late Archbishop of Tuam," who died in 1716.

of the World, hath by a strange Revolution, been the great *Uniter* of a most *Divided People.*"

Swift's brilliant appeal to self-interest, which he equated with national interest, won widespread support. But it was based on the fundamental flaw in Molyneux's *Case for Ireland:* the distinction between the Old Irish (the descendants of "the *Antient Race* of the *Irish*") and the Anglo-Irish (their English conquerors). Swift was only appealing for the Anglo-Irish establishment and had to refute Wood's accusation that the boycott was organized by papists and Jacobites. Though the Drapier argued that Irish Catholics "never once offered to stir in the Matter," Swift knew they were supporting the boycott out of economic self-interest. The Drapier claimed to speak for "the whole People of Ireland" in writing: "Were not the People of *Ireland* born as *Free* as those of *England?* How have they forfeited their Freedom? Is not their *Parliament* as fair a *Representative* of the *People* as that of *England?*" But Swift knew of the inequities in the Irish Parliament with the exclusion of Protestant dissenters and Irish Catholics*, and this awareness drove him to write an even greater piece of satire.

A MODEST PROPOSAL

Tormented by a triangular love affair and the deaths of the two women, Vanessa in 1723 and Stella in 1728, Jonathan Swift published in 1729 a pamphlet regarded as the greatest satirical essay of its kind, *A Modest Proposal for Preventing the Children of Ireland from Being a Burden to Their Parents or Country.* Driven by the inconsistencies in *The Drapier's Letters,* Swift proceeded to condemn "the whole People of Ireland": the landlords, the idle rich, male and female, the Irish poor, Protestant dissenters, papists, absentees, and merchants. The breadth of his scathing condemnations is incredible for both humanity and insight. Swift proposed to provide the children of poor parents exactly at one year old "in such a manner as instead of being a charge upon their parents or the parish, or wanting food and raiment for the rest of their lives, they shall on the contrary contribute to the feeding, and partly to the clothing, of many thousands." Swift wrote that he had been "assured by a very knowing American of my acquaintance in London, that a young healthy child well nursed is at a year old a most delicious, nourishing, and wholesome food, whether stewed, roasted, baked, or boiled." He admitted that this food would be "somewhat dear, and therefore very proper for landlords, who, as they have already devoured most of the parents, seem to have the best title to the children."

Swift said there were a number of advantages to his proposal:

1. It would "greatly lessen the number of papists, with whom we are yearly

---

*Perhaps one might argue that the British Parliament, with similar exclusions and its "rotten boroughs," was as unfair as the Irish Parliament.

overrun, being the principal breeders of the nation as well as our most dangerous enemies; and who stay at home on purpose to deliver the kingdom to the Pretender, hoping to take advantage by the absence of so many good protestants, who have chosen rather to leave their county, than stay at home and pay tithes against their conscience to an Episcopal curate.''

2. It would help poorer tenants pay their landlord's rent.

3. It would increase the ''tenderness of mothers toward their children'' when it was to the mother's ''annual profit instead of expense'' to ''bring the fattest child to the market.''

4. In anticipation of feminist liberation: ''Men would become as fond of their wives during the time of their pregnancy as they are now of their mares in foal, their cows in calf, their sows when they are ready to farrow; nor offer to beat or kick them (as is too frequent a practice) for fear of miscarriage.''

Swift finally and sarcastically dismissed the earlier ''expedients'' aimed at English tyranny. He despaired of ''teaching Landlords to have, at least, one Degree of Mercy toward their Tenants'' and of ''putting a Spirit of Honesty, Industry, and Skill into our Shopkeepers.'' In *A Modest Proposal,* ten years of warning turned into helpless frustration at the absurdity of the Irish situation. He warned the Irish people, both rich and poor, that they were not only victims but villains as they devoured themselves by their own selfishness. Jonathan Swift was far ahead of his time in his analysis of politics, economics, and their associated class psychology.

THE ANGLO-IRISH POLITICAL SYSTEM

Despite his temporary popularity when *The Drapier's Letters* first appeared, Swift saw little improvement for the whole people of Ireland in his lifetime. The political system almost guaranteed stagnation as it did in England. If the era of the Whig oligarchy under George I and George II in England was one of corruption, with seats in Parliament controlled by a handful of peers, the political scene in Ireland was much worse. In England, as the result of the Septennial Act of 1716, new Parliaments were ''elected'' at least every seven years. In Ireland, there was one Parliament during the reign of George I and one during the long reign of George II from 1727 to 1760. Between 1703 and 1767, the lord lieutenant was absent for long periods and rarely resident for more than six months of every two years. During his absence, three lord justices, usually the primate (the Anglican archbishop of Armagh), the speaker of the House of Commons, and the lord chancellor (who presided over the House of Lords), ran the government and controlled Parliament, as in England, though patronage. Even as late as 1783, some 109 landlords were involved in returning 215 members of the Irish House of Commons and thus controlled two-thirds of the 300-member body. Since Catholics and Presbyterians were excluded from voting, the Irish Parliament represented (in the modern sense) only a small percentage of the population.

ANGLO-IRISH CULTURE

The wealthy Protestant ascendancy, however, during Swift's lifetime, turned Dublin into one of the most elegant cities in Europe, with a patina of style and culture, mainly imported from England and the continent, against the background of writhing ignorance and inhumanity. The great library at Trinity College was completed, along with much of the new Parliament house, which was more spacious and elegant than "that heap of confusion at Westminster." Famous Italian musicians were imported, including Francesco Geminiani, who owned a fine house in Dublin; and in 1741 and 1742, G. F. Handel paid an extended visit to Dublin, where his *Messiah* premiered in the Music Hall on Fishamble Street on April 13, 1742.

Unlike Swift, most of the creative Anglo-Irishmen were off in London seeking fame and fortune. William Congreve (1670–1729), "the greatest English master of comedy," educated in Ireland and a friend of Swift's, produced *The Way of the World* on the London stage in 1700. Oliver Goldsmith (1728–1774), a sort of eighteenth-century Anglo-Irish "hippie" who would commemorate the village of his boyhood, Lissoy, Westmeath, in his famous poem "The Deserted Village," triumphed on the London stage with *She Stoops to Conquer*. And Thomas Sheridan (1719–1788), a godson of Jonathan Swift's, though a scholar and lecturer, became famous as an actor on the London stage. His son, Richard Brinsley Sheridan (1751–1816), who inherited from his grandfather's "Art of Punning" with Swift a keen sense of satire, dominated the London stage in the 1770s with his plays *The School for Scandal* and *The Rivals* and served, as a Radical, in Parliament, where he actively opposed the union of the Irish and English Parliaments in 1800. And the Dublin-born pianist-composer John Field (1782–1837), inventor of the nocturne, won fame not only in London but also on the continent and in Russia and inspired the young Chopin.

BERKELEY AND THE PEASANTRY

The seeds of intellectual and moral ferment Swift sowed among the Anglo-Irish were also nurtured in his lifetime by his friend, Bishop George Berkeley (1685–1753). This great philosopher who asserted that it is mind, not matter, that creates, spent several years in Rhode Island after being left half of the property in the estate of Swift's Vanessa. Upon returning to Ireland, Berkeley was named Anglican bishop of Cloyne, where he published three volumes of *The Querist* (1735–1737). In this journal Berkeley presented in epigrammatic form the essence of what Swift had been writing for fifteen years. Reflecting on his years in America, Berkeley found the Irish peasants "more destitute than savages, and more abject than negroes"; in fact American Negro slaves had a saying: "If a Negro was not Negro, Irishman would be Negro." Berkeley raised many questions: "Whether there be upon earth any Christian or civilized people as beggarly, wretched and destitute as the common Irish?" "Whether, nevertheless, there is any other people whose wants may be more easily supplied from home?" "Whether a foreigner could imagine that one-half of the people were starving in a country which sent out such plenty of provisions?''

Berkeley and Swift, unlike most of their fellow Anglo-Irishmen, could not ignore the terrible poverty of their Catholic countrymen. A series of small famines between 1727 and 1730 and a major famine during the winter of 1740–1741, the "year of the slaughter" that killed an estimated 200,000 to 400,000, occurred in a country whose English-dominated government encouraged the extension of pastureland and discouraged tillage, especially the growth of wheat that might compete with English wheat. "Go and preach to your own tenants to fall to the plough as fast as they can," Swift advised one country gentleman, "or else die with the guilt of having driven away half the inhabitants, and starving the rest." And the situation was made worse by the constant growth in population, despite the deaths and emigration, from about 2.5 million around 1700 to 4 million in the 1780s. The potato, which had become the staple crop of the rural poor during Cromwellian times because it could not be easily seized by marauding troops, nourished the population explosion because it was easy to grow, even in bad soil, and, along with a little buttermilk, provided a nutritious diet. But the potato crop was all that stood between most Irish peasants and famine.

SWIFT'S FINAL SOLUTION

In his final attack on the English domination of Ireland, circulated among friends in England, Swift commended the French recruiting of Irish brigades. Since 1692, tens of thousands of Irishmen had been fighting in the armies of France, Spain, and Austria. Descendants of these "wild geese" would become famous in various national histories, among them Marshal Patrice MacMahon, first president of the Third French Republic, Count Edward von Taaffe, Austrian chancellor, and Bernardo O'Higgins, liberator of Chile. And so again in the guise of a disinterested patriot, Swift parried his wit on England's Irish question and proposed what might be called a "final solution": the annihilation of Ireland itself.

When a Colonel Hennecy arrived in Dublin during the autumn of 1730 with the approval of King George II to recruit 750 Irish soldiers for the French army, Swift's Tory friends in London, Pulteney and Bolingbroke, attacked the Whig government of Walpole in their journal *The Craftsman.* The journal criticized the Walpole government for the recruiting scheme, though it said it was at least "a little more charitable than a *late project* for preventing *Irish Children* from being starv'd, by fattening them up, and selling them to the *Butcher.*" Upon reading this reference to his *Proposal,* Swift leapt into the fray.

Answer to the Craftsman facetiously attacked the journal's ignorance of Irish affairs: "In the seventeenth century, England had forbidden Ireland to export live cattle, to the subsequent disadvantage of both kingdoms. Now *The Craftsman,* unwilling to learn from this past mistake, was urging a similar restraint on the export of live men." But this exploit had many advantages: the more Irishmen were exported to the continent, the more land would be turned into pasture for lack of farmers. And so England would get more wool from Ireland and sell the Irish more grain. But this plan does not go far enough. Instead, all of Ireland should be converted into one large pasture with the only population an English army of occupation and peasant farmers to tend the livestock. The landlords would be required to live in England, and the annual surplus of shepherds would be shipped to America as a shield between the English settlers and the Indians. Swift had mastered the irony of the Irish dilemma, and his legacy to future generations is clear.

SWIFT'S LEGACY

In a speech celebrating the repeal of Poynings' Law and the Declaratory Act in 1782, Henry Grattan would proclaim: "Spirit of Swift! Spirit of Molyneux! Your genius has prevailed! Ireland is now a nation." But it was only a Protestant nation that would last a mere eighteen years. The full irony of Swift's writings and heritage were perhaps best appreciated by W. B. Yeats in the poem "Parnell." In lamenting the poor leadership of the Irish Free State after independence in 1922, with its civil war and factionalism, Yeats found no leader with Parnell's "heart" who had passed through "Jonathan Swift's dark grove," where he "plucked bitter wisdom that enriched his blood."

That "bitter wisdom," full of ironies and contradictions, is especially poignant for the politically and religiously schizophrenic Anglo-Irish Protestants, but, like so much of Irish literature, the message is universal. Ironically, Dean Swift left his estate to St. Patrick's Hospital in Dublin to treat mental illness and summarized his career in humorous verse:

> He gave the little Wealth he had,
> To build a House for Fools and Mad:
> And shew'd by one satyric Touch,
> No Nation wanted it so much:
> That Kingdom he hath left his Debtor,
> I wish it soon may have a Better.

A more serious epitaph in Latin, which Yeats called the greatest in history, Swift selected for his tomb in St. Patrick's Cathedral:

> Hic depositum est Corpus
> JONATHAN SWIFT S. T. D.
> Hujus Ecclesiae Cathedralis
> Decani,
> Ubi saeva Indignatio
> Ulterius
> Cor lacerare nequit.
> Abi Viator
> Et imitare, si poteris,
> Strenuum pro virili
> Libertatis Vindicatorem.*

*Here rests Jonathan Swift, dean of this cathedral, where bitter indignation can no longer rend the heart. Depart, traveler, and imitate, if you can, so strenuous a champion of liberty.

CHAPTER 4

The Age of Burke, 1750–1800

The statues of two prominent eighteenth-century Anglo-Irishmen, Edmund Burke and Henry Grattan, stand at the entrance to the British House of Commons at Westminster. Along with Wolfe Tone, a republican; Lord Castlereagh, architect of the Act of Union; and the virulently anti-Catholic earl of Clare, they represent the conflicting strains within the Anglo-Irish community, and their lives demonstrate why the "Protestant nation" was stillborn in 1782 and why the Act of Union of 1800 with Great Britain was inevitable.

EDMUND BURKE: EARLY RISE TO INFLUENCE

No person could symbolize Ireland during the second half of the eighteenth century the way Jonathan Swift had during the first. But Edmund Burke (1729–1797) was intimately involved not only in Irish matters but also in imperial matters and in policies bearing on the American and French revolutions that would weigh so

EDMUND BURKE
(1729–1797)

(Irish Tourist Board: Statue in front of Trinity College, Dublin)

heavily on Irish affairs. Burke's career is a microcosm of the dilemmas confronting the English and the Irish of all faiths between 1770 and 1800.

Edmund Burke was born in Dublin, the second of the fifteen children of Richard Burke and Mary Nagle, only four of whom survived infancy. Edmund was the child of a mixed marriage. His father, an attorney, was a member of the established Church of Ireland (a necessity to practice law); his mother was a Roman Catholic. As was common practice among the Dublin middle class in such cases, the sons were brought up in the religion of the father, and the daughters followed that of their mother. But from his mother, whom he loved deeply, he inherited his imagination, tenderness of heart, and capacity for feeling.

Because he was an asthmatic child, at the age of 6 he was sent to his mother's Catholic relatives in Ballyduff, County Cork, where he attended a Catholic "hedge school" conducted in the ruined castle of Monanimmy by a Master O'Halloran. Young Edmund experienced firsthand the inequity of the penal laws, and his spirit of religious toleration was enhanced at a boarding school in Ballitore, County Kildare, run by a kindly Quaker, Abraham Shackleton.

At the age of 15, imbued with a love of religion and tolerance, Burke entered Trinity College, Dublin, which was then limited to members of the Church of Ireland. With his intellectual exuberance and originality, he achieved no academic distinction: He "neither derived the benefits nor suffered the drawbacks of systematic intellectual discipline." But he did develop a great love for Ciceronian declamations, a passion he would put to good use in political oratory. And in his speeches before the debating club he founded, Burke revealed his lifelong preference for the "*via media . . .* rather than the theoretically perfect."

In 1750 Burke left Dublin to read law at London's Middle Temple. Though he loved the city, he was never happy with legal studies and refused to be called to the bar. When his lawyer father then cut off his allowance, Burke was on his own, and he eked out a living publishing philosophical studies and secretly becoming editor in 1758 of the *Annual Register,* a review of world affairs. From 1761 to 1764 he got his start in practical politics as private secretary to the Irish chief secretary in Dublin Castle.

Back in Ireland, Burke was forced to confront the popery laws. The long hapless Catholic peasantry was beginning to fight back, if only through anarchistic methods. The collectors of tithes for the Church of Ireland were being attacked by members of an organization known as Whiteboys who terrorized Munster, burning houses, maiming livestock, and torturing tithe collectors. Beginning in the 1760s, the Whiteboys would be succeeded by other secret societies, such as the Thrashers, the Defenders, the Molly Maguires, and the Ribbonmen. Always condemned by the Catholic church, these direct-action organizations were formed to deal with a variety of grievances: excessive rent, evictions, and tithes. Although many in the Dublin government viewed this rural violence as another papist plot, Burke viewed the violence outside Ulster, where the custom of tenant right prevailed for the Presbyterians, as a product of the penal laws against Catholics. As the Protestant landlords and the government ruthlessly suppressed the Whiteboys, Burke wrote to a friend how the landlords, even an Anglo-Irish lawyer of his acquaintance, had become "monsters of inhumanity."

But despite Burke's efforts, the first measure for "Irish Catholic relief" would not come until 1778, during the American Revolution. And Burke's new position, beginning in 1765, as private secretary to the prime minister, the marquis of Rockingham, would be helpful to the Irish Catholic cause. In addition, in 1766 he was elected to the British House of Commons from the "pocket borough" of Wendover and soon became a leading member of the "Rockingham Whig" opposition to Lord North's ministry from 1770 to 1782. Having supported the repeal of the Stamp Act and opposed the Townshend Acts, Burke would develop policies for the American colonies that would affect Irish politics.

Burke's position on America and Ireland was basically the same. Both were to be subordinate to British imperial policies, but those policies must be enlightened and not oppressive. And Burke would use Britain's loss of its American colonies to spur reform in Ireland. He came to favor a reformed Irish Parliament, free of the dominance of the Protestant ascendancy, with Catholic members in the Lords and Commons, that would legislate for itself in domestic matters.

THE AMERICAN REVOLUTION AND IRISH AUTONOMY

The shocking defeat of the British army at the Battle of Saratoga in October 1777 brought great pressure for Irish reform. The American Revolution had found Ireland in a state of economic depression, and the closing of the American markets in the spring of 1775 appeared to threaten Irish bankruptcy. In addition, sympathy for the American cause was especially strong among the "Scotch-Irish" of Ulster, who had tens of thousands of cousins in the colonies. In 1775 the lord lieutenant, the earl of Harcourt, wrote: "The presbyterians in the north are in their hearts Americans." And educated Catholic opinion, despite its dislike of republican principles, hoped the war would pressure the British Parliament for reform of the anti-Catholic penal laws.

At first the British government got military aid from Ireland, as the Irish Parliament approved the withdrawal of one-third of the 12,000 British troops stationed in Ireland for service in America. Burke was outraged: "Ireland has chosen, instead of being the arbiter of peace, to be a feeble party in a war, waged against the principles of her own liberties." But the Irish Parliament balked at a government proposal to replace the 4000 troops with foreign Protestant mercenaries, and support grew for a national militia.

John Paul Jones's successful raid into Belfast Lough in April 1778, when he captured a king's ship, led the people of Belfast to petition the lord lieutenant for troops to protect them against an invasion of America's allies, the French, who, in the view of the Presbyterians, were "the jealous enemies of our liberties and religion." When the petitioners failed, they began to organize their own local volunteer force. The movement soon spread throughout Ireland among the Protestants, with a few Catholic gentry and middle-class papists, into a national volunteer force, with the landlords as officers. By 1780, under Lord Charlemont, about 40,000 Irish Volunteers began to think of themselves as, more than a defense force, an instrument to press Irish grievances against Britain.

But the issue of Catholic civil rights had to be dealt with. Henry Grattan, leader of the emerging Protestant "Patriots," would assert that "the Irish Protestant could never be free till the Irish Catholic had ceased to be a slave." In 1778, after a similar bill was enacted for English Catholics, the government proposed a bill for Irish Catholics that would permit them to take leases for life or for any fixed term up to 999 years and also to inherit and bequeath land on the same terms as Protestants. The bill had been inspired by the *Tract on the Popery Laws,* written by Burke in 1761; and despite the opposition of many Protestant die-hards, the Irish Parliament approved the legislation with the support of Grattan's Patriots. "You are now," wrote Burke to the speaker of the Irish Commons, "beginning to have a country."

But religious tolerance was slow in coming, and anti-Catholic feeling was strong. When Burke proposed similar legislation for Scots Catholics, Lord George Gordon organized the Protestant Association of Scotland and England. During the "Gordon riots" of 1780, as many as 60,000 protesters held the British Parliament hostage in London and blocked relief for Scottish Catholics.

Meanwhile, British military losses in America went from bad to worse, and Lord Cornwallis surrendered to General Washington at Yorktown in 1781. As the British world "turned upside down," the Irish constitution of 1782 was implemented, and Ireland had a tenuous kind of independence for the first time in over 600 years. In March 1782 at Westminster, the Whigs replaced Lord North's Tories, and appointed the marquis of Rockingham as prime minister, Charles James Fox as leader of the House of Commons, and Edmund Burke as paymaster-general and a privy councilor. In May, Fox introduced bills that amended Poynings' Law and repealed the Declaratory Act. Upon approval, these acts of the British Parliament provided that the lord lieutenants of Ireland and their advisers at Dublin Castle could no longer initiate Irish legislation, that the British monarch could veto Irish bills but not amend them, that the British Parliament could not legislate for Ireland, and that the Irish courts had final jurisdiction and Irish judges had secure tenure. Britain, however, would have control over foreign policy and defense.

As the more democratic Irish Volunteers soon dissolved, sharp religious and class differences stifled the new "Protestant nation." Two prominent Patriots strongly differed over the extension of the franchise to Roman Catholics. Grattan supported the Catholic vote, and Henry Flood opposed it. And in 1783 the Irish Parliament, controlled by landlords, opposed both men's efforts for "more equal representation of the people in Parliament." Upper- and middle-class Catholics would look to Britain for Catholic relief, and middle-class Ulster Presbyterians would find themselves at odds with the Protestant landlords and peasants over political reform. And Belfast for a time would become known—as it turned out, wrongly—as "Little Boston." The British government, aided by the Anglo-Irish landlords, would pursue different policies after the French Revolution of 1789. For London, it was back to "divide and rule."

THE IMPACT OF THE FRENCH REVOLUTION

Edmund Burke was caught up in these conflicts from 1782 until his death in 1797. His principal concern was extension of the franchise to Irish Catholic voters. Burke, however, opposed parliamentary reform in England and still represented his "pocket borough" in the House of Commons. But Ireland was different, he argued. How can you deny representation in Parliament to the majority of a nation, he wondered? And though he quietly accepted the independent Irish Parliament of 1782, he was skeptical because control was left in the hands of the Protestant landlords. But he continued to work for Catholic relief, and his son Richard became the chief agent of the Catholic Committee of Ireland, at a large salary. Burke was typical of the upper- and middle-class Irish Catholics who were becoming "castle Catholics" in regarding the British government as a champion of Catholic rights. And the outbreak of the French Revolution signaled a renewed effort on Burke's part for Catholic relief.

While the Catholic Committee was controlled by Catholic gentry, they were content to have his son Richard as their secretary-agent, who reflected their anti--French Revolutionary sentiments. But after the election of more democratic middle-class Catholics to the committee in 1791, Richard Burke was replaced as secretary by a young Dublin Protestant barrister, Wolfe Tone. Tone, an avowed supporter of the French Revolution, hoped to unite the Catholic peasantry with democratic Protestant dissenters organizing in Ulster.

Class differences among Catholics and Protestants were smoothed over during the relative prosperity for the Irish economy between the end of the American Revolution and the war between Britain and France breaking out in 1793. But the Dublin riots of 1784 revealed how delicate Anglo-Irish relations were after 1782. A bill was introduced in the Irish House of Commons principally at the behest of woolen manufacturers to impose slight duties on British imports in order to put Irish manufacturers on a par in the domestic market. When the Irish Parliament defeated the measure out of fear of offending the British, a mob spirit swept Dublin for several weeks as merchants who sold British goods were tarred and feathered. The popular new British prime minister, William Pitt, then introduced measures in the British Parliament calling for virtually complete free trade between Ireland and Britain in return for Irish support of the British navy. But Burke, preoccupied with India in 1784 and at the time in political opposition to Pitt, joined the majority of British protectionists in killing the measure. The Irish Parliament also opposed using surplus Irish revenues to support the British navy.

In addition, part of Ireland was increasingly affected economically and politically by the industrial revolution. The linen industry flourished in Ulster; and beginning in the 1790s, especially in Belfast, an important cotton-spinning industry developed. And so northeastern Ulster by 1800 was becoming an outpost of industrial Britain, with Belfast having more in common, economically, with Manchester and Birmingham than with Dublin and the rest of Ireland.

But after 1789, in the words of the great historian of eighteenth-century Ireland, W. E. H. Lecky, the French Revolution "became the test of every man's political creed." Supporting the Revolution were principally middle-class radical Presbyterians of Belfast and a few middle-class Catholics, along with a handful of gentry and landlords. Opposing the Revolution were the Protestant ascendancy, the Catholic bishops, and most Presbyterian tenant farmers. The bulk of the Catholic peasants, with their own special grievances, were exploited by both sides. Even the "Catholic" Irish Brigade in the French army, led by Count Daniel O'Connell, uncle of the future Irish national hero, would become a regiment in George III's army in 1794 to fight and wait for the return of the *ancien régime* in France.

Despite his advocacy of Irish Catholic relief and economic reform to eliminate corruption, Edmund Burke opposed William Pitt's parliamentary reforms in 1785 and became a rather conservative Whig by the outbreak of the French Revolution. When in 1790 he published his anti-Jacobin tract, *Reflections on the Revolution in France,* Burke became a great hero to Pitt's Tories and to conservatives for the next two centuries. He could be ludicrously romantic in his defense of Marie Antoinette: "I thought ten thousand swords must have leaped from their scabbards to avenge even a look that threatened her with insult. But the age of chivalry is gone." But he was remarkably perceptive about the modern world ahead: "That of sophisters, economists, and calculators, has succeeded." Burke also reflected the intense Catholic fear of the Revolution:

> The murder of a king, or a queen, or a bishop, or a father, are only common homicide; and if the people are by any chance, or in any way, gainers by it, a sort of homicide much the most pardonable.

Replying to Burke in 1791, Thomas Paine published *The Rights of Man,* attacking Burke's "balance of the constitution" among king, lords, and commons. All hereditary government, whether by king or lords, was "an imposition on mankind," according to Paine; and since all power was derived from the people, a republican government should at once be established, with a representative legislature based on universal suffrage. When *The Rights of Man* was suppressed in England and Paine was tried for treason, he fled to France, where he was imprisoned during the Reign of Terror and barely escaped the guillotine.

Back in England, anti-Jacobin (radical French revolutionary) feeling gripped the country the way anti-Communist paranoia swept the United States during the 1950s. Antiradical mobs in Birmingham and Manchester attacked the homes of Painite Radicals. One Radical leader was tried for high treason for advocating "representative government," and habeas corpus was suspended and workingmen's associations banned throughout England. No wonder, then, that the British government should be concerned about Ireland!

In 1791 the Society of United Irishmen was founded in Belfast and soon spread to Dublin through the efforts of Wolfe Tone, secretary of the Catholic Committee. Tone referred to Tom Paine's *Rights of Man* as the "Koran" of Belfast, but he also noted that Ulster Protestant dissenters "have not come forward in support of Catholic Emancipation *save only in Belfast.*" Indeed, Tone and many of the United Irishmen were Enlightenment Deists, like Thomas Jefferson, and thus skeptical of all organized religions.

After the execution of Louis XVI on January 21, 1793, and France's declaration of war against Great Britain on February 1, the Irish government hastened to push through the Catholic Relief Act, which took two months. It extended the parliamentary franchise to Catholic "forty-shilling freeholders"* and permitted Catholics to hold most civil and military offices and to receive university degrees. But it did not permit Catholics to be elected to Parliament, and the Irish House of Commons overwhelmingly rejected in 1794 the United Irishmen's proposal for

---

*A lifetime leaseholder of a house or land with an annual rent of forty shillings.

parliamentary reform to eliminate "rotten" and "pocket" boroughs and to provide for more equal representation.

Burke denounced opponents of Catholic emancipation for "driving into Jacobinism" Roman Catholics "whose religious principles,—church polity, and habitual discipline,—might make them an invincible dyke against that inundation." By contrast, Wolfe Tone argued that the extension of the franchise in the 1793 act was only a "disgrace to our constitution and our country," when at election time "the wretched tribe of forty-shilling freeholders . . . [are] driven to their octennial market by their landlords."

DIVISIVE EVENTS: MAYNOOTH AND THE BATTLE OF THE DIAMOND

Unfortunately for Wolfe Tone, if most of England would resist French Revolutionary fervor, Ireland also was no haven for Jacobin ideas. And two events in 1795 illustrate why the British government and the Protestant ascendancy were able to divide their opposition: the subsidization of Maynooth Seminary and the Battle of the Diamond.

With the support of Burke, and Earl Fitzwilliam, the new Whig lord lieutenant, Henry Grattan, introduced a bill providing for Catholic emancipation (the admission of Catholics to the Irish Parliament) in February 1795. But the shrewd, dominant figure of the ascendancy, the reactionary John Fitzgibbon, earl of Clare and lord chancellor, with the support of the Irish cabinet and a huge majority of Tories in the Irish Parliament, forced Fitzwilliam's replacement as lord lieutenant by the more pliable Earl Camden. Had Fitzwilliam remained, with the support of Britain, according to Lecky, he might have persuaded the Irish Parliament to grant Catholic emancipation and have averted the "Risings of 1798." But Grattan's bill, supported by the Irish Whigs, was overwhelmingly defeated in May, and the government was looking for a palliative for Catholic opinion.

In this reactionary period in England and Ireland, William Pitt, panicked by French military successes, and Lord Clare came to view the Roman Catholic hierarchy as a bulwark against the spread of the contagion of the French Revolution. Consequently, on June 5, 1795, an act of the Irish Parliament partially endowed the Royal College of St. Patrick, at Maynooth, County Kildare. No longer would candidates for the Catholic priesthood have to study in continental seminaries.

The government endowment of Maynooth may have hardened the anti-Revolutionary sympathies of the Catholic bishops over the next century and a half, whether against United Irishmen, Fenians, or IRA. In addition, many of the early professors at Maynooth had been educated in Jansenistic seminaries on the continent, where they were taught a kind of Calvinistic Catholicism. Their student priests throughout Ireland (and later America, shaping American Catholicism) preached a moral puritanism that in stressing spiritual salvation viewed the body as evil and encouraged political conservatism.

This is not to say that in the 1790s the majority of Catholic peasants were politically conservative. But they also had no sense of nationality. Indeed, the situation the church hierarchy confronted with the Irish peasants was the prototype of the festering controversy in Roman Catholicism today over liberation theology, especially in Latin America. Father John Murphy, condemned by the bishops for leading the Wexford peasants in revolt in 1798, has hundreds of heirs throughout the clergy of South America.

But the Catholic peasant organizations of the 1790s were largely anarchistic in aim and merely encouraged Protestant peasants (tenant farmers) to organize against them. This short-term nearsightedness played into the hands of the Protestant ascendancy in 1795 in the famous Battle of the Diamond.

Sectarian strife had been a problem for much of the second half of the eighteenth century, but during the 1790s it became especially troublesome in southern Ulster, particularly in County Armagh, where there had been an increase of population and tougher competition for landholdings. Since Catholics had a lower standard of living than the Protestants, Catholics would work for lower wages as tenants. Fearful of losing their small holdings, the Protestants formed an organization known as the Peep O'Day Boys, who in armed bands raided the homes of Catholics to force them away from the locality. The Catholics set up a counterorganization, known as the Defenders, and frequent and fatal clashes occurred. The most famous took place at a crossroads known as the Diamond, near Loughall, County Armagh, on September 21, 1795. After the Peep O'Day Boys easily drove off the Defenders, the victorious Protestants that night formed the Orange Society, later named the Orange Order, after the Protestant victor of the Battle of the Boyne, William of Orange. The purpose of the Orange Order was to maintain the Protestant ascendancy and to terrorize the Catholics of Armagh, thousands of whom during the next few months fled to Connacht. Soon Protestant merchants and gentry began to join the Orange Order.

Nevertheless, thousands of Protestants in Belfast petitioned the Irish Parliament in February 1795 for Catholic emancipation and joined the United Irishmen. The government reacted quickly. The Irish House of Commons voted 143 to 19 against Grattan's motion to admit Catholics to Parliament, and shortly afterward, in the fall of 1796, voted 157 to 7 to suspend the Habeas Corpus Act, which suspension continued until June 1799.

DIVIDE AND RULE

In March 1797 General Gerard Lake, with the support of a militia of Catholic peasants, marched north to disarm Ulster. The Monaghan militia ran amuck through Belfast, burning and torturing, terrorizing anyone suspected of being a United Irishman, and thus broke the back of the organization. Furthermore, the majority of Ulster Presbyterians by that time had come to fear France and thus any alliance with Catholics.

By 1798 United Irishmen plans for a coordinated rising had fallen into disarray. Dublin Castle's secret service had a superior network of informers and arrested many of the leaders in March 1798. In May and June, with the arrest and death of Lord Edward Fitzgerald, the United Irishmen were left without a leader.

Nevertheless, sporadic uprisings occurred throughout Leinster. But only in County Wexford did the rebels have any success, capturing the towns of Wexford and Enniscorthy. Under the leadership of Father John Murphy, an opponent of the United Irishmen, the Wexford Rising, despite its initial success, was little more than a Catholic peasant uprising. After routing the North Cork militia and local yeomanry and slaughtering several hundred Protestants, the Wexford insurgents were defeated by British troops and Orange yeomen at Vinegar Hill on June 21, 1798 and the leaders were hanged.

Though discouraged by the failures in Leinster and reports that in Wexford the uprising had turned into a crusade against Protestants, on June 7 Henry Joy McCracken, a Belfast cotton manufacturer and one of the founders of the United Irishmen, led several thousand men in an attack on Antrim Town but was repulsed. Likewise Henry Munro, a Lisburn linen manufacturer, led 7000 men against Ballynahinch, County Down, but was defeated. And the Ulster uprising was over in ten days.

Only the West and the French were to be heard from, too little and too late. General Jean Humbert's army of 1000 Frenchmen landed at Killala Bay, County Mayo, on August 22, 1798. After routing government troops initially on August 27 in what was derisively known as the "Castlebar races," Humbert's small force was overwhelmed by British forces at Ballinamuck on September 8, and he surrendered to the new lord lieutenant, General Cornwallis, of Yorktown fame. And the last revolutionary gasp occurred in October, when a French invasion squadron was defeated off Lough Swilly, County Donegal. Seven of the ten French ships were captured, and Wolfe Tone, in the uniform of a French general, was arrested on landing at Buncrana on November 3. The Rising of '98 came to an end on November 19, when Tone committed suicide in a Dublin prison rather than be hanged as a traitor and not shot as an enemy officer, as he had requested.

Tone had long embraced the deistic and republican philosophy of the French Revolution and so completely misjudged his fellow Irishmen as to believe that they would abandon their religious and class hatreds. Instead of a united struggle against Britain, 1798 turned largely into a civil war between Catholic and Protestant. Nevertheless, Tone left a republican-revolutionary legacy that is still alive today and still confronting the same religious divisions with the same naivete. Every June 20 the IRA commemorates the birth of Wolfe Tone with a pilgrimage to his grave in Bodenstown Churchyard, County Kildare. And memories of '98 shaped a national consciousness with such ballads as "The Croppy Boy," "The Rising of the Moon," and President Kennedy's favorite, "Kelly, the Boy from Killanne." Indeed, the "Irish question" would be known around the world through one line of a Dion Boucicault ballad: "They are hanging men and women for the Wearing of the Green."

THE DRIVE TOWARD UNION WITH BRITAIN

Ireland at the turn of the nineteenth century was still a mere pawn in British plans, as the English fretted over Napoleon's success. The shrewd Anglo-Irish lord chancellor, the earl of Clare, who once referred to Irish Catholics as "the scum of the earth," knew where power lay and decided to lead the Protestant ascendancy away from Irish nationalism. In his view, the Anglo-Irish ascendancy could preserve their class and religious dominance in Ireland only by abolishing their Parliament of 500 years and supporting the Act of Union with Great Britain. The myth of a "Protestant nation" would be denied, and the stark reality of superior British power would once again confirm Ireland's status as a British colony.

Britain's wartime prime minister, William Pitt, had much bigger strategic concerns, but he was convinced that a legislative union between Britain and Ireland would not only serve Britain's imperial interests but also pacify Ireland. And through his lord lieutenant, the Marquis Cornwallis, and his Irish chief secretary, Viscount Castlereagh, Pitt would promise the Irish Catholic hierarchy to support Catholic emancipation once the two countries were united.

The Catholic bishops, especially the archbishop of Dublin, John Troy, were already predisposed to support the Act of Union because of the Maynooth grant and their antirevolutionary sentiments. In addition, in January 1799 the Catholic bishops secretly adopted resolutions in favor of state stipends for Catholic priests and a British government veto on the nomination of Catholic bishops.

The chief architect of the union was the first native Anglo-Irish chief secretary since the Glorious Revolution, Robert Stewart, Viscount Castlereagh. Ironically, young Lord Castlereagh was elected as a member of Parliament in 1790 for County Down, supporting Grattan's "popular" party and representing Presbyterian farmers and weavers against Dublin Castle and the marquis of Downshire. But like Lord Clare, he soon saw the opportunity for advancement on the government side, especially after his uncle, Earl Camden, became viceroy in 1795; and after holding minor office, Castlereagh was appointed chief secretary in 1798 with authority to negotiate the Act of Union.

Castlereagh's challenge lay in convincing the elite elements of Irish society. "The mass of the people of Ireland," remarked Cornwallis, "do not care one farthing about the union." Castlereagh's task was to build a majority in the Irish Parliament to vote the body into extinction or, as he put it, "to buy out, and secure to the Crown for ever, the fee simple of Irish corruption." Such "patronage" or "bribery" was the method of creating government majorities in England as well as Ireland, and even the idealist Burke would tolerate and benefit from the system. In fact, his friend, Sir Hercules Langrishe, whom Burke in his famous letter of 1792 prompted to introduce the bill for the Catholic franchise, voted for the union in 1800 and was paid 13,862 pounds (at least one million dollars today) to abandon his "interest" in the borough of Knocktopher, as its M.P.

Perhaps, the most dishonest part of Castlereagh's bargaining for the union was his understanding with the Roman Catholic elite that once the union was enacted, Pitt's government would introduce a bill for Catholic emancipation. But the earl of Clare, more accurately reading Irish and English Protestant opinion, forced Castlereagh to drop Catholic emancipation from the Act of Union. Clare had been the first politician to propose the union as a means of saving Ireland from a "popish democracy" because of the "fatal mistake" of giving certain Catholics the vote in 1793. He had bluntly warned his fellow Protestant landlords that "the Act by which most of us hold our estates was an Act of violence—an Act subverting the first principles of the Common Law in England and Ireland." When Clare got his way, Lord Cornwallis expressed his disappointment at the exclusion of Irish Catholics from the British Parliament: "I certainly wish that England could now make a union with the Irish nation, instead of making it with a party in Ireland."

Between January 1799 and January 1800 about one-fifth of the membership of the Irish House of Commons was changed through various forms of influence and intimidation. Even the last-minute appearance of Henry Grattan—dressed in a Volunteers uniform and absent since the House's rejection of parliamentary reform in 1797—failed to revive the Protestant Patriots. The myth of the "Protestant nation" was exposed for the sham it really was.

Back in England, with Edmund Burke's death in 1797, Irish Catholics had lost an articulate spokesman. Had he lived a few more years, he might have swayed his Tory friends to support Catholic emancipation as an antirevolutionary measure. But England, under the threat of Napoleon, had grown even more conservative than Burke. When George III refused to agree to Catholic emancipation for fear of violating his coronation oath to uphold the Protestant succession to the Throne (something that Burke had argued full civil rights for Catholics would not do), Pitt and Castlereagh were forced to resign, and the Irish Catholics were betrayed.

Without Catholic emancipation, the Irish Protestant ascendancy—"that junto of robbers," as Burke called them—could no longer be entirely blamed for Irish troubles. With the vainglorious declaration of the United Kingdom on January 1, 1801, the imperial Parliament of Westminster became directly responsible for Irish affairs, which even the most staunchly conservative apologists for Britain would admit was a curse as much as a blessing. Indeed, under the union, the Irish tail would constantly wag the English dog.

With great irony for Irish history, Edmund Burke wrote: "It is not about Popes but about potatoes that the minds of this unhappy people are agitated." Unfortunately, "No Popery" would still agitate many English Protestant minds, as British politicians, mimicking the earl of Clare, would "play the Orange card" of anti-Catholicism.

John Fitzgibbon, earl of Clare, would have little time to enjoy his new peerage in the British House of Lords, dying in 1802 at the age of 52. Married to the daughter of "Burn-Chapel" Whaley, who was known for his destruction of Catholic houses of worship in retaliation for peasant uprisings, Fitzgibbon, nicknamed "Fitzpetulant," even in death stirred up national hatred. His funeral procession through Dublin "was marked by some of the most unruly scenes ever witnessed in Ireland," which culminated when a dead cat was thrown on his coffin. Ironically, his portrait today adorns the halls of Trinity College, Dublin, where he peers down on a predominantly Irish Catholic student body, "the dregs of the people" in his words.

But most ironic is the inscription on the statue in the Statesmen's Corner of Westminster Abbey to "Robert Stewart, Second Marquis of Londonderry, Viscount Castlereagh (1769–1822)." The final words read: "Ireland will never forget the statesman of the legislative union."

PART II From Province to Nation-State, 1801–1921

by Lawrence J. McCaffrey

CHAPTER 5

Catholic Emancipation, 1801–1829

The Irish Parliament held its last session in College Green on August 2, 1800. On January 28, 1801, one hundred Irishmen took seats in the 658-member British House of Commons, and thirty-two Irish peers, including four Protestant bishops, entered the 360-member House of Lords. Despite the existence of a United Kingdom Parliament at Westminster, the merger of the Churches of Ireland and England, and the 1815 amalgamation of the two treasuries, Ireland was not as thoroughly integrated into the United Kingdom as the other two portions of the Celtic fringe, Scotland and Wales. The continuation of such positions as lord lieutenant, chief secretary, lord chancellor, and chancellor of the exchequer, over twenty government agencies supervising a multitude of civil servants, a military department, and separate courts and prison systems were remnants of nationhood.

The most glaring contrast between Ireland and Britain was the condition of the Irish Catholic majority. The Penal Laws had coerced most of the Catholic aristocracy and gentry into Protestantism, and restrictions on the acquisition of land had expanded the Catholic middle class. Although the position of the small Catholic upper class and the growing middle class had substantially improved by the time of

DANIEL O'CONNELL
1775–1847

Daniel O'Connell built modern Irish nationalism on the foundations of the Catholic Emancipation agitation. As a champion of human rights and freedom throughout the world, he implanted the values of liberal democracy in the soil of Irish nationalism. (Photo painted and engraved by R. M. Hodgetts, courtesy of the National Gallery of Ireland.)

the union, they were still deprived by remaining Penal Laws that kept them from a role in Irish political life and the professions. Both worked for Catholic emancipation to achieve equality with Anglo-Irish and British Protestants. In their effort to liberate themselves, upper- and middle-class Catholics had little empathy for the plight of the rural masses.

THE LIFE OF RURAL CATHOLIC IRELAND

The overwhelming majority of Irish Catholics were attached to the land as tenants at will or agricultural laborers. Few tenants had farms bigger than 15 acres. Far more numerous than farmers, agricultural laborers were fortunate to have a patch of land on which to erect a crude mud hut and to plant a potato garden. Small tenant farmers' cottages were often no better than those of the laborers. The floors were dirt, and vermin infested the thatch roofs. Windows to let in a bit of fresh air were rare. Since a pig was a valuable possession, in bad weather animals and people shared hearth and home. Such living conditions bred disease, resulting in an extremely high mortality rate, particularly among infants. If a person managed to survive childhood, the scourges of scurvy, cholera, tuberculosis, and malnutrition threatened to prevent the attainment of middle age. Defying poverty and disease and the lack of significant medical care, Ireland from the mid-eighteenth century until the Great Famine of the 1840s experienced a massive population increase. In 1781 the estimated number of people living in the country was 4,048,000. Sixty years later the census recorded the population at 8,175,000, a gain of slightly more than 100 percent.

Ireland's population explosion indicated frequent marriage and high fertility. Throughout time and place, poverty has increased the need for shared misery and stimulated sexual urges. Living within the confines of their religious and agrarian mores, Irish Catholics satisfied desires inside the marriage bond. For people as poor and as miserable as rural Irish Catholics, sex, the companionship of wives and husbands, and the joy of children, like good and even bad whiskey, were comforts and escapes in a normally hopeless existence.

Potatoes also figured in Ireland's population boom. An easy-to-cultivate vegetable, flourishing in less than excellent soil, the nutritious potato dominated the rural Irish menu. By the time of the Great Famine, most of the people ate only potatoes with a little milk or buttermilk to wash them down. Sometimes they were consumed half-cooked to prolong the digestive process. Potatoes made it possible to feed many from few resources, encouraging the young to marry and begin large families. But such reliance on a single food source posed the danger of crop failures. Beginning in the 1820s, Ireland experienced a series of famines, culminating in the "holocaust" of the 1840s.

The population explosion put too much strain on an already weak agrarian economy. Since there was no industry outside northeast Ulster to absorb the surplus population, tenant farmers had to emigrate, suffer downward mobility into the ranks of agricultural labor, or subdivide already too small holdings. As Irish farms decreased in size, agriculture gained in inefficiency. Following the decline in grain prices after the French Revolution and continuing for the rest of the century, Irish farming became more pasture than tillage, adding to the land shortage. Due to land hunger, landlords were able to raise rents beyond the value of farms and still find desperate souls willing to pay. Tenants with exorbitant rents were anxious to sublease parts of their holdings, also at excessive rates, to meet obligations to landlords.

Land pressure and its exploitation fostered avarice, evictions, class war, and violence. Since the landlords commanded the law and the authorities, a number of secret societies such as the Ribbonmen, Whiteboys, Molly Maguires, Terry Alts, and Defenders flourished. In individual instances and in epidemics of violence, they burned hayricks and maimed cattle to punish landlords for high rents and landgrabbers who occupied the farms of evicted tenants; they shot bailiffs of enemy landlords, harassed tithe collectors for an established church that served only 13 percent of the population, and even punished Catholic priests with reputations for charging too much for baptisms, weddings, and funerals. While tenant farmers and agricultural laborers frequently united in opposition against the landowning class, a number of secret societies were organized by laborers to protest the wages offered and conacre (potato patch) rents demanded by farmers.

In fiction form, William Carleton presented an insider's portrait of prefamine rural Ireland. His "Wildgoose Lodge" describes how agrarian terrorists could be cruel and indiscriminate in their violence at the expense of innocents. But secret societies did enforce a sort of moral economy where and when legal and political structures were indifferent to the plight of the rural masses.

Government responses to Irish violence indicated that Ireland was much more a colony than an integral part of the United Kingdom. Insurrection acts and coercion bills with house searches, curfews, sentences without jury trials, and suspensions of habeas corpus violated traditional British constitutional rights. In 1813 Sir Robert Peel, Irish chief secretary and Tory leader in the House of Commons, introduced a professional police force into Ireland. By 1867 it had evolved into the Royal Irish Constabulary. The half-police, half-soldier barracks-dwelling RIC became a model security force for the empire. The government also used the military in Ireland for law and order purposes. Among their police duties, soldiers assisted in tithe collection and escorting electors to the polls in hotly contested elections.

In Irish nationalist mythology and in British reformism, Irish landlords were the arm of British economic and social colonialism and the source of rural discontent and misery. As in Maria Edgeworth's *Castle Rackrent,* some landlords were reckless, improvident, and indifferent to the welfare of their estates. A considerable number were absentees living in Britain off their Irish rents. Absenteeism probably aggravated the social and economic dimension of the Irish question. Although not always the case, resident landlords were more likely to be interested in the quality of agriculture on their estates and the good of their tenants. It is difficult to prove that absentees were not as humane as residents, but they did deny to Ireland incomes derived from their property, thus hampering the development of domestic trades and industries. Absentees were more British than Irish in perspectives, and the loss of such a large proportion of the aristocracy retarded the development of a vital, intelligent, and influential Irish political, cultural, and economic opinion.

Irish nationalism and British reformism exaggerated landlord evils. They were scapegoats for complex social and economic problems. Many were kindly disposed to their tenants. Often well-intentioned landlords caused economic disasters. Reluctant to interfere with the mores of their tenants, they ignored farm subdivisions and inefficient farming. But the main problem with Irish landlordism was its alien rather than economic character. The landed aristocracy and gentry in other sections of the United Kingdom were often cruel to their tenants, but they shared religious and cultural values with them. They received natural acceptance as the leaders of British rural society. In Ireland, landlords and tenants were separated by religious and cultural barriers. Landlordism symbolized the passing of the Gaelic order, the oppression suffered by Catholic Ireland, and the triumph of British colonialism.

Relations between landlord and tenant were more cordial in Ulster than in Leinster, Munster, and Connacht. Ulster custom permitted a tenant to sell his interest in the farm, the result of improvements, when he left it. This was some protection against unfair rent increases and evictions. But in the south and west, if a tenant added to the value of his farm by draining, fencing, or fertilizing his fields or by repairing buildings, the landlord might raise his rent and evict him with no compensation if he could not meet the new demand. Consequently, Leinster, Munster, and Connacht farmers seldom improved their holdings, and the quality of Ulster agriculture was higher than in the remainder of the country. No doubt landlord-tenant contacts in Ulster were also more cordial because many farmers were Protestants (Anglicans) or Nonconformists like their landlords, and religious differences did not add to class and economic conflicts. In that way large areas of Ulster were more like Britain than Ireland.

Although the unhealthy condition of rural Ireland was apparent to all intelligent and impartial observers, politics, religion, and economic dogmas obstructed remedies. Both Whigs and Tories fought limitations on property rights, arguing that the Irish agrarian issue was moral rather than political. Laissez-faire dogmatism, so important in Whig and Radical circles, opposed proposed government emigration and public work programs to ease Irish poverty burdens. However, the British left was willing to give the Irish a greater voice in their own destiny through political reform, and it was sympathetic to equality between Catholic and Protestant peoples and their churches. But Tories were adamant in resisting any changes that might diminish Protestant ascendancy. They considered objections to the privileged position of Irish Protestantism and landlordism as assaults on property and traditional institutions. Concessions to Catholic grievances would encourage further Irish discontent and open doors to new demands for change. Radical victories in Ireland would jeopardize the union and inspire agitations against the status quo all over the United Kingdom.

THE EMERGENCE OF DANIEL O'CONNELL

Before Irish gentry and middle-class Irish Catholics could transform Whig and Radical good intentions into a constructive Irish policy and overcome Tory obstinacy, they had to mobilize the Catholic masses behind the demand for justice and equality. Demoralized farmers and laborers, whose hopes did not extend much beyond survival in this world and salvation in the next, were poor political material. Catholic Ireland needed a leader with the genius to lift its spirits and provide it with the expectations and confidence necessary for effective agitation. Daniel O'Connell was such a person. He created an Irish national opinion that forced British politicians to choose between the unpleasant alternatives of reform or a revolution endangering political, social, and economic structures throughout the United Kingdom.

O'Connell was more than the creator of modern Irish nationalism. No other Irish leader has had as much international importance. His main concern was Ireland, but the principles he defended, the goals of his efforts, and his agitation techniques had favorable consequences for liberal democracy throughout the world. In the reactionary age of Metternich, O'Connell was the most successful tribune of the people. He translated democratic theory into practice by mobilizing the Irish rural masses into a powerful nationalist bloc. Applying this new force, he forced concessions from an arrogant, aristocratic British government. In early nineteenth-century Europe, O'Connell was a much discussed personality: To the embattled left, he was a symbol of hope and a promise for the future; to the ascendant but nervous right, he was the enemy threatening entrenched privilege.

O'Connell was most hated by the British and Anglo-Irish establishments. Their newspapers and periodicals portrayed him as a mendacious, avaricious vulgarian inciting discontent in the public mind to collect money from ignorant, impoverished peasants. Conservative journalists and Tory politicians told the British public that O'Connell was the instigator of a vast conspiracy to subvert the empire and the constitution by detaching Ireland from Britain and by imposing popery on the British Isles. Since anti-Catholicism was the core of British nativism, O'Connell was a natural target for Tories manipulating Protestant passions to prevent economic and social change and to preserve the union with Ireland.

O'Connell's entry on the public stage made the Irish question the leading emotional issue dividing British political forces and public opinion. He instructed British politicians in the techniques of political organization and activity. His successors at the helm of Irish nationalism continued the lesson.

O'Connell was born on August 6, 1775, the son of Morgan and Catherine O'Connell, members of the Kerry Catholic gentry. Through the goodwill of Protestant neighbors, the O'Connells managed to hold on to their property through Penal times. They increased the family fortune through smuggling activities along the Kerry coast. Because Catholics were denied opportunities in Ireland, some O'Connells served Hapsburgs and Bourbons on the continent. O'Connell's uncle, Count Daniel, was a French general.

Following an Irish Catholic upper-class custom, Morgan and Catherine placed their infant son as a foster child in a peasant cottage for nursing and rearing. Learning and speaking the Irish language, participating in the religious devotions, games, and customs, and sharing the values of the people were good training for the future leader of Irish nationalism.

When O'Connell was still a boy, his childless uncle Maurice, head of the clan, adopted him as his heir. In 1791 Maurice sent his nephew to the continent for his secondary education. After the armies of the French Revolution closed two schools that he attended, St. Omer and Douai, O'Connell in 1793 transferred to a London academy. Since by then the Irish Parliament had opened the practice of law to Catholics, the young man decided to be a barrister, and in 1794 he enrolled in Lincoln's Inn. He transferred to the King's Inn, Dublin, two years later. In 1798 the Irish bar admitted O'Connell.

In O'Connell's day, legal studies were not rigorous, and he had time and leisure to read history, biography, fiction, poetry, theology, and essays on political and economic thought. William Godwin's belief that democratic moral force could change society impressed the young student. Thomas Paine bolstered his democratic faith and led him away from orthodox Christianity to Deism. Adam Smith made him a laissez-faire advocate. Though O'Connell eventually recovered his Catholic faith, he never rejected his commitment to human rights, democracy, religious tolerance, freedom of conscience, separation of church and state, and economic individualism. During the 1830s and 1840s he argued those causes in the British Parliament.

In Dublin, O'Connell became grand master of a Masonic lodge, visited the Irish Parliament, projected himself as a Catholic Grattan liberating his people, and dabbled with the Society of United Irishmen while at the same time drilling with a lawyer's yeoman corps organized to defend law and order. In 1798 O'Connell fled Dublin to avoid arrest. When the revolutions commenced, he was sick with fever in Kerry, but in his diary he denounced the events in Wexford: "Good God! What a brute man becomes when ignorant and oppressed! Oh liberty! what horrors are perpetrated in thy name! May every virtuous revolutionary remember the horrors of Wexford." O'Connell concluded that the Irish people were "not yet sufficiently enlightened to bear the sun of freedom." Revolution had released destructive passions in ignorant, frustrated people. Britain and the Irish establishment had responded to their rage with cruel repression and with the Act of Union. The uprising of '98 had decreased rather than enlarged Ireland's freedom.

O'Connell was not an ideological pacifist. He praised the leaders of the American Revolution and contributed money and the services of a son to Simón Bolívar, the liberator of Latin America. Believing that the British would always crush a peasant mob and then further restrict Irish liberties, O'Connell rejected physical force as the route to Irish freedom. He continued to argue that the only way Catholics should earn civil rights, and Ireland's independence, was through the pressures of moral force. He condemned secret agrarian societies and had little use for Robert Emmet, who became one of Ireland's most beloved heroes.

A younger brother of Thomas Addis Emmet, one of the founders of the

Society of United Irishmen, Robert Emmet, in 1803 led a Dublin insurrection crushed by the authorities. He was tried, convicted, and executed for treason. Before sentencing, Emmet made a speech defending his honor and condemning British oppression. He asked the young men of Ireland to listen to their country's cry for freedom and to vindicate his work and justify his sacrifice: "When my country takes her place among the nations of the earth, then and not until then, let my epitaph be written." Emmet's words and Thomas Moore's poetic tribute, "Oh Breathe Not His Name," made Emmet a martyr saint for Irish nationalists, but not to O'Connell. He wrote to a friend, "A man who could so cooly prepare so much bloodshed—so many murders—and such horrors of every kind has ceased to be an object of compassion."

In 1802 O'Connell married a distant cousin, Mary O'Connell. They had seven children who survived into adulthood. She provided him with a great deal of love, wise political advice, and the peace and security of a happy home. He loved her with passion and consistency.

When O'Connell began practicing his profession, times were difficult for Catholic lawyers. They had to be content with unimportant cases and small fees. But O'Connell worked hard and used his knowledge of the Irish people, as well as a quick mind, devastating wit, and oratorical skills, to become the best cross-examiner and persuader of juries in Ireland. His practice became so large that by 1828 he was earning over 6000 pounds a year.

In the courtroom, O'Connell promoted Irish nationalism. In addressing juries, he blamed British rule and the oppression of Catholics for Irish crimes and disorders. In 1805 O'Connell joined the Catholic Committee, working through petitions to Parliament to open political office for Catholics. He gave it much of his time and income. By 1812 he had replaced John Keogh as the most influential member of the organization.

Henry Grattan, leader of the Protestant nation and foe of the union, championed the Catholic emancipation cause in the House of Commons. He presented Catholic Committee petitions to his parliamentary colleagues. Emancipation enlisted the support of most Whigs and Radicals, and even a few Tories. On occasion it could command a House of Commons majority. But the Tory government, in its resistance to Irish and British Catholic and parliamentary opinion, could count on the king's Protestant conscience, the House of Lords, and British nativism to frustrate the Catholic civil rights effort. There was one possibility that Catholic emancipation might become law: a compromise that would give the government or a committee of respectable and loyal Catholic laymen a veto over papal appointments of United Kingdom bishops. This security was acceptable to most prominent Catholics in Britain and Ireland, a few of the Irish Catholic hierarchy, Grattan and the British Whigs, and even the pope. Many governments in Catholic countries controlled appointments to the episcopacy. Britain, however, was a Protestant country with an established church. But the pope wanted cordial relations with one of the world's major powers.

In 1813 Grattan introduced a Catholic emancipation bill with securities. Most of the leadership of the Catholic Committee approved of the measure. Joining a majority of the Irish Catholic hierarchy, O'Connell opposed Grattan's bill, killed it, and split the Catholic Committee. Why? He argued that government intervention in the affairs of the Catholic church would be detrimental to religion. His opposition to the veto was consistent with his Benthamite commitment to the separation of church and state, but his decision to oppose Grattan had political implications beyond the religious issue. O'Connell wanted to use the Catholic cause to create Catholic solidarity as a step toward national self-consciousness. The Catholic church, its hierarchy, and its clergy were instruments of nationality. Since most bishops and priests came from the strong farmer and shopkeeper classes, they had an affinity with the people. As a group they had been prevented by the Penal Laws from political participation, but their position made them natural leadership rivals to Anglo-Irish Protestant landlords. If the government could establish some influence over the appointment of Irish bishops, they could be turned into agents of British rule. It would be difficult, perhaps impossible, to organize an effective nationalist movement without the endorsement of the Catholic hierarchy and clergy. Therefore, O'Connell reasoned, it would be better to postpone emancipation to preserve the potential of something even more important, national freedom.

THE CATHOLIC ASSOCIATION AND THE BEGINNINGS OF MODERN IRISH NATIONALISM

In 1823 the division in the Catholic emancipation leadership ended when O'Connell and two of the leaders of the prosecurity wing, Sir Thomas Wyse and Richard Lalor Sheil, met at the home of O'Connell's son-in-law in the Wicklow Mountains and initiated a new organization, the Catholic Association. It took some time for the Association to catch on. For a while it was difficult to gather a quorum. Then, in 1824, O'Connell decided to broaden the base of the Catholic movement and at the same time add to its financial resources. He invited peasants and workers to join the organization as associate members for only a shilling a year. They could pay it a penny a month or only a farthing a week. Every Catholic parish in Ireland became a recruiting station for the Catholic Association. In sermons, priests told their flocks that they had an obligation to participate in the campaign for civil liberties and urged them to contribute their shillings, pennies, and farthings to the Association. Outside chapels, Catholic rent collectors set up tables to harvest the fruits of these sermons. A shilling was a small amount of money, but contributed by many, the result was thousands of pounds in the Association treasury. And to an Irish tenant farmer or a city or town worker, a shilling was a considerable expenditure. To make it, many had to give up tobacco or liquor, two escapes from the misery of poverty. Their sacrifice committed passions and emotions.

Most of the Irish masses could not even afford a shilling for Catholic emancipation. However, even agricultural laborers became moral supporters of the Association. Their presence at mass meetings added to the formidability of the emancipation agitation. Through it O'Connell took degraded and demoralized people, lifted them from their knees, and gave them hope, dignity, and a meaning for their lives. He disciplined their enthusiasm, arranged them into a powerful instrument of public opinion, educated them in the techniques of agitation, and grafted a nationality onto a religious loyalty, thus creating modern Irish nationalism. O'Connell, the Liberator, became the uncrowned king of Ireland.

From the beginning, it was evident that the Catholic Association was an unofficial Irish parliament. In addition to emancipation, it demanded repeal of the union, justice and security for tenant farmers, the end of tithes, and a democratic electorate voting by secret ballot. O'Connell insisted that his followers must use constitutional methods to achieve Catholic liberties and national independence, moral rather than physical force. But the emancipation agitation had revolutionary implications. Never before had a British government confronted a united, mobilized, and disciplined Catholic Ireland with high morale, commitment to a cause, and national determination. O'Connell's nonviolence implied the opposite. He warned British politicians that if they were not prepared to deal with men of moderation, the Irish masses might turn to leaders who advised physical force.

When the government outlawed the Catholic Association, O'Connell used his legal dexterity to reorganize it under new names and then expand its activities. The Association became a grievance committee, a propaganda agency against tithes, and a support group for mass education, tenant rights, expanded suffrage, the secret ballot, and parliamentary reform. In the process of agitating for Catholic emancipation, Irish nationalism took on its leader's liberalism.

While O'Connell was enlisting mass enthusiasm for Catholic emancipation, Thomas Wyse organized liberal clubs around the movement in cities and towns. They would continue to affect Irish politics long after the civil rights issue was settled. A superb tactician, Wyse decided to apply the power of the Catholic Association to the general election of 1826. In Waterford, the Association endorsed a proemancipation Protestant, Villiers Stuart, against Lord George Beresford. The Beresford family considered the Waterford seat private property. Priests helped the Association steel the courage of forty-shilling freehold voters to defy the wishes of their landlords. The Beresfords were defeated, and the Waterford example encouraged a number of other constituencies (Louth, Monaghan, Westmeath, Armagh, Cork City, Galway) to make emancipation a test for candidates. Again priests successfully competed with landlords for the farmer vote. The victories of 1826 elated the Association, added to the confidence of the Irish Catholic people in their leaders, frightened the Irish Protestant aristocracy, and worried the Tory government. Wellington and Peel understood that O'Connell had permanently diminished the influence of landlordism, rivaling it with Catholic clerical power. The former decided that emancipation would have to be the price of a successful United Kingdom. However, he wanted to avoid the appearance of surrender to agitation, and he hoped to work out an arrangement guaranteeing the loyalty of the Catholic clergy to Britain as part of an emancipation package.

Six months after the general election, Lord Liverpool resigned as prime minister for health reasons. George Canning took his place. Since he was sympathetic to Catholic emancipation, O'Connell slowed the pace of agitation to give him time to create and introduce a Catholic relief bill. But within months Canning was dead, and O'Connell's old enemies, Wellington, "the stunted corporal," and "Orange" Peel were back in office as prime minister and home secretary, respectively. Peel also led government forces in the House of Commons.

THE CATHOLIC VICTORY

Wellington appointed C. E. Vesey Fitzgerald, M.P. for Clare, to the Board of Trade presidency, forcing him to recontest his seat in a by-election. Fitzgerald was a popular landlord and a friend of Catholic emancipation. However, the Catholic Association decided to confront the issue of Catholic exclusion directly. Wyse and others persuaded O'Connell to challenge Fitzgerald. With the help of the priest-led forty-shilling voters, O'Connell defeated the government- and landlord-supported candidate.

The Clare results left Wellington and Peel with a variety of unpleasant questions and alternatives. After their great victory, would Irish Catholics passively stand aside if the government denied them civil equality and crushed the Association? More likely, they would become involved in a massive agitation to destroy the union. And there was a possibility that they might turn away from O'Connell's constitutional tactics toward physical force. In any event, if the government did not grant Catholic emancipation, governing Ireland would become an even more difficult task than it already was. If suppression of the Catholic movement and denial of its demand resulted in insurrection, many proemancipation M.P.'s in the House of Commons would blame the government, not Irish Catholics. In addition, there was considerable economic and social discontent in Britain, the consequence of industrialism and urbanization. It took the form of rioting, machine breaking, and demands for parliamentary reform. There was always the chance that rebellion in Ireland would increase British lawlessness.

To preserve peace and stability in Britain and Ireland, Wellington and Peel decided to ignore British no-popery and the right wing of their party and concede Catholic emancipation. The prime minister wanted to accompany it with payment of the Catholic clergy as a loyalty-wooing gesture. Peel talked him out of such a defiance of British nativism. Instead, the Catholic relief bill of 1829 revealed the government as a poor loser. In exchange for the Catholic opportunity to sit in Parliament, hold government office, and achieve professional distinctions, the forty-shilling freeholders lost their vote. Since landlords could no longer control it, tenant farmer suffrage seemed dangerous to the government. O'Connell accepted this defeat, arguing that the forty-shilling franchise without a secret ballot was not a free or reliable vote. He probably had other reasons for not defending the people who routed the Anglo-Irish Protestant ascendancy in 1826 and 1828. Knowing that upper- and middle-class British and Irish Catholics were more interested in their prospects than the rights of the people, he did not want to smash the Catholic Association as he had the Catholic Committee.

In addition to eliminating the forty-shilling franchise, there were other nasty reservations in the Wellington-Peel concession. The government forced O'Connell to recontest Clare (he won again, but at great expense), outlawed the Catholic Association, and forced Catholic M.P.'s to take an insulting oath of allegiance before taking seats at Westminster.

After the relief bill, Catholics could sit in the Lords and Commons and fill all offices in the United Kingdom except regent, lord chancellor, and lord lieutenant and lord chancellor of Ireland. Without the forty-shilling freeholders, the Irish electorate declined from somewhere over 100,000 to about 16,000. Even so, it was possible that Catholic voters could return a substantial number of their own to the House of Commons. Wellington expected emancipation to produce sixty Catholic M.P.'s. However, since members of Parliament did not have salaries, and given the high cost of political campaigns and London living, few Irish Catholics had the economic resources or the leisure to seek parliamentary careers. As late as 1874, after considerable franchise extensions and the secret ballot, a general election returned only forty-nine Catholic M.P.'s from Ireland. Fortunately, there were a few Protestant nationalists and liberals to speak at Westminster for Ireland's Catholic majority. Unfortunately, they were too few to make much of a difference.

THE CONSEQUENCES OF CATHOLIC EMANCIPATION

Although Catholic emancipation did make Irish Catholic opinion somewhat more important in Parliament, its immediate impact was greater on British than Irish politics. Right-wing Tory extremists fought Catholic relief to the bitter end, appealing to the anti-Catholic core of British nativism. When they lost, they never forgave Wellington and Peel, especially the latter, for their betrayal of the Protestant constitution. Peel had to give up his Oxford seat and find another one in Westbury. A number of the ultras began to urge parliamentary reform, claiming that the people were more dependably conservative than parliamentary aristocrats. They said that Parliament had surrendered to popery against the wishes of public opinion. And they joined the Whigs in 1830 to topple Wellington's government, clearing the way for a reform Parliament. Ultra-Tories in their pique were only playing with parliamentary reform because their instincts were as hostile to British democracy as they were to Irish nationalism. Whereas their flirtation with radicalism was of the moment, their distrust of Peel was permanent. It opened a fissure among the Tories that never closed completely, deepened under the stresses of Irish and economic policies during the 1840s, and finally divided them into progressive and reactionary factions.

Catholic emancipation changed British liberalism and radicalism as well as British conservatism. The Catholic Association became a model for United Kingdom popular movements and agitations. In their successful campaign for parliamentary reform, British radicals imitated O'Connell's ways of mobilizing public opinion, collecting funds, and intimidating the government with reform or revolution alternatives. Later, free traders successfully borrowed O'Connell's tactics in their eventually successful effort to repeal the corn laws.

Catholic emancipation nourished democracy beyond parliamentary and other reforms. It triumphed over George IV and the House of Lords, lessening the significance of monarchy and aristocracy. The Irish Catholic campaign for civil rights involved an early engagement in the long-term worldwide struggle for popular sovereignty. Daniel O'Connell in Ireland joined with Andrew Jackson in the United States as cocreators of modern political democracy.

Wellington and Peel conceded Catholic emancipation to preserve the union. But political equality had been delayed too long, granted under pressure and not as an act of justice, and enacted with humiliating strings attached. It therefore failed to merit the gratitude of Irish Catholics or divert them from nationalism.

Emancipation had little effect on the day-by-day lives of ordinary Catholics. It did not alleviate their poverty or economic insecurity or eliminate famine situations. They were not going to sit in Parliament or hold political office. But the events of the 1820s did introduce an element of hope into bleak lives. O'Connell and his success had demonstrated the potential of the pressure of organized mass opinion. Perhaps emancipation would be a prelude to economic improvements, social equality, democracy, even an Irish nation-state. The struggle for emancipation did establish and shape the structure and principles of modern Irish political nationalism. And thanks to the work of Wyse and others, it also contributed grass-roots organizations that would continue to be factors in reform and nationalist activities.

Unfortunately, emancipation's linkage of Irish and Catholic identities, intensified sectarian bitterness in Ireland. Following 1829, what was left of Protestant patriotism quickly faded. Certain that emancipation-derived nationalism represented a priest-led democracy, Protestants became fanatically attached to the union as security.

Although the campaign for Catholic emancipation and its triumph added to religious hostilities in Ireland, O'Connell had little choice but to emphasize the Irish-Catholic connections to mobilize a mass agitation to win Catholic civil rights and to initiate Irish nationalism. And it was necessary for him to bring in the priest as a local recruiting agent and as a counterforce to landlord influence.

It is true that post-1829 clericalism has often had a baneful impact on Irish affairs, but early nineteenth-century priests in Ireland were quite different from those on the continent. Originating from an oppressed people and serving an oppressed church, they were not defenders of the economic, social, or political privileges of the aristocracy. Two French travelers in Ireland, Gustave de Beaumont and Alexis de Tocqueville, observed how close priests were to their parishioners and how strongly they preached the political doctrine of popular sovereignty. They were disciples of John Locke rather than Bossuet.

Critics of the Irish clergy often exaggerate and misunderstand its role in politics. The respect the clergy received in religion did not carry over to politics. Priests were more lieutenants than leaders of popular movements. In that role, most of them accepted the liberal values of Irish nationalism. They learned that they had more standing with the people when they rode with rather than against the tides of nationalist sentiment. Clericalism surfaced as a problem only when in the absence of strong lay leadership, as in the period after O'Connell. When Irish Catholics committed themselves to a leader, the bishops and priests tagged along.

O'Connell's partial if not total integration of the values of Irish Catholicism with those of British liberalism had repercussions for the New World as well as the Old. Because of political lessons and values taught by O'Connell the Liberator, Irish pioneers of the American urban ghetto were able to overcome poverty, lack of technological skills, and the hostility of Anglo-American nativism to acquire power. Politics opened doors to economic opportunity and eventually respectability. By the close of the nineteenth century, Irish-American priests, politicians, and labor leaders were in charge of a powerful, city-based Catholic America. Because the Irish center of this force was Anglicized as well as Romanized, it could accommodate Catholicism in the United States to the American situation. The Irish played an important role in shaping a culturally pluralistic America by embracing a liberal political consensus.

CHAPTER 6
Repeal and British Politics, 1830–1845

O'CONNELL IN THE HOUSE OF COMMONS

When O'Connell entered the House of Commons in 1829, most British political experts predicted that at 54 he was too old to launch a successful parliamentary career. They said that a man had to be a skilled speaker and debater to command attention at Westminster and that O'Connell's earthiness, blarney, and invective might impress Irish peasants but would only antagonize British gentlemen.

Political pundits underestimated their man. O'Connell was immediately a powerful presence in the House of Commons. He played the parliamentary game with skill and dexterity. Occasionally his speeches were scurrilous—a tactic to bait opponents while pleasing the folks back home—but in general he adjusted his style to the House of Commons. Even his enemies had to concede that he was one of its leading debaters. He used his beautiful speaking voice to argue Irish grievances and passionately and reasonably to plead the case for Irish reform and repeal of the union.

O'Connell was also an advocate of British radicalism, serving as a spokesman for his friend, Jeremy Bentham, in Parliament. He was active in a variety of causes: a democratic electorate with a secret ballot, abolition of the House of Lords, an expansion of public participation in municipal government, laissez-faire and hostility to labor combinations as restraints on trade, prison and legal reform, Jewish emancipation, and the abolition of slavery throughout the British empire with full civil rights for blacks. O'Connell's Benthamism was appropriate to the British parliamentary and industrial systems but largely irrelevant to the needs of Irish Catholics suffering the burdens of manorialism. Still, they remained loyal to him. O'Connell had British political ambitions, sometimes fantasizing about the premiership, but British M.P.'s and their constituents could not hide their contempt for the tribune of Irish papists.

O'Connell commanded almost forty Repeal M.P.'s in the House of Commons. They constituted Ireland's first parliamentary party. In the early 1830s, when O'Connell emphasized the Repeal issue, Tory and Whig governments were equally determined on preserving the union. In fact, the Whig administration that took office in 1830 demonstrated more diligence in curtailing Irish nationalism than did Wellington and Peel. Whig leaders courted O'Connell's support with offers of government office, but Lord Anglesey, the lord lieutenant, and Lord Stanley, the chief secretary, outlawed all of his political organizations.

Whigs owed O'Connell for the passage of the 1832 reform bill. His influence was both direct and indirect. Radicals who led the reform agitation in Britain modeled their unions on the Catholic Association. Their newspapers reported and exaggerated discontent in Britain, warning the government that it had two choices: parliamentary reform or revolution. Not everyone in the government was convinced that revolution would follow a failure to reform, but like Wellington and Peel in 1829, they could not afford to take a chance.

O'Connell directly furthered parliamentary reform by supporting it with speeches and with the votes he and his followers cast in the Commons. O'Connell fought for the reform bill out of democratic principles and because he hoped that an improved British Parliament might concede justice to Ireland. However, the results of the measure were disappointing.

The Irish reform bill increased the Irish electorate to around 93,000 and Irish representation in the House of Commons to 105. But the numbers of voters were still smaller than before emancipation, and compared to other members of the United Kingdom, Ireland was shortchanged. A franchise including twenty-year leaseholders of property worth at least ten pounds as well as owners of property of the same value for tax purposes, did not radically increase the number of voters or begin to diminish aristocratic influence. As a result of the reform bill, one person in 115 voted in Irish county elections, contrasting to one in twenty-four in England, one in twenty-three in Wales, and one in forty-five in Scotland. In cities, the Irish franchise was one in twenty-two, in England and Wales it was one in seventeen, and in Scotland one in twenty-seven. British politicians replied to O'Connell's complaint that an increase of five M.P.'s did not adequately represent Ireland's rapidly multiplying population with the argument that Parliament represented property more than people. Despite his disappointment with Ireland's share of the reform bill, O'Connell stuck with the Whigs because he was sure that the Tories would be worse for Ireland, and he had hopes that the administrations of Lords Grey and Melbourne might see value in treating his country fairly.

Against his better judgment, at the urging of Fergus O'Connor, the future Chartist leader, O'Connell introduced an 1834 Repeal motion in the Commons. The support of only one British M.P. persuaded him that Parliament would never consider self-government for Ireland until it commanded the support of organized, massive, and disciplined agitation.

The first five years of the O'Connell-Whig collaboration brought few benefits to Ireland. Only Lord Stanley's 1831 Irish education bill establishing a state-supported system of national elementary schools was significant. To minimize religious conflict, they offered nondenominational instruction in secular subjects, but the various sects could supplement this with religious training for their own people. Protestants objected to this system of "Godlessness," which deprived them of an education monopoly. At the time, most bishops and priests welcomed the opportunity to raise the literacy and cultural levels of Catholics. Later, when the boldness and self-confidence of the hierarchy had increased, Archbishops Paul Cullen of Armagh and then Dublin, an ultramontane, and John MacHale of Tuam, a nationalist, led a fight against the schools. Cullen called them agents of Protestant proselytism; MacHale added the charge that they promoted British rule. Throughout the nineteenth century, cultural nationalists blasted the national schools as Anglicization vehicles and destroyers of the Irish language. When Catholics began to attack the system, Protestants began to defend it to prevent what Cullen and MacHale wanted, government aid for schools, which would be mostly Catholic. In reality there was little to criticize about the system. No doubt in 1831 the British government decided that after Catholic emancipation it was necessary to Anglicize the Irish masses. And to a certain extent the schools did that. In his autobiography, *An Only Child,* Frank O'Connor (Michael O'Donovan), the writer and critic, discussed how the schools he attended in early twentieth-century Cork City gave him English lifestyle models. Speaking of a later time, John Montague, the poet, in "A Grafted Tongue" complained that his school in Tyrone created a stutter by substituting English for his native language. However, English values also contained the liberal-democratic principles of O'Connell's nationalism. And the literacy that trained Irish emigrants to survive in more competitive societies also gave a reading audience to Irish political and cultural nationalism. National schools did spread English at the expense of Irish, but economic connections between Ireland and Britain and emigration to the English-speaking world doomed Irish as the vernacular anyway. Even religious complaints against the schools lacked validity. By the mid-nineteenth century they had in fact become denominational. In Catholic districts the priest headed the school board, while in Protestant or Dissenter territory the vicar or minister performed that function.

Ireland's system of national education also had British implications. In Ireland the government imposed state-supported, theoretically secular education at a time when it was afraid to take such a risk in Britain. The Irish experiment was a British Radical victory, increasing pressure for a program for state-financed non-denominational schools in Britain.

THE WHIG ALLIANCE

For five years the Whigs enjoyed the benefits of Irish nationalist support without the inconvenience of an open alliance. Then in 1835 the balance of political forces in the Commons compelled Whig leaders to come to specific terms with O'Connell. The Lichfield House Compact between Whigs and Repealers promised O'Connell Irish reforms in exchange for his efforts to keep the former in office and his promise to aid them in governing Ireland. This meant that O'Connell was abandoning repeal in return for reform. Tories denounced the Lichfield Compact as a corrupt bargain, and some Irish nationalists agreed. Lords Russell and Melbourne replied that the agreement with the Irish did not violate Whig principles, and O'Connell insisted that his arrangement with the Whigs was designed to advance Irish interests.

O'Connell's advocacy of repeal contained no inherent or unbending objections to the union in theory. He wanted an Irish Parliament because he believed that only a local legislature could solve the political, religious, social, and economic problems unique to Ireland. He knew that an Irish House of Commons would be dominated by members of the Protestant ascendancy. They were the only people in the country who could afford the luxury of political careers with heavy election expenses and service without compensation and who had the leisure to sit in Parliament. Protestants in an Irish Parliament, however, would have to respond to Catholic opinion and a Catholic electorate. Therefore, Irish Catholics would have more influence on a Parliament in Dublin than on one at Westminster. O'Connell also expected that time and pressure would bring changes increasing Catholic strength in an Irish legislature.

The Irish leader complained that under the union, Irish needs took second place to British concerns, but he was willing to let British politicians prove otherwise. O'Connell often told Irish audiences that he would accept the union as a permanent arrangement on the following conditions: Britain must treat Ireland as an equal partner, Parliament must discuss and solve Irish problems in an Irish, not a British context, and the United Kingdom must endeavor to promote Ireland's prosperity.

Except when stump-speaking to the Irish masses, O'Connell was not fanatic in his Irishness. He was little touched by the romantic cultural nationalism that began in the early nineteenth century on the continent, spread to Britain, and reached his own country in the form of the group known as Young Ireland. O'Connell was more concerned with the personal liberty, happiness, and economic security of his people than in such abstractions as national sovereignty or the folk soul. Though he doubted that the Protestant-dominated United Kingdom Parliament involved with Britain's booming industrial economy would ever have the patience, the sympathy, or the insight to cope with the difficulties of Catholic, underdeveloped, agrarian Ireland, in the Lichfield House Compact O'Connell gave British politicians another opportunity to demonstrate that the union could work for his country.

Melbourne's administration was responsible for the passage of three important pieces of Irish legislation. In 1838 Parliament commuted the tithe to a land tax, theoretically freeing most Catholics from the irritation of financing an alien religion, and enacted a law affecting the Irish poor that did not go into effect until 1842. The Irish municipal reform bill of 1840 opened city government to Catholic participation.

Like emancipation, the tithe act demonstrated the role of the Irish question as a catalyst defining and molding British politics. In early form, it would have applied surplus revenues of the Protestant Church of Ireland to Irish social needs. Lords Stanley and Graham considered such a proposal a despoilation and left the Whig fold. After a short period of independence, they became stalwarts in Peel's Conservative party.

Of the three Whig measures, the poor law was the best example of the insensitivity of a British Parliament legislating for Ireland. In 1833 the prime minister, Lord Grey, appointed an Irish commission to investigate the extent of poverty in Ireland and to recommend solutions. It included prominent Catholic, Protestant, and Presbyterian clergymen (both the Catholic and Protestant archbishops of Dublin were members). After two years of carefully gathering and evaluating evidence, the commission submitted a report rejecting for Ireland the British poor law system of placing paupers in government-supported workhouses. It noted that in Ireland poverty was not a disgrace and that the pauper had a social place in Irish society. Wandering beggars brought news and entertainment into rural cottages and offered the people an opportunity to practice Christian charity. The commissioners said that the Irish people would resent the government locking the poor up in workhouses as if they were guilty of crime. And the report emphasized that Ireland could not afford to imitate the British system. About 2.5 million Irish people, almost one-third the population, were impoverished. To institutionalize them would drain the financial resources of an extremely underdeveloped country, increasing rather than diminishing Irish poverty. Instead of a poor law, commissioners asked for more voluntary relief agencies and urged government public works and emigration projects. The former would provide employment and develop the economic potential of the country; the latter would siphon off the surplus population.

Lord John Russell, the Whig leader in the House of Commons, ignored the report. His utilitarian logic insisted that what was good for Britain would serve

Ireland. He sent George Nicholls, a British poor law official, to conduct another poverty investigation in Ireland. After only six months there, Nicholls recommended the British poor law system, and Parliament concurred.

O'Connell expressed dissatisfaction with the results of the Whig alliance. The tithe act fell far short of his demand for the disestablishment of the Protestant church in Ireland, and it did not prevent landlords from raising rents as a source for their tithe contribution. O'Connell was also disappointed when the government dropped the idea of applying surplus church revenue to social needs. His agreement with the Whigs prevented him from attacking the poor law with all the anger he felt. However, he did say that the bill was totally inappropriate to the Irish condition and voted against it. O'Connell also complained that the Whigs had done nothing to expand the Irish parliamentary franchise or to increase Irish seats in the House of Commons and not enough to destroy the Protestant monopoly of power in Dublin Castle.

O'Connell did realize that Thomas Drummond, the Whig undersecretary, had made efforts to bring a sectarian balance to the Irish situation. He told landlords that they had duties as well as rights and appointed Catholics to government, magisterial, and legal positions. Drummond also drove the anti-Catholic Orange Order underground, but the liberal and tolerant spirit in the Irish administration died with him in 1840.

LOBBYING FOR REPEAL

O'Connell decided to warn Melbourne in 1838 that from then on, Whigs would have to earn the support of Irish nationalist M.P.'s. He started the Precursor Society as a prelude to resuming Repeal agitation and again demanded substantial Irish reforms. When by 1840 it was evident that the Whigs would not author any constructive Irish legislation, O'Connell implemented his threat by creating the National Association, rechristened a year later as the Loyal National Repeal Association. Only a hundred people attended the first meeting at the Corn Exchange in Burgh Quay, Dublin, and just fifteen applied for membership. This apathy indicated that many nationalists feared that O'Connell's association with the Whigs revealed an insincerity regarding repeal and that the new organization was only an instrument to intimidate the Whigs.

O'Connell modeled the Repeal Association on its Catholic predecessor. Members paid annual dues of one pound. Contributors of 10 pounds or more became Volunteers and could wear uniforms similar to those of the 1782 Irish Volunteers. To achieve the same mass enthusiasm for repeal that emancipation had enjoyed, O'Connell again offered to farmers and workers a shilling associate membership in his organization. In city, town, village, and rural parishes, Repeal wardens, selected by the local clergy and approved by the Association, collected dues and sent them along with the names of contributors to Dublin headquarters. Wardens also established reading rooms where Repealers and potential recruits could read nationalist newspapers and pamphlets.

During its first three years, the Repeal Association had little impact on Irish opinion. Most of the energetic and bright Catholic lawyers who assisted O'Connell in the campaign for emancipation were now successes in their profession and were disinterested in repeal. Many, such as Richard Lalor Sheil, were House of Commons Whigs. Some held government office. Irish Catholic bishops remained nationalist in sentiment. But few of them believed that the British government would ever abandon the union. Prelates such as Daniel Murray, archbishop of Dublin, worried that Repeal raised false expectations among the people and distracted them from the realities and duties of their lives. Murray, and the majority of bishops who agreed with him, thought that O'Connell should concentrate his energies on the practical, winning Irish Catholic advances in the United Kingdom.

John MacHale, archbishop of Tuam, led the minority wing of the bishops active in the Repeal agitation. To keep their support and to win more converts from among the hierarchy, O'Connell became a vigorous opponent of government-sponsored nondenominational education. From that time on, Irish nationalism would be wedded to Catholic educational interests.

YOUNG IRELAND AND CULTURAL NATIONALISM

Fortunately for O'Connell and Repeal, a new talent source replaced the lawyers and bishops who defected from nationalism. On October 15, 1842, the first issue of the *Nation* appeared. This nationalist weekly was the product of the combined talents of Thomas Osborne Davis, John Blake Dillon, and Charles Gavan Duffy, three young men in their twenties, trained in the law, and experienced in journalism. Davis was Anglo-Irish Protestant; Dillon and Duffy were Catholics; Davis and Dillon had attended Trinity College, Dublin; Davis was from Dublin, Dillon from Mayo, and Duffy from Monaghan; all three were nationalists educated, to a large extent through Thomas Carlyle, in the romantic movement. They gave Irish nationalism the most powerful and influential newspaper voice that it ever had or ever would have, and they provided it with a cultural ideology.

Duffy, Dillon, and Davis launched the *Nation* to create an Irish cultural nationalist opinion and "to make it racy of the soil." They insisted that a nation was a spiritual as well as a geographic and political entity. Even more important than political independence, nationhood demanded cultural sovereignty. Young Irelanders, as those associated with the *Nation* were called, emphasized the spiritual qualities of peasant Ireland and ridiculed the materialism of urban, industrial Britain. They wanted to save their country from the cultural as well as the political and economic dimensions of British colonialism. They championed the Irish language as a defense against Anglicization, advocating its preservation where it still was the vernacular, and its revival where it had faded or disappeared. Since Young Ireland-

THOMAS OSBORNE DAVIS
1814–1845

Thomas Osborne Davis co-founded the Young Ireland Movement. In his editorial columns and his ballad poetry published in the *Nation,* he helped define the spirit and contents of Irish cultural nationalism. (Photo taken from Sir Charles Gavan Duffy, *Thomas Davis: The Memoirs of an Irish Patriot, 1840–46,* London, 1890.)

ers viewed the national school system as a strategy to replace the Irish with a British heritage, they took on the responsibility of educating the people to know and appreciate their culture and history.

The *Nation* attracted the talents of Thomas MacNevin, Daniel Owen Madden, John Mitchel, John O'Hagan, Thomas D'Arcy McGee, and Thomas Meagher. They extolled the quality of pre-Christian and early Christian Celtic culture and discussed the contributions of Irish missionaries to the spread of civilization. They wrote about Irish patriots who defended their country's independence against Danes, Normans, and Saxons. In addition to extolling the glories of an Irish past, Young Ireland tried to encourage a cultural revival in the present that would shape a promising future. The *Nation* printed the best in contemporary Irish writing, including William Carleton's prose and James Clarence Mangan's poetry. And it invited readers to submit stories, essays, poems, and ballads. Many of the nationalist songs that still stir Irish emotions at home and abroad first appeared in the *Nation* of the 1840s.

Dillon, Duffy, Davis, and their associates wanted to differentiate between the Catholic and Irish identities. In the *Nation,* the contributions of Protestants and Nonconformists to Ireland received equal treatment with those of Catholics. Young Irelanders pleaded for harmony between religious groups and stressed the common interests of Irish people from all creeds. This ecumenical spirit was expressed in Davis's "Anglo-Saxon and Celt":

> What matters that at different shrines
> We pray unto one God?
> What matters that at different times
> Our fathers won this sod?
> In fortune and in name we're bound
> By stronger links than steel;
> And neither can be safe nor sound
> But in each other's weal.

News coverage played a secondary role to the *Nation*'s cultural nationalism. It usually borrowed news stories from other papers. The *Nation* featured poetry, historical essays, biographical sketches, patriotic ballads, reviews, and exceptionally well written editorials. Its columns preached cultural and political nationalism, supported the Repeal Association, encouraged cooperation among Irishmen of all religions, classes, and ethnic origins, and advocated tenant rights, cultural and vocational education for the Irish people, and political change consistent with liberal democracy. Young Ireland's cultural nationalism had such an immediate impact on Irish national opinion that the *Nation* became a topic of discussion in Parliament. British M.P.'s recognized the talent of Young Irelanders but condemned their radical nationalist, anti-British ideology.

O'Connell welcomed Young Irelanders to the Repeal Association and the *Nation* to Repeal reading rooms, but he was a bit suspicious of his young allies and new lieutenants. Since O'Connell's nationalism concerned the bread-and-butter issues of politics, he never really understood the passionate, uncompromising cultural nationalism of Young Ireland. On political platforms, O'Connell told the Irish people that they were the most virtuous, handsome, and intelligent people in the world, living in its most beautiful and potentially fruitful country. His praise was designed to lift spirits demoralized by centuries of ignorance, poverty, and oppression. While O'Connell genuinely loved his own kind, he did not hate England, its people, or its culture. He admired Britain's technological leadership, constitution, political institutions, and liberal tradition and wanted them for his own country.

O'Connell's love of Ireland and the Irish—Catholic Protestant, and Nonconformist—did not include preoccupation with the Gaelic tradition. He was so concerned with Ireland's present and future that he had little interest in its past. He refused to emote over former defeats and misery. His modernist and utilitarian views were illustrated by his attitude toward the Irish language. Unlike the Young

Irelanders, he was a native speaker. Occasionally he spoke Irish at political meetings, sometimes to confuse police reporters, but he did not encourage efforts to preserve or revive Irish. To him it was a symbol of inferiority and an obstacle to progress.

Since the cosmopolitan O'Connell could not relate to the xenophobic spirit of cultural nationalism, which had spread throughout Europe and entered his own country, he distrusted the militant tone of the *Nation* and at times ridiculed its literary efforts and style (perhaps a reflection of his admiration of Charles Dickens). Young Irelanders, in turn, were often impatient with O'Connell's pragmatic flirtations with the Whigs, which compromised repeal for reform possibilities, with his vulgarity, and with his despotic control of Irish nationalism. They also thought that he antagonized Protestants through his linkage of Irish and Catholic.

On specific issues, such as Chartism, corn law repeal, and federalism, Young Ireland and O'Connell came to disagree. Young Ireland viewed the Chartists as representatives of the British democracy, a natural ally of Irish nationalism against the common enemy, British aristocracy. Chartists wanted to solve the social and economic problems of urban industrialism through political reform. Their "People's Charter" called for universal male suffrage, a secret ballot, equal electoral districts, the end of property qualifications for political office, annual Parliaments, and salaries for M.P.'s. O'Connell approved of these goals but he accused Chartists, particularly Fergus O'Connor, an old political foe, of advocating violence to achieve them. His attack on the corn laws was consistent with his utilitarian, free trade beliefs. The *Nation* argued that free trade benefited British industry but endangered Irish agriculture. At one time a *Nation* editorial suggested that a federal arrangement between Ireland and Britain might be a worthy substitute for repeal. Young Ireland withdrew from that position but said that it was prepared to work with Irish federalists in a common front against British rule. When O'Connell in 1844 announced that he would be inclined to accept a federal restructuring of the United Kingdom if British politicians made such an offer and Irish opinion was agreeable, the *Nation* denounced federalism as totally inadequate.

Despite Young Ireland's efforts and intention to blend the interests of Catholic, Protestant, and Nonconformist, Anglo-Irish, Scots-Irish, and Celt, the overwhelming majority of non-Catholics considered the group's cultural nationalism as much a bid for Catholic power as O'Connell's political nationalism. Their Britishness excluded any pride in things Irish before the English colonial presence. And for them, Irish history after that was a constant struggle for survival against the Catholic majority. To the Anglo-Irish and Scots-Irish, Celtic Ireland was Catholic Ireland. Their loyalty and their interests—religious, political, and economic—were invested in Britain.

While Young Ireland cultural nationalism made little impression on the Anglo-Irish or Scots-Irish community, it had massive appeal for members of the Catholic middle class. Their literary expression in the works of Gerald Griffin and John Banim revealed a serious identity crisis. They enjoyed economic prosperity but suffered the disdain of the Protestant aristocracy and middle class. And they had no affinity with Catholic peasants and agricultural laborers. Young Ireland told them that they were important people with a dignified and glorious historical tradition and cultural heritage.

THE SURGE OF REPEAL

Despite differences in temperament, policy, and procedure, Young Irelanders realized that O'Connell had the allegiance of the Irish masses and that without him the national movement would lose momentum. Therefore, they were gentle in criticizing him. They submitted to his leadership, and the *Nation* made a major contribution to the revival of national enthusiasm. Its influence extended beyond the 8000 weekly subscribers. The *Nation* was in Repeal reading rooms, and throughout Ireland illiterates crowded into thatch-roofed cottages to listen to the local scholar, often the national schoolteacher, read its poems, essays, and editorials.

During 1842, Repeal activities were practically suspended while O'Connell served as first Catholic lord mayor of Dublin. When 1843 began, O'Connell had completed his term, Sir Robert Peel was prime minister of a Conservative government, and the Repeal Association was meeting weekly at the Corn Exchange. But few people in Ireland or Britain considered the Repeal movement a serious threat to the continuation of the United Kingdom. British newspapers and periodicals described O'Connell as a deteriorating demagogue promoting repeal to keep his name before the Irish people so that he could line his pockets with their contributions. If that was his motive, he was unsuccessful. The Repeal Association's meager income showed public apathy to its work. Only the *Nation*'s success indicated the potential of Irish nationalism.

No doubt the sorry condition of the Repeal Association irritated O'Connell. He did love the limelight, and he needed the annual tribute he had received from the Irish people since Catholic emancipation. Their donations had permitted him to concentrate on their welfare instead of his law practice. The amount of the tribute had declined with repeal enthusiasm. However, for O'Connell, financial self-interest was of far less importance than the future of Ireland. And he worried that without mass energy and involvement in repeal, he could not effectively pressure the British government for change. So in January 1843 he decided to launch one more giant agitation for the restoration of the Irish Parliament or at least a considerable improvement in the Irish situation. He believed that he had the necessary ingredients at his disposal to arouse the Irish people from their lethargy.

Poverty, Protestant ascendancy, and peasant insecurity remained to perpetuate tensions between Irish Catholics and the British government. When the poor law went into effect in 1842, it raised a storm of opposition from all classes and creeds. There was resentment toward the workhouse test for poor relief and toward paying rates to support the new system. Repealers, Tories, and Whigs joined in denouncing the administration of the poor law, mainly the despotic power of the Central Board of Poor Law Commissioners, and complained about the expenses of operating a project designed for an industrial rather than an agrarian country.

The upper and middle classes expressed disapproval of the poor law in petitions to Parliament, platform orations, and letters to newspapers. Farmers often resorted to more spectacular and sometimes more violent methods. In many sections of the country they refused to pay rates, even when the army came to collect them. O'Connell recognized how anti-poor law feelings stimulated anti-British passions. So he encouraged the protest, including an anti-poor law plank as a major part of the Repeal platform. His strategy worked. In the spring of 1843, as anti-poor law activities tapered off, the Repeal Association grew in numbers and income.

Theobold Mathew, a Franciscan friar, was by 1843 the most popular and influential man in Ireland after O'Connell. He had enrolled between 4 and 5 million people in a temperance crusade. Almost every small village in Ireland had a local branch of the movement, complete with a reading room and a band with musical instruments and colorful uniforms. Even Protestant ascendancy newspapers praised Father Mathew's efforts to curb the tendency of the Irish masses to escape the realities of poverty in drink. O'Connell considered the discipline and the enthusiasm of temperance as Repeal potential. Father Mathew had continued the tradition of mass meetings that had started with the emancipation agitation and declined when O'Connell cozied up to the Whigs. The Repeal leader tried to entice teetotalers into Repeal by endorsing temperance. He said that it was the most powerful weapon in Repeal's arsenal of moral force and predicted that it would discipline Irish nationalism in its struggle against British tyranny.

Father Mathew wanted to avoid mixing temperance with Irish nationalism because it might alienate the British and Irish Protestants who had encouraged his efforts. However, he could not control the political loyalties of his followers or compete with O'Connell's charisma. During the Repeal campaign of 1843, temperance bands were an important feature at mass meetings, and the *Nation* was prominent in temperance reading rooms.

After O'Connell had maneuvered the anti-poor law protest and temperance into Repeal, he persuaded the Dublin corporation, along with other municipal and public bodies, such as poor law boards, to petition Parliament for repeal of the union. Government officials helped him mobilize Irish opinion behind the antiunion demand by a series of blunders. They awarded the Irish mail coach contract to a Scots company in preference to an Irish concern already holding it, thus forcing thousands of Dublin workers out of jobs in an employment-starved city. Then the government fired Dr. Phelan, one of the two Catholic poor law commissioners, without explanation. And when Parliament finally amended the poor law, it heeded gentry demands while ignoring the complaints of ordinary people.

During the 1843 Repeal agitation, the government pushed through Parliament an Irish arms bill that curtailed civil liberties, and the Irish lord chancellor, Sir Edward Sugden, dismissed magistrates attending Repeal meetings, although he conceded their legality. The arms bill and the dismissal of magistrates rallied a large number of Catholic barristers and solicitors to the Repeal Association, returning to O'Connell the support of an influential segment of the Catholic middle class that had largely abandoned him after Catholic emancipation.

In the spring of 1843, O'Connell began to hold public meetings to petition for repeal, choosing a different part of the country every week. They took place on Sunday afternoons, and hundreds of thousands attended. In the early morning roads were packed with Repealers who journeyed considerable distances to listen to the "Liberator." Priests said outdoor Masses on the the hillsides, and then the people sat down to eat their potato breakfasts. Parish priests and curates, local dignitaries, and temperance bands leading lines of marching Repealers met O'Connell's carriage as it approached the town. People detached the horses and pulled it by hand through the streets as women and children threw flowers in his path.

When he addressed the meetings, O'Connell told his audiences that they were the bravest, strongest, most patient, most virtuous people in the world. He promised them that before the year was out, Ireland would have its Parliament in College Green. They would win the independence of their country through the application of moral force. They would never fight except in self-defense. But that would not be necessary. Peel and Wellington would surrender to Irish national opinion as they did in 1829. O'Connell assured his followers that after Ireland had its own Parliament, there would be a reconciliation between classes and creeds. Tenant farmers would be secure on the land, trade and commerce would flourish, and culture would thrive. There would be freedom of conscience with no religious establishment. A free Ireland loyal to the crown would live in peace with its British neighbor as friends. O'Connell always encouraged loyalty to the queen. He said that even if "Orange" Peel and the "stunted corporal" denied justice to the Irish people, Victoria, who loved them, would use her royal prerogatives to establish an Irish legislature (it is difficult to accept that O'Connell actually believed such nonsense). In preparation for independence, O'Connell promised to summon a preliminary Parliament, the Council of Three Hundred, the same number as the old Irish Parliament, to meet in Dublin. He also announced his intention to establish arbitration courts so that the people could seek and find Irish rather than British justice. By the fall of the year, the arbitration courts were in operation, with surprising effectiveness.

The Monster Meetings, as the *Times* of London labeled them (the term caught on even among Repealers), were tremendous successes. Dues poured into the Repeal Association. For a time in the late spring and summer, the weekly Repeal rent exceeded 2000 pounds. Some of this money came from the Irish in Britain and the United States, although quite a few Irish-Americans were offended when O'Connell denounced slavery as a vile institution. They said that he should keep his nose out of American affairs. He replied that he did not want to liberate the Irish with money made from exploiting black slaves. O'Connell insisted that Irish nationalism represented a universal cry for human liberty and equality.

The surge of Repeal indicated by the Monster Meetings and the flow of shillings, pounds, and dollars to O'Connell's agitation horrified Irish Protestants.

To preserve the union and to protect Protestant ascendancy, they demanded that the government suppress Repeal. Earl De Grey, the anti-Catholic lord lieutenant, endorsed their plea.

COMBATING THE RISING TIDE

Peel and even De Grey were strangely unaware of the gradual but steady increase of Repeal enthusiasm in the early spring of 1843. Not until May did the prime minister realize the extent of O'Connell's challenge to British authority. When he did, Peel told the House of Commons that he would preserve the union at all costs. Wellington made the same pledge to the House of Lords. But the government found it difficult to deal directly with the agitation. Legislation designed to suppress the Repeal Association would also embrace the Anti–Corn Law League modeled on O'Connell's tactics for mobilizing public support. Peel did not want to unite radicals, free traders, and Irish nationalists in a common defense of civil and political liberties. Such an alliance would make O'Connell respectable in Britain and both the anti–corn law and Repeal agitations more difficult to control.

Since Peel had to reject an anti-Repeal strategy that could provide O'Connell with a British constituency, he was forced to respond to revitalized Irish nationalism with a public pose of calculated indifference. His refusal to react to O'Connell's boasts with coercive legislation or military might infuriated the reactionary, anti--Irish Catholic core of the Tory wing of the Conservative party, but his seeming indifference masked a strategy to destroy O'Connell's influence in Ireland and to eradicate the roots of Irish nationalism. By refusing to acknowledge the significance of Repeal by either coercion or immediate conciliation, Peel hoped to demonstrate to Irish Catholics that the scarcely veiled threats of their antiunion agitation would not intimidate the government into conceding repeal or reform. He hoped that once they realized that O'Connell could not deliver on any of his promises, they would lose confidence in him and his methods. Repeal would then dwindle into insignificance, and the British army could cope with any hotheads.

While Peel and the home secretary, Sir James Graham, waited for calculated indifference to deflate Repeal's balloon, they plotted a long-range Irish policy to satisfy some of the ambitions and needs of various components of the nationalist coalition, thus destroying antiunionism by eliminating the grievances that had created and nourished it. But Peel and Graham had no intention of initiating reform while Repeal was at full strength. Such a move would encourage Irish Catholics to believe that the government was susceptible to intimidation. They would then invest more loyalty in O'Connell, and he would intensify agitation. Peel wanted a coherent, long-term Irish policy, not an ill-considered, fearful response to Irish discontent. He wanted to lay the Irish question to permanent rest and to make the United Kingdom a true community of interests and allegiances.

Of course, there was the danger that O'Connell, faced with the necessity of retaining his influence with Irish Catholics, might commit himself to revolutionary conspiracy. There was also the possibility that he might lose the reins of Irish nationalism to more militant Repealers. To forestall these contingencies, Peel and Graham took out insurance policies against the failure of calculated indifference. They dispatched troops, weapons, ammunition, and other military supplies to Ireland, and arms were stored for possible use by Protestant yeomen. The prime minister and home secretary also decided to punish O'Connell and his chief lieutenants for their audacious challenge. Graham instructed Irish legal authorities to collect evidence indicating the seditious character of Repeal.

When Peel told Parliament in May that he was prepared to use military force to preserve the union, and when Sugden acted on this pledge by dismissing Repeal magistrates, O'Connell decided that the government was going to crush his movement. In an effort to persuade Westminster to reconsider the use of soldiers and to maintain the enthusiasm and confidence of his followers, he added a militant tone to his speeches. While addressing an audience in Mallow, County Cork, in June, O'Connell went so far as to suggest that he would lead a defensive war against British oppression.

By late summer, however, it dawned on O'Connell that Peel was out to demolish Repeal by undermining Irish Catholic confidence in his ability to deliver on promises of freedom and reform. He feared that if the prime minister's strategy succeeded, Repealers might reject constitutional agitation for physical force. To save them from the bullets and bayonets of the military, O'Connell softened the tone of his public statements, no longer guaranteeing Repeal in the near future. He said that it would be impossible to summon the Council of Three Hundred before the end of 1843. Instead of promising quick victories, O'Connell now asked Irish nationalists to support him in a long struggle for freedom. He warned them against counsels of violence, insisting that moral force could and would triumph over anti-Irish opinion in Britain.

THE DEFEAT OF REPEAL

By early autumn it was apparent that Peel's strategy of calculated indifference was wearing down Repeal. O'Connell was preparing his followers for short-term defeat, the Repeal rent had declined, and Irish farmers were neglecting agitation to concentrate on bringing in an abundant harvest. Now that the enemy was in retreat, the prime minister made ready to assume the offensive. He decided to institute prosecution for sedition against the Repeal leadership and sent Lord De Grey and Sugden to Dublin to supervise the arrest and trial of O'Connell and his lieutenants. They also received instructions to prevent the Clontarf Repeal rally on Sunday, October 8. It was to be the last Monster Meeting of 1843. A tremendous crowd was expected in the Dublin suburb. A large number of British Repealers were coming.

Late Saturday, October 7, De Grey proclaimed the Clontarf meeting on the grounds that the original announcement—written and distributed when O'Connell was not in Dublin—indicated that it was designed as a military demonstration to intimidate the government. Rather than risk a confrontation between soldiers and Repealers, O'Connell canceled the meeting. A week later, he and six others, including Charles Gavan Duffy, were arrested and charged with sedition and attempting to subvert the loyalty of her majesty's soldiers stationed in Ireland. (Because many soldiers in the British army were Irish, the government was always concerned that they could be infected with Irish nationalism.) In speeches O'Connell said that noncommissioned officers and privates would not heed orders to shoot their own people. In February 1844 a jury brought in a verdict of guilty, and the court sentenced the Repeal defendents to a year in prison and payment of a stiff fine. In September the law lords, in a 3-to-2 decision (three Whigs and two Tories), reversed the decision because the prosecution's indictment was improperly drawn, and the defendants were tried before a packed jury that excluded Catholics. O'Connell and his friends were released from Richmond Gaol. He received a hero's welcome. People pulled his carriage from the prison to his Merrion Square residence. Bonfires of celebration were lit on the hills of Ireland. But after his prison experience, though brief and comfortable, O'Connell lost his zeal for agitation. His decision to abandon the Clontarf meeting and his failure to exploit his legal vindication by intensifying nationalist activity did much to crush the Repeal spirit and to undermine confidence in constitutional methods. However, the 1843 Repeal defeat was not the consequence of faulty tactics so much as the Irish leader's misreading of the temper of the times.

Like many political leaders, O'Connell became a captive of past successes. In 1843 he expected Peel and Parliament to react to Repeal as they had to Catholic emancipation. In 1829 he had convinced Wellington and Peel that if they did not concede Catholic civil rights, extremists might push him aside, take control of popular agitation, and substitute physical for moral force. During the Repeal year he seemed to assume that if Peel again had to face the choices of concessions to Irish discontent or the chaos of rebellion, he would once more select the former. And if the prime minister refused to bow to expediency, perhaps, O'Connell hoped, the Whigs would exploit the Irish crisis to embarrass and perhaps topple the Conservative government. Once in power, he thought, Lords Russell and Palmerston would try to calm troubled Irish waters with a conciliation policy and a resumption of the Irish nationalist–Whig alliance.

Apparently, O'Connell failed to understand that although the Irish situation in 1843 was similar to that in 1829, things in Britain were different. During the 1820s and before, there was a considerable body of enlightened parliamentary opinion favorably disposed to emancipation. In 1829 Peel and Wellington knew that attempts to suppress the Catholic Association without conceding its objective would receive a rough reception in the House of Commons. Therefore, Irish physical resistance to government coercion would enjoy the sympathy of a respectable body of British opinion, and the seeds of rebellion might spread and take root in socially, economically, and politically disturbed Britain. Catholic emancipation was an Irish issue with United Kingdom implications.

In 1843 no respectable Tory, Whig, or Radical M.P. accepted Repeal as a solution to the Irish question. Both Tories and Whigs argued that an independent Ireland would weaken Britain's defenses and initiate a collapse of the empire. Tories also insisted that Repeal would place the Catholic democracy in a position to take revenge on the Protestant ascendancy. Radicals maintained that a properly managed union would bring peace and prosperity to Ireland. During the 1843 Repeal crisis, British anti-Catholic and unionist parliamentary opinion opposed Irish nationalism. Though Whigs and Radicals did not hesitate to exploit Irish discontent to embarrass the government with attacks on and inquiries into its administration of Irish affairs, Peel could depend on their support in his determination not to compromise the union.

When Peel challenged O'Connell on the Clontarf meeting, the Irish leader had no realistic choice but to back down. His nonviolent convictions, commitment to constitutionalism, and common sense would not permit him to lead his followers to slaughter in an engagement with British soldiers. But by surrendering to the government's ultimatum, O'Connell lost one of constitutional nationalism's most effective persuaders—the implied threat of rebellion if the government refused concessions to moderate opinion.

PEEL'S EFFORT TO INTEGRATE IRELAND INTO THE UNITED KINGDOM

Early in 1844 Peel and Graham were confident that Repeal had faded as a significant factor in Anglo-Irish affairs, and they could proceed with a comprehensive policy to destroy Irish nationalism by integrating Ireland into the United Kingdom. Although it included concessions to each of the clerical, agrarian, and middle-class components of the Repeal coalition, the main focus was the detachment of priests from popular agitations. Peel accepted a thesis, popular in British intellectual and political circles, that the Catholic hierarchy and clergy in Ireland had to promote the activities of demagogues because they were dependent on the ignorant anti-British masses for financial support. Before they could be persuaded to withdraw from politics, the government would have to provide them and their church with guaranteed incomes. But separating priests from nationalism presented risks. If not handled with tact and diplomacy, it would alienate British no-popery, Tories in the Conservative party, the Irish Catholic hierarchy and clergy, and even Rome.

The government began implementing its Irish policy by asking the pope, Gregory XVI, to forbid further excursions of bishops and priests into politics. Realizing the implications for all of Europe, and particularly for the multiethnic Hapsburg Empire, of a radical and nationalist Catholic hierarchy and clergy in Ireland, Prince Metternich, Austrian chancellor, endorsed the British request to Rome. Peel's emissary there told the pope that if the British government could obtain the cooperation of Irish bishops and priests for efforts to maintain the union and to preserve the social order, the prime minister's Irish initiatives might culminate in the endowment of the church in Ireland. Papal officials welcomed this prospect and the opportunity to establish friendly relations with the world's greatest power. So Cardinal Fransoni, prefect of propaganda, the agency supervising Catholicism in the United Kingdom, wrote to the Irish hierarchy advising against clerical political involvement, urging the concentration of priestly energies on spiritual matters. But only a handful of prelates gave heed to the Roman directive.

In the fall of 1844 the government launched the legislative phase of its Irish policy with a bill that permitted the Catholic church to inherit and bequeath property. The charitable bequests act was intended as a signal of the government's intention to extend justice to Irish Catholics. Peel also hoped to use bishops on the charitable bequests board as agents in his effort to convince Catholic clerical and middle-class opinion that cooperation with the British government promised more benefits than opposition.

O'Connell attacked the charitable bequests act because its provisions were inadequate in terms of inheritance and because it opened up the Catholic church in Ireland to British influences. Archbishop MacHale and a number of his allies in the hierarchy also criticized the act. Archbishop Murray of Dublin and his friends among the bishops accepted the British offer and agreed to sit on the charitable bequests board. This division intensified a split that had begun over the national schools in the 1830s. The feud in the hierarchy was bitter and personal, with MacHale accusing Murray of being a Dublin Castle bishop, a tool of British interests. Both sides frequently appealed to Rome.

In the spring of 1845 the government made another friendly gesture to the Irish Catholic clergy when it introduced a bill to increase the annual grant to the seminary at Maynooth and convert it to a permanent endowment. Every year when the grant was up for renewal, it touched off a binge of anti-Catholicism, embittering relations between Britain and Ireland. Peel hoped that the Maynooth bill would remove the seminary as an annual issue and at the same time assure Catholic bishops of the government's friendly intentions, thus smoothing the way for a more extensive endowment of Irish Catholicism. However, the bill generated so much no-popery, in and out of Parliament, that some of the effect of the government's generosity was lost, and Peel realized that he was restricted on what he could do to pacify Irish Catholicism. Nevertheless, he courageously resisted Protestant prejudice expressed by the Tories in his party, and with the support of Whigs, Radicals, and Repealers, he ushered the bill through Parliament.

After Maynooth, Peel directed attention to the educational needs of the Irish Catholic middle class, introducing an Irish colleges bill establishing three provincial colleges, in Cork, Galway, and Belfast, on the principle of nondenominational or mixed education. Peel expected that in a university environment, Protestants and Catholics would meet, socialize, and develop a middle-class solidarity. He also thought that an exposure to sophisticated, secular culture might free the sons of Catholic shopkeepers, professionals, and strong farmers from nationalism and clericalism, making them aware that they had interests independent of their religion and more relevant than Repeal.

In Parliament, the colleges bill met with minimum opposition. In Ireland, however, O'Connell attacked mixed education as offensive to Catholics and forced the hierarchy to condemn the provisions of the bill. Since O'Connell's position on the colleges proposal was inconsistent with his principles concerning freedom of conscience and Catholic-Protestant harmony, he probably opposed Peel's higher education measure to repay MacHale for his support in 1843, cementing the nationalism-Catholicism compact.

Young Irelanders approved of mixed education because they believed that the results would contradict Peel's anticipation. They predicted that Catholic-Protestant college contacts would lead Protestants toward nationality rather than lead Catholics away. The conflict over the colleges bill in the Repeal Association started an open feud between O'Connell and Young Ireland, eventually leading to the latter's secession.

On the urging of MacHale, the pope in 1847 and 1848 disapproved of the Queens colleges, the name given to the three provincial institutions. In 1850, at the Synod of Thurles, with Archbishop Cullen presiding, the Irish hierarchy forbade Catholics to attend the colleges or to accept administrative or teaching posts in them. The next year Rome concurred in the Thurles decision. In the 1850s Cullen established a Catholic University in Dublin with John Henry Newman as its first rector. Newman found it impossible to get along with the anti-intellectual Irish bishops. After contributing his brilliant views on higher education in *Idea of a University,* Newman returned to England. The Catholic university continued to exist without a government subsidy. It evolved into University College, Dublin, and in 1907 joined the Queens colleges in Cork and Galway as a constituent branch of the new National University of Ireland. Queen's College, Belfast, developed into an excellent twentieth-century university.

The colleges bill was the last portion of Peel's Irish policy to receive parliamentary approval. He attempted to conciliate Irish farmers by appointing a commission headed by an Irish landlord, Lord Devon, to investigate landlord-tenant relations and to recommend legislation improving the situation. Lord Stanley introduced a bill in the House of Lords, based on the findings of the Devon Commission, designed to establish a moderate tenant right. When many Whig and Conservative M.P.'s made it clear that they would not tolerate even a minor interference with property rights, the government dropped the measure.

In many ways Peel's Irish policy received affirmative results. Rome had condemned the nationalist involvement of bishops and priests, and several prelates were cooperating with government efforts to lighten the financial burdens of their church. The charitable bequests board gave Peel the opportunity to continue negotiations with some members of the hierarchy in his effort to demonstrate the potential benefits of the union. And despite the anti-Catholic bigotry provoked by the Maynooth bill, the Catholic hierarchy and clergy, and even O'Connell, appreciated

Peel's intentions and his fortitude in standing up to irrational fanaticism. Finally, although O'Connell and the bishops condemned the colleges bill, it did open a split in Irish nationalism, an ideological clash between Young and Old Ireland that eventually destroyed Repeal unity.

O'Connell did manage to limit Peel's achievements by reducing the success of his Irish policy. During the charitable bequests act controversy, he informed the Irish people that the British government was negotiating an arrangement with Rome at the expense of Irish national interests. This forced the bishops to publish the Fransoni letter, strengthening distrust of the British and creating suspicion of Roman motives. It also forced Archbishop Murray and British spokesmen to deny plans for a London-Rome concordat. By fostering Irish fear of an alliance between the Rome and the British government, O'Connell to a certain extent repaired the breach in Catholic nationalist unity opened by Peel's Irish policy and made the hierarchy cautious about overtures from the British government. British anti-Catholic reactions to the Maynooth bill also aided O'Connell's effort to maintain nationalist solidarity. This exhibition of religious bigotry demonstrated that Peel's Irish policy did not represent British attitudes toward the Irish. Even the split in Repeal ranks over the colleges bill did not appear all that serious in 1845. Old and Young Ireland were still united on the methods and aims of Repeal.

Of course, it is impossible to evaluate Peel's success by the only valid historical measure, its long-range impact on Anglo-Irish affairs. The 1845 potato blight devastated Ireland, inciting agrarian crime and discontent, persuading Peel to abandon, at least for a time, his project of integrating Ireland into the United Kingdom. He did send grain into the country to feed the people and used the famine as evidence that the corn laws had to be repealed. However, the prime minister, confronted with a rise in agrarian outrages, decided to substitute law and order for conciliation. In June 1846 he introduced a coercion bill. On the evening of June 29, the same day corn law repeal passed the House of Lords, protectionist Tories, in a vengeful mood, joined Whigs, Radicals, and Repealers to topple the Peel government on Irish coercion. But their break with Peel on agricultural protection was the conclusion of a division in the Conservative party that had started with Catholic emancipation and peaked on the Maynooth bill.

Since Peel's abortive effort to sabotage Irish nationalism contributed to the destruction of his administration, no British leader dared confront all the complexities of the Irish question until William E. H. Gladstone took office in 1868. By that time Irish nationalism had assumed an identity independent from the myriad of grievances that manufactured it. Short of self-government, solving the Irish question was no longer feasible.

CHAPTER 7

Famine and Fenianism, 1845–1870

O'Connell's liberal democratic political nationalism and Young Ireland's cultural nationalism complemented each other. Both moved Irish Catholics away from passivity and fatalism inherent in their Gaelic folk and religious traditions. O'Connell demonstrated that mass, disciplined agitation could change things. Young Ireland inspired a new folklore that provided the people with a sense of dignity and self-confidence. But after the collapse of the 1843 Repeal effort, differences in perspective and temperament inserted an ever-widening wedge between O'Connell and his young lieutenants at the *Nation*. Open conflict started when Davis and O'Connell battled verbally over the colleges bill in the Repeal Association. Although that quarrel was patched up, Young Irelanders, rigid in their ideological cultural nationalism, grew increasingly uncomfortable in alliance with the utilitarian O'Connell. When he came out of prison and indicated an indifference to resuming Repeal agitation, began flirting with federalism, and finally resumed his Whig associations, Young Irelanders criticized what they considered a cynical betrayal of nationalist principles.

The conjunction of nationalism with Catholicism was another issue in the O'Connell–Young Ireland controversy. Almost all the Young Irelanders were Catholics, but they believed that it was time to cut the close ties that bound repeal to the Catholic hierarchy and clergy. They argued that this association discouraged Protestants from participating in a coalition against British rule. They insisted that nationalism must be Irish, not sectarian. O'Connell believed in freedom of conscience and separation of church and state, but he also understood political reality. He had invited Protestants to join the national movement, even offering them its leadership. But he comprehended much better than young idealists that Protestants regarded the union as guarantor of their ascendancy position in Ireland. Therefore, it was not in their own interest to support repeal. O'Connell, more than anyone, knew that nationalism began in the struggle for Catholic civil rights and that the bishops and priests were the force that did so much to undermine the influence of Protestant landlords. He doubted that nationalism was yet strong enough to exist separately from Catholicism. Because Young Irelanders wanted to reduce the Catholic factor in Irish nationalism, some O'Connellites did not hesitate to portray them as secularists and anticlericals. This tactic turned most of the clergy in the Repeal Association against the young men.

THE IRISH CONFEDERATION

The feud between O'Connell and Young Ireland came to a head in July 1846. Worried that *Nation* articles extolling the patriotism of such revolutionaries as the United Irishmen of 1798 might provoke violence in a country made desperate by famine, O'Connell introduced a resolution in the Repeal Association demanding that every member must renounce physical force, no matter what the situation, as a method of achieving Irish freedom. Rather than adhere to the resolution, Young Ireland, led by Charles Gavan Duffy, Thomas Meagher, and William Smith O'Brien (Davis had died of scarlet fever in 1845) walked out of the Repeal Association and in January 1847 established the Irish Confederation as its rival.

William Smith O'Brien, a Protestant landlord from Clare, worked for Irish reform and justice as a Whig in the House of Commons. During the Repeal agitation of 1843, he decided that Irish interests would always take second place in the British Parliament. When the government arrested O'Connell and his chief lieutenants in October 1843, O'Brien joined the Repeal Association. His wife and mother pleaded with him not to mingle with nationalist riffraff. Although his mother disinherited him, O'Brien stuck to his principles. He was entrusted with the leadership of the Repeal Association while O'Connell was in prison. Young Irelanders formed a deep attachment to this man of strong conviction. He joined with them in withdrawing from the Association and was recognized as the chief of the Confederation.

The Irish Confederation had more talent than the Repeal Association and appealed to middle-class people, who formed branches in cities and towns.

However, O'Connell retained numbers for the Association. Most Irish nationalists followed their priests in remaining loyal to Old Ireland. Apathy marked the activities of the Association. O'Connell still placed confidence in the Whigs as Ireland's hope. During the famine crisis, he turned to them for help. In February 1847, as a fading old man with a voice not much louder than a whisper, he rose in the House of Commons and begged the British people to rescue his starving country. British M.P.'s listened and then ignored O'Connell's plea. Brokenhearted and sick, he set out for Rome in late March. In Paris he received the homage of French liberals, who expressed their gratitude for his contribution to the advance of liberal democracy. O'Connell never completed his journey. He died in Genoa on May 15, 1847. His heart was buried in Rome. His body rests in Dublin's Glasnevin cemetery beneath a gigantic round tower. O'Connell's favorite but not most talented son, John, took command of the Repeal Association.

Shortly after its beginning, the Confederation suffered a split over tactics. John Mitchel, an Ulster Unitarian and barrister, was at the center of the controversy. Mitchel began contributing to the *Nation* when it started in 1842. After Davis died, Duffy invited him to become assistant editor. He seceded with the other Young Irelanders from the Repeal Association and helped establish the Confederation. But by 1847 he had become disillusioned with constitutional nationalism and had lost confidence in the possibility of recruiting Protestants in any numbers for the self-government cause. Mitchel believed that they placed their property interests above all other considerations and that landowners were the economic dimension of British colonialism. Mitchel decided that landlordism must be destroyed and the property of Ireland distributed among its people. He insisted that a vital Irish nationalism must revolve around the land question.

Mitchel's convictions were inspired by James Fintan Lalor, an occasional contributor to the *Nation*. Lalor came from a prominent nationalist family. His father, Patrick, was an active antitithe agitator in the 1830s. His younger brother, Peter, a Repealer, emigrated to Australia, became an important leader there in the labor movement, and held office as a minister in the Victoria government. A hunchback recluse, Lalor not only lacked the extrovert personality of his father and sibling, but he also did not share their enthusiasm for repeal. He believed that land was the most important aspect of the Irish question and deserved priority over the independence demand. In 1843 Lalor wrote Peel to say that he could derail Repeal with concessions to the farmer's need for economic justice and security.

Impressed with Lalor's mind but unaware of his anti-Repeal advice to the British government, Duffy invited him to express his ideas in the *Nation*. In a series of letters to the paper, Lalor said that the agrarian issue was of more immediate importance than repeal and that the only way that Irish nationalism could hang on to the support of tenant farmers was by endorsing their cause. He ridiculed O'Connell's agitation tactics and his distinction between legal and illegal methods. With considerable insight, Lalor pointed out that since British authorities defined legal and illegal, constitutional nationalism would always be limited by enemy restrictions. He insisted that the Irish people should base their liberation strategy on only one consideration, the best interests of their country. Lalor suggested refusal to pay rents as a strategem to destroy landlordism, the foundation of British rule in Ireland. Fascinated with this logic, Mitchel in early 1848 recommended a variation of Lalor's plan, a campaign against payment of poor rates.

With his landlord background, William Smith O'Brien was shocked by the ideas of Lalor and Mitchel. He believed in the potential of Protestant nationalism and feared that wild, antiproperty talk would destroy its prospects. When Duffy agreed with O'Brien, Mitchel resigned from the *Nation*. In a Confederation debate, Duffy opposed nonpayment of rates and suggested a strategy alternative: the formation of an independent Irish party in the British Parliament. It would publicize Irish grievances and attempt to convert British opinion to the necessity of Repeal. If the Irish party failed to make an impression at Westminster and if Britain remained hostile to improving the situation in Ireland, then, said Duffy, Irish M.P.'s should retaliate by obstructing the passage of British legislation through Parliament. He recommended that while the Irish party was presenting Ireland's case before the parliamentary forum, nationalists at home should organize and use their voting power to win control over local government agencies. If the Irish M.P.'s were ejected from the House of Commons for obstruction, Duffy indicated that they could return home to an Ireland under nationalist domination. In that case, Britain would have to surrender to a united and disciplined national opinion in charge of parliamentary representation, city corporations, poor law boards, and grand juries and capable of mobilizing effective passive resistance to alien rule in Ireland.

REPEAL TO REVOLUTION

When the Confederation adopted Duffy's proposal, Mitchel resigned and began, with the assistance of Devin Reilly, to publish a nationalist weekly, *The United Irishmen*. It advised readers to prepare for revolution by collecting weapons and practicing their use. Mitchel's editorials insisted that the British must be driven out of Ireland and their puppets, the landlords, with them. In an Irish Republic, "the land of Ireland would belong to the people of Ireland," a slogan coined by Lalor. The February 1848 revolution in France and its spread throughout western and eastern Europe altered the attitude of Young Irelanders toward physical force. When the news from Paris reached Dublin, they decided that a new day of liberty had dawned for all of Europe, including Ireland. Mitchel rejoined the Confederation, *Nation* editorials took on the same militant tone as those in *The United Irishmen*, Smith O'Brien and others attempted to enlist John O'Connell and Irish conservatives in a national front, and contacts were made with friends of Irish freedom in the United States and Britain (the Chartists). O'Brien led a delegation to Paris to congratulate the leaders of the Second Republic on their victory and to secure their aid for an Irish uprising, and Confederate clubs throughout the country were advised to gather arms and prepare for combat. Although O'Brien was ready to lead a rebellion against Britain, he had no intention of making war on Irish property. This conservatism decided Mitchel again to leave the Confederation.

In May the government, attempting to prevent an insurrection, arrested O'Brien, Mitchel, and Meagher. When juries failed to agree that O'Brien and Meagher were guilty of sedition, the government released them. But a packed jury, applying a new coercion bill, decided that Mitchel had committed treason and sentenced him to fourteen years' transportation in Tasmania. Meanwhile, revolutionary planning made little headway. The Confederation did not persuade John O'Connell or Protestant leaders to cooperate in an effort to end British rule; Catholic bishops and priests remained hostile to Young Ireland and loyal to O'Connell's nonviolence; French Republicans, eager to win British recognition of their new government, refused military assistance for Irish nationalism; and Irish peasants, demoralized by hunger, fever, and emigration, were not good revolutionary material.

In July, however, the government's arrest of Duffy, seizure of the *Nation's* office, and suspension of habeas corpus pushed Young Ireland into insurrection, but it had neither the leadership nor the materials for victory. A sincere patriot and a brave man, O'Brien lacked the essential ruthlessness and indifference to property rights to lead a peasant uprising against the landlord establishment. The small number that answered the call to arms came with pikes to battle policemen and soldiers with rifles. O'Brien told members of his motley army that they must not cut down trees on landlord property for road barricades and that they must bring their own food supply rather than forage off the country. Toward the end of May, the Young Ireland revolution came to a pitiful end. The constabulary routed O'Brien's small force in Widow McCormick's Ballingarry, County Tipperary, cabbage patch and arrested him. After juries decided that he and many of his companions had committed treason and sentenced them to death, the government transported them to Tasmania instead. Other Young Irelanders were on the run, looking for a means of escape to France or the United States. Young Irelanders did not just fade away. They might have failed at revolution, but their accomplishments in many things and in many places proved that they were an extraordinarily talented group. Thomas D'Arcy McGee helped create the federated Dominion of Canada and served it as a cabinet minister. Duffy became important in Australia and was prime minister of Victoria. Thomas Francis Meagher was a brigadier general in the Union army during the American Civil War and was appointed governor of the Montana territory. John Blake Dillon returned from an American exile to play a prominent part in Irish politics during the 1860s. Thomas O'Hagan became lord chancellor of Ireland. John Martin, Mitchel's brother-in-law, was an early leader of the Home Rule movement. Other Young Irelanders, including James Stephens, John O'Mahoney, Michael Doheny, and Charles Kickham, created Irish revolutionary republicanism in the United Kingdom and in the United States. As a journalist in the latter, John Mitchel opposed abolitionism and was a Confederate propagandist in the Civil War. During the 1870s Tipperary voters twice elected him their M.P., but as a convicted felon, he was denied a seat in Parliament. Mitchel was an Irish example of the ideological divide between liberalism and cultural nationalism, a distinction made clear on the continent during the revolutions of 1848. Unlike most Irish nationalists, Mitchel could not harmonize nationalism with liberalism. His defense of American slavery indicated that he did not equate individual freedom and dignity with national sovereignty. Mitchel was the complete opposite of O'Connell, who associated the Irish freedom effort with the universal struggle for individual liberty and equality.

In a time of crisis, Young Ireland had been rejected by the priests and people, then defeated by soldiers and the constabulary. But in the history of Irish nationalism, martyrology has been as important as victories. Young Irelanders joined Robert Emmet in the pantheon of defeated but noble and articulate defenders of their country. In the long run, Young Ireland captured the mind of Irish nationalism. While the *Nation's* message would inspire Fenians, Home Rulers, Gaelic Leaguers, writers of the Literary Revival, and Sinn Feiners, in the late 1840s it seemed of little significance to a country devastated by the tortures of famine.

FAMINE

In 1845 a potato fungus from North America arrived in Ireland via Europe, causing a massive famine that persisted with great intensity until 1849. Its effects lingered into 1851. During the "Great Hunger" at least a million and a half people died of starvation or the side effects of malnutrition—cholera, fever, and scurvy; many millions more came close to death; and at least another million crossed the Atlantic in fever-filled coffin ships or swarmed across the Irish Sea to Liverpool, Glasgow, and Cardiff. Most who arrived in Liverpool went on to America.

Nineteenth-century Irish nationalists argued, and there are still people in Ireland and Irish America who hold this view, that Ireland suffered so much and lost so many people during the famine because the British government used it to solve the Irish question through population extermination. This is too simplistic an explanation for a complex situation. Most of the misery of the famine was the product of an inefficient and unproductive agricultural system that preceded the union. There is no reason to believe, considering the economic ideologies of the time, that the aristocracy and gentry in an Irish Parliament would have responded much differently to the famine than did people from the same classes in the British Parliament. Death, disease, and emigration were also the consequences of a population explosion produced by the agricultural system and dependence on the potato. When the famine began to strike down the Irish people, British officials in Ireland worked energetically to mitigate the disaster. Often they contributed their own money to feed the poor. A number of British physicians fell victim to fever while treating the sick. Britons, including the queen and members of the royal family, donated to famine relief. British religious groups, particularly the Quakers, raised relief funds, ministered to the sick, and distributed food to the hungry. The government spent a fortune attempting to soften the blow of the famine. In the first year, Peel's administration spent 8 million pounds on famine relief.

In contrast to Peel's effort, the Whig government's famine response gave Irish nationalists reason to raise the genocide charge. At a time when the Irish were dying of hunger or disease or fleeing the country, Britain was the most prosperous country in the world. Its politicians did not use the full resources of the United Kingdom to save Ireland. Committed to laissez-faire dogmatism, they did not provide enough food to meet the Irish need or design the sort of public works projects that would provide food-buying income while at the same time stimulating the economy. Government officials argued that famine relief should not interfere with normal commercial activity, compete with private business, discourage personal initiative, make the Irish people psychologically dependent on government charity, or interfere with private property or private responsibility. They appeared to believe that the Irish famine was a beneficial Malthusian disaster. In its darkest hours, Nassau Senior, a famous economist high in the counsels of the Whig administration, lamented that in 1848 only a million would die from famine causes, and that was not sufficient to solve the Irish surplus population problem. Charles Edward Trevelyan, undersecretary of the treasury and the person most responsible for the government's relief program, decided that the famine was divine retribution on a wicked, perverse people.

There are similarities between the famine of the 1840s and the Holocaust of the 1930s and 1940s. The Jews and the Irish were both victims of what Albert Camus in *The Plague* described as ideological murder. Certainly the Nazis were more ruthless, heartless, and consistent in the application of racist principles than Trevelyan and his colleagues were in their anti–Irish Catholicism or in their enforcement of the dogmas of political economy. But Irish people dying of hunger or fever or crowded into the bowels of an emigrant ship, abused by heartless captains and crews, exploited by runners and hostel keepers in Liverpool, New York, Boston, and New Orleans, would have had scant consolation in knowing that their predicament was not the result of racism but a price they must pay to retain a free enterprise economy and to restore a "proper" population balance.

The famine was the most significant episode in modern Irish history, destroying whatever chance Peel's policy might have had to conciliate Catholic opinion. It left the Irish with bitter memories and focused and intensified their hatred of British rule as the source of their miseries. These recollections and emotions were passed on to children and grandchildren. The famine also influenced the development and personality of Catholicism in Ireland; pushed the agrarian dimension of the Irish question to the forefront, with important economic and political consequences; and, through emigration, transported Irish nationalism throughout the English-speaking world, especially to the United States.

THE CONSOLIDATION OF IRISH CATHOLICISM

When British government pressure in the late eighteenth century persuaded the Irish Parliament to begin rolling back the Penal Laws, Irish Catholicism began to lose its timidity and tentativeness, shedding the trappings of a ghetto religion. (It became less Anglo-Protestant and more Continental Catholic in observance.) Devotions such as the Rosary and the Stations of the Cross became popular in the eighteenth century. In the early nineteenth, old chapels were repaired and new ones constructed. Parish missions became increasingly common. Post-Tridentine discipline, dogma, and liturgy spread through Irish Catholicism. The successful campaign for Catholic emancipation instilled confidence and courage in the hierarchy and clergy, completing the change in the Church's stance from defensive to aggressive. Because of indifference, ignorance, and poverty (lack of decent clothes to wear), many people did not attend Mass or receive the sacraments in a church setting (large numbers did at stations held in private homes). Still, the prefamine Irish were better churchgoers than continental Catholics.

While Irish Catholicism on the eve of the famine was increasingly assertive and devotional, most of the post-Penal religious enthusiasm and reform took place in Anglicized cities, towns, and the prosperous agricultural sections of Leinster and Munster. West of the Shannon, in the poorer, more Gaelic parts of the country, superstition continued to compete with Catholic orthodoxy, religious observance was spotty and casual, and there was a shortage of priests and chapels. Everywhere in Ireland the church was afflicted by a split in the hierarchy between the Murray and MacHale factions; a clergy that was contentious, insubordinate, and less than well educated; and a laity largely ignorant of Catholic beliefs.

The famine was a catalyst in the movement of Irish Catholicism toward Roman discipline, devotionalism, and centralization. Most of the famine casualties came from the poorest, most unenlightened element in the population, people who knew the least about their religion and practiced it spasmodically. With their passing, through death or emigration, the church found it easier to instruct and control those who remained, and the clergy and chapel facilities increased in proportion to the decline of the laity. Catholicism also had a role in famine-induced changes in marriage and reproduction patterns. When the famine survivors became aware that overpopulation and subdivision of land contributed to the Great Hunger, they determined to control numbers through a more thoughtful approach to marriage. The result was prolonged periods of and sometimes permanent celibacy. Catholic morality gave spiritual and psychological support for this difficult decision. If social and economic necessities attached the Irish more closely to their church, it also made puritanism a prominent feature of their religion. Perhaps it contributes to the Irish alcohol addiction as sublimation. Of course, the pub is a great refuge from the depressing damp and cold of the Irish climate as well as a substitute for the company of women. People on the next island, the English, Scots, and Welsh, also are hearty drinkers.

The impact of the famine on Irish Catholicism set the stage for the entry of Paul Cullen. He became the most powerful personality in Ireland in the period between O'Connell and Charles Stewart Parnell. The son of a substantial Kildare yeoman farmer, with priests on both sides of the family, Cullen attended the Propaganda College in Rome for seminary training and doctoral studies. He became a papal court favorite and its adviser on Irish affairs. Appointed rector of the Irish College in 1832, Cullen was the intermediary between the Irish hierarchy and the Curia. More nationalistic in his youth, prior to Mazzini's ouster of the pope from Rome, than in middle or old age, Cullen tipped off O'Connell on the Fransoni directive. In 1849 Pius IX sent his good friend Cullen back to Ireland as archbishop of Armagh, primate, and apostolic delegate. Three years later he replaced Murray as Dublin's archbishop. In 1866 Cullen became the first Irish cardinal. His importance was apparent in 1870, when he designed Vatican I's papal infallibility formula.

Cullen returned to Ireland determined to engineer an ultramontane triumph over competing forms of Gallicanism: Murray's cooperation with the government, MacHale's alliance with nationalism. With the exception of much of Ulster and MacHale's Tuam, Cullen managed to select bishops and to impose his will on the hierarchy. As part of the Romanization process, he built large numbers of churches and schools; achieved public displays of unity in the hierarchy; improved the discipline and training of priests; promoted a rapid increase in religious vocations, both for Irish and missionary purposes; expanded Catholic education, including the foundations of a university; defeated an English-financed Protestant evangelical crusade to proselytize Irish Catholics; and completed a "devotional revolution" that made the Irish the most pious, generous, and dedicated Catholics in western Europe.

Cullen disliked and distrusted the English, even those who were Catholic, and all Protestants, but he was also hostile to lay and clerical nationalism. When he came to Ireland, he associated Young Ireland with Mazzini's anticlericalism. Later he would link the Fenians with Garibaldi and the Carbonari. In Cullen's opinion, Irish nationalism's liberal inclusiveness and tolerance constituted a more dangerous threat to ultramontanism than the hereditary Anglo-Saxon and Anglo-Irish Protestant enemies. To him, there was no distinction between Irish and Catholic identities—faith and fatherland were inseparable. What was good for the church was good for the country.

What Cullen never understood was that the success of his effort to unify, discipline, and dogmatically and liturgically Romanize the Irish church owed as much to the advance of Irish nationalism, with its religious and cultural identity connections, as it did to his leadership ability. The Irish wore their religion as an identity badge. As they increased their commitment to nationality, they intensified their Catholicism. However, stronger Catholics did not mean weaker nationalists. Cullen and other bishops found out that in politics, they could only lead where people wanted to go. The Irish loved their religion, treasuring it as culture as well as

PAUL CARDINAL CULLEN
1852–1878

Paul Cullen's primary commitment to the interests of the Catholic church made him unpopular with Irish nationalists, but as Archbishop of Armagh (1849–1852) and Archbishop of Dublin (1852–1878) he led the "Devotional Revolution" that shaped the spirit, content, and structure of modern Irish Catholicism. (Courtesy of the National Library of Ireland.)

faith; respected their priests, listening to and obeying them on matters of dogma; but retained their allegiance to the principles and objectives of Irish nationalism. At the Dedalus family's Christmas dinner in James Joyce's *Portrait of the Artist as a Young Man,* Mrs. Riordan, bitterly denounces John Casey, the ex-Fenian and Parnellite anticlerical, as a renegade Catholic. In anger, he replies: "And I may tell you ma'am, that I, if you mean me, am no renegade Catholic, I am a Catholic as my father was and his father before him again when we gave up our lives rather than sell our faith."

LAND AND POLITICS

Catholicism remained the nucleus of Irish identity, but emancipation and Peel's Irish policy did much to reduce the religious dimension of the Irish question. Because of the famine, land emerged as the most pressing and emotional issue in nationalist politics.

After the fiasco at Ballingarry, Charles Gavan Duffy was the only Young Ireland leader left in the country. The government tried him five times on treason charges, but brilliant courtroom tactics by his attorney, Isaac Butt, and the inability of juries to reach a unanimous decision freed him from prison and saved him from transport to Van Diemen's Land (Tasmania). After his release, Duffy revived the *Nation* and with new colleagues—Dr. John Gray, Protestant part owner of the leading daily nationalist newspaper, *The Freeman's Journal,* and Frederick Lucas, owner and editor of the *Tablet,* a Catholic weekly—he set out to combine the ideas of Lalor and Mitchel with the strategy he proposed to the Irish Confederation as a new program for Irish nationalism.

Duffy and his friends proposed an independent Irish party in the House of Commons dedicated to a tenant right solution to agrarian discontent. They believed that a concentration on the plight of farmers all over the country would unite Protestants in Ulster in common cause with rural Catholics from all over Ireland. A precedent of Catholic-Protestant cooperation would break down barriers of suspicion and animosity, clearing the way for an ecumenical Irish nationalism incorporating all the people.

Duffy, Gray, and Lucas were appealing to famine-intensified farmer security concerns both north and south, Catholic, Anglican, and Presbyterian. The demand for economic and social justice did not express desperate poverty. In fact, as British political economists predicted, the famine benefited its survivors, especially in the fertile sectors of Leinster, Munster, and Ulster. Famine death and emigration population decreases most affected the agricultural laboring and marginal tenant-farming classes. Continuing emigration kept reducing Irish numbers. After the famine, farmers came to outnumber laborers, and farms grew larger. Throughout the 1850s, 1860s, and well into the 1870s, harvests tended to be good, agricultural prices rose, rents were relatively stable, and evictions were rare. These factors and dollar gifts from sons and daughters in the United States lifted the rural Irish standard of living. Cottages became roomier and sturdier; people wore better clothing and supplemented potatoes with cereals, bread, butter, vegetables, eggs, and occasionally meat and fish. National school education, a demanding Catholicism, and better food and housing produced a much more sophisticated, disciplined, and healthier peasantry than the prefamine variety.

Tenant right was most consistently advocated in areas where people were experiencing economic and social improvements, rather than along the Atlantic coast or in mountainous Catholic Ulster, where the soil was poor and rocky and fields were small, and the potato still sustained life. Therefore, tenant right organizations articulated rising expectations, a determination not to fall back into a prefamine survival situation and mentality.

Encouraged by Duffy, Lucas, and Gray, representatives of tenant right clubs from all over Ireland began to discuss shared problems and goals. These conversations resulted in the Irish Tenant League, with the stated objectives of fair rents established by impartial evaluation, secure tenures, and the right of tenants to sell their interest in the farm they occupied when leaving (Ulster custom). The political activation of Irish farmers persuaded a number of M.P.'s to combine in an Irish party committed to independent opposition in the House of Commons and to tenant right. In July 1852 a general election returned forty-eight Irish party M.P.'s, but within a few months of this spectacular victory, it began to disintegrate.

The Achilles heel of the party was the Tenant League–Irish Brigade coalition. Ridiculed as the "Pope's Brass Band," the Brigade was the organized response of a group of Liberal Irish M.P.'s to Lord John Russell's 1851 bill threatening to prosecute and penalize Catholic clergymen who took United Kingdom geographic ecclesiastical titles. In exploiting the anti-Catholic hysteria following Pius IX's decision to create a diocesan structure for an Irish-immigrant-enriched British church, Russell's bill indicated that the Whigs were prepared to outdo the Tories at their no-popery game.

Insulted by the Whig courtship of prejudice, George Henry Moore, M.P., son of the George Moore in Thomas Flanagan's novel *The Year of the French* and the father of a future distinguished writer, George Moore, gathered a small group of Irish M.P.'s to punish Russell by voting with the opposition to destroy the government. The passage of the ecclesiastical titles bill (it was never really enforced, and the Catholic church used different geographic titles from the Church of England's) so aroused Irish Catholic opinion that Moore decided to retain the Brigade as an independent party. To give it constituency backing, in August 1851 Brigade M.P.'s established the Catholic Defense Association of Great Britain and Ireland.

Gray's *Freeman's Journal* endorsed the Brigade and its constituency organization. Duffy respected Moore's integrity and talent but did not find the same qualities in some of his Brigade colleagues. However, in August 1851 he helped William Sharman Crawford, M.P., an Ulster Protestant champion of federalism and the outstanding parliamentary promoter of tenant right legislation, complete an alliance between the Brigade and the Tenant League. It gave the League additional strength in Parliament without associating the nondenominational tenant right movement with the Brigade's Catholic concerns.

Shortly after the general election, two Brigade members of the independent Irish party, William Keogh and John Sadlier, broke their independent opposition pledge and accepted office in Lord Aberdeen's Peelite-Whig coalition government. This apostasy did not offend Archbishop Cullen or some other bishops. They wanted cooperation with Aberdeen, hoping to win concessions for the Catholic church, particularly in education, and were pleased to have Catholics such as Sadlier and Keogh in office.

Duffy blamed the defection of Sadlier and Keogh and the anti-independent opposition stance of prominent members of the Catholic hierarchy for the collapse of the Irish party. By 1855 he had lost confidence in the movement and in his ability to shape the future of Irish nationalism. Duffy sold the *Nation* to A. M. Sullivan, a young nationalist from West Cork, and sailed to Australia, where he played an important part in that nation's political development. When an old man, he returned to Ireland as Sir Charles Gavan Duffy, blessed the Home Rule movement, and molded Irish popular history in books on Thomas Davis, Young Ireland, and the independent Irish party.

Duffy's historical interpretations made Cullen a villain in the mythology of Irish nationalism. While it is true that the approval of Cullen and other prelates of the Sadlier-Keogh "treachery," their enmity to independent opposition, and Cullen's instructions to Irish priests to stay out of politics did damage Irish party prospects, other factors, perhaps more important, contributed to its demise. Aberdeen's government attracted considerable support from Ulster Protestant tenant farmers. Common famine suffering created common cause, but when times improved, ancient sectarian animosities reemerged and defeated peasant-class solidarity. And it must be remembered that relations between landlords and tenants were more harmonious in Ulster than in the other provinces.

Landlordism also had a political resurgence in the 1850s. With the Catholic hierarchy split on such matters as independent opposition and the priority of tenant right, landlords were able to muster the votes to return fifty-seven Conservative Irish M.P.'s in the general election of 1859. Tenant insecurity, their deference to the upper classes, and the absence of a secret ballot meant that the owners of large estates could still control Catholic as well as Protestant votes.

Landlord success in the 1859 general election also owed something to the pro-Cavour, antipapal position of Lords Palmerston and Russell. Reacting to this Whig support for Italian nationalism's menace to the papal states, Nicholas Patrick Cardinal Wiseman, archbishop of Westminster, and some Irish prelates urged Irish voters in Britain and Ireland to support Lord Derby and the Conservatives.

In addition to the conduct of bishops and priests, the independent Irish party's difficulty in finding quality candidates assisted the resurgence of landlord political power. As previously observed, prohibitive election costs and London living expenses without a salary made politics an upper-class avocation. Most Irishmen in a position to pursue parliamentary careers were landlords hostile to the economic, political, and religious interests of Irish Catholics. Candidates willing to gamble small fortunes to represent nationalist, tenant right, or Catholic causes could not be expected to keep preelection pledges once separated from constituents by the Irish Sea. Irishmen eager for status, prestige, and wealth often sold their services to any government in exchange for office.

By 1858 the independent Irish party numbered an ineffectual twelve. A year later it was officially dissolved. Led by John Blake Dillon, most of its M.P.'s moved to the Liberal benches in 1866. In the 1860s a number of Irish Liberal M.P.'s, including George Henry Moore and Dillon, cooperated with Cullen and other bishops in the National Association. Its goals were government aid to Catholic education, disestablishment of the Protestant church, and tenant right. Because of Cullen and the bad experience of the independent Irish party, the Association lacked a mass constituency, but through its alliances with John Bright's Reform League and the Society for the Liberation of the Church from State Patronage and Control, two British radical organizations, it did influence William E. H. Gladstone's perspective on the Irish question. However, in the 1860s Irish nationalism was moving in an anticonstitutional direction, and emigration was instrumental in this shift.

THE AMERICAN DIMENSION

Irish emigrants were scattered throughout the English-speaking world, but most ended up in the United States. Before 1820 the majority of those who left Ireland for North America were Ulster Presbyterians irritated by British restrictions on Irish economic development and the ascendancy of the Church of Ireland. After that date, periodic famines, rural violence, and population pressures on a primitive and static economy transformed emigration into a primarily Catholic affair. The famine institutionalized it as a safety valve, with parents raising most of their children for export. From 1845 to 1891 more than 3 million Irish, mostly young and single, entered the United States. By the end of the nineteenth century, more women than men were leaving for America.

Irish emigrants were not prepared psychologically or vocationally for life in industrial societies. As the most underprivileged people in urban Britain and the United States, they did the hard, unpleasant work that Anglo-Americans and Britons were too proud or perhaps too weak to do. The Irish dug canals; built railroads; mined coal, silver, gold, and copper; lifted cargo on the docks; soldiered all over the British Empire and on the American frontier; and scrubbed the floors, washed the dishes, and took care of children in the homes of the well-to-do. Anglo-Protestants in Britain and in Boston, New York, and Philadelphia despised dirty, ignorant Irish papists, and the British and American working class did not welcome their labor competition. Rejected by host communities, the Irish huddled in slum ghettos, spawning a large proportion of juvenile delinquents, petty thieves, alcoholics, depressives, and schizophrenics. Many immigrants blamed their American misfortunes on the British oppression that forced them into exile. And they responded to alienation with a nationalism more fanatic than the Irish-in-Ireland variety. As Thomas N. Brown has observed: "in the alembic of America the parochial peasant was transformed into a passionate Irish nationalist."

This emigration-scattered Irish nationalism multiplied its challenge to Britain. Although economic realities necessitated emigration as an Irish safety valve, nationalist leaders blamed the diaspora on British misgovernment. When the Irish began to achieve economic and social mobility in the United States, their success also fed Irish nationalist propaganda. It argued that Irish genius flourished when emancipated from British tyranny.

Irish Catholicism's acceptance of liberal democracy and the political skills Irish immigrants brought from Ireland led to Irish-American progress. O'Connell's instructions on Anglo-Protestant political values and on operating within its constitutional traditions and structures made it possible for the Irish to adjust to the American political system and consensus and then lead other Catholic ethnics into a similar accommodation. Political power and the leadership of Catholic America resulted in economic and social advances and eventual respectability, but the process was long and uneven.

In early Irish America the dominant impulse of nationalism was an alienation response to poverty, social disorder, and Anglo-American Protestant nativism. Because Anglo-Americans emphasized Catholicism as the main feature of the "ugly" Irish cultural and social profile, and because in the United States nativism destroyed fraternal links between Irish Catholics and Irish Protestants and Dissenters, the twin identities, Irish and Catholic, became stronger than in the United Kingdom. Consequently, Irish nationalism evolved more exclusively Catholic in America than in Ireland. Anglo-Irish and Scots-Irish Americans melded into Anglo-America. When it came, economic progress in the United States did not necessarily eliminate the Irish inferiority complex. Irish-Americans with substantial incomes and good educations were classical examples of what the Chicago school of sociology in the 1920s described as marginal men. They longed to participate in the social activities of Anglo-Protestant America. When rejected, they returned to the subordinate Irish cultural community as leaders, determined to demonstrate its significance and achieve its acceptance. Young Ireland's cultural nationalism was as good for the ego of Irish-Americans as it was for the Irish in Ireland. It told them that they were an honorable people with a cultural heritage as rich and a history as glorious and values more spiritual than Anglos. So in economically and socially mobile Irish America, nationalism developed a respectability as well as an anti-British purpose. Associating their status problem with Ireland's bondage, many middle-class Irish-Americans believed that the liberation of their homeland would culminate in American acceptability.

Irish-American nationalism employed two strategies. One pressured American foreign policy to move in an anti-British direction; the other used the United States as a supply station for freedom efforts in Ireland. Although Irish-Americans have been the most talented politicians in the United States, they have not been particularly effective in influencing foreign policy. Occasionally non-Irish candidates for office have played to an Irish grandstand to gather votes, but Anglo-American Protestants have defeated Irish-American maneuvers to provoke antagonism between the United States and their cultural mother country, Britain.

Irish strategy successes partially compensated for Washington failures. Without the American connection, nationalism in Ireland might have perished. In addition to organization, passion, dollars, and pressures on Britain, Irish America affected the personality of Irish nationalism. Nationalist commitments in Ireland to democratic principles and values were strengthened through associations with American republicanism and democracy. In 1887 Lord Spencer, an influential Liberal peer, discussed the importance of the Ireland-America connection:

> The Irish peasantry still live in poor hovels, often in the same room with animals; they have few modern comforts; and yet they are in close communication with those who live at ease in the cities and farms of the United States. They are also imbued with the advanced political notions of the American republic and are sufficiently educated to read the latest political doctrines in the press which circulates them. Their social condition at home is a hundred years behind their state of mental and political culture.

Anglo-Irish landlords and Catholic priests were also apprehensive about the impact of American examples. After 1860 they observed that people had become more assertive and less deferential to their social or religious betters, attributing this arrogance to the American contents of Fenianism.

FENIANISM

Fenianism emerged in 1858 from the New York–based Emmet Monument Association, dedicated to writing Robert Emmet's epitaph in the form of an Irish nation. John O'Mahony and Michael Doheny, veterans of 1848, led the association. They and James Stephens managed to escape British clutches after Ballingarry. Doheny made it to New York; Stephens and O'Mahony found work, respectively, as translator and English teacher in Paris, where they absorbed the teachings of 1848 refugees from other European revolutions.

In Paris, O'Mahony and Stephens decided on a revolutionary movement to establish a democratic Irish republic. Ideologically socialists, they agreed to submerge economic issues, still entertaining the Young Ireland notion that Protestant property owners could become Irish nationalists. This fantasy deprived Republicanism of a significant economic content.

Invited by Doheny, O'Mahony left Paris in 1854 for New York to recruit Irish-Americans for revolutionary conspiracy. Stephens concentrated his mobilizing efforts in Ireland and Britain. In 1858 he initiated the Irish Republican Brotherhood (IRB) and incorporated Jeremiah O'Donovan Rossa's Cork-centered Phoenix Society. It represented the dashing Gaelic speaker's determination to raise Ireland from the ashes of British conquest. This was in the same year that O'Mahony transformed the Emmet Monument Association into the American branch of Republicanism. Since he was a Gaelic scholar and an admirer of the legendary sagas featuring warriors called Fianna, O'Mahony decided to name it the Fenian Brotherhood. *Fenianism* became the popular term for Irish Republicanism on both sides of the Atlantic.

To ensure secrecy, Stephens and O'Mahony organized Fenianism into circles commanded by a centre. Circles were subdivided into cells under the command of captains with authority over sergeants in charge of privates. Lower-rank Republicans knew only cell comrades. IRB members took secrecy oaths. To avoid offending American Catholic bishops, Fenians took a pledge. Despite security measures, informers and spies infested and infiltrated Republicanism.

Stephens was head centre of the IRB and chief organizer of the Irish Republic. O'Mahony was Fenian head centre. Stephens considered himself in charge of the total Republican movement. Irish-Americans did not always honor that claim.

The IRB in Ireland and the Fenians in the United States both had about 50,000 members, but many more Irish-Americans were contributing sympathizers. In 1865 the American Irish donated about $228,000 to the cause. The next year they increased their contribution to over $500,000. During the War between the States, many Irish-Americans enlisted in the Union and Confederate armies, hoping to use their combat training and experience against the British at some later date.

Fenianism was more than politics and nationalism. As previously mentioned, in the United States it involved working-class alienation and a quest for middle-class respectability. Like Young Irelanders, many IRB leaders were journalists. Striving for fame and glory, these lower-middle-class young men were blocked by the O'Connellite and Young Ireland establishments. By moving beyond Repeal and independent opposition to revolutionary Republicanism, they found a position in Irish nationalism.

Despite the reluctance of Stephens and O'Mahoney to emphasize the economic aspects of the Irish question, Republicanism did exhibit class frustrations and interests. In America it included unskilled working-class rage and the expectations of the economically mobile. In Ireland city and town artisans and shop assistants, suspended between the working class and the middle class, joined the IRB. In the late 1860s it took root in rural Ireland, particularly Connacht and Catholic Ulster, whence it became a significant force in the land war of the 1870s and 1880s.

In Ireland and the United States, Fenianism also offered recreational opportunities for fun-starved people. Life in class-structured, agrarian, Catholic puritan Ireland was dull and monotonous. This, as well as economic hardship, stimulated emigration. Fenians sponsored athletic activities, reading rooms with discussion groups, outings, and walking tours in the mountains. They gathered at horse races and fairs and formed musical organizations. In the United States, the Fenian Brotherhood, and later the Clan na Gael, sponsored picnics and clambakes with barrels of beer to wash down the food. After the meal, there were colorful patriotic speeches and, even better, music and dancing. Finley Peter Dunne, the Chicago journalist initiator of American urban ethnic literature, observed in the 1890s that if Ireland could have been liberated by picnics, it would have become an empire.

In Ireland the IRB did not get the approval of John Martin or William Smith O'Brien, two returnees from Australian exile. In the United States other Young Irelanders, such as Thomas Meagher, condemned Fenianism. John Mitchel first opposed then later approved. Because of his hostility, Fenians assassinated Thomas D'Arcy McGee in 1867 on the steps of the Canadian Parliament in Ottawa. In the *Nation*, A. M. Sullivan identified the IRB with agrarian secret societies in a blanket denouncement of physical force. Catholic bishops, led by Cullen, were the most powerful enemies of Republicanism. They attacked its secret character and commitment to the violent destruction of British rule. To Cullen, Fenians were dangerous secularists, enemies of throne and altar, radicals inspired by the excessively democratic and turbulent environment of the United States, and Irish disciples of Mazzini, Cavour, and Garibaldi. The Catholic hierarchy also had high hopes that Gladstone's Liberal party would disestablish the Protestant church and endow Catholic education. They feared that physical-force nationalism in Ireland would so alienate British opinion that Gladstone would shy away from Irish reform. No doubt the bishops also were concerned with the recreational side of Fenianism. They did not like social functions outside the control of the parish priest, particularly if they involved contacts between young men and women. David Moriarity, bishop of Kerry, said that "hell wasn't hot enough or eternity long enough" to punish Fenians properly.

Clerical hostility introduced a strong anticlerical note into Republicanism. In its newspaper, *The Irish People,* Charles J. Kickham replied to the hierarchy. Kickham, a devout Catholic, was author of such popular novels as *Knocknagow* and *Sally Cavanaugh.* His descriptions of peasant Ireland were much more romantic than those of Carleton, but insightful all the same, and they contributed to the mainstream of Irish cultural nationalism. Kickham ranked with Thomas Moore and Thomas Davis in the hearts of Irish exiles in America. Speaking then from a position of powerful influence, Kickham said that the Irish people should respect and listen to bishops and priests when they discussed religion but that clerical authority stopped on the frontiers of politics. He reminded readers that bishops had supported the treachery of Sadlier and Keogh and warned that some of them would sell the liberty of their country for government educational grants. He advised Irish Catholics to love God and His church but also to love their country. He assured them that there was no conflict in these affections.

From the original condemnation of the Fenians in 1858 until 1865, Cullen managed to keep his fellow bishops and priests away from Republicanism. However, there were a few exceptions. Since most of the clergy came from the farmer and shopkeeper classes, they shared the grievances of their kin. Some were bold enough to defy superiors by offering prayers for and sympathy to the IRB. In 1861, for example, Patrick Lavelle, a Mayo priest, spoke at the Glasnevin burial of Terence Belew McManus after Cullen displayed coolness to a Fenian-staged Catholic funeral for the 1848 veteran who had died in San Francisco. Lavelle was shielded by Archbishop MacHale, who, though he never went so far as to endorse Fenianism, remained on good terms with Republicans and accepted their charity.

After Appomattox, Fenians began to prepare for war on Britain. Irish-Americans who had recently commanded troops in the War between the States infiltrated Ireland and began to train members of the IRB. John Devoy initiated an effort to recruit Irish soldiers in the British army stationed in Ireland for the IRB. Several thousand may have joined. American pressure forced Stephens to plan an uprising for 1866, but a factional dispute in American Republicanism cut off supplies to Ireland. In 1865 a national Fenian convention in Philadelphia adopted a new constitution abolishing the head centre, replacing him with a president responsible to a general Congress divided into a Senate and a House of Delegates. Colonel William R. Roberts, head of the Senate, dictated a new strategy for Fenianism. Instead of participating in an Irish revolution, American Fenians would attack British Canada, holding it hostage for Ireland's freedom. This would leave the Irish in Ireland to conduct and supply their own war against the British. Lacking proper equipment, Stephens refused to repeat the fiasco of 1848. Meanwhile, a spy in the offices of *The Irish People* turned over incriminating evidence to the government. The authorities shut down the paper and arrested its staff, along with Stephens. Devoy engineered the head centre's prison escape. Stephens then went to the United States to end the feud between O'Mahony and the Senate wing and to get weapons for an Irish revolution. However, his arrogant and abrasive personality exacerbated rather than ended conflict within American Fenianism. Blaming Stephens for indecisiveness in regard to an Irish revolution, in December 1866 American Fenians deposed him as Republican head centre. An Irish-American, Colonel Thomas J. Kelly, took his place.

While Stephens's American mission was collapsing, the government took the IRB by surprise. It transferred Irish soldiers stationed in their own country elsewhere, suspended habeas corpus, and arrested a number of Republican leaders. In a futile gesture of defiance, Kerry Fenians took the field in February 1867, and others in Dublin, Cork, Tipperary, Limerick, and Clare followed the next month. Without adequate weapons, these little Fenian bands were easily routed by the British army and the Royal Irish Constabulary.

After 1865 a growing number of priests, influenced by traditional grievances, particularly those concerned with land, a decreasing American influence on the IRB, and the fact that Republicanism had been defeated and was more of a legend than a reality, began to view Fenianism with some sympathy. Cullen feared that the clergy was becoming unmanageable on the issue. When news got out that British prison authorities were brutal to Fenian convicts, and when in 1867 the British legal system executed three young Irishmen (W. P. Allen, Michael Larkin, and Michael O'Brien), after a trial in an atmosphere of tremendous anti-Irish feeling, for allegedly killing a police constable in a Manchester rescue of Colonel Kelly from a police van, there was a massive wave of pro-Fenian sentiment in Ireland. Prayers rose from the Catholic altars of Ireland for the Manchester martyrs. Some bishops joined the Amnesty Association working to commute Republican prison sentences. But the British government was active in Rome. Assisted by Bishop Moriarity, and with promises of benefits to the church in Ireland, Lord Odo Russell, the British representative, persuaded Pius IX to issue an official condemnation of the IRB.

Actually, Rome's pro-British interference in Irish affairs antagonized Irish nationalism, making the Fenians more popular. Trying to exploit a more friendly climate of opinion and to increase efficiency, Republicans reorganized their movement on both sides of the Atlantic. Physical-force nationalism best represented Irish America's approach to liberating Ireland from British colonialism. In Ireland people came to respect Fenians for their sacrifice and their bravery—they were added to the list of martyred patriots, but revolutionary Republicanism was and remained a minority voice. Fenianism added democratic and egalitarian impulses to Irish nationalism, but its mainstream continued to seek self-government with some British connection by constitutional means. After 1870 it found expression in Home Rule.

GLADSTONE'S INITIAL RESPONSE TO THE IRISH QUESTION

Fenianism not only colored the personality of Irish nationalism, but along with the alliance between the National Association and the British Liberation Society, it decided William Ewart Gladstone, who organized the Liberal party from a coalition of Whigs, Radicals, and Peelites, to address the Irish question. Taking office after the 1868 general election, he decided to follow the lead of his mentor, Peel, by initiating a policy of attempting to destroy Irish nationalism by eliminating the social, economic, and religious grievances of its constituency. In 1869 the prime minister disestablished the Protestant Church of Ireland. The next year he pushed a land act through Parliament. It was a conservative effort to achieve tenant farmer security by forcing landlords to compensate evictees for improvements they had made and inconvenience they had suffered. The land act applied in all instances of eviction except for nonpayment of rent. Gladstone believed that the expense of ousting tenants from their holdings would force landlords to think twice before clearing estates. Both the disestablishment and land acts contained land purchase possibilities. The government offered tenants on church property loans to buy their holdings. John Bright added an important clause to the land act, providing government loans up to two-thirds of the purchase price for tenants who wanted their own farms.

As an instrument of security, the land act failed. Since landlords could evict without compensation if rents were not paid, it encouraged them to raise rents to get rid of poor tenants. Loans provided by the disestablishment act created about 6000 peasant proprietors, but the terms of the Bright clause did not attract much tenant farmer enthusiasm. In fact, with the severe agricultural depression that began in the late 1870s, peasant conditions worsened, and many tenant farmers were evicted for nonpayment of rent.

Though inadequate for its purpose, the land act was a precedent weakening resistance to government control of property rights, paving the way for more meaningful legislation in the 1880s. And the disestablishment act and Bright clause pointed to a final solution of the land problem, peasant proprietorship. The disestablishment act was a British liberal rejection of Protestant ascendancy in Ireland. And the refusal of dual establishment by Cullen and other Catholic bishops, despite the wishes of Rome, meant that Irish Catholicism had accepted the separation of church and state, a principle of Irish nationalism. Since the land act was the first major government reversal of the traditional rights of landed property, it had major implications for Britain as well as Ireland. By expanding government areas of responsibility, the land act was a significant step in the progress of British liberalism from its early nineteenth-century laissez-faire start to its late nineteenth- and early twentieth-century collectivist climax.

Although Gladstone agreed with Irish Catholic complaints that they were denied higher education opportunities and facilities, as leader of a party dependent on the votes of British Nonconformists, he could hardly endow the Catholic University in Dublin. And it would be imprudent and inconsistent to follow the disestablishment of Irish Protestantism with an endowment of Catholic education. In 1873 the prime minister presented to Parliament a solution to the Irish higher education dilemma. His Irish university bill proposed converting Dublin University from a Protestant institution to a national one by expanding it to include a Catholic college as well as Trinity. The university would offer no lectures or examinations in such controversially sectarian subjects as theology, history, or moral philosophy. The affiliated colleges, however, would be free to offer courses and diplomas in them.

Since the Irish Catholic hierarchy had been fighting nondenominational higher education beginning with the Queens colleges in the late 1840s, they rejected Gladstone's offer as inadequate. They argued that since the government supported Protestant Oxford and Cambridge and the disestablishment act left Trinity a well-financed center of Protestant studies, a nonendowed Catholic college within Dublin University would be a disadvantaged institution without funds to attract good students or faculty. Influenced by the bishop's criticism of the university bill, a large number of Irish Liberal M.P.'s voted against it and defeated it, forcing Gladstone to call a general election in January 1874. Expanded by the 1867 reform bill and emancipated by the 1872 ballot act, the British electorate returned a Conservative majority. Benjamin Disraeli succeeded Gladstone as prime minister. In Ireland, the contest between Liberals and Conservatives was of minor importance compared to the success of Home Rule, which sent fifty-nine M.P.'s to the House of Commons.

CHAPTER 8

Home Rule and the Land War, 1870–1882

ISAAC BUTT AND HOME RULE

Isaac Butt created the Home Rule movement. He was born in 1813, the son of a Protestant rector in Donegal. At Trinity College, Dublin, Butt was a brilliant student, and he cofounded and edited *The Dublin University Magazine,* the best of nineteenth-century Irish conservative periodicals. After graduation in 1836, Butt stayed on at Trinity to teach political economy while he studied law at the King's Inn. As a young barrister, his was the most intelligent voice of Irish unionism and Protestant ascendancy. In 1843 Alderman Butt debated Repeal with O'Connell in the Dublin corporation, arguing that by including Ireland in the United Kingdom, the union promoted it from province to world power. At the same time that Butt exalted the union, he complained that British laissez-faire endangered the Irish economy. From an economic protectionist he evolved into a political nationalist. This process was evident in Butt's 1847 pamphlet *Famine in the Land.* In it, he attacked the Whig laissez-faire approach to hunger and death in Ireland. As a substitute, he recommended strong government action, including public works to provide employment while advancing Ireland's economic potential, improved transportation facilities to encourage Irish industry and agriculture, and a government-sponsored and -financed emigration program to relieve population pressure.

In 1848 Butt defended Young Ireland rebels, telling juries that British insensitivity to the famine disaster had exasperated the patience of idealists. He insisted that the Irish people had a constitutional right to agitate for repeal. He also suggested that an Irish legislature supervising local affairs might be the best solution to the Irish question.

As a liberal Conservative M.P. in the 1850s and a pamphleteer in the 1860s, Butt abandoned Protestant ascendancy and proposed constructive unionism. He suggested tenant right, denominational education, and a dual Catholic and Protestant religious establishment as conservative responses to Irish religious pluralism and economic discontent. During those two decades, Butt worked closely with Catholic bishops and the leaders of tenant right organizations.

In 1867, without charge, Butt defended Fenians in court. Then he became president of the Amnesty Association, petitioning for their parole from prison. Since he was by this time convinced that the Westminster Parliament could not reconcile the priorities of industrial Britain with those of agrarian Ireland, Butt came out for a local legislature to manage Irish business. As a conservative in the school of Edmund Burke, he also believed that a domestic parliament might isolate Ireland from the secularism and radicalism sweeping Britain. But he did not want self-government to come through the democratic, egalitarian, and violent auspices of Fenianism. It was time, he believed, for a conservative constitutional attempt at legislative independence.

Butt discussed his ideas with George Henry Moore. Together they decided that constitutional nationalism should replace repeal with federalism as its objective. Since the Union victory in the American Civil War, federalism had developed a clientele among British intellectuals and politicians. They were responsible for the 1867 North American act establishing the Dominion of Canada with a federal constitution to harmonize relations between Anglos and French. Moore and Butt thought that Britain might be prepared to apply the same logic to the Irish situation.

Moore died in early 1870, leaving Butt with the task of founding a federalist organization. He met with forty-nine prominent Dubliners, mostly Protestants, on May 19, 1870, and their discussion led to the Home Government Association, which had its first meeting at the Rotunda on September 1. The HGA was a private organization dedicated to uniting Irish Catholics and Protestants behind Home Rule and persuading British and Irish opinion that a federal arrangement between the two islands would be a permanent and satisfactory conclusion to centuries of animosity. To secure the allegiance and allay the fears of Irish Protestants, the HGA confined itself to one issue, Home Rule. All other subjects were barred from its meetings.

In *Irish Federalism* (1870), Butt assured Irish and British readers that Home Rule was a conservative proposal. He pointed out that their religion made Irish Catholics orderly and deferential. Frustrations with British misrule had led them into paths of rebellion. But once governed by their own Parliament, they would be the most loyal members of the British empire, following the lead of a Protestant aristocracy and gentry. He told the British that Home Rule meant Irish-British friendship and Irish Protestants that it would lead to religious and class reconciliation in Ireland. Butt informed his coreligionists that they would have significant influence in an Irish House of Commons and control over an Irish House of Lords. This would prevent the domination of the Catholic majority. But he warned them that if they rejected this opportunity to join Catholics in a common national cause, they could expect little consideration in a future Irish state.

Irish Republicanism responded to federalism in a variety of ways. Charles J. Kickham, president of the IRB's Supreme Council, did not oppose alternatives to Irish freedom. He told Butt that he would neither publicly endorse nor oppose Home Rule. Therefore, many IRB members worked in the HGA. Some, such as Joseph Biggar and John O'Connor Powers, were Home Rule M.P.'s while serving on the Supreme Council. British Republicans admired Butt for his legal defense of the Fenians and his work with the Amnesty Association. They established a number of HGA branches in British cities. Things were different in America. Founded by Joseph Carroll in 1867, the Clan na Gael superseded the Fenian Brotherhood. Under the direction of John Devoy, who arrived in the United States in 1871 after his release from a British prison, the Clan refused to cooperate with the "corruptions" of parliamentary nationalism. Since Irish-American money funded Republicanism in Ireland, the Clan forced Kickham in 1876 to expel IRB members trafficking with federalism.

From the beginning, federalism enjoyed successes. The Dublin corporation, poor law boards, town councils, tenant right organizations, and many newspapers, including the influential Protestant Tory *Evening Mail,* declared for Home Rule. In England and Scotland branches of the HGA multiplied so rapidly that in 1873 it was necessary to create an umbrella organization, the Home Rule Confederation of Great Britain, with Butt as president. From January 1871 to August 1873 federalism acquired a parliamentary representation of fourteen. Eight came from by-election victories; six were converts from Liberal ranks. Turmoil in the by-elections between Home Rule people and priests and pro-Gladstone priests convinced Parliament in 1872 that it was time to legislate the secret ballot.

Home Rule advances were limited by its failure to enlist significant numbers from the Protestant community or from the Catholic hierarchy and clergy. Fondly recalling their eighteenth-century nation, hating Gladstone's liberalism, thinking that their position might be more stable in an Irish than a British Parliament, in its early days some Protestants, mostly from the commercial class but a few from the aristocracy and gentry, signed on with the HGA. Later, when they decided that an expanded Irish suffrage combined with a secret ballot and an aggressive and assertive Catholicism projected a Catholic peasant democracy beyond the control of the Protestant upper and middle class, they returned to staunch unionism.

Butt's main recruiting focus was Protestant Ireland, but he also bid for the participation of the Catholic hierarchy and clergy, knowing their importance to the advance of any nationalist movement. Convinced, however, that he would endow the Catholic University in Dublin, the bishops were in Gladstone's camp. They worried that Irish nationalism diverted attention from the education issue, and some of them rejected Home Rule as a Protestant effort to diminish Catholic influence and to frustrate Gladstone's effort to bring religious and social justice to Ireland. Hierarchical antipathy discouraged many priests from association with the HGA. Some politicians also avoided a movement displeasing to the bishops. As previously mentioned, Home Rule candidates at by-elections often encountered clerical opposition. They usually won but their victories and the accompanying bitterness and violence (some priests were stoned) did nothing to improve the bishops' opinion of federalism.

Gladstone's university bill disappointed the expectations of the hierarchy, warming some of them to Home Rule. Several prelates said that legislative independence was the best route to government-sponsored denominational education. A few went so far as to praise Butt and his program, encouraging priests to enroll in the HGA.

A number of federalists interpreted by-election victories, and clerical approval of Home Rule principles, as indications that it was time to replace the HGA with an organization more open to the public. In October and early November 1873 some 25,000 people signed a requisition summoning a national conference to discuss and organize Home Rule's future. From November 18 to 21, the national conference was in session in Dublin's Rotunda. Nine hundred delegates approved a resolution calling for a federal arrangement between Ireland and Britain, insisting on the responsibility of nationalist M.P.'s to their constituents and future national conferences and replacing the Home Government Association with the Home Rule League, with Butt as president. League dues were a pound a year, but borrowing from O'Connell, it established an associate membership for only a shilling.

The inadequacies of Gladstone's Irish legislation promoted public support for federalism. In addition to the disappointment of bishops and priests with the university bill, tenant farmers soon realized that the land act did little to increase their security. Although the mild platform of the League did not address economic, religious, or social issues, priests and farmers sought an outlet for their frustrations in federalism. They appeared to accept its idealistic assumptions that an Irish Parliament would be able to create an Ireland united in spirit and purpose.

In January 1874 Gladstone called a general election. In Britain the Liberals lost, and Benjamin Disraeli became prime minister of a Conservative government. In Ireland voters returned fifty-nine Home Rulers. Shortly after the election, they met in Dublin and organized the Irish Home Rule parliamentary party. It mirrored the conservatism of Butt, who as chairman rejected Charles Gavan Duffy's idea of a completely independent, strongly disciplined Irish party voting as a bloc on all Irish matters. He said that Home Rule M.P.'s were not of one mind on British, imperial, or even Irish issues and that independent opposition would signal that they were allied to the Liberals. According to Butt, tight discipline would force inflexibility on land and religion, convincing Protestants that Irish nationalism was inextricably tied to Catholic ambitions and agrarian radicalism. He asked party members to function as a unit only on federalism. In other things they could vote according to private interests and consciences.

Butt realized that his efforts to avoid offending Protestant concerns might anger Catholics. To compensate, he urged Home Rule M.P.'s as individuals, not party members, to support his efforts to amend the land act, enlarge the Irish suffrage, and gain government funds for Catholic education. Butt's strategy was too subtle. Not many nationalists or unionists made the effort to sort out the differences between individual parliamentary conduct of Home Rule M.P.'s and their party's public image.

To impress British parliamentary and public opinion with Home Rule's conservative character, Butt's House of Commons strategy was conciliatory. He instructed Irish party M.P.'s to be gentlemen in debate and discussion, always to respect parliamentary procedures and traditions, and to demonstrate loyalty to the crown, empire, and constitution.

Two years after its spectacular start, the Irish party was in shambles. It suffered from weak leadership, unsatisfactory personnel, and a restricted platform. Butt was an intelligent and generous man lacking leadership qualities. He was too kind and jovial to be a disciplinarian, and he admired the British and their system too much to oppose them effectively. An extravagant and dissolute lifestyle left him financially embarrassed. During the 1860s he spent time in debtor's prison. Because of shaky finances, Butt had to spend much time practicing law, to the neglect of Home Rule. The Irish people did not contribute with the same generosity to a Butt tribute as they had to O'Connell's. Because of his drinking and womanizing, Butt's Home Rule colleagues were afraid to send him on an American fund-raising tour. To remain solvent, he had to rely on the generosity of Mitchel Henry, Galway landowner, and William Shaw, Cork banker, two Protestant conservative Home Rule M.P.'s.

In recruiting parliamentary candidates, the Home Rule party was in the same fix as the tenant right party of the 1850s. They both had to accept whoever came along. Election expenses, London residences while Parliament was in session, and the lack of salary excluded many sincere, talented nationalists from politics. Often those who declared themselves as such in election campaigns were opportunists. Once elected, their love of Ireland lessened and their self-interest increased. Absenteeism became a notorious party problem. A number of Irish reform bills were defeated for the lack of Home Rule votes. And Butt did not chastise party members who failed in their duties.

When tested, Butt's conciliation policy failed. British politicians were not impressed with Home Rule's logic, considering it just another attempt to destroy the union and disrupt the empire. The freedom of action of Irish party M.P.'s offended all shades of Irish opinion. Most Protestants remained convinced that Catholicism, agrarian radicalism, and nationalism were one package. The vast majority of Irish Catholics insisted that tenant right and religious education were part of the national demand. They found it increasingly difficult to give their enthusiasm to a movement that isolated political from other grievances.

Criticisms of the Irish party performance that began in 1874 were widespread by the close of the 1876 parliamentary session. Tenant righters and their newspaper, *The Kilkenny Journal,* and denominational education advocates, through *The Galway Vindicator,* accused Home Rule M.P.'s of indifference to their causes. Some suggested shelving federalism for a national movement more involved in agrarian and Catholic issues. T. D. Sullivan, of the *Nation,* still the most important voice of nationalist journalism, branded Butt's parliamentary policy of conciliation a failure and suggested obstruction as an alternative. He said that it would be an appropriate response to the indifference of British politicians to the Irish question. Most other nationalist newspapers seconded the *Nation.* And when the Home Rule Confederation of Great Britain held its annual convention in Dublin in July 1876, delegates passed a resolution expressing loyalty to Butt but demanding more discipline and energy from the Irish party. Butt assented to the resolution, committing Home Rule M.P.'s to a more resolute course of action in the next session of Parliament.

THE EMERGENCE OF CHARLES STEWART PARNELL

Butt did not keep his promise. In 1877 his leadership of the Irish party remained passive, and the conduct of most of its members apathetic. But the obstructive tactics of Joseph Biggar and Charles Stewart Parnell diverted attention from the sorry record of so many of their colleagues. Biggar, head of a Belfast Protestant provision firm, was a member of the IRB's Supreme Council when he joined the HGA. Cavan voters elected him their M.P. in 1874. In 1877 the IRB expelled him for his association with constitutional nationalism. That same year he became a Catholic. During the parliamentary session of 1875, Biggar experimented with obstruction by reading at length from blue books to delay passage of an Irish coercion bill. Butt was outraged that the M.P. from Cavan disregarded his instruction that Home Rulers should be gentlemen and play the British parliamentary game.

Charles Stewart Parnell was born in 1846 at Avondale, County Wicklow, into an Anglo-Irish Protestant gentry family. Parnell's great-grandfather, Sir John, was active in the eighteenth-century Protestant patriot Parliament. In 1793 he objected to concessions to Catholics. Seven years later he opposed the Act of Union. Parnell's grandfather, William, and his father, John Henry, played the role of country gentlemen rather than politicians. They were nationalist in sympathy, friendly to Catholicism, and good to their tenants. Parnell's mother, Delia Tudor Stewart, was an American from New Jersey. Her father was a retired commodore in the United States navy. Parnell attended Magdalene College, Cambridge, concentrating on mathematics. Because of a tussle with a railway porter, he was dismissed before earning a degree. Despite his Cambridge experience, English speech patterns, love of cricket, and an aloof manner associated with the British establishment, Parnell inherited his family's antipathy to things English and devotion to Irish interests.

CHARLES STEWART PARNELL
1846–1891

As President of the National Land League and Chairman of the Irish Parliamentary Party, Charles Stewart Parnell made Home Rule and the Irish Question the dominant issue in British politics. His decline and fall led to a messiah myth and cult that inspired Irish literature and a new generation of intense nationalists. (Photo taken from R. Barry O'Brien, *The Life of Charles Stewart Parnell,* London, 1910.)

When Parnell contested County Dublin in 1874, Butt welcomed the young Protestant landlord as the ideal Home Ruler. He lost, but in 1875 Meath electors chose him to take the place of the deceased Joseph Martin, secretary of the Home Rule League. During the first two years of his parliamentary experience, Parnell seldom spoke, but he was always present for debates and divisions, and he kept close contact with his constituents. In this period he was studying the parliamentary process and learned his lesson well. He was particularly impressed with Biggar's obstruction tactics in 1875.

During the 1877 Parliament, Parnell and Biggar, joined by a handful of other Home Rule M.P.'s, impeded Disraeli's legislative schedule with motions to adjourn or to report progress and with amendments to almost every bill on the docket.

Though some of the amendments were constructive, they forced long discussions that seriously delayed the government's timetable.

Responding to their tactics, British newspapers and periodicals characterized Parnell and Biggar as uncouth Irish ruffians. Butt accused them of insubordination and party disunity. He said that obstruction was a negative approach that would increase anti-Irish British nativism by encouraging the opinion that the Irish were too savage and incompetent for self-government.

In a debate conducted mainly in the columns of *The Freeman's Journal,* Parnell and Biggar denied that their consistent attention to parliamentary duties, frequent motions, and numerous amendments were attempts to paralyze the British government. They insisted that they were working to achieve proper and detailed consideration of important issues at times when people were attentive and in their seats in the House of Commons. Parnell argued that if thoughtful analysis and discussion of legislation delayed the government's schedule, this was evidence that the docket was too crowded. He suggested a solution: Home Rule for Ireland and other portions of the United Kingdom. He, like Butt, thought that the Scots, the Welsh, and the English should also manage their affairs in local legislatures with common interests supervised by the imperial Parliament.

In defending what he and Biggar were doing in the House of Commons, Parnell ridiculed Butt's notion that reason and politeness would persuade British politicians to concede reform and legislative independence to Ireland. He said that Liberals and Conservatives seldom took the time to listen to Irish points of view, no matter how well presented. What really counted in the House of Commons was party strength and discipline, and the Irish party was small, demoralized, and disorganized. Parnell pointed out that the only way Home Rule could triumph in Parliament was through the support of one of the British parties. That could be achieved, he said, through intimidation, not reason. He argued that Home Rule M.P.'s must make their presence felt by dedicated attention to duty and by influencing legislation that directly touched Britain and the empire. They must present Parliament with clear choices: Home Rule for Ireland or persistent Irish interference in British and imperial affairs. Parnell told the Irish people that if his active parliamentary policy failed, they might as well abandon hope in constitutional methods.

Obstruction or conciliation was the issue discussed in newspapers, nationalist organizations, Irish party meetings, and tenant right societies and on political platforms. Butt fought with unusual energy, though with decreasing effect, as Parnell's attraction grew within nationalist opinion. Most Home Rule newspapers praised the man who stood up to the British and recommended his defiance to the Irish party. In 1877 the Home Rule Confederation of Great Britain ousted Butt as its president and elected Parnell in his place. Sensing the mood of nationalist Ireland, a growing number of Butt's friends urged him to compromise with Parnell by adopting a more vigorous parliamentary strategy. It was the despised absentee and Whig elements in the party that remained loyal to the chairman. Parnell partisans forced the Home Rule League to summon another national conference to decide the question of parliamentary strategy. Held in January 1878, it retained Butt as president but instructed him to unify the party and to pursue an energetic parliamentary effort.

THE NEW DEPARTURE

The popularity of Parnell and Biggar with the Irish people compelled the Clan na Gael to reevaluate parliamentary nationalism. Clan leaders decided that an Irish party led by a man with Parnell's qualities could advance Irish freedom. They were interested in reaching an understanding with him as part of a "New Departure" strategy. Clansmen such as John Devoy and John Boyle O'Reilly, editor of *The Boston Pilot,* a Catholic nationalist publication, were sure that Britain would actively take the Turkish side in the war against Russia. This would give Irish nationalism the opportunity to exploit Britain's preoccupation with a foreign enemy. They hoped to repeat 1782, when Britain, fighting for survival against Bourbon France and Spain in the American war, submitted to armed Ireland's demand for parliamentary sovereignty. American Republicans were in a poor position, however, to mobilize the Irish people. Too many years of subterranean conspiracy had cut them off from the mainstream.

Patrick Ford, Galway native and editor of *The Irish World,* a paper published in New York but widely circulated in both Ireland and Irish America, advised a way for the Republican movement to capture the hearts and minds of the people. He rejected the notion of William Smith O'Brien, James Stephens, and Isaac Butt that Irish nationalism should avoid offending Protestants by espousing causes associated with the Irish Catholic majority. He agreed with O'Connell, James Fintan Lalor, John Mitchel, and the Charles Gavan Duffy of the 1850s that Irish nationalism could recruit mass enthusiasm only by concentrating on the economic and social concerns of its constituency. Ford, a Henry George single-tax socialist, appealed to Irish-Americans by attacking industrial capitalism and courted the Irish in Ireland by denouncing landlordism. According to Ford, Irish-American and Irish nationalisms had a common enemy, exploitative property on both sides of the Atlantic. He finally persuaded Devoy and other Clan leaders that the only way Republicanism could enlist and mobilize mass support for revolution in Ireland was through a war on landlordism.

Ford's view was particularly appropriate to the Irish situation of the late 1870s. Inexpensive American and Canadian grain swamped a free trade United Kingdom market, bringing down the prices of agricultural goods and thereby ending prosperity for British and Irish farmers. Conditions were particularly bad in Ireland, where horrible weather resulted in a series of meager harvests. People on the small farms and rocky soil of the overcrowded, potato-dependent west suffered most from the economic downturn. But times were difficult all over. Many tenants could not pay rents and suffered evictions. Emigration approached famine-times proportions. This new economic calamity increased the irrelevancy of the one-issue Irish party.

The New Departure emerged as a two dimension effort to bring the Republican movement into association with majority nationalist opinion. A campaign against landlordism was designed as a device to arouse passion among a politically apathetic peasantry in the throes of agricultural depression. Republican involvement in the troubles of the rural masses was also an approach to an alliance with the Parnell segment of the Irish party. According to the New Departure design, Ireland would be free when the peasant masses became ardent nationalists and a significant number of Irish M.P.'s committed themselves to separation from Britain. At the right time, hopefully 1882, the centenary of the Protestant patriot victory, Parnell would demand immediate Home Rule in the House of Commons. When the British refused, as they surely would, he and his colleagues would withdraw from Westminster and establish an Irish republic supported by a militant peasantry armed by Irish America.

In October 1878 the Clan na Gael offered Parnell alliance terms, including the substitution of a general commitment to self-government for federalism; energetic efforts to replace landlordism with peasant proprietorship, while accepting legislation to abolish arbitrary evictions as an interim concession; an Irish party united on all Irish and imperial issues pursuing an aggressive policy in the House of Commons; and "advocacy of all struggling nationalities in the British Empire and elsewhere."

Parnell was not as interested in, sympathetic to, or informed about tenant farmer problems as Butt. However, he did realize the merit of combining the agrarian and Home Rule movements and recognized the importance of Irish-American funds for Irish nationalism. But he was reluctant to conclude an alliance with the Clan on its terms. Parnell did not want to become a pawn of Irish-Americans or to offend Catholic bishops by a close association with revolutionary Republicanism. While waiting for a more favorable time to reach an accord with Irish America, Parnell and his colleagues in the active wing of the Irish party involved themselves in the agrarian phase of the New Departure. At one tenant right meeting, John O'Connor Power, ex-IRB Supreme Council M.P. for Mayo, echoed James Fintan Lalor's slogan, "The Land of Ireland for the People of Ireland." Copying Patrick Ford's American theme, some Parnellites, speaking in the cities of England and Scotland, said that it was time for an alliance between the British working class and Irish tenant farmers in a democratic thrust against the enemies and exploiters of the poor: Irish landlords and British industrialists.

THE DECLINE OF BUTT'S VERSION OF HOME RULE

Although Parnell never concluded a working relationship with the Clan until 1879, Butt in 1878 already believed that such a compact existed and that it was designed to destroy constitutional nationalism. In the autumn he addressed a manifesto to the Irish people, warning that obstruction would lead to the expulsion of Irish M.P.'s from the House of Commons, the disenfranchisement of nationalist voters, and the resurgence of physical-force nationalism followed by bloody defeat on the battlefield.

Butt's message had a small audience. His parliamentary activities in 1878 did much to discredit him with nationalists. In exchange for an Irish intermediate education bill, providing scholarships for Catholic secondary school students, he pledged support for the government's foreign and imperial policies. True to his bargain and to his proimperial convictions, Butt defended Disraeli's actions at the Congress of Berlin against verbal jabs from the Liberal benches. In December, when Parliament discussed a crisis in Afghanistan involving tensions between Britain and Russia, he rejected a suggestion by some of the Home Rule M.P.'s that the party add an amendment to the queen's speech asking for a redress of Irish grievances. Butt said that it would jeopardize national security and cast doubt that Irish nationalists were patriotic supporters of crown and empire.

Nationalist newspapers expressed shock that the champion of Home Rule would defend Tory imperialism. Even newspapers that had previously sided with Butt in his conflict with Parnell disowned him for encouraging a British administration "avowedly hostile to the claims of Ireland."

When the annual meeting of the Home Rule League convened on February 4, 1879, T. D. Sullivan gave notice of two resolutions. The first censured Butt for violating the Irish party pledge by personally negotiating with the government on the education question; the second insisted on increased activity and vigilant parliamentary attendance from Home Rule M.P.'s. Butt persuaded Sullivan to drop the censure move, but the second resolution passed by eight votes. Butt left the meeting an ill man, leaning on the arm of his son. He died of a stroke on May 5, 1879.

Parnell made no move to replace Butt as president of the impoverished, tottering Home Rule League or as chairman of an apathetic, lackluster Irish party. He concentrated on the land agitation and on the energetic Irish in Britain and Irish-American wings of Irish nationalism. Command of Home Rule in Ireland could wait for a more auspicious occasion.

Home Rule M.P.'s elected William Shaw, M.P. from Cork, Nonconformist clergyman and successful banker, to succeed Butt as party head. He failed to improve its undistinguished performance. Meanwhile Parnell, pointing to the next general election, helped Michael Davitt launch the National Land League in October 1879. Davitt, a native of County Mayo, moved as a child to Britain with his family. An industrial accident deprived him of an arm but did not keep him from Fenianism. In 1870 he was sentenced to fifteen years of penal servitude but was released in 1878. On an American lecture tour he became a convert to the New Departure, returning to Ireland to initiate its agrarian phase with the Land League of Mayo. It evolved into the National Land League. Realizing that Parnell had more charisma than he and that an Anglo-Protestant landlord would make a good front man for the league, Davitt turned over its presidency to the Home Ruler.

From January to March 1880 Parnell was in the United States completing an alliance with the Clan na Gael on his own terms and soliciting funds for the Land

League. During his stay he spoke to a joint session of Congress on the Irish situation and established an American branch of the Land League. Parnell arrived back in Ireland in time to contest and win three seats in the general election. Altogether, Irish voters returned sixty-one Home Rulers, most of them Parnellites. In the April 26 election for party chairman, Parnell defeated Shaw twenty-three votes to eighteen, ending the era of Butt's conciliation policy, commencing the ten-year Parnell domination over the forces of Irish nationalism at home and abroad.

Shaw and about twenty of his followers could not accept the new regime. They sat in the House of Commons as independent nationalists tied to the Liberals. Most lost to Parnellites in the 1885 general election. In the 1880s, John O'Connor Power and F. Hugh O'Donnell, two of his former obstructionist colleagues, decided that they were more qualified for leadership than Parnell and seceded from the party.

THE LAND WAR

When Parnell took charge of the Irish party, he was focusing more on the land agitation than on Home Rule. Irish-Americans were so generously endowing the Land League that by March 1880 it had a balance in excess of 20,000 pounds. Davitt's solution to the agrarian aspect of the Irish question was land nationalization, but the league asked for peasant proprietorship. However, as the prosperous farmers from Leinster and Munster joined the agitation and outnumbered the league's first recruits, the more radical peasants from the rocky fields of Connacht, the old and more conservative tenant right demand became more prominent. Since the league inherited the traditions of secret societies and Fenianism, the agrarian agitation sometimes crossed the frontier of violence. While Parnell and his lieutenants did a remarkable job of limiting bloodshed and destruction, they urged tenants to hang on to their farms, not to occupy those of evicted members of their own class, and not to pay unjust rents. In July 1880 John Dillon, 29-year-old son of John Blake Dillon, recently elected M.P. for Tipperary, brilliant Parnell lieutenant, and militant Land Leaguer, advised its members to refuse rent payments, to purchase arms, to march to meetings in military formation, and to hold back their friendship from those involved with landlordism. Two months later, in an Ennis, County Clare, speech, Parnell expanded on Dillon's ideas. He told his farmer audience that they should not use violence against the agents of landlordism or land-grabbers.

> I wish to point out to you a very much better way—a more Christian and charitable way, which will give the lost man an opportunity of repenting. When a man takes a farm from which another has been evicted, you must shun him on the roadside when you meet him—you must shun him in the streets of the town—you must shun him in the shop—you must shun him on the fair green and in the market place, and even in the place of worship, by leaving him alone, by putting him in moral Coventry, by isolating him from the rest of the country, as if he were the leper of old—you must show him your detestation of the crime he committed.

The rent strike and shunning suggestions were melded into a policy and first applied to Lord Erne's estate in Mayo where Captain Charles Boycott was agent. Ostracism was so effective in driving off house servants and field hands that Orangemen from the north, protected by soldiers, had to bring in the harvest at a net loss. The English language had a new word: Shunning became *boycotting*.

Although Parnell had mustered the most powerful agitation in Ireland since the Repeal movement of the 1840s, and not even O'Connell had so stirred the west, two important elements in Irish nationalism held back from the land war. Although the Clan na Gael initiated the New Departure and was the senior partner in the Revolutionary Directory (1877) with the IRB, Kickham and the Supreme Council rejected the Land League because they thought it divided Ireland by class and religion. The IRB insisted that nothing must distract Ireland from its priority cause, independence. A sovereign Irish nation would reconcile economic, social, and religious differences. Compared with Catholic bishops and priests in other places, those in Ireland had been liberal on property rights and duties, supporting tenant right. But many thought that abolition of landlordism was too radical, and they were uneasy about the Fenian elements and flashes of violence in the land war. Even John MacHale, the prelate most associated with nationalism, condemned the Land League.

The reluctance of the bishops and priests to become involved with the Land League created a local leadership vacuum filled by shopkeepers in the towns. They had kinship, customer, and money-lending ties with farmers. Most shopkeepers had peasant origins; many continued to till the soil. Their town residences and their economic associations with and visits to cities gave them an aura of sophistication and knowledge that rivaled that of the clergy. When priests discovered that the peasantry was marching on ahead of them with a new class of leaders, they quickly caught up, but they had to share power and influence with the shopkeepers.

Despite the rage of British politicians, journalists, and Irish Protestants and despite government coercion, the land campaign continued, bordering on the fringes of insurrection. Land League militancy and the turbulence in Ireland persuaded Gladstone, who replaced Disraeli as prime minister after the 1880 Liberal election victory, that he must again try Irish reform. He decided to mix kindness with firmness. Despite the obstruction tactics of Irish party M.P.'s, the government passed a strong peace preservation act. After the House of Lords vetoed a measure to compensate evicted tenants, in August 1881 Gladstone, with the queen's influence, maneuvered a land act through Parliament. It established the Three F's so long sought by tenant righters: "fixity of tenure, fair rents, and free sale." Though it did not destroy landlordism, the land act, by creating a sort of dual ownership of land, made it untenable. Gladstone's measure also weakened laissez-faire economics throughout the United Kingdom by establishing precedents for government limitations on property rights.

Parnell rejected the land act as inadequate because it did not include over 100,000 tenants in arrears of rent (one-third of the farmers in Ireland, two-thirds in Mayo) or leaseholders. Parnell also knew that it was unwise for a leader of Irish nationalism to be enthusiastic about or grateful for British concessions that were considered compensations for part injustices by the Irish people. And he was aware that to radicals in the Land League, the act stopped short of their objective, the destruction of landlordism.

Parnell continued the agrarian agitation even after the land act was law, hoping to force further reforms and to influence tribunals to decide on the lowest possible rent obligations. Finally, in October 1881, Gladstone and the Irish chief secretary, W. E. Forster, lost patience and employed the peace preservation act to incarcerate Parnell and his chief lieutenants in Dublin's Kilmainham Gaol. The Irish leader retaliated with orders to Irish farmers not to pay rent. The no-rent manifesto was opposed by influential bishops and priests, and few tenants responded to its appeal.

Imprisonment was a favor to Parnell, increasing his popularity as a victim of British oppression, removing him from the land war when he needed time to ponder the future direction of Irish nationalism. Now that agrarian agitation had mobilized and impassioned the Irish people, and most of them accepted the tenant right land act, it was time to refocus their attention on Home Rule. To do this he had to subdue radicals determined to continue the war on landlordism. Gladstone relieved Parnell's problems by outlawing the Land League while Parnell was in Kilmainham.

By the spring of 1882 both Parnell and Gladstone wanted the Irish leader out of prison. Although the no-rent manifesto fell on deaf ears, crimes and outrages increased while Parnell was out of circulation. During that time there were fourteen murders and sixty-one murder attempts in Ireland. Gladstone realized that Parnell had restrained agrarian violence and that it would be better to have him back in charge of the Irish situation. Although his captivity was relatively comfortable, Parnell's physical and emotional states, never the most stable, were deteriorating under confinement. His superstitious conviction that green was unlucky was constantly provoked by sweaters and scarves in that color knitted by the patriotic women of Ireland and sent to his cell. What troubled Parnell most was the fading health of his infant daughter, Claude Sophie (she eventually died), and the anxiety of her mother, his lover, Katherine O'Shea.

In April, Joseph Chamberlain, a cabinet minister, using his friend Captain William O'Shea, Katherine's husband, as intermediary, began release negotiations with Parnell. What he considered a betrayal of law and order angered Forster, who resigned as chief secretary, but an arrangement, known as the Kilmainham Treaty, was reached. Parnell accepted the 1881 act as "a practical settlement of the land question" and agreed to cooperate with the Liberals in reform efforts in Ireland and other regions of the United Kingdom. In exchange, Gladstone introduced and passed an arrears act that guaranteed 800,000 pounds in rent money to restore evicted tenants and to include them and leaseholders in the benefits of the land act. There was also a tacit agreement that the Liberals would end coercion. On May 2, 1882, Parnell and his friends left Kilmainham.

The Kilmainham Treaty promised an era of good feeling and cooperation between British Liberals and Irish nationalists. Unfortunately, a shocking incident in Dublin postponed that hope. Although Parnell had captured majority Irish-American opinion and loyalty, elements in the Clan na Gael closely associated with anarchism were sponsoring and subsidizing violence in Ireland. Irish-American money and manpower participation went into schemes to blow up such scenic and historic sites in Britain as London Bridge (the dynamiters demolished themselves instead of the bridge). An IRB breakaway group, the Invincibles, got Irish-American funding for plots to assassinate British officials. Three days after Parnell left Kilmainham, they stabbed to death Lord Frederick Cavendish, Forster's replacement as chief secretary and Gladstone's nephew by marriage, who had just arrived in Dublin that day, and his undersecretary, T. H. Burke, near the viceregal lodge in Phoenix Park. Parnell was so disgusted by this atrocity that he offered to resign as Home Rule leader and to retire to private life. Gladstone persuaded him to stay on as chairman of the Irish party, but the prime minister heeded the anger of British opinion by renewing coercion.

CHAPTER 9

Home Rule and British Politics, 1882–1906

THE IRISH PARTY: STRONG AND SOLID AT LAST

With the land issue temporarily settled and British reactions to the Phoenix Park murders subsiding, Parnell was ready to redirect Irish attention to Home Rule. Although Gladstone had done him the favor of outlawing the Fenian-tainted Land League in 1881, the Ladies Land League still existed to express agrarian radicalism. Much to the consternation of its president, his sister Fanny, Parnell terminated the organization in 1882. He then appropriated the funds of the defunct Land League and added them to new American money to restructure the Irish party. He recruited bright, energetic young men as parliamentary candidates. In the Young Ireland and Fenian traditions, many of them were journalists. The Irish party paid their election expenses and gave them a living allowance so they could survive in London when Parliament was in session. An efficient election machinery, Irish-American money, good candidates, the secret ballot, and the 1884 reform bill, which created a household rural male suffrage, guaranteed Irish constitutional nationalism eighty-five Westminster seats. No longer was it hostage to political opportunism. Parnell's party was disciplined. Its M.P.'s pledged solidarity on all Irish issues before the House of Commons. A parliamentary committee of sixteen M.P.'s, dominated by Parnell and his chief lieutenants, decided party policy. During the 1880s, Home Rulers were the most efficient, best-organized party in the House of Commons. Their front benches displayed as much talent as either of the two British parties. They inspired the reorganization of both the Liberals and the Conservatives.

During Butt's leadership, Home Rule nationalism never tapped into the nationalist loyalties of the Roman Catholic hierarchy and clergy. Cullen was still able to concentrate their attention on Catholic interests. Parnell and circumstances changed the situation. At his death in 1878, Cullen left a church structurally, economically, and spiritually sound. Shortly after, Irish Catholicism got caught between Irish nationalism, energized by the land war and Parnell's leadership, and Pope Leo XIII's ambition to achieve a diplomatic relationship with Britain.

In courting the British government, the pope tried to remove Irish bishops and priests from agrarian and nationalist populism. His pro-British policy infuriated many Irish Catholics, threatening the survival of the Irish-Catholic identity blend. To prevent Irish Catholic estrangement from Rome and true to their own patriotism, Archbishops William J. Walsh (Dublin) and Thomas William Croke (Cashel) warned Leo of the danger of sacrificing Irish Catholicism to papal foreign policy and kept the bishops and priests loyal to Irish nationalism.

Croke and Walsh renewed the Catholic-nationalist alliance first negotiated between O'Connell and MacHale in the 1840s. As a result, a large majority of the bishops recognized the Irish parliamentary party as the voice of the Irish nation and endorsed its effort to liberate Ireland through constitutional means. In exchange, Parnell, like O'Connell, accepted the hierarchy's right to control the spiritual life of the laity through a system of state-financed denominational education.

Parnell knew that the continued health and progress of the Irish party necessitated a strong constituency as well as Catholic support in Ireland and the continued mobilization of Irish nationalism throughout the English-speaking world. He replaced the apathetic, nearly bankrupt Home Rule League with the Irish National League. Irish-Americans and the Irish in Britain created branches. In Ireland the League functioned as a powerful election machine. In Britain and the United States it collected funds for Home Rule nationalism. British Home Rulers also worked for the election of English and Scots M.P.'s friendly to Irish self-government. From 1885 until 1921, Thomas Power O'Connor, an Irish journalist working in England, was Home Rule M.P. for the Scotland division of Liverpool and a power in the Irish party. Irish-American Leaguers tried to influence Washington to take a friendly view toward Home Rule for Ireland.

Obstruction had been a short-range parliamentary tactic to concentrate the attention of the Irish people on the active wing of the Irish party and to discredit Butt's conciliation policy. After New House of Commons procedure rules limited the potential of obstruction, the Irish party, increased in size and improved in efficiency, had a much better strategy, balance of power. In 1885 Home Rule votes forced the Liberals out of office and supported a conservative minority administration. Its prime minister, Lord Salisbury, promised not to renew the Irish coercion bill. The Conservatives also agreed to initiate a new program of land purchase and to investigate some measure of local self-government for Ireland. They appointed Lord Carnarvon, who supported a mild form of Irish Home Rule, as lord lieutenant and passed the Ashbourne Act, providing a tenant loan fund of 5 million pounds at 4 percent interest so that they could purchase their farms.

Liberals won the general election of 1885 in Britain, but eighty-six Home Rule M.P.s kept the Conservatives in office. Parnell had more confidence in what Randolph Churchill, the champion of Tory democracy and a young man on the move in the Conservative party, might do for Ireland than he did in the intentions of Joseph Chamberlain, the Birmingham radical who appeared to be an heir apparent to Gladstone. Chamberlain's devolved government ideas for Ireland were far short of Parnell's notion of Irish sovereignty. But in December 1885 Herbert Gladstone announced his father's conversion to Home Rule. Since Salisbury had no intention of topping Gladstone's gesture, the Conservatives abandoned their effort to conciliate Irish nationalism. They made preservation of the union the main plank in their platform and introduced an Irish coercion bill. The Irish party immediately dismissed them from office, and Gladstone returned as prime minister committed to Irish Home Rule.

GLADSTONE'S PURSUIT OF HOME RULE

Gladstone's adoption of Home Rule gave British Liberalism Irish nationalist support at a time when Tory imperialism had an appeal to the newly enfranchised British masses. However, there was more than opportunism involved in the Gladstone conversion. He had endorsed the efforts of emerging nationalities throughout the world and was on record as saying that British rule should encourage self-government in colonial situations. A post-1885 election report by James Bryce that Ireland was on the brink of social disintegration was the final push in Gladstone's journey to Irish self-government.

Gladstone's historical and philosophical arguments for Home Rule were similar to Isaac Butt's. He focused on the long preunion Irish parliamentary tradition, particularly in the era of Grattan's Parliament, emphasing its Protestant patriotism. Gladstone argued that the union had magnified class and sectarian divisions in Ireland. He promised that Irish self-government would be a conservative solution to the Irish question because Irish Catholics would follow the guidance of a mostly Protestant aristocracy and gentry. Gladstone agreed with the Irish party that Irish Protestant unionism was narrow Orange factionalism.

Gladstone's 1886 Home Rule bill proposed a two-order Irish assembly (he did not want to use the word *parliament* because of its separatist connotations). The first order of 103 members would include 28 appointed peers and 75 elected by a narrow, high-property franchise. Democracy was the intended base of the second order, with 204 members representing popular opinion. Although both orders would deliberate collectively, they would vote separately, giving the upper classes a veto over the will of the Irish majority. The proposed assembly was denied the power to legislate on matters dealing with religious endowments, customs, excise, defense, foreign policy, and empire. In time the police would come under the control of the Irish government. It also would select and pay the salaries of judges, but court verdicts would be subject to review by the British privy council, which could also decide on the constitutionality of Irish assembly legislation. Although Ireland was to contribute one-fifteenth of the costs of empire, it would lose its parliamentary representation at Westminster unless it became necessary to revise the provisions of the Home Rule bill. Gladstone wanted to complement Home Rule with a land purchase solution to the agrarian issue, but such a suggestion was far too radical for many members of his own party.

British opponents of the bill and Irish unionists argued that the high Irish contribution to imperial expenses could wreck the Home Rule experiment and make the Irish more anti-British than ever. They also pointed out that since 40 percent of Irish taxes would be collected by the British government for the imperial contribution, denying Irish representation at Westminster was taxation without representation. British and Irish unionist enemies of Home Rule had more serious objections to Gladstone's proposal. They said that it was a surrender to Irish extremism and endangered Britain's security and the permanence of empire. Irish party M.P.'s also opposed certain segments of the bill: the denial of tariff protection, the high imperial contribution, temporary British control of the Royal Irish Constabulary, voting by orders in the assembly, and taxation without representation. But Home Rule M.P.'s had little choice but to defend and support Gladstone's bill. The weakness of Irish constitutional nationalism was that the senior partner in the union, Britain, would ultimately define the quantity and quality of Irish self-government. And the Irish party knew that it was either Gladstone's proposal or nothing at all.

Gladstone would have entertained an amendment restoring Irish representation at Westminster, but the first Home Rule bill never reached the committee stage, suffering defeat on its second reading. The fatal blows came from within the Liberal party. The Whig faction, led by Lord Hartington, refused to stomach Home Rule. And Chamberlain, convinced that Home Rule threatened the continuation of empire, angry that Parnell had rejected devolution as an alternative to Home Rule, and bitter because he thought he deserved more cabinet influence, persuaded some of his radical colleagues to reject Gladstone's proposal. On June 8, 1886, ninety-three Liberals, mostly Whigs, joined British and Irish conservatives in opposing the Home Rule bill, defeating it, 343 to 313.

After his defeat, Gladstone dissolved Parliament and took the Home Rule issue to the British electorate. Conservatives marshaled anti-Irish Catholic opinion against Liberals. When the votes were tabulated, they won 316 seats, Liberal Unionist defectors from Gladstone 78, Home Rule Liberals 191, and the Irish party 85. With Liberal Unionist support, Lord Salisbury was able to form a Conservative government.

ASPECTS OF THE IRISH-LIBERAL ALLIANCE

The events of 1886 indicated that the Irish-Liberal alliance was the most important development in late nineteenth-century British politics. While it made the Irish question the dominant issue, it also compromised the independence of the Irish party. From 1885 on, Home Rule rested on the fortunes of British Liberalism, and Parnell and his colleagues had no other choice but to uphold their allies in the House of Commons. The Irish nationalist–British Liberal compact also redefined British politics.

During and after 1886, many Liberal politicians and some historians have suggested that Gladstone made a tactical blunder when he tied his party to Irish nationalism. They argue that with the British economy failing after 1870, Liberals would have been better off concentrating on the social question to keep the working-class vote. However, when Gladstone committed British Liberalism to Irish self-government, he clarified its ideological content. Before 1886 there were still too many representatives of the Whig aristocracy in the Liberal party to permit an uncompromising commitment to political, social, and economic reform. Policy tensions within the party tarnished its image as a progress vehicle and blocked efforts to enlist the loyalty of the recently enfranchised working class. Whigs who could not tolerate the Home Rule alliance left the Liberal party, called themselves Liberal Unionists, and finally found a home in the Conservative fold. They felt comfortable with people who shared their views concerning class distinctions, property rights, and the glory of empire.

Before the Irish-Liberal alliance, the British party system reflected hereditary allegiances more than principles. By pruning the Liberal party of its Whig–landed aristocracy tradition, Home Rule made social, economic, and imperial issues more significant in the contest between Liberals and Conservatives. Association with Irish nationalism made it easier for Liberals to make commitments to democracy and social change. Home Rule M.P.'s were more interested in the welfare of Irish peasants than British industrial workers and were more committed to denominational education, friendlier to the brewing and distilling industries, and less supportive of free trade than Liberals. However, they were also stronger on democracy and government involvement in social change than their British allies. Thus the Irish-Liberal connection was natural and served mutual interests.

While Home Rule moved Liberals left, it sent Conservatives in the opposite direction. The Whig addition strengthened Conservatives in the House of Commons and reinforced their commitment to property, tradition, aristocracy, and empire. The Liberal commitment to Home Rule gave the Conservatives an opportunity to exploit the prejudices and loyalties of British nativism in the quest for votes. Much of the attack on Home Rule appealed to anti-Catholicism with the slogan "Home Rule is Rome Rule." And Conservatives insisted that Irish self-government was the beginning of a domino process, beginning with the disruption of the United Kingdom, culminating in the destruction of the empire. To emphasize that the Home

Rule debate involved social structure, the Protestant Constitution, British security, and the empire, Conservatives changed the name of their party to Unionist.

Home Rule polarized politics more clearly in Ulster than in Britain. There the population density of non-Catholics was higher than in other portions of Ireland, slightly over 50 percent, most of it concentrated in the region around Belfast. Because of the even sectarian divide, bitter memories of ancient and modern struggles for land and power, Ulster's politics were the most paranoid in the United Kingdom.

Beginning with eighteenth-century linen factories and shipyards, Belfast and northeast Ulster became an extension of the British industrial complex, adding an economic motive to the contents of Ulster unionism. Wealthy landlords and factory barons led Ulster Toryism. Protestant and Presbyterian tenant farmers, industrial workers, and middle-class professionals despised Catholics but found common social and economic cause with them in the Liberal party.

Starting with Home Rule, some Ulster Catholics, particularly in the border counties where they were most numerous, began to drift to the Irish party, but Ulster Liberalism continued to be significant and ecumenical in numbers if not entirely in spirit. During the land war, a small number of Protestants and Presbyterians joined the Land League, and, of course, all Ulster tenants profited by its achievement. But when Parnell pulled Irish popular agitation back into the path of Home Rule and concluded an alliance with Gladstone, there were for all practical purposes only two parties in Ireland: nationalist and unionist. After 1886 Ulster politics lost its economic and social content. The fate of the union dominated all other issues.

From the first Home Rule bill through the third, British Conservatives played the "Orange card" as a key part of their strategy to frustrate the Irish-Liberal alliance, preserve the union, retain the status quo, protect property interests, and maintain the empire. In the general election of 1886, Lord Randolph Churchill, privately contemptuous of Ulster Anglicans and Nonconformists, cynically appealed to their prejudices. He went to Belfast and told them to resist Home Rule to the point of defying Parliament. He said, "Ulster will fight and Ulster will be right." Well into the twentieth century, Churchill clones would make the same appeal to Ulster fanaticism.

Gladstone would continue to publicly interpret Ulster unionist opposition to Home Rule as a contradiction of the Grattan Protestant patriot tradition and as selfish Orange factionalism. Nationalists started out thinking that way but came to realize the almost unanimous Ulster Protestant and Presbyterian antipathy to Irish self-government. But they rejected it as an inadequate expression of Ulster's geography and people. Home Rulers pointed out that five of Ulster's nine counties had Catholic majorities and that the other four had large minorities. Often nationalist M.P.'s had a 17-to-16 majority in the province's parliamentary representation.

Gladstone and the Irish party were anticipating an Ulster Unionist bid for separate treatment in any Home Rule settlement. However, since Ulster Protestants were more interested in preventing Home Rule for any part of Ireland and did not want to desert their coreligionists in other parts of the country, they never presented a partition plan for themselves. Despite their frequent threats of violence, they planned to resist a Dublin government passively before resorting to force.

THE FALL OF PARNELL

After 1886 the Irish party continued to perform effectively for its constituents, but the exigencies of the Liberal alliance restricted its independence and flamboyance. Distracted by his relationship with Katherine O'Shea, Parnell left much of the party leadership tasks to such talented lieutenants as John Dillon, William O'Brien, Timothy Harrington, Thomas Sexton, and Timothy Healy. Because of the Liberal connection, Parnell found it necessary to soften the public tone of Irish nationalism. This caution was evident in his reluctance to support the Plan of Campaign authored by Harrington, Dillon, and O'Brien.

Agricultural hard times did not end with the 1882 land act. For many farmers, paying rent was difficult. Harrington, Dillon, and O'Brien advised them to request further rent reductions. If landlords refused to comply, the three M.P.'s suggested that tenants place the rents they were prepared to pay in a fund to assist victims of evictions. This strategy became the Plan of Campaign and swept the country. Unionist government coercion and the arrest of the radical Home Rule M.P.'s provoked violence. To avoid antagonizing British public opinion and diverting Irish agitation away from Home Rule, Parnell did not participate in the new war on landlordism. Only grudgingly did he contribute Irish party funds to the relief of evictees.

Parnell's decision not to become involved in the Plan of Campaign did not damage his Irish popularity, and by 1890 he had acquired considerable respectability in British circles. In 1887 the *Times* of London published a series of articles called "Parnell and Crime," claiming that the Home Rule leader and his lieutenants had instigated agrarian outrages in Ireland. One of these articles reproduced a letter supposedly signed by Parnell condoning the 1882 Phoenix Park murders of Cavendish and Burke. The *Times*'s attack on Parnell's integrity raised a groundswell of animosity toward him throughout Britain. Indifferent to what the British thought of him, he ignored the Unionist *Times*'s effort to discredit him. However, one of Parnell's former Irish party colleagues who became his opponent, F. Hugh O'Donnell, took offense at his inclusion in the *Times*'s charges and sued for libel. During the trial, the *Times*'s attorney offered more incriminating letters allegedly signed by Parnell.

Parnell decided to take action against the paper. Since he had no confidence in the justice of British courts and juries in cases involving Irish nationalists, he asked the government for a parliamentary committee of inquiry to investigate the authenticity of the letters. The Unionist government said no but did appoint three judges to investigate the total context of the *Times*'s accusations against the Irish leader and his movement. The hearing discovered that the *Times* had, in good faith, purchased the Parnell letters from Richard Pigott, a Dublin journalist with shady credentials in nationalist circles. In a February 1889 cross-examination of Pigott, Charles Russell, Parnell's counsel, proved that Pigott had forged the letters. The forger left the courtroom and Britain and committed suicide in a Madrid hotel room. The respectable *Times* was in disgrace. Irish nationalist opinion was jubilant that its leader had evaded and exposed a vile Unionist plot to damage his and Home Rule's reputation. Many Britons with notions of justice and fair play believed that Parnell had almost become a victim of a foul conspiracy involving the *Times,* the Conservatives, and the Liberal Unionists.

When Parnell entered the House of Commons following the exposure of the Pigott forgeries, he received a standing ovation from the Liberal and Home Rule benches. But only ten months after this triumph, Parnell was on the road to ruin. On December 24, 1889, Captain William O'Shea, his one-time friend and former Irish party M.P., sued his wife, Katherine, for divorce on grounds of adultery, naming the Home Rule leader as correspondent. Though not a public item, Parnell's relationship with Mrs. O'Shea was not exactly a secret. They had been lovers since 1880 and during that time had three children, two of whom survived. Liberal leaders knew of the relationship, and Mrs. O'Shea played a role in the Kilmainham Treaty negotiations. A number of Home Rule M.P.'s were also aware of the Parnell-O'Shea connection. During the 1886 general election, Joseph Biggar and Timothy Healy went to Galway and told voters to reject captain O'Shea as a Home Rule candidate because Parnell was prepared to let him avoid taking the party pledge. However, in the Victorian period, there was considerable difference between a quiet affair and a public scandal. A messy divorce case could ruin a political career. It had destroyed the prospects of Sir Charles Dilke, a likely successor to Gladstone as leader of the Liberal party.

After the announcement of the pending divorce case, Parnell told Irish party colleagues that evidence would prove his relationship with Katherine O'Shea honorable. Many nationalists believed that O'Shea's charges, like the *Times*'s accusation, was a Unionist scheme to ruin Home Rule and its chief. Some public bodies in Ireland passed resolutions endorsing Parnell's leadership of nationalism, and the divorce case dropped from public discussion for over ten months.

In the courtroom O'Shea presented himself as the victim of betrayal by wife and friend. Historical evidence rejects this claim. The Galway seat appears as a payoff for O'Shea's passive acceptance of his wife's relationship with Parnell. O'Shea's own conduct with other women was far from correct. Katherine intended to divorce her husband and marry Parnell but was reluctant to do so while her wealthy aunt, Mrs. Benjamin Wood, was alive. Mrs. Wood made a substantial financial contribution to the O'Shea household and might have cut Katherine out of her will if she divorced the captain. When Mrs. Wood died in 1889, Katherine agreed to buy a divorce from William for 20,000 pounds. The estate, however, was tied up in legal tangles. Hungry for money and bitter at not getting it, the captain decided that Katherine was swindling him out of his silence fee. In vengence, he initiated the divorce. Chamberlain, bitter against Parnell, encouraged him.

Planning to marry as soon as possible, Parnell and Mrs. O'Shea decided not to contest the divorce when it came to trial. Consequently, O'Shea's testimony, the only evidence presented, portrayed Parnell as an unscrupulous fiend who had invaded a friend's home and seduced his wife. The judge gave the verdict and custody of the O'Shea children, including Parnell's two, to the captain.

Nationalist Ireland's first reaction to the divorce was pro-Parnell. The Irish National League met and pledged continuing loyalty to his leadership. But there were negative reactions. In *The Labour World,* Michael Davitt asked him to resign as party chairman. Henry Cardinal Manning, archbishop of Westminster, intermediary in negotiations between Gladstone and the Irish Catholic hierarchy, and resenter of a Protestant leader of Irish nationalism, advised the Liberal leader and the bishops to repudiate Parnell. The most powerful anti-Parnell force was British righteous, Nonconformist opinion, a large part of the Liberal electorate. Its leaders gave Gladstone an ultimatum: disassociate British Liberalism from the adulterous champion of Irish nationalism or lose the next election. Gladstone had to accept political realities.

On November 24, Gladstone informed John Morley, the most pro-Irish Liberal, and Justin McCarthy, prominent essayist and vice-chairman of the Irish party, that for the sake of the Irish-Liberal alliance and Home Rule, Parnell must remove himself as party leader. The next day the Irish party met to elect its chairman for the coming parliamentary session. Morley failed to contact Parnell before the gathering, but McCarthy delivered Gladstone's message. Parnell ignored it, and McCarthy did not mention it at the party meeting. Home Rule M.P.'s, unconscious of the issue at stake, unanimously reelected Parnell as their leader. When Gladstone made his position public the next day, a large number of Irish M.P.'s persuaded Parnell to call another party meeting on the leadership question. From December 1 to 6, Home Rule M.P.'s gathered in committee room 15 of the House of Commons and vigorously, and at times nastily, debated whether they should retain or reject the man who relit the flame of Irish constitutional nationalism and forced the Liberals into a Home Rule commitment.

If Parnell had been a selfless, dedicated patriot, logic and integrity would have forced his resignation to save Home Rule. He would have continued as a power in the Irish party. Perhaps, as Gladstone suggested, time would have permitted him to regain the leadership. But powerful politicians are seldom selfless. Parnell was a man of intense pride and power lust. His ego and ruthlessness had carved his political fortune and the success of Home Rule. He considered himself leader of the Irish nation not through election but through conquest. He had triumphed over Butt, the Fenian tradition, and apathy in the ranks of nationalism. He was the "uncrowned king" of Ireland, and he was not going to abandon his throne at the dictate of the British puritan conscience or its public spokesman, William Ewart Gladstone.

John Redmond, Parnell's most articulate party defender, argued that if Home Rule M.P.'s deposed their leader on the orders of Gladstone, they would publicly surrender their independence and acknowledge themselves as Liberal satellites.

Parnell told his colleagues that if they were going to sell him out, they had better make sure that Gladstone promised a better Home Rule bill than the 1886 version as a price. Anti-Parnellites countered that when Parnell consummated the Liberal alliance, the identities and welfare of the Liberal and Irish parties became one; the fate of Home Rule was in the hands of the British Liberal electorate, and it had spoken. Gladstone had no choice but to obey, and the Irish party had no option but to replace Parnell with a new leader.

Some prominent Irish party M.P.'s were fund-collecting in the United States during the leadership crisis. The two most prominent, O'Brien and Dillon, could not return home because the government would arrest them under the crimes act for their role in the Plan of Campaign. They and most of the other members of the American delegation supported the demand that Parnell resign. On December 6, Justin McCarthy left committee room 15 with forty-four other Home Rule M.P.'s, leaving Parnell with twenty-seven followers. Anti-Parnellites reassembled in another place and elected McCarthy party chairman.

Parnell refused to surrender to the wishes of the party majority, deciding to appeal to the Irish people. His choice interjected the influence of the Catholic bishops and priests into the leadership controversy. On December 4, during the committee room 15 discussion, the bishops had issued a manifesto asking the laity to reject Parnell as their spokesman. It did not affect the Irish party, which made a political, not a moral decision. The hierarchy and clergy, by contrast, emphasized the moral issue rather than the future of the Liberal alliance. They could not be less pious and sanctimonious than British Nonconformists and Protestants, who denounced Parnell as a public sinner and as an enemy of the sanctity of marriage.

In 1891 Parnell put his prestige on the line in three by-elections. Sometimes he appealed to the Fenian element, suggesting that if he failed to achieve self-government through constitutional methods, he would join in a physical-force attack on British tyranny. Parnell never worked harder or more courageously than he did in campaigning for his candidates. But he could not compete with the combination of bishops and priests, the anti-Parnellite majority in the Irish party, and Gladstone and the Liberal alliance. Parnellite candidates lost all the by-elections, and their chief ruined his health speaking on political platforms in the Irish cold and damp. On October 6, 1891, he died of rheumatic fever in the Brighton, England, residence that he shared with his wife Katherine. After a large and emotional Dublin funeral, largely managed by his Fenian following, Parnell was laid to rest near O'Connell in Glasnevin. He left behind a shattered Irish party, a disillusioned and divided Irish national opinion, and the powerful myth of martyred messiah to inspire future generations, particularly the literati. Parnell as myth was almost as powerful as the Parnell of reality.

To serious students of Irish history, it seems strange that the cold, neurotic Parnell retains more popularity in contemporary Ireland than the warm, articulate, and charismatic O'Connell. To the champions of physical-force nationalism that finally severed the chains of the union, Parnell appears as a sterner, more uncompromising foe of British colonialism than O'Connell. And his leadership of the

Land League and his last campaign appeal to the Fenian tradition gave Parnell a revolutionary image. To Parnellite writers such as William Butler Yeats, James Joyce, and Sean O'Faolain, their hero was not only a martyr sacrificed on the altar of British anti-Irish nationalism but also a victim of Catholic authoritarianism and puritanism. To them Parnell appeared as a symbol of artistic resistance to the forces of narrow-minded oppression.

THE EBB AND FLOW OF HOME RULE ENTHUSIASM

In 1893, during his fourth and final administration, Gladstone introduced a second Home Rule bill. Again he proposed a two-house chamber, one of 48 elected by a restricted franchise, the other of 103 more democratically constructed. Deadlocks between them that lasted two years would be resolved by an absolute majority of the two chambers. Most of the provisions and restrictions of the 1893 bill were similar to those of 1886 except that Gladstone lowered Ireland's imperial contribution from one-fifteenth to one-twentieth and retained Irish M.P.'s at Westminster for discussion of Irish and imperial matters. An amendment to the bill kept Irish M.P.'s in Parliament for all debates and votes. Because of the combined Liberal-Irish majority, Home Rule passed through the House of Commons, but the House of Lords crushed it. Gladstone wanted to dissolve Parliament and take the House of Lords veto power issue to the electorate. When other Liberal leaders disagreed with Gladstone on the House of Lords strategy and on naval expenditures, he resigned as prime minister.

Lord Rosebery, the new prime minister, was an advocate of a strong national defense and of empire, but he was indifferent to Irish nationalism. Shortly after assuming command, he made it clear that Ireland was not a Liberal priority. Rosebery said that his party would not introduce another Home Rule bill until British public opinion clearly favored Irish self-government. But the Liberals were not long for office. Because of divisions within the cabinet, House of Lords vetoes of House of Common bills, and a slim Liberal majority, Rosebery in late 1895 turned over the government to Unionists. A general election confirmed them in office with a large majority.

Opposition strengthened Rosebery's conviction that Home Rule alienated British public opinion. He wanted his party to be associated with concern for social problems resulting from a retreating British industrial economy and nationalism, imperialism, and militarism sweeping through the world following the emergence of Germany, Italy, and Japan as major powers. The conduct of Irish nationalist M.P.'s offended Liberal jingoism. As the first victims of British colonialism, the Irish ridiculed the humanitarian cant and hypocrisy of its apologia. And during the 1899–1902 war in South Africa, Irish nationalist M.P. sympathy for the Boers angered British majority opinion, propelling some Liberals farther away from the Irish alliance. While most agreed with John Morley that Home Rule was a moral commitment for their party, they believed that it should be postponed until a more favorable time. Now, they decided, the party should address issues more dear to the hearts of the British middle and working classes.

Irish nationalism was in poor condition to respond to the Liberal retreat from Home Rule. The Irish party was in shambles, divided into Parnellite and anti-Parnellite wings. John Redmond led the small Parnellite group of seven M.P.'s in 1892, eleven in 1895. Despite a meager parliamentary representation, it had considerable constituency support, much of its coming from the IRB. Justin McCarthy led the anti-Parnellite majority until 1895, when John Dillon succeeded him. The anti-Parnellite faction had serious problems. Nationalists in Ireland, Britain, the United States, Australia, and Canada were disillusioned by the division in the Irish party and were no longer generous in money contributions. Without Parnell's firm hand and the deference he received from party members, his brilliant lieutenants—Dillon, Tim Healy, and William O'Brien—disagreed on policies. Dillon, once a strong agrarian radical, came to fear that continued emphasis on land distracted attention from Home Rule. But William O'Brien insisted that the party continue to focus on the needs of tenant farmers, particularly in the west. Dillon believed in a strongly centralized Irish party in the O'Connell and Parnell mode. Tim Healy insisted that constituency organizations have more say in the selection of parliamentary candidates and in Home Rule policy. He won much clerical support for his decentralization program by promising priests major roles on the local Home Rule level. While Dillon managed to maintain his control of the party, he did so by forcing Healy and O'Brien to its fringes and sometimes into independent opposition.

TRYING TO KILL HOME RULE WITH KINDNESS

With the Liberals lukewarm on Home Rule and Irish nationalism confused, divided, and demoralized, the Unionists decided on a comprehensive Irish program. From 1886 to 1892 and then from 1895 until 1902, Lord Salisbury was prime minister. His nephew, Arthur J. Balfour, was Irish chief secretary from 1887 to 1891. He developed the Unionist Irish strategy and continued to guide it when his brother, Gerald, was chief secretary, 1895–1900, and from 1902 to 1905 when he was prime minister. Both Salisbury and the Balfours refused to accept Home Rule as an answer to the Irish question. They believed that the racial instability of the Celtic personality made Irish Catholics unfit for self-determination, and they were convinced that Home Rule would begin to unravel the United Kingdom and the empire.

British Unionism pledged a strong commitment to Irish Anglicans and Nonconformists, promising that they would never be placed under the domination of a Catholic majority. Unionists also emphasized law and order. Balfour believed that Ireland needed strong government. His efficient use of the crimes act to suppress agrarian outrage and agitation earned him the sobriquet "Bloody Balfour." The insult was a bit unfair. Balfour did not believe that commitments to resolute government and Irish Unionists contradicted the need for Irish reform. Most historians of the period have accepted Gerald Balfour's description of Unionist Irish policy as an attempt "to kill Home Rule with kindness." There was some of that, but it had other, perhaps more tactically important purposes. Salisbury and Balfour were also determined to calm Ireland so that they could more easily govern the United Kingdom and the empire. They also wanted to satisfy the Liberal Unionists who deserted Gladstone on Home Rule but retained a concern for constructive change in Ireland. British Conservative leaders also needed to keep Ulster Protestants divided by religion (Anglican and Presbyterian) and class (landlord and tenant, factory owner and industrial worker) under one Unionist umbrella. Salisbury and Balfour also intended to demonstrate that a British government could deal with Irish problems, proving Home Rule unnecessary. This would diminish its British constituency and hurt the Liberals still associated, if reluctantly, with Irish nationalism.

No matter what its motivation, Unionist legislation transformed the Irish political, economic, and social scene. Despite the 1881 land act and another land purchase scheme, the 1885 Ashbourne Act, Irish agriculture remained depressed, with the familiar scenario of agitation, violence, and evictions. In 1887 Balfour introduced a land act lowering rents to harmonize with agricultural prices and increased protection against eviction. He followed the next year with another land purchase bill, the first in a series leading to the Wyndham Act of 1903, named after its author, Charles Wyndham, the Irish chief secretary. It encouraged tenants to buy their farms with interest rates so low (3-¼ percent) and the repayment period so long (68-½ years) that their financial obligations were no higher than their rents. The government gave the landlords an incentive to sell with a 12 percent cash bonus. In 1909 the Liberal government amended Wyndham's measure with even more generous terms and compulsory sales in certain instances. Land purchase was the final solution to the agrarian dimension of the Irish question. The 1903 and 1909 bills created 200,000 peasant proprietors. Their farms comprised about half of Ireland's arable land.

Balfour realized that poverty in Ireland was a problem that went beyond landownership. In 1891 he established the Congested Districts Board to provide poor relief and to stimulate economic growth in the most depressed areas of the country. Most of the board's activities were in Connacht, but Kerry, Cork, and Donegal also benefited. With government subsidies, the board developed cottage industries such as spinning and weaving, fishing, and agriculture. Much of the progress was achieved through technical and agricultural education programs. The board consolidated many small holdings into more efficient ones, placed poor farmers on them, and then taught the new occupants modern agricultural methods. In 1899 Gerald Balfour established the Department of Agricultural and Technical Instruction (DATI) for Ireland with Horace Plunkett, Unionist creator of the Irish Agricultural Cooperative Movement, as vice-president and guiding hand. The department was in charge of agricultural and technical instruction, fisheries, prevention of animal and plant diseases, the National Library, and the National Museum. Perhaps peasant proprietorship, the Congested Districts Board, and the DATI projects retarded modernization by keeping Ireland in an agrarian mold, but they did raise the rural standard of living and introduced some economic vigor. Still, its rocky soil, uneconomic farm units, relatively primitive agricultural methods, conservative resistance to change, and Gaelic-Catholic fatalism kept the west of Ireland one of the most impoverished, unproductive parts of Europe. Although the results did not match its intentions, the Congested Districts Board was probably the most humane example of British rule in nineteenth-century Ireland.

In addition to the various programs associated with the Congested Districts Board and the DATI, Unionists initiated public works projects to provide employment while stimulating and improving the Irish economy. They involved railroad construction, road and bridge building, and drainage. Although their ultimate objective in reform legislation was to encourage rural prosperity through self-help rather than dependence on government intervention, Unionists, who had warned against the socialist implications of Home Rule and the Liberal party's approach to Ireland and the British social problem, established welfare state precedents in Ireland far in advance of anything yet attempted in Britain.

While refusing to relent in their objections to Home Rule, Unionists did make a major concession in Irish demands for self-determination. Their 1898 local government act stripped the Protestant landlord–dominated grand juries of all fiscal and administrative powers and responsibilities, transferring them to urban, rural, and county councils elected by a democratic franchise including women voters. This legislation turned over local government to the Catholic nationalist majority in every section of Ireland except northeastern Ulster, which became the last enclave of Irish Protestant political power. But instead of substituting for an Irish parliament, urban, rural, and county councils gave nationalists political experience and whetted their appetite for more influence over their destiny.

When the Unionists left office in December 1906, theirs and previous Liberal legislation had eliminated almost all of the economic, political, and religious grievances that combined to manufacture the Irish question and fuel Irish nationalism. Nevertheless, the demand for Home Rule, more muted than in Parnell's time, remained. Irish nationalism by the close of the nineteenth century had assumed an identity independent of the complaints that conceived and sustained it. From O'Connell's time, the Irish nation existed as a Catholic community. Parnell increased its intention to become an Irish state. No British concession, whether it be Liberal or Conservative, could deter that resolve.

CHAPTER 10

Currents and Crises in Irish Nationalism, 1880–1914

A REUNIFIED BUT AGING IRISH PARTY

After a decade of division, in 1900 the Irish party reunited with John Redmond in the chair. John Dillon graciously agreed to serve as his chief lieutenant. Under the new arrangement, the United Irish League replaced the Parnellite Irish National League and the anti-Parnellite Irish National Federation as the Home Rule constituency organization. William O'Brien created the United Irish League in 1898 to pressure the British government into dividing and distributing large grazing ranches in the west among Irish peasants to slow the rush of emigration.

Not all Home Rule M.P.'s were happily assimilated into the Irish party. Healy still insisted on Home Rule decentralization, with more power to local constituencies. O'Brien continued to focus on the land question, believing that landlord-peasant cooperation on land purchase could lead to collaboration on other issues, including self-government. Redmond wanted to make the party as inclusive as possible but finally bowed to Dillon's determination to maintain a tightly controlled Home Rule party and organization concentrating on self-government. As a result, the party expelled Healy, and O'Brien left. They, their followers, and a few other dissidents numbered eleven independent nationalists after the last 1910 general election.

Despite the O'Brien-Healy disaffections, the end of the Parnellite–anti-Parnellite feud improved Home Rule prospects in the House of Commons and opened Irish purses at home and abroad to the party. To all appearances, Home Rule nationalism was in a healthy condition. However, there was a slowly expanding gap between the politicians at Westminster and the people back home, particularly the younger generation.

For all their talent and integrity, Redmond, Dillon, and their colleagues lacked Parnell's charisma. The trauma of Irish nationalism in the 1890s, with its feuds and splits, and the conviction of many that the Irish party had betrayed its leader to appease the Liberals renewed cynicism concerning constitutional nationalism that did not completely vanish with party unification. And in addition to the O'Brien and Healy independent opposition, after 1890 many problems nagged the Irish party. Some critics said that it was a Catholic lobby; others ridiculed it as a Liberal pawn. Since Home Rule M.P.'s had to insist that the union was a disaster and that only a native parliament could rescue Ireland from injustice and misgovernment, they could not take proper credit for their substantial efforts and successes in the House of Commons. They could not dwell on the reality that they had forced British politicians to pass constructive legislation to improve the condition of the Irish people.

By 1900 the Irish party had lost the bloom of youth and had become a familiar part of the nationalist landscape. Parliamentary experience and the restrictions of the Liberal alliance had transformed the energetic young firebrands, almost revolutionaries, who followed Parnell in the turbulent 1880s into cautious, prudent, sophisticated, practical, and pragmatic politicians. They never sold their convictions for place or profit or shirked their constituent obligations, but over the years Home Rule M.P.'s slowly, almost imperceptibly and unconsciously, were integrated into the British political system. They enjoyed the give-and-take of parliamentary debate, appreciated the corridors of power, admired and respected British institutions, and liked the British people. Since Westminster was a long and tedious journey from their Irish bases of power, it was easy for them to lose touch with the nuances of Irish life. The introverted Redmond was sometimes insensitive to the undercurrents of Irish opinion. He and many other Home Rule M.P.'s did not comprehend the implications of a revived cultural nationalism or the depths of urban poverty and misery.

ENGLISH AND IRISH RACISM

In many ways, the new enthusiasm for Irish cultural nationalism responded to Anglo-Saxon racism. Before the late nineteenth century, British anti-Irish prejudice was rooted mostly in religion. British and Anglo-Irish Protestants and Ulster Presbyterians believed that they were superior to Catholics, who were caught in the authoritarian and superstitious clutches of popery. With the decline of religious conviction in the British upper and middle classes, a racism implicit in sectarian arrogance became overt in a pseudoscientific ideology. Contrasts between Anglo-Saxon and Celt seemed a more rational explanation of British superiority and Irish inferiority than distinctions between Catholic and Protestant. Anglo-Saxonism was one manifestation of racial nationalism sweeping through the Western world. Gaelic or Irish-Ireland enthusiasm demonstrated that the Irish also acquired the virus.

British intellectuals and scholars drew on social Darwinism for their Anglo-Saxon racist apologia. Distinguished historians such as Edward A. Freeman, James A. Froude, William Stubbs, Goldwin Smith, and John R. Green claimed that the ancestors of the Britons of their day enshrined the concept of liberty originating in the forests of Germany in the British constitution. Scientists and social scientists measured skulls, jawbones, and other parts of the human anatomy and then ranked primates in such a way that Anglo-Saxons were on top and the Irish near the bottom, just above apes and blacks. Journalists simplified the "wisdom" of scholars and intellectuals and passed it on to their readers. British politicians of all persuasions referred to the Irish question in racist terms. Disraeli and Salisbury thought the Irish so savage that they were as incapable of managing their own affairs as the Hottentots. An advanced Liberal such as Charles Dilke and even the founders of the Fabian Society, Sidney and Beatrice Webb, considered the Irish an inferior species. The Webbs thought Home Rule necessary "to depopulate the country of this detestable race."

Anglo-Saxon racism was another communication barrier between the English and the Irish. Since British Protestants believed Irish Catholics intellectually and morally inferior, they refused to listen disinterestedly to their grievances and demands for self-government. They patronized Irish Catholics as feminine or child-like in their dispositions, needing the guidance of masculine, benevolent Anglo-Saxon masters.

Racism in Britain and among the Anglicans and Presbyterians in their own country invited the Irish to reply with Celticism. Although Young Ireland in the 1840s insisted that the Irish were morally, intellectually, artistically, and spiritually superior to materialistic Anglo-Saxons, official Irish nationalism continued to reject as important the sectarian or ethnic differences among the Irish population. Tenant right, Land League, and Home Rule movements kept emphasizing the common Irishness of all the people living in the country. But after the Parnell era, Irish nationalism began to assume a more racist tone.

IRISH-IRELAND

The cynicism stemming from the conflict between Parnellites and anti-Parnellites turned many young people from political to cultural nationalism. By diminishing Irish economic and political discontent, progressive Unionism also contributed to the revival of Irish cultural nationalism by freeing Irish energies to concentrate on cultural concerns. But the most important ingredient in the late nineteenth-century Celticism was an Anglo-Irish Protestant search for identity in a rapidly changing Ireland.

The vast majority of Anglo-Irish Protestants responded with ultra-Britishness to an advancing Irish nationalism indoctrinated with American egalitarianism and Republicanism, fueled by agrarian radicalism, and joined in alliance with the Liberals. However, two of their scholar intellectuals, Samuel Ferguson (1810–1886) and Standish O'Grady (1846–1928), thought this shortsighted. As an alternative reaction, they urged their coreligionists to find common ground with Catholics in a mutual appreciation of Ireland's Gaelic heritage. In contrast to Young Irelanders, Ferguson and O'Grady offered Irish cultural identity as a substitute for, rather than a supplement to, political nationalism. They thought that a wide appreciation for the aristocratic Gaelic tradition would sustain Protestant influence and the union by weaning Catholics away from democratic nationalism. They also expected that united in a unique cultural solidarity, Ireland would not need self-expression in Home Rule.

Ferguson and O'Grady initiated and inspired scholarly research into the Gaelic past and translations of its literature. Their efforts did not coax Anglo-Protestant Ireland out of its mental fortress into an accommodation with the majority population. And they did not distract Catholics from their goals of "the land of Ireland for the people of Ireland" and self-government. But they did reactivate cultural nationalism.

Unlike O'Grady and Ferguson, almost all of the Anglo-Irish Protestant scholars and writers they inspired were friendly to political nationalism. Douglas Hyde, the first president of the Gaelic League, and William Butler Yeats and colleagues in the literary renaissance were hostile to the British connection. Though not politically active in Home Rule, they blamed British rule for suppressing a creative, distinct, and significant culture.

Founded in 1893 by Eoin MacNeill, an Ulster Catholic scholar, and Hyde, the Gaelic League promoted the Young Ireland tenet that it took more than political sovereignty to make a nation. In its effort to emancipate Ireland from cultural Anglicization, the league was even more involved with the Irish language than Young Ireland was. Gaelic Leaguers insisted that language was more than a means of communication: it expressed cultural values and a mind set. They argued that if the Irish were to be truly free, they must reject the English tongue as a badge of slavery and think and speak Irish.

The league reprinted ancient Gaelic literature and encouraged contemporary writing in Irish. Many members of the urban middle class, even people who never bothered to learn Irish or knew it only superficially, enrolled in the Gaelic League. A large number of its members cycled off to remote Irish-speaking districts or crossed over to the Aran Islands off the coasts of Clare and Galway to polish language skills in conversations with native speakers. They were also enthusiastic about Irish folk music and dancing.

Gaelic scholarship and the language movement inspired such a high quality of literature that at the turn of the century, little, poverty-stricken Dublin became one of the world's literary capitals. In their glorification of the simple, unsophisticated Irish peasant as a person with great folk wisdom and spiritual sensitivity while attacking the baneful materialism of Anglo-Saxon urban industrialism, writers, like Gaelic Leaguers, were in the Young Ireland tradition. In attempting to preserve the innocence of the peasant soul, they believed they were maintaining the essence of a superior Gaelic culture that would flourish again. The writers also hoped that a culturally revived and restored Ireland would serve as a messiah redeeming the world from the greed and utilitarianism of Anglo-Saxonism.

Despite its powerful impact, turn-of-the-century cultural nationalism was saturated with contradiction. The Gaelic League and Michael Cusack's Gaelic Athletic Association (1884) represented exclusivity. Fostering such "ancient" Irish sports as Gaelic football, hurling, and camogie (a version of women's field hockey), the GAA spread throughout rural and small-town Ireland. It was so intolerant of things English that participants in rugby, soccer, or field hockey games were banned or expelled from the GAA. Gaelic Leaguers also mobilized against "foreign" influences, labeling those indifferent to their ends and means as "West Briton" or "Shoneen" (little John Bulls). This xenophobia and provincialism estranged the young James Joyce from Irish-Ireland nationalism.

Within cultural nationalism, there were conflicting perceptions of literature's place. Leaders of the Gaelic League and the GAA expected writers to function as propagandists for an Irish Ireland. Hyde also insisted that an authentic national literature must be in Irish. Writers such as Yeats, John Millington Synge, and Lady Augusta Gregory drew on the Gaelic tradition for themes and inspiration but would not abandon the flexibility of English and its wide reading audience. They were experimenting with a literature in English instructed by the Irish experience, insight, and perspective. And they insisted on the artist's duty and right to present creations in an honest way. Opposing views of the role of literature provoked two riots at the Abbey theatre. Many nationalists in the audience expressing patriotism and an exaggerated notion of peasant virtue, believed that Synge's 1907 *Playboy of the Western World* insulted Irish peasants and women (the word *shift*, a woman's undergarment, was used) and attempted to stop its performance. Later, the play received a similar reception from Irish-Americans. In 1926 some viewers of Sean O'Casey's *Plough and the Stars* complained that it defamed the Dublin working class. In both instances, Irish-Ireland nationalism defended the mob against the artist.

Although the literary renaissance occasionally scandalized and antagonized Irish-Irelanders, it strengthened Irish cultural nationalism. Audiences and critics were hostile to the pagan tones of Yeats's *Countess Cathleen,* but they applauded his *Cathleen ni Houlhihan* as the quintessential representation of the spirit of Irish nationalism. To reading and theater audiences throughout the world, Irish writers disproved the myths of Anglo-Saxon racism, demonstrating that the Irish possessed a unique and interesting cultural identity. And it was world opinion that eventually

WILLIAM BUTLER YEATS
1865–1939

William Butler Yeats was the dominant personality in the Irish Literary Revival which perpetuated the cultural nationalism of Young Ireland and articulated it to a world opinion that pressured the British government into conceding dominion status to twenty-six Irish counties. (Courtesy of Bord Failte-Irish Tourist Board)

helped persuade the British that Irish genius deserved to develop and flourish in an atmosphere of political sovereignty.

From Young Ireland to the Gaelic League, cultural nationalism was intended as an alternative to Catholic nationalism, something with appeal for all the people. At first Catholic bishops and priests distrusted the nondenominational element in the cultural revival as they had in Young Ireland. They dreaded the prospect of an Irish Ireland separated from the Catholic heritage. They came to realize, however, that they shared many of the hopes, fears, and values of Irish-Ireland proponents. Both groups worried about the impact of British culture and the American feedback on Ireland. Both wanted to isolate their country from the effects of urban industrialism. Catholic leaders exploited Irish-Ireland Anglophobia and diverted its hope for a culturally monolithic, religiously pluralistic Irish-Ireland into an essentially Catholic Ireland. They were assisted by the determination of Anglo-Irish Protestants and Scots-Irish Presbyterians to remain British. So what began as inclusive ended exclusive, increasing the cultural dimension of a mental partition that preceded one of place.

AN ALTERNATIVE TO HOME RULE

Irish Ireland's emphasis on multidimensional nationalism; the generation gap between Irish party M.P.'s and young people caught up in the mystique of Parnell, the fallen messiah, the rebel against British colonialism and Irish Catholic clericalism; and the beginnings of urban social and economic radicalism encouraged political alternatives to Home Rule. In 1898 Arthur Griffith began to present a *Sinn Fein* ("We Ourselves") program in his paper, the *United Irishman*. It synthesized (1) the arbitration courts and the proposed Council of Three Hundred of O'Connell's Repeal agitation of the 1840s; (2) C. G. Duffy's and the New Departure's suggestions that at an appropriate moment, Irish M.P.'s should withdraw from Westminster and establish a legislature in Dublin; (3) Griffith's interpretation of Austro-Hungarian history; (4) the protectionist theories of the German economist Friedrich List; and (5) the values of Irish Ireland.

By preference, Griffith was a Republican, but he did not believe that Britain would concede total separation or that Ireland would have the strength to force it. His Sinn Fein program was a compromise between a republic and Home Rule. He proposed dual monarchy, like Austria and Hungary, as a reasonable conclusion to the centuries-old conflict between British colonialism and Irish nationalism. As a persuasive tactic, Griffith urged passive resistance to British authority rather than the submissiveness of parliamentarism or the futility of revolution. For the future Irish nation-state, Griffith recommended cultural and economic self-sufficiency through Irish-Ireland nationalism and a protectionist economy.

In many ways Griffith was an unpleasant fellow. Imitating his hero, John Mitchel, he projected a provincial nationalism. Anti-Negro and anti-Semitic, Griffith had no compassion for non-Irish victims of oppression. The economic and cultural aspects of his Sinn Fein program were similarly narrow. He insisted that the writers of the renaissance should place their patriotism above their art. His plans for Irish industrial development were procapital and antilabor.

Except for arranging patriotic funerals, the Irish Republican Brotherhood had been a relatively ineffective force in Irish nationalism since the rise of Parnell. Without the financing and the prodding of the Clan na Gael, it might have vanished from the Irish scene. But after the turn of the century, new leaders gave the IRB a sudden burst of energy. Thomas J. Clarke, a veteran of British prisons and a friend of John Devoy, returned to Dublin from America. His tobacco shop off Parnell Square became a focus of Republican conspiracy. Bulmer Hobson and Denis McCullough from Belfast and Sean MacDermott from Leitrim via Glasgow learned from Clarke and began to energize and discipline the IRB. Although there were only about 1500 in the movement, the membership magnified its significance by infiltrating the Gaelic League, the Gaelic Athletic Association, and Sinn Fein when it became an organization in 1905. Republicans persuaded Griffith to make the Constitution of 1783, which was close to dual monarchy, his minimum demand and to keep his options open for something more.

LABOR RESTIVENESS

Throughout the nineteenth century, Irish nationalism had focused on the economic and social grievances of tenant farmers while ignoring the condition of agricultural and urban laborers. Irish working-class people lived in the most socially wretched cities in the United Kingdom, particularly those dwelling in Dublin. Most of them inhabited the overcrowded, rat-and-vermin-infested tenements of Sean O'Casey's plays. Diets of tea, jam, and bread produced unhealthy bodies. Tuberculosis was an Irish urban and rural scourge, and the infant mortality rate was appalling. In a country with little industry, few natural resources, and a low level of capital investment, the urban working class suffered from unemployment or partial employment at low wages. Poverty, hunger, disease, and filth bred alcoholism, depression, and prostitution. Formulated in the tradition of agrarian protest and dependent on Catholic middle-class financing, the Irish party neither understood nor responded to the urban problem. Workers turned to militant labor unionism inspired by socialism.

In 1908 James Larkin, a Liverpool-born Irishman with syndicalist leanings, organized the Irish Transport Workers Union. Another syndicalist, Edinburgh-born-and-raised James Connolly, was his chief lieutenant. Ultimately, they unionized about 10,000 workers and, through strikes, won significant concessions from Dublin employers. But in 1913, led by William Martin Murphy, a close associate of Tim Healy, proprietor of the important *Irish Independent* and the wealthiest man in Ireland, with extensive economic interests throughout the United Kingdom and the empire, the employers combine in an all-out war on the ITWU. When it struck Murphy's United Tramway Company, the employer combine retaliated by locking out 25,000 employees. After four months of hunger, police brutality, and the hostility of the Catholic hierarchy and clergy, Larkin had to surrender. Workers returned to their jobs on the bosses' terms.

The 1913 labor dispute revealed the frustrations and poverty of Irish urban life, exposed the shortcomings of the Irish party as a representative of working-class interests, and indicated that nationalism in Britain and Ireland was more powerful than socialism or class solidarity. During the strike and lockout, Home Rule M.P.'s avoided the capital-labor dispute. Generally they were probusiness and frightened of Larkin's radicalism, but they despised Murphy because he and his newspaper encouraged Healy's attacks on the Irish party. As the strike dragged on, British Trade Union Congress support for Irish workers grew lukewarm, suggesting that it shared the establishment's anti-Irish prejudices. As a result of Murphy's victory and the inadequacy of BTUC backing, Ireland's working-class movement became more nationalist and less socialist.

After the workers returned to their jobs, Larkin left Ireland for America to raise funds for his depleted union treasury. He remained there for a number of years, organizing workers in the United States, promoting its young Communist party, and encouraging anti-British activities during World War I. In his absence, Connolly took charge of the Irish trade union movement. He created a "citizen army" to protect workers against future police brutality. More of a nationalist than

Larkin, Connolly committed Irish labor and socialism to revolution on the road to a worker's republic.

REFORM UNDER THE LIBERALS

Despite new forces and perceptions in Irish nationalism and a growing urban social problem, the Home Rule movement at the turn of the century was far from collapse. Members of the IRB had infiltrated portions of Gaelic cultural nationalism and Sinn Fein, but Republicanism and dual monarchy had small constituencies. Gaelic Leaguers, members of the Gaelic Athletic Association, and writers of the literary renaissance did not see themselves as contradictions to Home Rule. They and the overwhelming majority of the people were Irish party constituents. More bland than in the days of Parnell, the Irish party was nevertheless an able body of politicians. It was safe as long as it continued to be effective at Westminster. The Liberal alliance continued to be both the strength and the weakness of the party, and thus pressures external rather than internal to Irish nationalism destroyed it.

The human and financial costs of the Boer War, a steadily declining British commercial and industrial economy, and the concern that Unionists might further injure trade and manufacturing with protective tariffs resulted in a Liberal House of Commons majority of 224 in the 1906 general election. Comfortably free from the pressures of Irish nationalism, aware of its divisiveness in Britain, and determined to cater to the social and economic demands of the British electorate, Liberal leaders decided to keep Home Rule low on their list of priorities. They did, however, present one concession to Irish nationalism. In 1907 Sir Henry Campbell-Bannerman, the prime minister, offered the Irish party devolution as a step in the direction of Home Rule. He proposed an Irish Council of eighty-two elected and twenty-nine appointed representatives, financed by a generous government subsidy, to assume the responsibilities of administering existing agencies and boards. Campbell-Bannerman told Home Rule M.P.'s that the Irish Council would provide nationalists with an opportunity to demonstrate to the British that they could govern themselves.

Redmond suspected Liberal motives, fearing that the Irish Council would be a substitute for Home Rule rather than a prelude to it. Nevertheless, he presented the prime minister's offer to a national convention, which agreed with him and rejected it. Some Catholic bishops had a separate motive for asking the national convention to scorn Campbell-Bannermman's scheme. They worried that the Irish Council might lead to lay interference with Catholic education. After the convention, Redmond told the Liberals that Irish nationalism would accept nothing less from them than Home Rule.

Defeated in their effort to compromise and postpone Home Rule, Liberals turned to less volatile Irish subjects, settling the university issue and improving land purchase. Arthur Balfour was a strong champion of Catholic higher education, arguing, as Sir Robert Peel once did, that university experiences and degrees would make the Irish Catholic middle class more cosmopolitan and sophisticated and thus less nationalist. In 1897 he suggested that the government finance three Irish universities: Trinity as Protestant, Queen's in Belfast as Presbyterian, and a national university, predominantly Catholic. Like Gladstone, he thought the government should not endow instruction in such controversial subjects as modern history, moral philosophy, or theology, but the individual religions could finance faculties in those areas. The Unionist leadership gave Balfour little support for his university proposal, and he never introduced it as a government measure. Later George Wyndham wanted to create a Catholic college in Dublin University and to establish Queen's in Belfast as a predominantly Presbyterian university, but Trinity College blocked such a move.

In 1908, the Liberals, through the cooperation of the chief secretary, Augustine Birrell, and Archbishop William Walsh of Dublin, satisfied Catholic higher education demands by establishing the National University of Ireland, including the Queen's College's Cork and Galway campuses and the Jesuit University College, Dublin. The two Queen's Colleges changed their name to University Colleges Cork and Galway. Queen's College, Belfast became Queen's University, serving the needs of a mostly Presbyterian student body. A year later, the Liberals smoothed out some of the wrinkles in the Wyndham land act, increasing the money available for tenant loans, insisting on compulsory sale in certain circumstances, and speeding the process of peasant proprietorship.

The Liberals' Irish policy paled in comparison to their British reform legislation. During their first three years in office, they concentrated on British social and economic problems resulting from a declining industrial economy that featured unimaginative leadership, static technology, increasing foreign competition, and an ever-widening unfavorable trade balance. Since a large portion of the upper and middle classes continued to enjoy overseas investment income, workers and their families bore most of the burden of the faltering economy. Their insecurity and discontent nurtured militant, syndicalist trade unionism and provided a constituency for the new Labour party, which managed to win twenty-nine seats in 1906.

To calm the working class and to prevent its mass defection to socialism, Liberal legislation laid the foundations of the welfare state—old-age pensions, health insurance, unemployment compensation, employer's liability, and labor exchanges. This comprehensive program of social reform put great pressure on a budget already strained by heavy spending on the fleet to match German naval expenditure. The chancellor of the exchequer, David Lloyd George, once a Welsh Home Ruler, decided that the rich should pay for both national defense and social welfare. In his search for tax revenues, he borrowed ideas from Fabian socialism. The government imposed substantial duties on unearned land profits and high income taxes on wealth. It also raised inheritance taxes. In increasing revenues, Lloyd George satisfied the puritan, Nonconformist section of Liberalism by punishing vice with heavy duties on the use of beer, spirits, and tobacco. Although the Irish party disliked the negative impact of the budget on Irish distilling and brewing, it remained loyal to the alliance by voting for the Liberal measure.

Beginning with Lord Randolph Churchill's 1886 encouragement of Orange violence against Home Rule, British Conservatives became constitutionally reckless in their efforts to defeat the Irish-Liberal alliance and social reform. In 1893 they employed the veto power of the House of Lords to defeat the second Home Rule bill. Following their massive defeat in 1906, Arthur Balfour and other Unionist party leaders decided that the only way that they could obstruct the Liberal's welfare program was to return to the Lords veto strategy. Given the mandate that the electorate had given the Liberals at the polls, this was a risky tactic, placing the aristocracy in the path of advancing democracy.

THE HOUSE OF LORDS CRISIS AND HOME RULE

In 1909 the House of Lords violated centuries of constitutional tradition by vetoing a House of Commons budget. Responding, the Liberals took the issue of the Lords to the country in general elections in January and December 1910. This first reduced the Liberal Commons margin over the Unionists to two seats; the second left the two parties even, at 272 seats apiece, placing the government under obligation to the Irish and Labour parties, who controlled the balance of power.

Obviously, the House of Lords was more popular with the public than the Liberals had anticipated, but other factors also influenced election results. Many traditional middle-class Liberals were unhappy with their party's welfare state financed by a soak-the-rich policy. And since the 1910 elections increased Labour party strength in the Commons to forty-two, it seemed apparent that middle-of-the-road liberalism was no more appealing to working-class radicals than to middle-class property owners. In addition, a large number of the lower class resented Nonconformist, middle-class Liberals taxing their pints and their smokes, the simple pleasures of the poor. No doubt, many Britons were apprehensive over German military and naval power and diplomatic arrogance. Perhaps they concluded that Unionist champions of imperialism and militarism were more likely than Liberals to conduct an aggressive foreign policy and to modernize the armed forces.

Ireland also figured in the 1910 election campaigns. Unionist politicians and newspapers warned that Home Rule would follow from a lessening of the Lords' power. Before the December election, Herbert H. Asquith, Campbell-Bannerman's successor as Liberal prime minister, promised in Dublin that Irish self-government would follow a curbing of the veto power of the peers. Without a doubt, traditional anti-Irish Catholic nativism hurt the Liberals at the polls, but the Unionist charge that the two elections failed to produce a Home Rule parliamentary majority was false. Forty-two Labour M.P.'s gave Home Rule 314 British votes in the Commons, compared to 254 against (19 of the 272 Unionist M.P.'s were from Ireland: 17 from Ulster, 2 from Trinity College). Altogether, after the December election, Home Rule had a majority of 125 in the Commons. Since it was a major issue in both 1910 contests, this majority was a considerable accomplishment for Irish nationalism.

When Asquith seemed reluctant to move against the Lords, Redmond gave notice that the Irish party would not vote for the budget unless the Liberals carried out their pledge to reform the upper house. Consequently, the government in February 1911 introduced and passed the Parliament Act, limiting the Lords' veto of a bill to three consecutive sessions or two years. King George V's message that if necessary he would pack the Lords with Liberal peers to fulfill the will of the people nudged the Unionist majority in the upper house to surrender its absolute veto power. Thanks to the pressure of Irish nationalism, in 1911 Britain took a major step toward democracy.

THE BRINK OF CIVIL WAR

After the Parliament Act removed the last constitutional obstacle to an Irish Parliament, Asquith, in the spring of 1912, presented the third Home Rule bill to the House of Commons. He said that since the Parliament at Westminster was swamped with more business than it could properly manage, Home Rule for Ireland was the beginning of a federal structure for the entire United Kingdom. The Liberals offered Ireland a mild measure of self-government, establishing an Irish Parliament with a democratically elected Commons and an appointed Senate. Forty-two Irish M.P.'s—thirty-four nationalists and eight Unionists—would remain at Westminster to represent Ireland's financial and imperial interests. The British government would retain jurisdiction of the Royal Irish Constabulary for six years before turning it over to Irish control. There were other restrictions on Irish sovereignty. Britain retained management of Irish revenues, and the Dublin Parliament could not impose tariffs (a 10 percent rise in customs was permitted), conduct an independent foreign policy, or legislate matters of religion. This last limitation indicated Britain's determination to protect Ireland's non-Catholics. They received other considerations as well: Ulster was to be overrepresented in the Irish Commons, and it was expected that the Crown would appoint a disproportionately large number of Protestants and Presbyterians to the Senate.

Despite its many barriers to real independence, John Redmond accepted the government's offer as a settlement of the Irish claim to self-government. He seemed to speak for the overwhelming nationalist majority. Even Sinn Feiners and Irish-Irelanders said they were content with the third Home Rule bill. Irish party M.P.'s could take pride in their accomplishment. They had completed the work of O'Connell and Parnell within the framework and rules of the British constitutional system. And no doubt Redmond and his colleagues realized that once Home Rule was in place, it could be renegotiated over time to expand the possibilities of the Irish Parliament.

Sir Edward Carson, Dublin barrister, M.P. for Trinity College, and leader of the Irish Unionist Council, and Sir James Craig, spokesman for Ulster Unionism, gave a firm no to Home Rule. They told the House of Commons that their people would always remain loyal to the union and the British constitution. They described Home Rule as a knife pointed at the heart of Ulster, insisting that it would destroy the economy and the liberties of Anglicans and Nonconformists by imposing the rule of Catholic politicians only interested in the agrarian economy and religious culture of the other three provinces.

To prove that they were not bluffing, Carson and Craig left the halls of Parliament and went to Ulster, where they obtained the signatures, some in blood, of 471,000 Unionist zealots to a "solemn league and covenant" to use

> all means which may be found necessary to defeat the present conspiracy to set up a Home Rule Parliament in Ireland. And in the event of such a Parliament being forced upon us we further solemnly pledge to refuse to accept its authority.

Carson then organized an Ulster provisional government to go into operation the day Home Rule became law. He also raised an Ulster volunteer army to resist the imposition of Dublin rule on the north. Craig announced that if necessary, Ulster Protestants were ready to swear allegiance to the German Kaiser in preference to the control of an Irish Catholic Parliament.

British Conservatives decided to exploit Ulster fanaticism and paranoia to destroy the Liberal government, checkmate Irish nationalism, and preserve the United Kingdom and, in their opinion, the empire. Arthur Balfour's successor as Unionist party leader, Andrew Bonar Law, had an Ulster Presbyterian heritage. He promised Ulster Unionists that his party would support their resistance to Home Rule even if it was unconstitutional and posed the menace of civil war. Seconding Bonar Law, Irish nationalism's old enemy, the *Times* of London, assured Ulster non-Catholics that they had the approval "of the whole force of the Conservative and Unionist Party."

Previous British governments had transported and jailed Irish nationalists for less defiance of the constitution than that of Carson, Craig, and Bonar Law. Asquith, however, was reluctant to prosecute British and Irish Unionist leaders when British public opinion was so split on Home Rule, especially since Europe was close to a wide-scale war. Redmond advised the prime minister not to take action against Carson and Craig because they were only bluffing and martyrdom would enhance their prestige in the eyes of their followers. And he told Irish nationalists to remain calm because "the ship of Home Rule would sail safely into port, borne on the tide of British Liberal opinion." Rationality, calmness, and decency might have been assets in most political situations, but in Ireland's relations with Britain and Ulster Unionism, they were fatal flaws. Redmond never seemed to comprehend the lunatic quality of British Unionist strategy or the vacillating mentality of British Liberals.

As Home Rule proceeded on a three-session, two-year trip through Parliament, violence became more plausible and probable. British Conservatives were so furious with Liberals for enacting the welfare state, curbing the House of Lords, and jeopardizing the United Kingdom and the empire with Home Rule that their support of Ulster Unionism became more aggressive. Lord Milner, a British Empire proconsul, begged Carson to commence the armed struggle. He also persuaded 2 million Britons to sign a solemn league and covenant in support of Ulster's resistance to Home Rule. F. E. Smith, the future Lord Birkenhead, outdid his party leader, Bonar Law, when he assured Carson that British Conservatives would be in his corner if the Home Rule crisis evolved into civil war. Treason under the guise of some higher law became fashionable. A. V. Dicey, the distinguished Oxford professor of constitutional law, rationalized Ulster Unionist intent to disobey an act of Parliament; Geoffrey Dawson, editor of the *Times,* propagandized Ulster defiance; Rudyard Kipling poeticized "loyal Ulster"; and Waldorf Astor and Lord Rothschild donated a great deal of money to the Ulster Volunteers.

Army generals and lesser officers, Unionist in conviction, Conservative by class and family connections, joined the conspiracy against law and order. Field Marshal Earl Roberts recommended Lieutenant General George Richardson to Carson for the position of Ulster Volunteer commander. Orangeman Sir Henry Wilson, director of military operations, revealed confidential information to Bonar Law and Carson and advised them to resist Home Rule by sabotaging a military operation bill in the Commons. In March 1914 some 144 British officers stationed at the Curragh, County Kildare, said that they would resign their commissions rather than enforce Home Rule in Ulster. Officers in Britain expressed a similar sentiment; some threatened to offer their skills to the Ulster Volunteers.

Weighing the possibility of an Ulster Unionist insurrection, disloyalty in the army, and a war mood on the continent, cabinet members began to flinch. In 1912, when planning the Home Rule bill, Liberal leaders did discuss the possibility of appeasing Ulster Unionism with partition. They decided to keep it as a last-ditch option. In June 1912 T. G. Agar-Robartes, a Liberal M.P., tried to amend the Home Rule bill, moving that the four Protestant majority counties of Ulster— Antrim, Armagh, Down, and Londonderry—be excluded from the government's proposal. Carson and Craig voted for the amendment, believing that Home Rule could not survive without such a large portion of Ulster, but the Agar-Robartes amendment failed. In the autumn of 1913 Lord Loreborn, a prominent Liberal peer and a consistent friend of the Irish alliance, recommended a constitutional conference to settle the Irish crisis, implying that partition could be the solution. Winston Churchill, in his Liberal phase as first lord of the admiralty, suggested excluding Unionist Ulster from Home Rule because "Orange bitters and Irish whiskey will not mix." Redmond reacted with a rejection of partition and an offer to grant Ulster considerable autonomy within a Home Rule Ireland. Carson also refused partition because, as he said, Ulster Protestants and Presbyterians were selfless people trying to save all of Ireland from the political and economic disaster of Home Rule.

Aware that Ulster and British Unionists were intimidating the Liberal government, dimming the prospects for a united Home Rule Ireland, some nationalists decided on adopting Orange tactics to demonstrate to Westminster politicians that they were just as determined to fight for the Irish nation as Ulster Unionists were to fight against it. In November 1913 the Irish Republican Brotherhood took the lead in creating the Irish Volunteers, masking its role by selecting Eoin MacNeill, Celtic scholar and founding father of the Gaelic League, as Volunteer president.

At first Redmond thought the Irish Volunteers divisive and violence-prone. But after he pondered the psychologically coercive impact of Ulster defiance on the Liberal government, he decided to incorporate them into the Home Rule offensive. In April 1914 the Irish party leader began negotiations with the Volunteer command, insisting that the Irish party control half its executive. Although IRB influences in the organization continued strong, in July the Volunteers expanded their executive committee from twenty-five to fifty, giving the Irish party half the representation. Between January and May 1914, Volunteer membership skyrocketed from 10,000 to 100,000. After its official collaboration with the Irish party about 15,000 a week joined so that by September there were about 180,000 Volunteers. Redmond's blessing, participation, and appeal for American money increased Volunteer membership, prestige, and funding. With three unofficial armies in existence—the Ulster and Irish Volunteers and Connolly's citizen Army—Ireland, like the entire United Kingdom, stood on the brink of a violent disaster.

By 1914 Asquith, always lukewarm on Home Rule, and most of the cabinet had decided on partition as an an escape from the Ulster dilemma. Suddenly aware of the potential results of his irresponsible and reckless words and conduct, Bonar Law also was ready to satisfy Ulster with exclusion from the Home Rule bill. Even Carson apparently retreated from his all-or-nothing position. He said that he would accept partition if it involved all nine Ulster counties, an unreasonable demand since five of them had Catholic majorities, and at the time seventeen Home Rule and sixteen Unionist M.P.'s represented the province.

For obvious reasons, Redmond could not endorse a divided Ireland. At the same time, he could not repudiate the Liberal alliance and bring down the government. A general election might return a Unionist administration or lead to a coalition government, indifferent or hostile to Home Rule and independent of Irish party pressure. And it might be a long time before nationalists in the House of Commons would again hold the balance of power. With the consent of his party colleagues and Ulster Catholic bishops, Redmond offered Liberals and Unionists a partition compromise: Ulster counties could vote themselves out of Home Rule for six years. In addition, he insisted on plebiscites for two Catholic nationalist majority cities, Derry and Newry in south Down. While this Liberal-approved concession was presented as an opportunity for Catholic nationalists to prove to Ulster Unionists that Irish self-government would work and to assure Home Rulers that partition was transitional rather than permanent, Redmond must have known that he had surrendered a united Ireland. Within the alloted six years a general election would take place. A probable Unionist victory in the next general election would convert a temporary into a final arrangement. The result would be a Home Rule Ireland of twenty-eight counties plus Newry and Derry and a truncated four-county Ulster as a British province. This was not a pleasing prospect for any nationalist, but it was much better than a twenty-three-county Home Rule Ireland.

Carson chose to ignore the reality of Redmond's concession. He continued to insist on a nine-county exclusion, obviously still hoping to keep the United Kingdom intact. In July 1914 George V, trying to avert civil war, asked the leaders of all parties and factions to settle the Ulster crisis in conference. Redmond, Dillon, Carson, Craig, Asquith, Lloyd George, Lord Lansdowne, and Bonar Law met from July 21 to 23 at Buckingham Palace but failed to agree on the time limit or the boundaries of partition. The government then introduced an amending bill in the Lords calling for the temporary exclusion of the four Ulster Unionist majority counties, minus Newry and Derry, from Home Rule. But the Unionist majority in the upper house altered it to exclude permanently all of Ulster and returned it to the Commons. Asquith scheduled a discussion of the amending bill and the Lords' changes for July 27. Violence in Ireland delayed the government's time table.

To deter civil war, in December 1913 the government forbade the importation of arms into Ireland. Four months later the Ulster Volunteers defied this ban by smuggling 20,000 rifles and 2 million rounds of ammunition into Larne from Germany. This bold gesture embarrassed the authorities and made the Ulster Volunteers a much more formidable force. Impressed by the Ulster Volunteers' coup, and determined to balance the intimidation factor, on July 26 the Irish Volunteers landed 900 rifles and 125,000 rounds of ammunition at Howth, a fishing village close to Dublin, and on August 1 an additional 600 rifles and 20,000 rounds of ammunition at Kilcoole, County Wicklow. They also made their purchases in Germany. Alerted by police, British soldiers, the King's Own Scottish Borderers' marched out to disarm the Volunteers returning from Howth. When they met on the Howth road, the front ranks of the Volunteers held off the soldiers with their rifle butts while their comrades disappeared into fields and byways carrying guns and bullets.

When the frustrated Borderers returned to Dublin, people on Bachelor's Walk, a narrow road along the river Liffey, taunted them. When some threw stones, a few soldiers lost control of their emotions and fired into the crowd, killing three and wounding thirty-six. The next day at Westminster, Redmond posed a reasonable question. Why, he asked, could Ulster Volunteers openly parade with loaded guns while British soldiers were attempting to disarm Irish Volunteers? Redmond's challenge forced an official inquiry into the Bachelor's Walk incident, delaying consideration of the amending bill. The inquiry led to scapegoat censures of the assistant commissioner of the Dublin police and the Borderers commanding officer.

THE UNION TEMPORARILY PRESERVED BY A FOREIGN WAR

Before the House of Commons could return to Home Rule, Austria declared war on Serbia, Russia mobilized, Germany declared war on Russia and France and issued an ultimatum to Belgium demanding troop passage through that small, neutral country. Perhaps the Germans thought that Britain was so involved with the possibility of civil war over the Ulster crisis that it would not intervene on the continent. If so, they were wrong. On August 3 Sir Edward Grey, the foreign secretary, informed the Commons that Britain would honor its obligation to defend Belgium's neutrality. Redmond, without consulting his colleagues, then rose and said that the government could withdraw troops from Ireland because the Irish Volunteers would join the Ulster Volunteers in defense of their common homeland. Both Unionists and Liberals rose and cheered his generosity and patriotism.

Following entry into World War I, Liberals attempted to pacify Ireland by settling the Home Rule issue without disturbing United Kingdom morale and unity. To please nationalists, the House of Commons passed the Home Rule bill for the third time, placing it on the statute books, but to appease Unionists, a suspensory bill delayed its application for the war's duration.

World War I might have saved Britain from the destruction of civil war. But its politicians evaded rather than escaped the Ulster dimension of the Home Rule problem. In August 1914 Liberal, Conservative, Irish party, and Ulster Unionist M.P.'s failed to grasp the significance of the crisis that they had passed through. When British Conservatives encouraged and cooperated with Ulster Unionist defiance of the parliamentary process and when Liberals surrendered to intimidation, they weakened the credibility of constitutional Irish nationalism. In refusing to award the Irish party the trophy of victory that it had fairly won in the parliamentary game, British politicians proved the thesis of Irish physical-force nationalism. They announced that the union was a farce, that the constitution did not apply to Ireland, and that they would only concede self-government to violence. Ulster Unionism; British anti-Irish Catholic nativism, manipulated by Conservative politicians, intellectuals, and journalists; and Liberal timidity had created an Irish revolutionary situation. After 1914 the case of Irish freedom moved from the halls of Westminster to the hills, glens, and streets of Ireland. Guns and grenades, not parliamentary debates and roll calls, would determine the verdict.

CHAPTER 11

Wars of Liberation, 1914–1921

BLOOD SACRIFICE

Like the American president, Woodrow Wilson, and unlike the European politicians, diplomats, generals, and admirals who created World War I, John Redmond viewed it as a contest between good and evil. He believed that German and Hapsburg authoritarianism, militarism, irresponsible imperialism, and disregard for small nations menaced Western civilization. Redmond told Irish nationalists that they had an obligation to help Britain and France preserve liberal democracy and the freedom of small nations such as Belgium. He said that an Irish sacrifice for international justice would persuade Britain to concede all-Ireland Home Rule when peace came. Sinn Feiners, Irish-Irelanders, and the IRB disputed Redmond. They could not see Britain, the oppressor of Ireland, as the champion of democracy or the rights of small nations. They pleaded with Irishmen not to shed their blood and risk their lives for the power and glory of the British Empire.

In August 1914 approximately 12,000 of the 180,000 Irish Volunteers refused to go along with Redmond's version of the war. The majority wing that did took the name National Volunteers. Many of its members joined the British armed forces. Dissidents continued to call themselves Irish Volunteers. Eoin MacNeill still commanded them as an unwitting front man for the IRB. MacNeill wanted to preserve the Volunteers as a strong and ready force to persuade Britain after the war that Irish nationalists were determined on united Ireland Home Rule; the IRB wanted to use them as a weapon of revolution. Patrick Pearse, IRB director of organization, barrister by profession, poet by inclination, and master of St. Enda's, a boys' school featuring instruction in Irish, was the main link between the Republican military council and the Irish Volunteers.

Pearse, who had shifted his allegiance from Home Rule to Republicanism, and two of his poet friends, Joseph Mary Plunkett and Thomas MacDonagh, represented the assimilation of Catholic with Irish Ireland. They insisted on an Ireland "Gaelic as well as free" and weaved Catholic atonement and redemption themes into a revolutionary ideology. Pearse and his associates argued for revolution as salvation rather than victory. They insisted that Ireland needed a blood sacrifice to wash away the sinful corruption of parliamentary politics and Anglo-Saxon culture. British soldiers would slaughter Irish rebels, but victory like a phoenix would rise from the ashes of defeat. Martyrs' blood would cleanse the Irish soul, and a new, stronger, purer generation of Irish youth would drive the British out and de-Anglicize the country.

Soon after Britain entered World War I, Irish Republicans in harmony with the Clan na Gael began revolutionary preparations. They decided to fight before the war on the continent concluded so as to earn a place at the peace conference. John Devoy contacted the German ambassador in Washington, who promised aid from his government for an Irish insurrection. Sir Roger Casement, an Ulster Protestant knighted for his humanitarian efforts for the British consular service in Africa and South America, went to Germany via the United States to recruit Irish prisoners of war for an Irish brigade to fight for the freedom of their own country. Irish-American nationalists, Irish POWs, and the German government did not take the British-accented Casement very seriously. Other Republican envoys had a stronger impact on Berlin and returned to Ireland with solid offers of arms and ammunition.

James Connolly was also planning revolution, but not a romantic blood sacrifice. He believed victory possible. Although there were only 200 in the Citizen Army, Connolly was certain that a Dublin rising would spark the entire country. According to his thinking, the British, occupied with the war in France and reluctant to destroy property in putting down an Irish insurrection, would evacuate Ireland, clearing the path for a socialist republic. To avoid competitive planning and split allegiances, the IRB in January 1916 concluded an alliance with Connolly, and he joined its military council.

From August 1914 to April 1916 the Irish Volunteers and the Citizen Army drilled in the Dublin and Wicklow mountains and held public reviews in Dublin streets. At the same time, Republicans and Sinn Feiners were pleading with Irishmen not to join the British armed forces. Their speakers and newspapers said that Irish victims of colonialism had no place in a struggle between competing forms of imperialism. They should remain at home and prepare for the coming struggle for Irish freedom. Attempting to avoid another bloody incident like Bachelor's Walk, British authorities ignored the parades and maneuvers, but they did jail or deport leaders of the antirecruiting campaign. They also shut down extremist nationalist newspapers; most of them, however, quickly reappeared under new names.

For a while Redmond's support for the war effort did not seriously damage his reputation among Irish nationalists, but the conduct of British politicians and generals gradually eroded his popularity. Lord Horatio Herbert Kitchener at the war office permitted the Ulster Volunteers to enter the army as a separate division with their own officers and insignia, the Red Hand of Ulster. He denied a similar privilege to the National Volunteers. Kitchener's Unionist prejudices, as well as heavy Irish casualties at Gallipoli and on the western front, widened the antiwar circle in Ireland and discouraged Irish enlistments.

Continued British failures and the slaughter in France provoked extensive political and newspaper criticism of government policy. To gain popular support for the war effort, Asquith created a coalition cabinet. He invited Unionists, Labourites, and leaders of the Irish party to join. Consistent with the principles of his party, Redmond refused to participate in a British government, but Home Rule enemies Carson, Craig, and Bonar Law did enter the coalition. Its composition increased Irish nationalist distrust of the intentions and integrity of the government.

Meanwhile, the military council of the IRB in conjunction with the Clan na Gael selected Easter Sunday, April 23, 1916, as an appropriate day for an uprising. Germany promised military equipment. Pearse persuaded an unknowing MacNeill to summon a general review of all Volunteer units with full equipment for April 23. Plunkett and some of his friends distributed a fake document, indicating the intention of British authorities to raid the headquarters of the Irish Volunteers, the Citizen Army, Sinn Fein, and the Gaelic League and to arrest their leaders. This forgery, which may in fact have represented British intentions accurately, was used by the IRB to convince MacNeill and the Volunteers that they would be fighting a defensive war rather than starting a rebellion.

On Holy Thursday, Bulmer Hobson discovered the revolutionary scheme. He informed MacNeill, and they tried to prevent a futile slaughter. MacNeill insisted that the Volunteers existed to demonstrate the intensity of the Irish people's fervor for freedom and only as a revolutionary force if Britain refused postwar Home Rule. He argued that an insurrection that did not first determine British intentions and had little chance of success would be ''immoral.'' Hobson protested that Pearse and his allies were violating the 1873 IRB constitution. It said that a majority of the Irish people must decide the time, occasion, and appropriateness of revolution. Hobson denied that a military junta such as the military council spoke for the IRB membership or the Irish people.

Since Hobson was a powerful, stubborn, and persuasive personality, his old friend, Sean McDermott, pulled out a revolver and had him detained until the fighting started. Pearse and MacDonagh told MacNeill that because a German ship was on the seas bringing arms and ammunition to the Volunteers, it was too late to cancel the revolution. This argument decided MacNeill to turn the Volunteers over to the military council. But the next day the authorities arrested Casement on the Kerry coast after he came ashore from a German submarine to warn Volunteer leaders that German assistance would be too negligible to produce victory. Also on Good Friday, the German ship *Aud* arrived off Kerry with a supply of weapons. Confused orders and inefficiency prevented the Volunteers from unloading the cargo. While the *Aud* waited, a British warship intercepted it. To avoid the disgrace of capture, the captain scuttled his ship, sending its contents of obsolete Russian armaments, captured on the eastern front, to the depths of the Atlantic.

When MacNeill learned of Casement's capture and the fate of the *Aud* on Holy Saturday, he canceled orders for the Easter Sunday maneuvers. Knowing that they would get little support from the rest of the country but determined on their redemptive blood sacrifice, Pearse and his associates proceeded with the insurrection. Even Connolly, who once thought victory possible, must have realized the suicidal nature of the venture. But Pearse seemed to have persuaded him that some Irish nationalists must give up their lives to restore self-respect to the Irish people. Using the Calvary model, Connolly wrote, "Without the shedding of blood there is no redemption."

On Easter Monday morning, while most Dubliners were still enjoying the holiday season, a grim band of 1528 rebels, including 27 women, quietly marched through the streets of the city, seizing the General post office and other strategic places. They almost captured Dublin Castle, the seat of British administration in Ireland. Over the post office rebels hoisted a Republican tricolor—orange for the Protestant tradition, green for the Catholic, and white for the bond of love and cooperation that should exist between them. From the balcony, Pearse read a proclamation declaring an independent republic dedicated to social reform and to the civil liberties and equality of all its citizens regardless of creed.

If Pearse indoctrinated Connolly with his political theology of blood sacrifice, Connolly instructed Pearse in socialist principles. The affirmation of "the right of the people to the ownership of Ireland" was inspired by Connolly as well as James Fintan Lalor. It is ironic that while Connolly has lived in the memory and song of the Irish nation, even in the name of a Dublin railway station, his social ideology has had small impact on postrevolutionary Irish thought or action.

For six days the Citizen Army and the Volunteers fought the Royal Irish Constabulary, the Dublin Metropolitan police, and the British army, quickly reinforced with men and equipment. The fighting killed 508 people (300 civilians, 132 soldiers and policemen, and 76 rebels) and wounded 2520 (2000 civilians, 400 soldiers and policemen, and 120 nationalists). Republicans fought with courage in a hopeless endeavor. Their enemy had superior forces and equipment. And Connolly's socialism proved naive: "Britannia's sons with their long-range guns" did not hesitate to bombard Dublin with fire and shell.

Since most of the Irish had relatives or friends fighting with the British in France, they were hostile to the Easter Week rebels as cowardly traitors. When Connolly, Pearse, and their comrades surrendered on April 29 and British soldiers herded them off to jail, Dubliners cursed, jeered, even spit on them. In denouncing the rebellion, Redmond described its participants as German dupes and reaffirmed Irish support for the war effort.

Considering the mood of Irish opinion, the government should have punished the rebels with prison, making them more pitiful than heroic. But after twenty months of slaughter on the western front, with hundreds of thousands of their young men dead or wounded and with no end in sight, the British were frustrated. They were in no mood to react to Easter Week in a calm and dispassionate manner. They wanted vengence on Irish backstabbers. Therefore, the authorities decided not to imprison leaders of the Volunteers and Citizen Army as misguided fools. Instead, they turned them over to military courts for trial and punishment. Over a ten-day period, under the direction of General Sir John Maxwell, firing squads executed fifteen rebels, including Pearse, Connolly, and the other five signers of the Republican Proclamation. Although he was wounded in the post office, soldiers strapped Connolly into a chair and shot him. In addition to the executions, British soldiers angrily assaulted citizens in the Dublin streets. An officer murdered F. Sheehy Skeffington, a prominent pacifist and champion of women's suffrage with no connection to the uprising. And the authorities seized and transported over 2000 Sinn Feiners and Republicans, including Eoin MacNeill, many of them completely innocent of revolutionary conspiracy, to British prisons, often without trial. The British tried Casement for treason in England. During the proceedings, the government released the contents of his diary, containing evidence that Casement was a promiscuous homosexual. This disclosure was designed to influence opinion, particularly in the United States, against Easter Week Republicans. A jury found Casement guilty, and the government executed him on August 3, 1916.

Considered in the historical context of Anglo-Irish relations, although understandable, the British reaction to an Irish rebellion while the United Kingdom was involved in a war of survival on the continent was shortsighted. It offered a lesson in barbarous vengence rather than measured justice as the Irish public reconsidered Easter Week. The "backstabbers," "dirty bowsers," and "hooligans" became martyred heroes. People began to read and quote the poems of Pearse, Plunkett, and MacDonagh, whose pictures, along with Connolly's, appeared in Irish homes. British insensitivity translated blood sacrifice from poetry into reality. As Yeats described it in his "Easter 1916" poem, "All changed, changed utterly: a terrible beauty is born."

Shifting Irish opinion and appeals from leaders of the Irish party were factors in a belated glimmer of reason in Britain's Irish policy. So were war considerations. The army needed more Irish cannon fodder on the western front and help from the United States to defeat Germany. Irish public reactions to the executions had a negative effect on recruiting, and the Irish vote, offended by British responses to Easter Week, was an important element in American politics, particularly with a Democratic administration in office. Asquith assigned Lloyd George, soon to replace him as prime minister, the task of pacifying Ireland. The "Welsh Wizard" offered Redmond immediate Home Rule with the exclusion of six Ulster counties—

Antrim, Armagh, Derry, Down, Fermanagh, and Tyrone—until a permanent partition boundary could be determined after the war. The Irish leader was prepared to make this major concession to the partition lobby until he discovered that Lloyd George had promised Carson that the arrangement would be permanent.

When Lloyd George's duplicity combined with Ulster Unionist obstinancy to wreck immediate Home Rule, the government attempted to appease Irish nationalist opinion by releasing the internees. They returned to Ireland as heroes, especially Eamon de Valera, the only Easter Week commandant not executed. Born in New York, the son of an Irish mother and a Spanish-Cuban father, de Valera was raised and educated in Ireland, became an ardent Gaelic Leaguer, taught mathematics in a Dublin secondary school and in a teacher's training college, joined and then left the IRB, and enlisted in the Volunteers. On Easter Monday he commanded the Volunteer force in Boland's flour mill. For the duration of the insurrection it successfully prevented British reinforcements landing at Bray from reaching Dublin. Some historians have said that de Valera's technical American citizenship spared his life in 1916. But his survival owed more to the British realization that the executions were counterproductive than to his birth in the United States.

In 1917 the Volunteers took over Sinn Fein and used it as a political front to hamper British army recruiting and to defeat the Irish party. By the end of the war, Sinn Feiners had won six by-elections but refused to sit in the British Parliament. Changing Irish politics should have instructed the British that the Irish party no longer controlled nationalist opinion and that the next general election would present a completely new Irish situation.

After entering the war in April 1917, the United States advised the British that the enthusiasm of its contribution would be related to an improvement in Irish affairs. As prime minister, Lloyd George once more approached Redmond, offering immediate Home Rule with the permanent exclusion of the four Ulster Unionist counties plus Fermanagh and Tyrone. The Irish leader said no. The most he was prepared to concede was the 1914 compromise: temporary exclusion of Ulster counties that decided by plebescite to remain outside the jurisdiction of a Dublin Parliament. And as in 1914, he insisted that the cities of Derry and Newry be treated separately from their counties. This offer was unsatisfactory to Carson, Craig, and the British Unionists in the coalition government. To relieve the stalemate, Redmond suggested to Lloyd George the convening of an Irish convention, including all interested parties—Home Rulers, Unionists, and Sinn Feiners—to work out mutually satisfactory terms for Irish self-government. The prime minister agreed to the suggestion and told Redmond to proceed.

The Irish convention met in Dublin from July 1917 to April 1918. Sinn Fein refused an invitation to participate, and Ulster Unionists obstructed rather than contributed to conciliation. Accepting the inevitability of some sort of Home Rule, southern Unionists were more open-minded, asking only that Westminster continue supervising customs, excises, and defenses. Eager to cooperate, Redmond accepted those conditions. In so doing, he alienated a significant portion of the nationalist community, particularly the Catholic bishops.

A month before the convention adjourned in failure, an exhausted and disillusioned Redmond died after what seemed a routine gallbladder operation. He did not have to witness the destruction of a party he had served so long and well. John Dillon replaced him as chairman, to face the impossible task of attempting to save Home Rule nationalism in the wake of Easter Week.

At the close of 1917, with Russia out of the war and German strength concentrated on the western front, Britain was unsure of how long it would take the United States to mobilize its manpower fully, and Lloyd George and his colleagues decided to draft Irishmen. When Parliament authorized conscription for Ireland in April 1918, Dillon led the Irish party out of the House of Commons and joined Sinn Fein, trade unionists, and the Catholic hierarchy in a united nationalist front against forced military service. It increased Republican respectability, speeded the rebuilding of the Volunteers, and goaded Britain into more coercion. On the flimsiest charges, including trumped-up accusations of collaborating with the Germans, officials deported and arrested some Sinn Feiners (including de Valera) and closed down a number of Republican newspapers. But when the war ended on November 11, 1918, the government still had not enforced conscription in Ireland.

THE ANGLO-IRISH WAR

The post-Armistice general election in December 1918 gave a substantial parliamentary majority to Lloyd George's Unionist-dominated coalition government over Labour and Asquith Liberals. In Ireland, however, Sinn Fein won seventy-three seats to only six for the Irish party and twenty-six for the Unionists. Except for the two Trinity College seats, all of the Unionist victories were in Ulster. Only two Irish party candidates—Captain William Redmond, John's son, and Joseph Devlin from Belfast—won in direct contests with Sinn Feiners. In an East Mayo confrontation between the leaders of Home Rule and Republicanism, de Valera defeated Dillon by an almost two-to-one margin. Sinn Fein success owed much to the preelection Representation of the People Act, which extended the franchise to include all men over 21 and women over 30, expanding the number of Irish voters from 701,475 in 1910 to 1,936,673. Since the Irish party in contested constituencies actually increased its vote, it seems that previous voters and their wives stayed with Home Rule while younger people declared for Sinn Fein.

Victorious Sinn Feiners refused to enter the British Parliament. Instead, they assembled at the Mansion House in Dublin as Dáil Éireann, the legislative expression of the Irish Republic. It established arbitration courts (shades of O'Connell) as an alternative to British justice, an Industrial Disputes Board to mediate labor-management conflicts, and a Land Bank to provide land purchase loans. It also sent delegates to the Versailles Peace Conference to obtain international recognition of the Irish Republic. They made little impression on Anglophile Woodrow Wilson. Despite the piety of his Fourteen Points, he did not think Ireland met his requirements for national self-determination.

In February 1919 two members of the Sinn Fein executive committee, Michael Collins and Harry Boland, arranged de Valera's escape from Lincoln gaol in England. On his return to Ireland, the Dail elected him its president. In June de Valera left for the United States to solicit funds for and acceptance of the Irish Republic. Arthur Griffith, who in 1917 had relinquished the Sinn Fein presidency to de Valera, served as acting president of the Dáil in his absence. Although de Valera managed to collect a considerable amount of money during his tour of the United States, he did not persuade Democratic or Republican politicians to add planks recognizing the Irish Republic to their 1920 national convention platforms. And he had personality clashes with such strong Clan na Gael leaders as John Devoy and Judge Daniel Cohalan. Many of the Clan were more interested in preserving Irish power in American politics than in liberating Ireland. Devoy and Cohalan thought de Valera too conciliatory toward British interests. They resented his willingness to have Ireland assume a subordinate geographic sphere-of-interest position to Britain, similar to the one Cuba had with the United States.

While de Valera was having American problems, Collins emerged as the strongman of the Sinn Fein executive committee. He was minister of finance, but his real power came from his role as leader of the IRB and adjutant general and Volunteer director of organization. Collins resisted Dáil control of the IRB, which he kept independent of the Volunteers. Cathal Brugha, minister of defense and Volunteer chief of staff, resented the existence of a secret army free from Dáil supervision. No doubt jealously played a role in the frequent clashes between the two men. Collins's handsomeness and dashing personality, his brilliant intelligence network and operations, and his daring evasions of capture made him the Scarlet Pimpernel of Irish Republicanism. His glamour overshadowed Brugha's solid but less colorful contributions.

The connection of the Dáil with the Volunteers and the IRB became more critical in January 1919 when Sinn Fein's passive resistance to British authority evolved into a guerrilla war of liberation. Dressed as civilians, members of the Irish Republican Army, the new name for the Volunteers, ambushed military lorries, captured arms, assassinated suspected spies and informers, and shot soldiers and policemen. They concentrated their efforts on the paramilitary Royal Irish Constabulary, destroying barracks, seizing weapons, and killing constables. Even before the Anglo-Irish War began, events in Ireland demoralized and depleted the RIC. The IRA completed its destruction. Many constables resigned out of either fear or reluctance to fight against their own flesh and blood. The collapse of the RIC turned over large sections of the country to the IRA. Although Lloyd George and other British government ministers described IRA tactics as murder, a guerrilla approach was the only practical strategy for a small nation at war with a great power.

Britain met terrorism with counterterrorism, recruiting ex–World War I servicemen, often sadists or psychologically scarred combat veterans bored with civilian life, to reinforce the diminishing RIC. Their uniforms of dark green caps and khaki pants gave them the name Black and Tans. Later the government enlisted

ex–army officers as RIC Auxiliaries. Tans and Auxiliaries often tortured and sometimes murdered IRA prisoners, and they looted and burned towns, demolishing a
section of Cork. But compared to some later armies of occupation, including the
American in Vietnam, British atrocities were relatively restricted. Even the Tans
were reluctant to molest women.

In responding to Irish Republicanism, the British were confounded by their
own World War I propaganda on rights and self-determination for small nations. As
coauthors of the peace treaties, they had dismembered the German, Austro-Hungarian, and Turkish empires. This resulted in a plethora of Arab and Slavic nations.
During the Anglo-Irish conflict, world opinion began to ask if the British Empire
was any more sacred than those it had defeated. Were the Irish, the people of the
literary renaissance and the leaders of Catholic America, less deserving of independence than Arabs, Czechs, Slovaks, Croats, Serbs, or Poles?

Since Britain refused to accept the Sinn Fein election victory as a mandate for
an Irish Republic, its leaders insisted that they were engaged not in a war but in a
police action to suppress illegal terror and to restore law and order. This distinction
restricted the amount of force they could apply in Ireland. They were trying to
contain rather than annihilate Republicans, hoping to coerce them into negotiations
that would lead to a settlement short of an Irish Republic.

If the IRA was a courageous and troublesome foe, British and world opinion
was an even more difficult challenge for the British government. When it came to
propaganda, the Irish were more persuasive than the British. They successfully
exploited postwar anti-imperialism. Influential voices from all over the world
regarded Ireland as a gallant little nation standing up to a bully. Black and Tan and
Auxiliary tactics damaged Britain's reputation as a civilized power, even shocking
large and important sections of British opinion. During the early stages of the
Anglo-Irish War, most Britons were indifferent to events in Ireland. But Irish
propagandists and British journalists turned apathy into concern. Labour, Liberal,
even a few Conservative M.P.'s; Anglican, Catholic, and Nonconformist clergymen; journalists; trade unionists; businessmen; university professors; distinguished literati; and some members of the aristocracy criticized government Irish
policy. Many joined the Peace with Ireland Council, demanding an end to British
barbarism and accommodation with Irish nationalism. Council members argued that
while concessions to the Irish might weaken the fabric of the empire and the
Commonwealth, the risk was preferable to the erosion of Britain's image
throughout the civilized world. In addition to mounting British criticism of the
government's approach to Ireland, Commonwealth leaders pressured Lloyd George
to come to terms with Irish nationalism.

END OF A WAR, START OF A NATION

"We are all Home Rulers today," said the *Times* in March 1919. Unfortunately,
British politicians and their constituents failed to realize that the 1914 failure to

award the Irish party its properly earned constitutional victory and Easter Week and its aftermath had escalated the demand of Irish nationalism beyond Home Rule. But in 1920 Lloyd George returned to it as his solution to the Irish crisis. Parliament passed a bill creating Home Rule parliaments for the six Ulster counties of Antrim, Armagh, Derry, Down, Fermanagh, and Tyrone and for the other twenty-six. It also included a Council of Ireland to administer mutual services between North and South and to function as a bridge of reconciliation and eventual unity between them. The bill retained Nationalist and Unionist M.P.'s at Westminster.

Although Ulster Unionists had rejected Home Rule for all of Ireland, they seized it for themselves as an opportunity to create "a Protestant nation for a Protestant people." In the South, Sinn Fein took advantage of the elections for a Dublin Parliament to demonstrate to Britain and the world that Irish opinion remained Republican. So the Anglo-Irish War continued with its ambushes, assassinations, burnings, lootings, torture, night raids, curfews, and general atmosphere of violence and terror. Republicans added another weapon to focus attention on their determination when Terence MacSwiney, lord mayor of Cork, died in October 1920 of a hunger strike in Brixton Prison. The anti-British chorus of world opinion swelled to the point where Lloyd George was forced to negotiate with Sinn Fein. On July 11, 1922, a state of truce, preliminary to negotiations, began between Britain and Irish Republicans. In the thirty months of the Anglo-Irish War, the IRA had killed 230 soldiers and policemen and wounded 369; British military and police forces had killed 752 and wounded 866 of the IRA. Republicans may have suffered the most casualties, but they won the propaganda war that brought their enemy to the settlement table.

During July talks in London and in subsequent correspondence, Lloyd George offered de Valera Dominion status with the following reservations: Irish nationalists would have to accept partition, maintain free trade with Britain, contribute to the British war debt, limit the size of their army in conformity with the British military establishment, permit the continued existence of British air and naval bases in their country, and allow the British armed forces to recruit in Ireland. Although the prime minister warned that if Republicans rejected his offer they could expect all-out war, de Valera said no. He did, however, indicate that he was not a doctrinaire Republican and said that he would submit the British proposal for Dáil discussion.

The Dáil agreed with de Valera that Dominion status was inadequate, but Lloyd George kept communications open. He scheduled, and de Valera agreed to, an October treaty conference in London. In a still puzzling and controversial decision, de Valera decided not to attend. Did he think a republic was impossible to achieve? Did he send others who would have to take the blame for failure? There are other possible explanations. Perhaps he thought that since he and Lloyd George were at loggerheads, other Republicans would be more persuasive. Or did he believe that in Dublin he would be more effective than in London? There he could restrain hotheaded, no-compromise Republicans, and he could control the tempo of the London negotiations. Since the Irish envoys would have to refer all offers back to Dublin for discussion and advisement, they would be less likely to cave in to the pressure of operating in enemy territory. Whatever his reasons, de Valera stayed home while Collins, Griffith, George Gavan Duffy, Eamon Duggan, and Robert Barton went to London. Barton's cousin, English-born Robert Erskine Childers, accompanied the delegation as its secretary. Author of the classic spy-adventure novel *The Riddle of the Sands,* Childers and his American wife, Molly Osgood, had in July 1914 smuggled guns into Howth on their yacht, the *Asgard.* In World War I he served in the British navy and earned the Distinguished Service Cross. During the Anglo-Irish War, Childers was a member of the Dáil and minister for propaganda. As a dedicated Republican, he served as de Valera's London watchdog. The Irish envoys arrived for discussions with vague instructions. As plenipotentiaries, they had the authority to negotiate and conclude a treaty with Britain, but at the same time they carried orders not to sign anything without first consulting the Dáil cabinet.

In London, unsophisticated Sinn Feiners negotiated with tough and tested politicians skilled in all the nuances of pressure diplomacy: Lloyd George, Austen Chamberlain, Lord Birkenhead, and Winston Churchill. And they were caught in the middle between British party politics and Republican fanaticism in Ireland. Lloyd George's coalition government was dominated by anti-Irish Unionists. They would not tolerate too generous an offer to Sinn Fein.

The prime minister resubmitted his proposal for conditional Dominion status. If they would have accepted it without partition, Collins, Griffith, and their colleagues would have had him in a quandary. Instead of concentrating on the divided-Ireland issue, they made a serious tactical blunder by focusing on their abstract, almost metaphysical objection to taking an oath of allegiance to the British Crown. Coalition Conservatives were loyal to Northern Ireland unionists, but British public opinion would not have tolerated a resumption of the war with Ireland over partition. By contrast, Britons were as passionately devoted to the symbols of monarchy and empire as Sinn Fein was to the tokens of Republicanism. They insisted that Ireland must remain in association with Britain through mutual allegiance to the Crown.

When the British insisted on the oath of allegiance, the Irish suggested an alternative arrangement, external association. This de Valera–conceived plan proposed that the Irish Republic would recognize the Crown as head of an association of states comprising the British Commonwealth. Following World War II Britain accepted external association in the Commonwealth for the republics of India and Pakistan, but in 1921 such a concept was too *avant garde* for Lloyd George and company. But instead of a flat no to de Valera, they offered an oath of allegiance that would place primary loyalty to Ireland rather than the Crown.

Frustrated by stalemated negotiations, Lloyd George tried a two-pronged blitz on the weary Irish delegation. He split the Northern Ireland and oath of allegiance issues, concentrating first on partition, where his position was the weakest. He told Irish envoys that he could not persuade Ulster Anglicans and Presbyterians or British Conservatives in the coalition to accept a united Ireland and that any effort to do so would return Anglo-Irish relations to where they were in 1912. Lloyd George then got Griffith to agree to a posttreaty boundary commission to redefine the border between the two Irelands on the basis of residents' preferences. He suggested that the boundary commission would shrink Northern Ireland to a small enclave around Belfast, and he predicted that its geographic and economic nonviability and heavy British taxes would lead to a united Ireland.

After evading the shoals of partition, Lloyd George returned to the Dominion offer. In early December 1921 the Irish envoys presented it to the Dáil. Led by Cathal Brugha and Austin Stack, Republican extremists rejected the modified oath of allegiance to the Crown. De Valera told the envoys to return to London and negotiate a treaty on the principle of external association. They did so, but Lloyd George bluntly told them either to accept Dominion status or prepare for war against the might of the British Empire. Griffith found the British offer compatible with his original dual-monarchy Sinn Fein program. Collins knew that just before the truce, the IRA had reached the point of exhaustion and that the cessation of hostilities had further eroded the Irish will to return to the inconvenience and hardship of war. Since he believed that Ireland could not resist unrestricted British military power and was convinced that Dominion status, even with its reservations, was a major British concession and a firm foundation on which to build complete Irish sovereignty, Collins joined Griffith in accepting Lloyd George's terms. They persuaded their colleagues, except Childers, to join them. With little enthusiasm and many doubts, on December 6, 1921, the Irish envoys signed the treaty establishing a twenty-six-county Irish Free State as a Dominion within the British Commonwealth.

In early January 1922 the Dáil debated the treaty in the Senate chamber of University College, Dublin. In leading the opposition, de Valera insisted that it betrayed the Republic and perpetuated British colonialism in Ireland. Collins replied that the Free State was a considerable improvement on Home Rule. He said that the Irish people could expand on Dominion status; it was a beginning, not an end. After a long and increasingly bitter verbal battle that barely touched on partition, the Dáil ratified the treaty, 64 to 57. A defeated de Valera resigned as president of the Dáil. The protreaty majority elected Griffith as his successor. Within a few weeks, British officials began to relinquish the instruments of government and to depart from their oldest colony, a country they had occupied for almost 800 years.

From the distance of time and influenced by the contemporary situation in Northern Ireland, some historians have argued that Easter Week and the Anglo-Irish War have not justified the human sacrifice involved. Revisionists argue that if they had never happened, a post–World War I British government would have put a Home Rule Ireland into operation and that it could have evolved into a Dominion, even a republic. They say that even though revolutionary nationalism provided a shortcut to national sovereignty, it left the country divided and established and sanctified the cult of the gunman that has afflicted constitutional government in Ireland ever since. But in all fairness to the Sinn Fein envoys in London, it must be remembered that the treaty only confirmed the psychological, cultural, religious, and physical reality of two Irelands. In light of the Anglican and Nonconformist sectarianism and British loyalism of Ulster Unionism and the Catholic roots and the post-1880 Gaelic emphasis and pretensions in Irish nationalism, a divided Ireland was close to inevitable. However, the revisionists are probably right when they maintain that the post–World War I attitudes of British opinion and the changing natures of the empire and Commonwealth promised Home Rule for Ireland and its development into something more for most of the country.

Revisionist conjectures ignore the importance of myth and legend in the making of a nation. Like the American Revolution, the Irish versions provided heroes and examples of sacrifice and courage that helped sustain and inspire a people in times of difficulty. Because patriots died for independence, it became more precious to Irish citizens. Despite the ifs and might-have-beens of revisionism, Easter Week, the Anglo-Irish war, and the treaty creating the Free State altered Irish, British, and, to a certain extent, world history. As the first victim of imperialism and colonialism to wage a successful twentieth-century war of liberation, Ireland inspired similar efforts in other places. And posttreaty Ireland continued to be a relevant experiment in national development. Britain and the world watched to see if the Irish had the patience, fortitude, and skills to convert nationalist ideology and tradition into a stable economic, social, and political community.

PART III   *From Free State to Republic, 1922–1988*

by Thomas E. Hachey

CHAPTER 12

The Irish Free State, 1922–1932: A Reluctant Dominion

ESTABLISHING THE NEW STATE

In the debate over the treaty that would create the new Irish Free State, the Sinn Fein assembly very probably confirmed the view of those in Britain who had always believed that the Irish were unsuited for self-government. Men and women who had endured months and years of adversity together while fighting the common foe of English rule were seen shouting abuse at one another during the so-called treaty debate in the Dáil. Ultimately, the treaty was ratified by the narrow margin of 64 votes to 57, and that divisive schism within the Irish nationalist movement actually foreshadowed what were to become permanent political alignments. The divisions that separated the treaty party (Cumann na nGaedheal from 1923 to 1933 and Fine Gael thereafter) from the antitreaty party (retaining the name Sinn Fein until 1926, when de Valera founded Fianna Fáil) were not temporary disagreements. Their differences have endured to the present day.

Eamon de Valera resigned the presidency of the Dáil on January 9, 1922, and the following day Arthur Griffith was elected in his place and nominated a new cabinet. Doctrinaire Republicans promptly joined de Valera, who then permanently withdrew from the Dáil, leaving that assembly to its slim majority of troubled survivors. The antitreaty people, now in political exile, continued to insist that an Irish Republic had been declared in 1916, that it had been ratified in 1919, and that every member of the Dáil had sworn allegiance to it in 1921. The republic was inviolable, went the argument, and not only was it treason to attempt to disestablish it, but it was also beyond the competence of anyone—even a majority in the Dáil— to do so.

These were not the best of times in which to launch the first attempt at Irish self-government in nearly 800 years. Military barracks and arms depots were being quickly taken over by local IRA forces as soon as the British evacuated them, but whether those forces were in fact loyal to the supporters of the Free State or to the fancied republic was anyone's guess. The IRA had never given more than nominal allegiance to the Dáil, and it had often acted in defiance of its own leadership. What direction the army might take seemed uncertain, but the danger that it posed to democratic governance was without question. The IRA was now better armed than ever before, and many young recruits had taken their place at the side of veteran gunmen, now local folk heroes, whose ill-disguised impatience with any government authority did not bode well. It was fortunate for Michael Collins that the secret Irish Republican Brotherhood, which pervaded a large part of the IRA, was still very much under his control. This gave Collins the loyal organizational network he needed to rally support for the Free State within the IRA, and it provided, even for Collins, the justification for believing that the establishment of the Free State was but a temporary and transitional step toward the ultimate goal of a republic. This reasoning helped Collins and his senior military officer, Richard Mulcahy, to win over about half of the IRA in support of the treaty. These men were then armed, given uniforms, and organized into what became the Free State Army. The uneasy relations between the new army and the antitreaty forces, who often occupied different premises in the same towns throughout the countryside, was further complicated by the fact that so many men on both sides had been close comrades a short time earlier.

One of the more persistent myths about this period in Irish history has been the widely accepted belief that Eamon de Valera was to blame for the civil war that began in 1922. But the responsibility was not his. Perhaps his antitreaty attitude did help to provide a focus for the opponents of the Free State, but antitreaty members within the IRA looked to their military leaders, to men like Liam Lynch, Ernie O'Malley, and Sean Moylan, rather than to de Valera. If anything, de Valera spent considerable energy attempting to negotiate a political compromise with the new leaders of Dáil Éireann, even though he did warn that he would do everything in his power "to see [that] this established Republic is not disestablished."

In April 1922 a group of antitreaty officers occupied the Four Courts, a government building in the heart of Dublin. It was located just a few hundred yards down the same road from where Irish blood had first been spilled by British guns at Bachelor's Walk on the eve of World War I. This time, however, both the rebels and the authorities were Irish. Collins tried for two months to negotiate a peaceful withdrawal from the Four Courts. Then, on June 22, Field Marshall Sir Henry Wilson was assassinated on his own doorstep in London by men who were apprehended and identified as members of the IRA. A furious Prime Minister Lloyd George wrote Michael Collins demanding action against the Four Courts occupants whom the British chose to believe were responsible. The irony is that the assassins not only had no orders from the antitreaty IRA leadership, but they may quite possibly have been acting on a still unrescinded order that Collins himself had issued while the Anglo-Irish War was in progress.

Contributing to the sense of urgency in this situation was the fact that the time was fast approaching when a general election would have to be held. Under the provisions of the treaty, a new parliament was to be elected for the purpose of hammering out a constitution for the Irish Free State. The treaty required at minimum the ratification of a document that specifically acknowledged Dominion status, and it mandated that this should be done before the end of 1922. As tensions heightened, Lloyd George recalled home General Sir Neville Macready and instructed him to prepare for an assault on the Four Courts. Neither Macready nor Lloyd George really preferred that course of action, however, as they feared it might have the effect of uniting the protreaty and antitreaty groups in Ireland against their old nemesis, the British. Meanwhile, the deputy chief of staff of the protreaty army was kidnapped by men from the Four Courts garrison. Just what their objective was is unclear, but the immediate consequence was a challenge that Collins could not afford to ignore. He decided that the insurgents, headed by Rory O'Connor, would have to be flushed from their quarters, and he accepted the loan of British military artillery, repeatedly offered earlier by Colonial Secretary Winston Churchill, to complete the task.

The attack on the Four Courts went on for two days until the flames so consumed the building that the garrison was compelled to surrender. Many regard this event as the beginning of the Civil War, but in truth the country had been drifting in that direction for several months. What it did do, of course, was polarize the conflict, whereupon the political opponents of the treaty promptly joined the military types in an atmosphere of increasing violence. Many of the leading figures in the old Sinn Fein Republic, such as Cathal Brugha, Austen Stack, Countess Markievicz, and Eamon de Valera, quickly volunteered for service in the antitreaty army, now popularly known as the Irregulars. At the outset of hostilities, there were a few battles in central Dublin that the Free State forces won without much difficulty, but the conflict soon gave way to guerrilla warfare in the hills and bogs. During the ten-month-long civil war that followed, the Free State army drove the Irregulars from one strong point after another without ever being able to render the knockout blow. As is often true of civil wars, the most enduring cost of the hostilities for the country was in the enmities that were produced and then perpetuated by the tactics employed by both sides. No fewer than seventy-seven captured Irregulars were put to death during the struggle as evidence of the Free State's determination to reestablish its authority.

Although the provisional government eventually "won" the Civil War, at least in the sense that the Irregulars were compelled to cease and desist in their armed resistance after May 1923, the peace was obtained at an incredibly heavy price. More than 600 people lost their lives, and 3000 others were wounded. The cost for the Dublin government in putting down the rebellion was almost 20 million pounds, money that might have been put to productive use in restoring Irish agriculture, industry, and social services. Moreover, the violence had taken a heavy toll on Irish leadership. On August 12, 1922, Arthur Griffith, president of the provisional Free State government, worn out by the tension and fatigue from which he had been suffering since the treaty negotiations, died of a cerebral hemorrhage at the age of 50. Ten days later, Michael Collins, commander in chief of the Free State army, was killed in an ambush while on an inspection tour of his military postings in West Cork. He was struck down by a ricochet in a gun battle at Béal na mBláth, a spot within walking distance of his birthplace, only two months before his thirty-second birthday. Thus in less than a fortnight the Free State had lost its chief architects and principal signatories to the Anglo-Irish treaty.

Despite these setbacks, the Dublin government continued its relentless campaign against the Irregulars. William Cosgrave succeeded Griffith as president, and he, together with Kevin O'Higgins, the minister for home affairs, and Richard Mulcahy, minister for defense, attempted to fill the leadership vacuum created by the death of Collins. A different temper now guided the Dublin government. While Collins had been inclined to view the Civil War as a tragic conflict between former comrades, Cosgrave and O'Higgins perceived it as a clash between civil law and anarchy. In October, special emergency powers were given to the army for the purpose of conducting military courts and imposing the death penalty for a wide range of offenses, including the unauthorized possession of arms. By the end of 1922 no fewer than 12,000 people had been interned. Meanwhile, Erskine Childers, Rory O'Connor, Liam Mellows, and other heroes of the Irish War for Independence, now Irregulars and prisoners of war, were executed by Irish government authorities. The new state would show no mercy to those who continued to threaten its existence.

On December 6, 1922 (the first anniversary of the treaty), the provisional government was dissolved and the Irish Free State came formally into being. A few months earlier, de Valera had been elected by Irregular political sympathizers as president of the true Irish Republic, and it was expected that he would lead a government in exile. But the Irregular fighting forces ignored de Valera's attempts to negotiate an armistice and followed instead their uncompromising combat leader, Liam Lynch. When Lynch was killed in action on April 10, however, de Valera did convince the fallen commandant's more amenable successor, Frank Aiken, to terminate hostilities. De Valera then tried to secure a ceasefire with Dublin on favorable terms, but when the government refused to consider any of his proposals, he issued this proclamation to his followers on May 24:

> Soldiers of the Republic, Legion of the Rearguard: The Republic can no longer be
> defended successfully by your arms. Further sacrifice of life would now be vain and

continuance of the struggle in arms unwise in the national interest and prejudicial to the future of our cause. Military victory must be allowed to rest for the moment with those who have destroyed the Republic.

What is perhaps most remarkable about this sudden cessation of hostilities, after ten months of vicious attacks and reprisals, is that it was not accompanied by any joint negotiations or formal exchanges between the combatants. There were no peace talks, no agreed terms, and no surrender. The Republican Irregulars simply stopped fighting, hid their arms, and went ''on the run'' as fugitives from justice. There was no declared amnesty, nor was there any surrender of principle. The republic may have suffered a reversal, but in the eyes of its supporters, it was still the only legitimate form of government for the Irish people. And it was precisely this legacy of dissent and animosity that would prove most difficult of all for the Free State government to eradicate. The bitterness caused by the Civil War had pitted family against family and had left indelible scars on the new state.

There was no spirit of triumph, no glee over having vanquished the enemy among the Free State ministers who now sought to bring back an atmosphere of normalcy within the country. The provisional government, which had taken over from the British, was in a precarious enough economic situation before the outbreak of civil war. Conditions thereafter were considerably worse. Thousands of acres of land were lying uncultivated, and unemployment and poverty were widespread. The systematic destruction of vital links in the railway system by the Irregulars, for example, was but one of the factors that made economic recovery immeasurably more difficult than it might otherwise have been in the absence of an internecine struggle. Indeed, the promise of great achievement, which had inspired so many Irish nationalists in the 1919–1921 War for Irish Independence, now gave way to intense frustration and demoralizing cynicism.

Aside from the legacy of hatred and bitterness the Civil War also had an immutable impact on the configuration of Irish party politics, which is unique to that country and bears no resemblance to the right/left, conservative/socialist divide so characteristic of British and European politics throughout this century. Indeed, for more than a generation the Civil War would contribute to the unnatural polarization around the treaty issue, with the resulting consequence that social and economic considerations suffered from inattention and neglect. And within that divisive and enduring dialogue over the treaty, Free Staters might be seen to be reasonable men pragmatically attempting to create a viable political community while, by contrast, Republicans might appear as simple-minded fanatics without regard for political necessity or reality.

There were, however, treaty opponents who embraced Republicanism in response to what they perceived as the betrayal by the Free State government of the sacred policies embraced in the democratic program that had been unanimously ratified by the First Dáil in 1919. That document, which among other things, had declared that ''all rights to private property must be subordinated to the public right and welfare,'' had been a hastily contrived expedient by Sinn Fein nationalists to win the favor and support of the tiny Labour and Socialist followings. Most of the nationalist leadership espoused more bourgeois interests and, not surprisingly, this came as a profound disappointment for those on the political left in 1923. For these true believers in a new social order for Ireland, the Free State represented a counter-revolutionary cabal that had deserted the people in exchange for the support of the Catholic, clerical, landowner, shopkeeper, and Protestant Unionist classes. There could be no reconciliation with people who were so antithetical to the vision of men like James Connolly, and the socialists remained a minority within a minority as they joined the Republicans in political exile. But it would be more than a generation later before this left wing of the advanced nationalist movement would come to the fore.

Perhaps the most compelling problem to confront the new state was not any of these internal ideological issues, however, but rather that of the Northern Ireland question. The subject of partition had been totally eclipsed by the Dominion versus republic arguments during the Dáil debate on the treaty, but during the Civil War the Republicans succeeded in making the division of Ireland a political controversy once again. What seemed to give the dispute a special sense of urgency was the overt Protestant oppression of Catholic nationalists in Northern Ireland. Indeed, the campaign of Protestant violence in the Six Counties would extend, intermittently, until 1935, during which time hundreds would be killed and thousands more wounded, almost all of them Catholic. For the unrepentant Republicans, who had just lost the Civil War, the pogroms in the North were indisputable evidence of Britain's continuing imperialism in Ireland, as well as dramatic proof of the unfinished business of Irish nationalism.

During the treaty negotiations, it will be recalled, British Prime Minister Lloyd George had persuaded the Irish delegation to accept what he characterized as the necessary but temporary exclusion of the Six Counties from the new Dominion. He promised that if the North refused to form part of a united Ireland, a Boundary Commission would be created to determine the frontiers between the two regions. Therefore, although Article 12 of the treaty contained a proviso permitting Northern Ireland to opt out of the anticipated union, Lloyd George led both Griffith and Collins to expect that the Boundary Commission appointed by the London government would so drastically reduce the size of the Ulster region as to make it economically unfeasible to remain apart. At least that was the tacit, if unwritten, understanding in 1921. Who could tell, then, that by the end of the next year, both Griffith and Collins would be dead and Lloyd George would be displaced as Britain's prime minister?

Northern Ireland exercised its right under Article 12 and, on December 7, 1922, opted out of a united Ireland. William Cosgrave, the new head of government in the Free State, was just then preoccupied with the problem of consolidating his government in the twenty-six counties and with suppressing the Civil War insurgency. Meanwhile, the new British Conservative prime minister, Andrew Bonar Law, was forced to resign within the year due to ill health. He was succeeded by Stanley Baldwin, a man who keenly distrusted Lloyd George and who could be expected to find suspect any agreement that the latter might have entered into. And Baldwin himself was out of office for a time in 1923 when Ramsay MacDonald assumed the premiership of a short-lived Labour government. Baldwin returned to power in 1924, but it is hardly surprising, given the political instability in England during the early 1920s, that scant attention was paid to the Northern Ireland question for several years.

Indeed, it was not until October 1924 that Cosgrave and Baldwin got around to establishing the repeatedly postponed Boundary Commission under the neutral chairmanship of Justice Richard Feetham of the South African Supreme Court. J. R. Fisher, a prominent Northern Unionist, was nominated by the British government to represent Northern Ireland, and Eoin MacNeill, the Free State minister of education who hailed from a Catholic family in Ulster's County Antrim, was selected to be Dublin's representative. For most of 1925 the commission met with individuals and groups on both sides of the border, and it took testimony and collected evidence without ever indicating what action was in fact contemplated. Then, in early November 1925, the *Morning Post,* a British newspaper, leaked a story that caused an instant sensation and led to Eoin MacNeill's resignation from the commission. According to the *Morning Post,* a ruling was imminent that would leave the frontier much as before except that an important section of County Donegal, in the Free State, would be given over to Northern Ireland.

No one doubted the integrity of Eoin MacNeill, nor the loyalty of that celebrated patriot, but even he could scarcely escape the wrath of his indignant colleagues in the Dáil. And it was before that assembly that MacNeill stood and explained how he had foolishly agreed in principle to a joint report of the commission before knowing what it was going to contain. He did so, he said, in the mistaken belief that Judge Feetham shared his interpretation of Article 12, and he resigned when he found out otherwise, since he could not possibly subscribe to the report about to be issued.

MacNeill's resignation from the commission did not preclude his two fellow members of that body from publishing their findings, and that possibility caused great consternation and anxiety throughout the Free State government—for good reason. The publication of the Boundary Commission report would, according to the Judicial Committee of the Privy Council, give it the force of law. Eoin MacNeill resigned in disgrace from the Executive Council, and for a time it seemed possible that the entire Cosgrave government would fall.

It was in this atmosphere of crisis, then, that an Irish delegation traveled on November 28 to London, where it met with both British and Northern Ireland representatives. The price that the Irish had to pay to prevent the promulgation of the commission's report was adherence to a tripartite agreement that was signed in London on December 3, 1925. Under its terms, the Free State accepted the existing frontier of Northern Ireland and in return, Britain absolved both the Dublin and Belfast governments of their obligations to the British debt. Moreover, the Council of Ireland, which had been established under the provisions of the 1920 Government of Ireland Act as a conduit through which to promote Irish unity, was eliminated. The abolition of the council was no real tragedy, since it had never functioned anyway, and the expressed intent of the tripartite agreement, calling for direct negotiations between the two Irelands over matters of mutual concern, was doubtless a more rational structure for any future negotiations between North and South. Yet the distrust and suspicion with which each community viewed the other made the prospects for constructive dialogue extremely remote.

What the Boundary Commission scandal did, despite the fact that the report itself was suppressed until 1969, was to heighten anxieties that were already intense within the Free State owing to a crisis within the army at about the same time. In March 1924 the government decided to reduce the size of the Free State army, which had expanded to 60,000 men owing to the Civil War situation. The demobilization was to involve almost 2000 officers and over 35,000 men. That order was keenly resented by many veteran soldiers who had fought in defense of the treaty more out of loyalty to the memory of Michael Collins and to his vision of an eventual republic than to any Free State leader or principle. To be sure, a number of these old IRA men knew no trade other than soldiering, and they were neither favorably disposed nor well equipped to assume civilian jobs. The response from some of these malcontents was an ultimatum, dated March 6, 1924, signed by two officers, Liam Tobin and C. F. Dalton, that was dispatched to the government.

Even in the chaotic days of postrevolutionary Ireland, this was a startling development. The ultimatum demanded (1) an immediate end to demobilization; (2) the removal of the army's internal controlling body, namely the Army Council; and (3) some guarantee of the government's intention to achieve an Irish Republic. The Free State government responded quickly, arresting all of the document's signatories and appointing General Eoin O'Duffy, the commissioner of the civic guards (the police), as commandant of the army. Kevin O'Higgins, who assumed full responsibility for the government during the incapacitating illness of President Cosgrave at this time, sought to minimize the damage to the state with an approach that reflected firmness and impartiality. He promised an inquiry into army administration and assured that a number of deserting officers who had refused to return to their posts, following the government's initial sanctions, would be judged to have simply "retired" from the army. Last, O'Higgins promised to ensure the implementation of an army service pension scheme.

The so-called army mutiny was short-lived, but there can be no underestimating the threat it represented to the life of the young state. Kevin O'Higgins and his Executive Council colleagues redressed what they felt to be genuine grievances, but they insisted on the resignation of three senior officers and were about to make the same demand of General Richard Mulcahy, the minister of defense, who was also implicated, when he resigned of his own accord. The question of who possessed ultimate control in the state, the civil authorities or the army, was decisively resolved. As O'Higgins himself remarked, "Those who take the pay and wear the uniform of the state, be they soldiers or police, must be non-political servants of the state."

Despite the Civil War of 1922–1923, and the army mutiny and Boundary Commission crises of 1924–1925, the Free State had survived—but it was still endangered. In March 1926 the government concluded with Britain the so-called ultimate financial agreement, which became the occasion of yet another political emergency for the Cosgrave government. The sense of that agreement had been confirmed by the Irish Free State as early as 1923, when it committed Dublin to pay the British government the land annuities that were owed due to the land legislation of the late nineteenth and early twentieth centuries. In addition, the Free State acknowledged responsibility for the payment of certain Royal Irish Constabulary pensions. The total cost of these twin obligations was approximately 5 million pounds a year. Even in the best of times the agreement would have been controversial, all the more so because it had not been submitted for parliamentary approval. Cosgrave may have felt that he had no choice but to honor his government's earlier pledge, but his political enemies were quick to exploit the dissatisfaction that most people felt over this pact with the British.

In that same month of March 1926, the Sinn Fein party organization met to discuss a new departure in basic strategy. Ever since 1922 the antitreaty Republicans, calling themselves the Sinn Fein party, had boycotted participation in the Dáil because of the oath to the Crown that members were obliged to take upon admission to that assembly. Party leader Eamon de Valera, however, declared his readiness to discuss joining the Dáil now that a full convention of the IRA, on November 25, had formally withdrawn its allegiance to him as president of that still revered abstraction, the Irish Republic. To IRA militants, the Sinn Fein leader had not been vigorous enough in advancing the day when partition might be ended by force. De Valera's response was to urge Sinn Fein, at its March meeting, to enter the Dáil in parliamentary opposition to the hated Cumann na nGaedheal ("Community of Irishmen") party then in power. The motion generated a furious debate in which Sinn Fein purists made it abundantly clear that many within the party were still opposed to legitimizing the "usurper" legislature through association with true Republicans like themselves. Thus repudiated by Sinn Fein, as he had been previously by the IRA, de Valera broke with his old comrades and launched a new party only two months later, which he named Fianna Fáil ("warriors of Fál," the term *Fál* being a poetic symbol for Ireland). Most of de Valera's more moderate Sinn Fein associates joined him, as did other admirers from outside that party. It was an auspicious turn of events.

Republicanism was scarcely dead in Ireland. Despite their recent military defeat and their subsequent suppression by the law, Republicans had made an impressive showing at the time of the first general election under the new Irish Free State Constitution in August 1923. Cumann na nGaedheal won 63 of the 153 seats in the Dáil, but the Sinn Fein Republicans secured 44 seats and over 27 percent of the popular vote. Yet de Valera and his colleagues steadfastly refused to enter a Dáil that they had repudiated. Fianna Fáil had expressed a new willingness to participate in democratic opposition, but the question of the oath remained an obstacle.

Whether or not it could be overcome was a question that would not take long to resolve. The next general election was due in 1927.

The timing of the electoral contest did not favor Cosgrave's government. Not only had it just concluded the highly unpopular financial agreement with Britain, but the government had also introduced a new public safety act in its uncompromising quest to impose law and order on a still turbulent society. The act provided for powers of detention and suspension of habeas corpus in response to the successive IRA attacks against police barracks in late 1926. And almost as if to add insult to injury, the government alienated a diverse and vocal constituency with the Intoxicating Liquor Act, the purpose of which was to reduce the number of licensed pubs and to limit the hours during which they could operate.

Fianna Fáil, of course, sought to fan the flames of discontent. The new party accused its opponents of being pro-British and attacked what were said to be the government's ruinous economic policies. If elected to power, Fianna Fáil promised to remove the oath, dismantle the treaty, withhold the land annuities, protect the small farmer, foster manufacturing industries, and extend social services.

As it happened, the real winners of the June 1927 campaign were a multiplicity of small parties. Cumann na nGaedheal dropped from the 63 seats it had won in 1923 to 47, while Fianna Fáil's 44 seats represented no gain over the Sinn Fein position in 1923. But Labour took 22 seats, Farmers 11, National League 8, Sinn Fein 5, and Independent Republicans 2. In addition to these parties, which suggested that the proportional representation system of election was destined to fragment political alignments in Ireland, 14 independent deputies were elected.

For the first time it was then possible for Fianna Fáil to seize control of the government, assuming that it acted in coalition with a few of the minor parties. Given the charged emotions on all sides, it is difficult to say whether there could have been a peaceful transfer of power, with the preservation of democratic government, at that moment in 1927. A crisis was averted, however, when de Valera and his followers were denied admission to the Dáil after they refused to take the obligatory oath. Without Fianna Fáil to contend with, Cosgrave again formed a government with support from farmers and independents. Any hope that political tranquility might follow once Cosgrave had been given a new lease in office was quickly dashed two weeks later, on July 10, with the assassination of Kevin O'Higgins.

Perhaps no person since Michael Collins had had so commanding a presence in the Irish government. He was, at the age of 35, the most forceful and dynamic member of the cabinet, and many Republicans saw him as their real nemesis far more than they did Cosgrave. O'Higgins's power in the new government was evident from the fact that he had held three portfolios; that of vice-president, minister for justice, and minister for external affairs. No one admitted responsibility for his killing, and some Republican leaders, like de Valera, condemned it in the strongest possible terms. All the same, the government responded with the passage of the harshest public safety act to date (ultimately repealed in December 1928), which authorized severe penalties for membership in specifically proscribed organizations, granted the police extreme latitude in any search that they might conduct, and established a special court that was empowered to impose the death sentence or life imprisonment for unlawful possession of firearms.

Events within the Dáil were no less dramatic. An electoral amendment act was passed that henceforth would require every candidate for the Dáil or Seanad (the less important upper house of the Irish parliament), upon nomination, to sign an affidavit that he or she would take the oath, if elected. Failure to do so would disqualify the person from his or her seat. The purpose of such legislation, of course, was to put an end to the abstentionist policy of Fianna Fáil. De Valera and his followers were suddenly confronted with the need to choose between either giving up all meaningful political action or taking the oath and entering the Dáil. For a man who had spent from August 1923 to July 1924 in jail primarily because he had sought to substitute a republic for the Free State, Eamon de Valera was not easily reconciled to taking the hated oath simply to gain admission to a parliament that he regarded as illegal. But on this occasion he permitted his political pragmatism to prevail over his lofty idealism and, on August 10, 1927, he took the oath and led his party into the Dáil. Yet even then de Valera, whose reputation for semantical distinctions was well deserved, insisted that the oath was an empty formula that could be taken by Fianna Fáil members "without being involved, or without involving their nation, in obligations of loyalty to the English Crown."

In the long term, Fianna Fáil's entry into the Dáil would prove to be a significant development if only because that action compelled the second-largest party in the state to accept a fully responsible role in the parliamentary system. It also helped to ensure peaceful changes of administration in the future. But the immediate consequence was to threaten Cosgrave's political survival, particularly when Labour deputies joined with Fianna Fáil in a vote of no confidence in the government. Balloting on that motion resulted in a tie, and the government was able to prevail only because the chairman could, and did, cast a tie-breaking vote. The margin of victory, however, was much too close for Cosgrave to govern effectively, and he decided to call for a general election, the second within a year, in September 1927.

The political issues remained unchanged, but the response of the electorate had the effect of restructuring the Dáil membership. Hardest hit were the smaller parties. The National League was almost wiped out, as it lost 6 of its 8 seats, and Sinn Fein representation disappeared entirely. Correspondingly, the Farmers fell from 11 seats to 6, while Labour, suffering from internal strife between moderates and extremists, lost 9. The beneficiaries of these losses were the two big parties: Cumann na nGaedheal won 67 seats and Fianna Fáil 57. Some interpreted the results as voter disenchantment with the way in which smaller parties had engaged in power maneuvering. Others saw it as an expressed preference by the electorate for the stability of a two-party system over the uncertainties of proportional representation if left unchecked. Whatever their thinking, the Irish had succeeded in bringing accountability into the affairs of government through the established parliamentary means of a legitimate oppositional party. Fianna Fáil promptly began establishing a constituency organization second to none throughout the Free State, and in 1931 de Valera founded *The Irish Press* as the party newspaper. It would soon boast a circulation of 100,000, which was proof enough, if any was needed, that a new political force was emerging.

IRISH SOCIAL, ECONOMIC, AND CULTURAL LIFE IN THE 1920s

Against the backdrop of political uncertainty, life in the Irish Free State was anything but the utopia some revolutionary idealists might have expected. The country was without any important natural resources, or at least none that were known or could be easily retrieved during the 1920s. Partition had deprived the Free State of the only industrially developed portion of the island, and the Civil War had squandered funds that might otherwise have been used to help build the economy.

Men like D. P. Moran and Arthur Griffith had once preached the doctrine of a self-sufficient Ireland achieved through protective tariffs and subsidies to industry and agriculture. Free State politicians, however, soon realized the necessity of making theories conform to reality, given the reciprocal responsibilities and trade concessions that Dominion status implied. Moreover, the Commonwealth notwithstanding, the plain fact was that geography and history had integrated Ireland into the British economy, and Dublin had little choice but to remain a part of the latter's economic complex. Britain was the natural market for Irish agriculture, and over 90 percent of all Irish trade was with the United Kingdom. Hence any attempt to impose tariffs that would protect Irish industries could be met by British reprisals against Irish agriculture, with potentially devastating consequences for the Free State.

As it was, Irish agriculture was floundering in a state of inertia by the time the War for Independence ended in 1921. Part of the problem may have been attributable to the residues of the landlord system, which had debilitated the energies of the Irish farmer. More significant was the static condition that pervaded agricultural life in Ireland. While other countries during the late nineteenth and early twentieth centuries had been applying technology to agriculture and thereby increasing food production substantially, the yield from Irish farms improved only marginally. It was not until 1927 that the government established the Agricultural Credit Corporation for the purpose of making loans to farmers needing overall improvements. And although reforms of this kind did in fact halt the pace of the economic recession that had plagued Ireland in the early 1920s, progress was still retarded by instinctively conservative farmers, who resisted experimentation and seemed content with subsistence production levels. The halcyon days of agricultural prosperity, which were as much a boon to the merchant as to the farmer in an earlier time, were now but distant memories.

By contrast, the
d from the urban
look with little
century Ireland.
ial activist Irish
ences.

Irish literature.
of the 1920s,
nd emigration;
smen and their
which were an
Irish rule had

olution, many
priests as the
nfronting the
ean O'Casey
y, the nerves
ncing it all.''
he pressures
he influence
omic policy
at Catholic
Irish imag-
ected place
oortrayal of
ity became

tate, it has
ish would
vent, were
rarchy, it
ated those
composed
s encour-
925; and
n, it was
alliance.
ss than 7
ose who
t was a
religion
for the

the domestic industries, which were often
industrial jobs frequently earned less than
, though the cost of living was roughly the
i counting partial and temporary jobs in
out 6 percent through most of the 1920s.
, and others sought new lives in the United
fore persisted as a demoralizing dimension
the effect of functioning as a safety valve,
tical discontent, emigration also deprived the
intelligence, ambition, and energy.

the otherwise dismal economic malaise. A
Carlow, and it became in time an important
enterprise was the state-sponsored Shannon
harnessing the flow of the country's longest
outside Limerick. German engineers and Irish
nd the Free State government established the
just two years before the Shannon Scheme was
or since has had such a profound impact on the
nt of Ireland, especially in the rural areas and
ly populated regions, such as Sligo, Kilkenny,
electricity until the 1920s, and in Dublin itself no
mes was serviced by this marvelous new energy.
in Ireland, even if the pace sometimes seemed

sttreaty Ireland was the dominant influence Catholi-
mores, values, and culture. Bishops and priests had
ues since the days of O'Connell, and before, but that
nce welcome to intellectuals or to members of the
leed, most of the important Irish writers have charac-
tive force in Irish life. Unlike the upper-class Anglo-
y renaissance, the majority of postrevolutionary Irish
lass or lower-middle-class Catholic families. Nearly all
ome degree in the cultural and revolutionary nationalist
lists whose sympathies reflected their class origins and
m the ascendancy writers, who, like the Catholic hier-
vative on social issues.
re far more real than imagined. Sean O'Casey, a Dublin
l been a member of the Gaelic League and the Citizen
d Frank O'Connor learned their nationalism in Cork City
talented writer, brilliant teacher, and Irish-Ireland pro-
joined the Republican forces during the Civil War. Their
utopian republic, which would respond to the poverty and

privations that were suffered by so many of the Irish people.
literary renaissance writers attempted to isolate and inoculate Irelan
materialism of the outside world. Theirs was a romantic, backwar(
or no concern for the social or economic problems of twentieth-
They were respected but not imitated by the new generation of so(
writers, whose perceptions had been informed by their own experi

Disillusionment was a dominant theme of postrevolutionary
Authors and playwrights who observed and evaluated the Ireland
1930s, 1940s, and early 1950s saw the stagnant economy, poverty, a
the power and profit motives of the priests, politicians, and busines
resistance to social and economic progress; and the censorship laws,
affront to artistic spirit. They concluded that the shift from British to
changed little for the better and some things perhaps for the worse.

If there was a villain to be held responsible for the failed rev(
writers thought it to be the Catholic church. They saw bishops and
nucleus of a conservative coalition that prevented Ireland from c(
social and economic problems that were demoralizing the nation. S
referred to the Catholic seminary at Maynooth as "the brain, the bod
and the tissue of the land, controlling two-thirds of the country, influe
Sean O'Faolain also complained about clerical power independent of
of democratic opinion. He argued, for instance, that bishops abused
they had over a devout laity in order to dictate political, social, and eco(
to the politicians in Dublin. Other Irish writers contended th
authoritarianism, anti-intellectualism, and puritanism had enslaved the
ination and intellect. Since Irish literature continued to enjoy a resp
among sophisticated readers the world over, this uncomplimentary (
posttreaty Ireland and the role of the Catholic church within that commu(
widely accepted.

Although the Irish Free State's constitution was that of a secular s
been said that this may have been more the consequence of what the Br(
require rather than to what the Irish might aspire. Affairs of state, in any e
not very long administered in any purely secular spirit. The Catholic hi(
should be remembered, had supported the treaty and had excommunic(
who opposed it in the civil war. The government therefore appeared to be
of "better Catholics" than its opponents, and some ministers and deputi(
aged this image of themselves. A law preventing divorce was passed in
although there is no evidence that the bishops had requested the legislati(
congenial to them all the same, and it further strengthened the church-state
For some in the new state's tiny Protestant minority, which was perhaps le
percent of the total population, the divorce law confirmed the old fears of th
had equated Home Rule with "Rome rule." And to other Protestants,
betrayal of the constitution, which had stressed freedom of conscience and
and, unlike the later Constitution of 1937, had recognized no special positio(

Catholic church. But Protestants remained generally passive, even as the divorce law was succeeded by further sectarian legislation against contraception. Nor were there many audible protests from this minority community when the Dáil approved the Irish Censorship of Publications Act of 1929 for the purpose of excluding "immoral and obscene" literature. Acquiescence did not mean approval, however, and most Protestants balanced their guarded criticisms with expressions of support for the government precisely because they felt that to do otherwise might help the Republican cause, which to them represented a still greater threat to position and property.

The writers were therefore correct in their view that Catholic power was very much a reality in Ireland. Contributing to this circumstance was the historical connection between the Irish and Catholic identities and the deep piety of the Catholic majority in the Free State whose respect for their hierarchy and clergy gave the church a considerable influence over the passage of legislation. And Irish politicians have indeed legislated Catholic morality on substantive issues, such as divorce, contraception, and abortion, as well as on lesser matters, like drinking hours and dance hall licenses. What the Irish legal and political systems have not done is to leave much room for private conscience and morality.

Despite their unchallenged authority among the laity and their indisputable influence on the government, some Catholic bishops still worried during the 1920s that the moral fabric of society was unraveling in an era of rapidly developing mass media. Their concern was misplaced, for the great majority of the faithful would continue to be loyal adherents of a very pietistic, devotional Catholicism until the 1960s. Ireland's Catholic population simply was not terribly receptive to the increasingly libertarian climate that had pervaded other postwar western societies. And the reasons for this are attributable not only to the power of the church but also to the fact that Irish Catholicism was ideally adapted to the Irish social reality of the time. The regularized rites and practices of the faithful had helped, in the period following the famine, to engender a sense of national identity. The devotional exercises became for many Irish men and women an external expression of the differences that set them apart from other inhabitants of the British Isles. It served the needs of a nascent Irish nationalism, therefore, at a moment when the Gaelic language and culture of the past were in rapid decline.

It is easy to understand why some people have characterized the Irish Free State, with its homogeneous religious constituency and its active institutional church, as a theocracy. But that term does not best describe posttreaty Ireland. Calling it a Catholic confessional state would be more accurate. Irish nationalism grew out of a liberal democratic as well as a Catholic tradition. Catholic influence was only effectively operative when it reflected the climate and goals of nationalist opinion. Church and state have clashed openly only once since the treaty, and that was over the 1951 "mother and child health scheme," (discussed in Chapter 13) which the hierarchy declared to be against Catholic and social teaching on the rights of the family and of the church in education. Otherwise, bishops and priests have suffered occasional defeats since 1922 whenever their ambitions have run counter to the liberal democratic spirit of Irish nationalism.

Further proof of the essentially democratic nature of the Irish Free State is evident from the way in which the Anglo-Irish Protestants have been treated. They have retained their civil rights, they continue to own a percentage of the national wealth that is hugely disproportionate to their numbers, and they are still prominent in cultural and political affairs. Indeeed, they have furnished the country with two of its six presidents to date. Such tolerance and liberalism had not been automatically assumed by the Church of Ireland delegation that visited with Michael Collins on May 12, 1922, to inquire whether or not the Protestant minority would be permitted to live in the twenty-six counties. Collins's firm assurance that they were welcome to remain and would have the protection of the new state must have been reassuring to those petitioners. The promise, in any event, was fully honored in the years thereafter.

Critics have argued that Catholic triumphalism became, all the same, a hallmark of the Irish Free State and that the 1922 Irish constitution, which insisted on the separation of church and state, was itself an illustration of how actual practice could differ from abstract theory. But successive centuries of British repression of and discrimination against Irish Catholics make it hardly surprising that there was a certain sense of Irish triumphalism. Moreover, those who would deride that spirit would do well to recall that it was precisely that kind of prejudice and discrimination, of an anti-Catholic variety, that became the given condition of the portion of the island that was to remain a part of the United Kingdom. And as for constitutional theory and practice, it might be noted that Irish legislation concerning divorce, birth control, and abortion was more representative of democratic public opinion than it was of clerical politicking. The bishops were indeed conservative, even reactionary in some instances, but there was also a xenophobic hostility toward the outside influences of modernism within Irish society that derived equally from the Gaelic and Irish-Ireland movements.

The Gaelic has never been so controversial as the Catholic component in Irish nationalism, but it has provoked considerable discussion and criticism. So, too, the Irish-Ireland ideology inspired enthusiasm, dedication, and a sense of purpose to the liberation movement. Cumann na nGael leaders implemented Patrick Pearse's proclaimed objective to make "Ireland Gaelic as well as free." And although less than one-tenth of the Irish population could speak Irish in 1922, the Free State constitution established it as the "national language." Yet this commitment to cultural orthodoxy by Cosgrave's party made good political sense. On the one hand, enthusiastic support of the language revival would dispute the presumption of Republicans that they were the sole custodians of true nationalism. On the other, two key ministers of these years, Ernest Blythe (of finance) and Eoin MacNeill (of education, until the end of 1925), were avid enthusiasts of the cause. In addition, Richard Mulcahy, who for a time served as minister of defense, was chairman of the Gaeltacht Commission of 1925. It was the purpose of the commission to preserve the Gaeltacht—the Irish-speaking districts of Waterford, Cork, Kerry, Galway, Mayo, and Donegal—as an inspiration and source of instruction for the rest of the country. Indeed, the commission pronounced it a national duty "to uphold and foster the Irish language, the central and most distinctive feature of the tradition which is Irish nationality."

A strategy for the linguistic transformation of the Free State was undertaken by the government in the following way. The compulsory teaching of Irish was to be adopted by the National University, with the ultimate objective of extending the requirement to the secondary and elementary school levels as soon as it became practical to do so. In the meantime, proficiency in the Irish language was required of all civil servants and members of the army and police force (Garda Síochana). Preference was to be given, for example, to native speakers hired by the government, and it was decreed that Irish should be used in official business, during Dáil debates, and for legal proceedings whenever possible. The language was a fixture in the school curriculum as early as 1928, and it became a requirement for all certificate examinations by 1934. Indeed, the necessity for students to earn a pass in Gaelic before becoming eligible for the school-leaving certificate would persist until 1973.

It was an ambitious but unrealistic scheme. The custodians and evangelicals of the Gaeltacht Commission mistakenly assumed that popular support for their program could be obtained through government-sponsored prizes, bonuses, and scholarships. They also failed to recognize that the hereditary education patterns of Gaeltacht people were quite foreign to the secondary and postsecondary school programs that were intended to open new careers for these native speakers. Last, very few people outside the schools could or would speak Gaelic. There was therefore no reinforcement in the community at large for what children spent almost half of their school time acquiring painfully in the classroom. The futility of the language revival was conceded in the Department of Education report of 1929, which read in part:

> As far as the general use of Irish is concerned, little progress seems to have been made in the last ten years. It appears to be true that very few pupils speak Irish outside school hours, and a still smaller number can be still classified as Irish speakers a few years after leaving school. . . . English is the language of their sports and pastimes and of the means of earning their livelihood, while Irish remains a school subject closely allied to lessons and examinations. Under such circumstances it is inevitable that a very considerable part of the work done by the schools must fail to bear fruit.

Neither this report nor any of the similar testimony that was given over the next several years had the slightest effect on the government, which continued, undaunted, to strive for the unachievable. Cumann na nGael was displaced from power in 1932, but the new government had its own zealots. Indeed, Thomas Derrig, minister of education from 1932 through 1948, was obsessed with the campaign for Gaelicization. When elementary school teachers complained to him in

1934 that the time given to compulsory Irish was impoverishing primary education, Derrig responded by *reducing* the teaching time available for English, mathematics, and science in order to allow for a greater concentration on Irish. But it was all to no avail. English remains today the spoken language and means of communication for most Irish citizens, and people continue to leave the Gaeltacht and settle in English-speaking places in Ireland and the United Kingdom. Nevertheless, the Irish-Ireland movement continues as a powerful lobby. Its supporters contend that Irish independence requires cultural integrity as well as political sovereignty. And although the Irish people have continued to resist using the Irish language, a majority of them still piously pay lip service to the Irish-Ireland ideal. However irrational such behavior may appear to an outsider, most Irish citizens justify that ambivalence as a reasonable compromise between the deference that they feel is owed to the quest for national identity and the conformity that they feel is essential for surviving in a non-Gaelic world.

Sean O'Faolain, an Irish novelist and critic whose nationalist credentials were impeccable, carried out a brave and desperate campaign some years later in his journal, *The Bell*, in which he wrote: "The sum of our [Irish] local history is that long before 1900 we had become part and parcel of the general world process—with a distinct English pigmentation." And other intellectuals, who were otherwise friendly to the Irish-language movement, have argued that it has reinforced the thinking that divides Catholics in the South from Protestants in the North. They insist that Irish Ireland represents an exclusive, Catholic, provincial, puritanical, and culturally anti-intellectual and isolationist perspective. If, therefore, the Anglo-Irish had been guilty of a dismissive contemptuousness toward Irish nationalism that reflected an offensive blend of insecurity and class snobbery, Irish-language fanatics had responded in kind by proposing a theory of Irish nationality that denied full spiritual assimilation with the Irish nation to the Anglo-Irishman with his English manner and Protestant faith.

Hence it was not the deprivation of civil rights or the appropriation of private property that precipitated the exodus of many Protestants from the twenty-six counties upon the establishment of the Irish Free State. There was none of the panic, for example, that years later would accompany the departure of French pieds noirs from North Africa. The guarantees that Collins had promised to Protestants were respected and enforced by the Cosgrave government. No fewer than twenty-four Protestants, including sixteen who were former Unionists, were appointed to the Senate by Cosgrave and his colleagues. Despite these gestures of reassurance, however, Protestants still continued to leave. Political oppression may not have been a concern of theirs, but cultural intolerance decidedly was.

Anglo-Irish anxieties were perhaps inevitable in any event. Before the partition of the country in 1920, that minority had taken comfort in the knowledge that Protestants comprised one-quarter of the population of the entire island. In the new Irish state, however, they totaled slightly more than 7 percent. And the sense of isolation was still more intense in Connaught and Munster, where the Protestants accounted for only 2.6 and 3.6 percent, respectively, of the population. The emotional state of Anglo-Ireland was reflected in a number of novels that appeared in the 1920s and early 1930s that employed the Big House as the prism through which successive authors portrayed the socially disintegrated world of the Protestant ascendancy. Edith Somerville's *Big House of Inver* (1925) and Elizabeth Bowen's *Lost September* (1929) are typical of this genre, employing the metaphor of the emptiness of spaces in the house, contrasting it with the space between the house, the landscape, and society, in order to describe the emotional isolation of the Anglo-Irish community. In the period between 1911 and 1926, the Protestant population in the twenty-six southern counties declined by about one-third as an ever-increasing number of Protestant professional men, civil servants, and small farmers moved to different parts of the United Kingdom. Some of these people very probably left because of the violence during the insurgency years, but a good number of them moved because of the cultural and intellectual climate. The closing of the Maunsel publishing company in 1926 must have seemed symbolic to those who recalled how that firm had once published the works of many writers associated with the literary renaissance. P. L. Dickinson's book, *The Dublin of Yesterday* (1929), conveys the sense of bitterness and betrayal that Anglo-Irish men and women took with them into exile and how they truly believed that the Ireland they had known was no longer hospitable to their kind.

THE IRISH CONSTITUTION: BLUEPRINT FOR DEMOCRACY AT HOME AND EQUALITY ABROAD

Irish nationalists who were charged with the task of constructing a government in 1922 may perhaps have felt a bit alien themselves in the circumstances. None of their dreams had been fulfilled. Not the Gaelic League's Irish-speaking nation, nor Yeats's literacy-conscious people, nor Redmond's home rule for a united Ireland, nor Connolly's worker's democracy, nor Griffith's economically self-sufficient dual monarchy, nor de Valera's and Collins's republic. What they had instead was a truncated twenty-six-county domain with imposed liabilities, such as land annuity payments and occupied naval ports, which no other British Dominion had been forced to endure. Compelled to accept Commonwealth membership, the Irish proceeded to draft a constitution that both fulfilled the conditions of the treaty and permitted the new state a notably amended version of the Westminster model of government.

Adopting a written constitution was in itself a marked departure from the British example. Other differences included electing the lower house of parliament through a system of proportional representation; a formal Bill of Rights; initiative and referendum; and extern ministers chosen for their skills in political, economic, and cultural matters. Except for the Bill of Rights, these innovative departures from the Westminster model were intended to make the Irish parliament more responsive to the electorate and less susceptible to the corruptive influence of vested interests. In practice, however, initiative and referendum soon retreated before the power of parliamentary majorities, and the experiment of extern ministers proved to be short-lived. Even proportional representation, which was intended to redress the anti-democratic tendencies associated with traditional party politics, failed to survive in any meaningful form. Initially, that system had encouraged a variety of political organizations, but the treaty controversy and the civil war polarized Irish politics around two major factions. Consequently, party considerations dominated the Irish parliamentary process as they did throughout the English-speaking world.

Differences between the Irish and British forms of government were nevertheless rather unremarkable, aside from the innovations just noted. The Irish equivalent of the British cabinet was called the executive council, and the prime minister was described as the president of that council. The Oireachtas (Parliament) contained two chambers: The Dáil and the Seanad Éireann (Senate), whose relations were broadly comparable to the relations between the British House of Commons and House of Lords.

The Dáil, or lower house, was therefore predominant, while the Senate, or upper house, could suspend legislation for nine months, suggest amendments to bills, and initiate legislation in certain areas. Members of the Dáil, numbering 153 in all, were elected by universal adult suffrage under the proportional representation (single transferable vote) method of voting. The Senate was comprised of sixty members, half of whom were appointed by the president of the executive council, the other half elected by the Dáil. Presiding nominally over this government was the governor general, who represented the British crown.

From 1922 to 1932, William T. Cosgrave, leader of the protreaty Cumann na nGaedheal party, served as president of the executive council. He had become head of government quite by accident and had none of the charisma of Collins or the magnetism of de Valera. Personally unambitious and politically unspectacular, he nonetheless was an honest, intelligent, and efficient administrator who deserves much of the credit for placing the new state on solid political and institutional foundations. Cosgrave's government created a police force, preserved the integrity of the civil service, reorganized local government, put down the incipient 1924 army mutiny, and stabilized the economy. Social services suffered, unemployment continued unabated, and the flow of emigration went unchecked, but Cosgrave's conservative fiscal programs had the support of the protreaty constituency of businessmen and large farmers, and the health of the Irish economy earned for it good credit and investment ratings from bankers and financiers. Cumann na nGaedheal succeeded in maintaining the political momentum on the domestic front until 1927, when a combination of unpopular policies and organizational deficiencies began to jeopardize the party's control over a restive electorate.

Yet it was not on the domestic front but in Commonwealth and foreign relations that Cumann na nGaedheal enjoyed its most significant and enduring triumphs. After being denied a republic and being compelled to enter the Commonwealth as a British Dominion, the subsequent performance of the Free State within the confines of that organization made Ireland something of a Trojan Horse. It must be remembered, of course, that the Irish-led campaign for Dominion sovereignty during the postwar decade was not exclusively Dublin-orchestrated. The other Dominions, after all, had grown greatly in power and self-confidence as the result of the war, and this was bound to reflect itself sooner or later in constitutional advance. But led by Kevin O'Higgins, Patrick McGilligan, and Desmond Fitzgerald, the Irish were the best-briefed and most articulate delegates attending the imperial conferences of the 1920s and 1930s. Their leadership, often shared by Canada and South Africa, helped to produce substantive changes in the concept and operation of the Commonwealth. The British Parliament abandoned any claim to legislate henceforth for the Dominions, and members of the Commonwealth no longer had to abide by treaties that Britain negotiated bilaterally with foreign powers. These momentous reforms, which helped to untangle the confused constitutional anomalies that existed between Great Britain and the Commonwealth of Nations, led ultimately to the passage of the Statute of Westminster by the imperial Parliament on December 11, 1931. That ruling defined Dominion status as a free association of sovereign and equal states united in common allegiance to the same monarch. The statute was later described as having "put the goblet of freedom into Ireland's hands, to be drained at her discretion."

Outside the Commonwealth and in the forum of world affairs, Cosgrave's government deported itself with an independence indicative of the latent Republican ambitions that Dublin's ministers hardly sought to disguise. The Free State, for example, joined the League of Nations in 1923, much to London's disapproval, and then proceeded in 1924 to register the Anglo-Irish Treaty with that body despite protests from the British, who regarded Dominion relations as an internal matter for the Commonwealth. Dublin further insisted on having separate diplomatic representation abroad and moved thereafter to appoint Irish ambassadors to the United States, Canada, France, Italy, and the Vatican. Acting more like nationals of a sovereign nation than a Dominion, Free State citizens traveled abroad on Irish passports. And although those instruments did bear the seal and signature of the British king, the irony was that Britain was now conceding the main essentials of de Valera's proposed external association, which London had emphatically refused to consider in 1921.

Republicans, however, remained unimpressed with these successes of Free State diplomats and continued to concentrate on the symbols of British influence in Ireland rather than the reality of Irish sovereignty. As one might expect, this was especially true of the IRA, which had become, for all intents and purposes, a military organization committed to the establishment of a republic that embraced all thirty-two counties of Ireland. A part of that organization espoused left-wing political views that were inimical to the ruling bourgeois interests of Cumann na nGaedheal. They took their inspiration from James Connolly and exploited the discontent felt by many over such issues as unemployement, poverty, and the payment of land annuities. What may seem more surprising was the fact that the newly minted parliamentary republicans, Fianna Fáil, should have been equally disdainful of the Free State's gains. Instead of acknowledging that the Cosgrave government had begun to use the treaty as "the freedom to achieve freedom," as Collins had promised, de Valera and his colleagues continued to castigate their opponents as heretics, traitors, and usurpers. Irish majority opinion was deemed irrelevant by these ideologues, who judged that the people had "no right to surrender their independence at the ballot box . . . no right to do wrong." Quite naturally, perhaps, some degree of political posturing was behind this rhetoric by Fianna Fáil spokesmen, who knew that the government was in trouble and were determined to make the most of it.

Cosgrave and his colleagues were caught in an economic and political morass that was both international and local. A severe economic depression caused financial dislocation the world over, especially during the years 1929–1931. The Wall Street Crash of 1929 had resonating echoes in Ireland as elsewhere. These took many forms, including reduced remittances home from the emigrants in America and a sharp decline in the export of cattle and dairy products. Factories closed and investment in Ireland nearly halted as the unemployed population soared from 20,000 to 30,000 between 1929 and 1932.

While the internationally generated economic crisis was still at its height, the Cosgrave government was suddenly confronted with a domestic security threat more lethal to the survival of the state than fiscal default. It began with Ireland's own version of the red scare, which, in retrospect, was of small consequence compared with the incipient militancy of several other IRA groups that had a fearsome potential for violence and destruction. The radicalization of left-wing elements of the IRA by men like Peadar O'Donnell and Seán MacBride led to a new organization in 1931, Saor Eire, whose professed purpose was the overthrow of capitalism and the formation of a workers' and farmers' revolutionary republic. Denounced as Marxist by the Cosgrave government, it was suppressed only a few months after its inception even though most of Saor Eire's members were more likely socialists than communists. The latter did not emerge as a party until 1933 and failed persistently thereafter to have any influence on Irish public opinion. Typical of the more dangerous revolutionary groups was the Comairle na Poblachta (Central Council of the Republic), which engaged in crimes of violence and intimidation, particularly against jury members sitting in judgment of Republican defendants. To meet these threats, the Cosgrave government, in the face of bitter opposition from Fianna Fáil in the Dáil, passed legislation that banned, in addition to Saor Eire, the IRA and ten other organizations.

Outrages like the murder of a Garda superintendent in Tipperary during March 1931 convinced Cumann na nGaedheal that drastic countermeasures were necessary, but the party leadership knew that it was also entering a political mine field. Accordingly, they set about, as they had in 1922, obtaining advance episcopal endorsement for what they intended. The bishops were no less sensitive to political nuances, however, and they now perceived Fianna Fáil as a more moderate Republican alternative to anything that had existed eight years before. Mindful that this party had a reasonable chance of soon coming to power, the hierarchy muted its denunciation of IRA radical organizations. Cosgrave's party therefore took the brunt of criticisms that inevitably grew out of the government's rather draconian Constitution Bill (Amendment No. 17). It provided for a military tribunal of five members with the power to punish political crime by use of the death penalty, if necessary, with appeal only to the executive council. And the council itself was given authority to declare associations unlawful without reference to the Dáil. Finally, the police were given wide powers of arrest and detention. The severity and comprehensiveness of these rather totalitarian methods shocked many people more than the comparatively isolated IRA atrocities, and the tide of public opinion began to flow against the government.

Against this backdrop, the most important election in Free State history was about to take place. The Dáil was not legally obligated to call for a general election until October 1932, but Cosgrave decided for his own reasons to hold a snap election in February of that year. His motives may have been influenced by the impending International Eucharistic Congress scheduled for Dublin at the end of June and by the Imperial Economic Conference slated for Ottawa in late July and early August. The president of the executive council hoped to obtain, if at all possible, a positive expression of public support prior to appearing before either of these two groups. And he hoped that an early election might help distract attention from criticisms of his repression of groups threatening public disorder.

Fianna Fáil already had put together a remarkably efficient political machine. The energies and the enthusiasm of the voluntary workers, whose allegiance to de Valera was intense, formed a vital ingredient in the party's success. De Valera did not conduct a strident campaign, and he cunningly avoided using hyperbolic attacks against his opponents that might alienate undecided voters. Instead, he enticed the electorate with the pledge that if elected, he would abolish the oath and other offensive features of the 1921 treaty. He also appealed to the farmers by declaring that under his administration, land annuities would no longer be paid to Britain but would instead be retained in the state treasury for domestic use. With a platform that promised something for nearly everybody, de Valera committed Fianna Fáil to a vigorous program of economic self-sufficiency that was calculated to win the favor of agricultural and industrial interests.

Cumann na nGaedheal responded by stressing its achievements in safeguarding the institutions of the state. That theme, however, failed to give the momentum to Cosgrave's party, which then turned to the desperate tactics of a smear campaign. Patrick McGilligan, for instance, publicly suggested a Bolshevik influence in the ranks of the Republicans, and Richard Mulcahy proclaimed that Marxists were behind de Valera's quest for power. Advertising posters appeared everywhere warning that a vote for Fianna Fáil was a vote for IRA violence and communist stooges.

When the election results were tallied, Fianna Fáil emerged as the largest single party with 72 seats as against 57 for Cumann na nGaedheal. Nevertheless, there were also 11 Independents, 7 Labour, 2 Independent Labour, and 4 Farmers to be taken into account. De Valera was able to fashion a bloc of 79 supporters, while Cosgrave could summon only 74 at best. William Cosgrave was thus compelled to step down, and de Valera became the leader of the new government. Few people would have expected the transition of power in this decade-young democracy to follow so peacefully and uneventfully. Fewer still, given the narrowness of victory, could possibly have imagined that a sixteen-year dynasty had just been inaugurated.

CHAPTER 13

The de Valera Era, 1932–1959: Continuity and Change in Irish Life

DISMANTLING THE TREATY AND SUPPLANTING THE FREE STATE

The name Eamon de Valera can evoke to this day a strong and spontaneous response throughout most parts of Ireland. And the sentiment conveyed by that response will vary from unswerving loyalty and unmeasured devotion, on the one hand, to profound bitterness and hostility, on the other. Such has been the legacy of this man, who, upon coming to power in 1932, had already been a nationally prominent figure for over fifteen years. Yet he was to embark upon a career as head of government for twenty of the Irish state's first thirty-seven years of existence, whereupon he would become head of state (Uachtarán) for another fourteen years. His towering presence, like that of O'Connell and Parnell before him, so dominated the life of the nation that it is not inappropriate to view this period in the making of modern Ireland as the "age of de Valera."

This new era began as William Cosgrave's came to an end. Cosgrave had labored effectively for ten years to extend the frontiers of Dominion sovereignty,

EAMON DE VALERA
1882–1976

Eamon de Valera was the dominant personality in post-Treaty Ireland. During his many years as Taoiseach he altered the Treaty and led Ireland on the road from Free State to Republic. His neutrality policy during World War II was the ultimate test of Irish independence. (Courtesy of the National Library of Ireland)

but he had done so in strict accordance with the spirit of the Anglo-Irish Treaty, as well as with the letter of the Commonwealth agreements that culminated in the 1931 Statute of Westminster. Fianna Fáil was now in power, however, and if there were some signs of anxiety among that party's opponents in the Dáil, the feeling of apprehension in London was almost palpable. De Valera was neither interested in defining Dominion status nor in refashioning Commonwealth relationships. He made it abundantly clear, upon taking office, that his ultimate aim was an Irish Republic that would be in association with the British Commonwealth of Nations and would recognize the British monarch as head of that association. Indeed, that affirmation prompted Prime Minister Ramsay MacDonald to respond immediately with the creation of an Irish Situation Committee for the specific purpose of monitoring the activities of the de Valera government and remediating any differences with it. The committee included a number of cabinet ministers and senior civil servants, and it met on a regular basis from 1932 to the Anglo-Irish Agreements of 1938. That high-level and sustained scrutiny of the Dublin government by London is indicative of just how important the Irish Free State was to British interests.

Eamon de Valera began his promised attack on the provisions of the 1921 Anglo-Irish Treaty within days of assuming office in March 1932. His immediate targets were the oath of allegiance to the Crown, which he desired to have removed completely from the constitution, and the suspension of land annuity payments to the United Kingdom. These annuities were annual payments of about 3 million pounds made by Irish farmers in repayment of money lent to them under the Land Purchase Acts of 1891–1909. Beginning in 1923, the annuities had been transmitted each half-year by the Free State government to the British National Debt Commissioners. A subsequent agreement negotiated with Britain in 1925 obligated the Dublin government to pay 250,000 pounds per annum, over a period of sixty years, as compensation for property damage in Ireland between 1919 and 1925. De Valera believed that these obligations were contractually invalid because they had never been ratified by the Dáil. He further insisted that the annuities represented a contingent liability for a share of the United Kingdom's public debt, a responsibility for which the British, in 1925, had agreed not to hold the Irish accountable. Efforts to resolve this difference between the two governments broke down in June 1932. The British responded by promptly imposing duties of 20 percent on Irish cattle and on Irish agricultural exports to the United Kingdom for the purpose of recovering the revenue owed to the Exchequer by the Irish Free State. Dublin retaliated by imposing tariffs of its own on imports from Britain, and there ensued a trade war that escalated in the months and years that followed until a negotiated settlement was eventually reached in 1938.

On the subject of the oath of allegiance, de Valera was equally assertive. He declared it a relic of medievalism and an intolerable burden that the Irish people would no longer endure. J. H. Thomas, secretary of state for the Dominions, was appalled by the suggestion that the oath was no longer obligatory because of a general election and a change of government in the Irish Free State. De Valera remained unimpressed by this expression of moral outrage from London, and his bill to remove the oath was ratified in the Dáil in May 1932. It was not until a year later, however, that the bill became law, owing to the fact that the Seanod sought to amend and then to delay its implementation. Meanwhile, another general election was held in January 1933. Fianna Fáil proceeded to capture half the seats in the Dáil and, with the support of eight Labour members, now enjoyed a working majority of sixteen. When, therefore, de Valera returned to the attack in the new year, it was from a position of increased strength, and the oath removal bill quickly passed a third reading in the Dáil and came before the Seanod. Under the law, the upper house now could do no more than retard the bill's progress for sixty days after which, on May 2, 1933, it became law. Dominions Secretary J. H. Thomas, who irreverently but memorably described de Valera as "the Spanish onion in the Irish stew," loudly protested that the withholding of the annuities, together with the removal of the oath, represented nothing less than a full-scale assault on the whole 1921 Anglo-Irish Treaty settlement.

As the trade war intensified and the dispute over the unpaid annuities continued, de Valera launched yet another attack against the treaty with a campaign of calculated affronts against the office of governor general. The incumbent, James MacNeill, had had a distinguished career in the Indian civil service and had served, for a time, as high commissioner for the Irish Free State in London. Appointed during the Cosgrave administration in 1928, Governor General MacNeill found himself excluded from nearly all official functions once de Valera took control of the government. That may have demoralized MacNeill, but it did not dispose of him, and de Valera therefore exercised his right to ask the king for the governor general's dismissal. Once accomplished, de Valera sought and obtained the appointment of Donald Buckley as MacNeill's successor. Buckley was a country shopkeeper, an Irish-language enthusiast, and a Fianna Fáil loyalist. The fact that he had no particular credentials to recommend him for the office of governor general was perhaps what de Valera found most attractive about his appointment. In any case, Buckley refused to move into the official residence and instead made his home the simple Dublin suburban house provided him by the Irish government. He never appeared at public functions and restricted his official role to that of signing acts of parliament until the office of governor general, which de Valera had succeeded in reducing to ridicule, was entirely abolished in 1937.

Still more controversial was the new Irish government's view toward appeals to the Judicial Committee of the Privy Council. There was no specific guarantee for this provision in the 1921 treaty, but that instrument all the same had defined the relationship between the Irish Free State and the United Kingdom as being essentially that of the Canadian model. Insofar as Canada in 1921 did not possess the right to abolish by legislation the right of appeal to the Privy Council, it seemed to follow that the Irish Free State did not have it either. But even as early as 1922, Free State leaders had insisted that the model Ireland would follow in this regard would be that of South Africa, not Canada, whereby only exceptional Irish court cases involving international issues might be appealed to London. Dominions Secretary J. H. Thomas reacted with astonished indignation to the 1933 Free State Act abolishing the appeal to the Privy Council. The progressive elimination of the Crown and Imperial Parliament from the constitution was, he warned, all part of an ill-disguised plan for the establishment of an all-Ireland republic that would be associated only tangentially with the British Commonwealth of Nations. And that, of course, went contrary to the principle of free association under the Crown agreed to at the Imperial Conference of 1926 and, therefore, was totally unacceptable to His Majesty's government. Thomas also emphasized that the Irish Free State enjoyed all the privileges that derived from Commonwealth status, and he reminded Dublin that these privileges carried with them responsibilities.

Since the Dominions secretary had inferred that the Irish Free State could not reasonably expect to have it both ways, de Valera immediately asked whether the Free State would be released from its responsibilities if it was willing to forgo the privileges. He also wondered whether or not London was prepared to accept Ireland's right "to exist as a distinct and independent nation" and if the British contemplated making war on the Irish people if they chose to sever their connection with the Commonwealth. The Dominions secretary's reply reflected his sense of exasperation as he rejected de Valera's view that the 1921 Anglo-Irish Treaty had imposed Dominion status upon the Irish Free State. His Majesty's government therefore felt no need to respond to so hypothetical a question based on a fallacious understanding of history. Thomas concluded his rejoinder by remarking that Ireland's free intercourse on equal terms with other members of the Commonwealth, together with the guarantees affirmed in the Statute of Westminster, constituted the most obvious proof of the fact of Irish freedom.

Indeed it did, as events made clear shortly after the Irish unilaterally abrogated the appeal procedure. In June 1935 the Judicial Committee of the Privy Council considered, on appeal, a test case intended to resolve whether or not Irish legislation abolishing the appeal was valid. The finding of the Judicial Committee was that the Irish Free State Parliament, as a direct consequence of the Statute of Westminster, did in fact possess the necessary power to repudiate the provisions of the 1921 Anglo-Irish Treaty. That judgment effectively cut the ground from under the British government's feet by rendering Dublin's initiative legally unimpeachable. Disheartened by this unexpected reversal, British Attorney General Sir Thomas Inskip scornfully remarked that a legal power did not confer a moral right and that there had to be some obligations that are binding other than legal obligations.

From the British viewpoint, one can perhaps understand the bewilderment and frustration that was felt in London over the apparent contradictions of Free State policy. Cosgrave, after all, had declared in 1931 that his government regarded the 1921 Anglo-Irish Treaty as a mutually binding agreement. Without that affirmation, it is doubtful that the Statute of Westminster would have been ratified so readily by the House of Commons. Both the British government and Cosgrave, who was now the opposition leader in the Dáil Éireann, accused de Valera of acting dishonorably. Fianna Fáil, quite naturally, viewed the matter from an entirely different perspective. Members of that party had never regarded the treaty settlement as either just or honorable, nor did they accept as normal the Dublin government's subsequent relationship with the United Kingdom and the Commonwealth, since that relationship had been adopted by the Dáil Éireann under duress.

Meanwhile, de Valera lost no time in further demonstrating the independence of action that the Judicial Committee of the Privy Council had conceded was Dublin's right under the Statute of Westminster. Under his leadership in 1935, the Dáil passed the Irish Nationality and Citizenship Act and the Aliens Act. What the first of these laws did was to define Irish citizenship so that it allowed for reciprocal citizenship between the Free State and other countries. It also repudiated the view that Irish citizens were British subjects, which occasioned yet another angry response from the Dominions secretary. The second of these laws, the Aliens Act, added insult to injury by declaring that British subjects in the Free State were aliens. Yet insofar as British subjects were exempted from the actual application of the law by an Executive Council decree, the Aliens (Exemption) Order, the London government chose not to lodge any official protest. There could be, however, no doubt about what de Valera really intended by insisting on external association with the Commonwealth rather than membership in it and by arguing for reciprocal citizenship in preference to common citizenship. In an address before the Dáil only a few months earlier, in November 1934, the Irish premier had asserted that the language of his recommended legislation would require no change whatever if the whole of Ireland were to be declared an independent republic the following day. It was an accurate enough statement, given the implications of the Free State's constitutional initiatives since 1932, but it did nothing to placate the anxious concerns of officials in London.

Throughout this period of political difficulty, the economic war between the two countries persisted. Punitive and protectionist trade policies were having a ruinous effect on the Free State economy. Irish agricultural exports, the major part of which went to Britain, fell from 35 million pounds in 1929 to just under 14 million pounds in 1935. And the cattle industry, the very lifeblood of the country's economy, was threatened with collapse. Although the economic war provided the opportunity for pursuing de Valera's cherished ambition of economic self-sufficiency, as increased tillage and expanded industrialization were undertaken, the effort proved less than successful. Even allowing for the complicating effects of the general collapse of world agriculture prices at this time, the reduced income of Irish farmers was directly attributable to British tariffs. Moreover, the economically depressed agricultural community's reduced purchasing power had a direct impact on the growth of domestic industries. Lenin once observed that facts are stubborn, and it was an incontrovertible fact that Irish exports were utterly reliant on the British market. A diligent but costly campaign by de Valera to find alternative markets for Irish products, in which subsidies and bounties were paid irrespective of the profit or loss factor, failed cataclysmically. Six years of trial and error resulted only in a very modest redirection of the Irish export trade. For example, in 1929 only 6 percent of the Irish Free State's exports went to non-British countries; by 1935 that figure had increased only to 7 percent. One object lesson that some Irishmen drew from this experience was that regardless of the political relationship between the United Kingdom and the Irish Free State, the latter simply was in no position to endure the cost of economic insularity.

Although British ministers could and did find alternative sources of foodstuffs, the United Kingdom was seriously affected by the precipitous decline in its trade with the Irish Free State. As 1934 drew to a close, it became increasingly clear that some movement toward mediation would be in the best interests of both countries. The United Kingdom could preach about the principle of treaty obligations and the Irish Free State might aspire to the ideal of national self-sufficiency, but the economic lessons of this unwelcome experience could not be ignored indefinitely.

Under the terms of the so-called coal-cattle pact, which took effect at the beginning of 1935, the British quotas on Irish cattle imports were raised a third in return for a promise by the Free State that it would purchase all of its coal from the United Kingdom. The compromise was gratefully accepted by both sides for very good reasons. The Irish cattle industry was in a state of critical decline, and the British coal market in Ireland was in peril of being lost forever. Irish representatives were already in Germany and Poland negotiating for coal and, had this undertaking resulted in a trade agreement, Irish furnaces would have had to be converted at considerable expense to accommodate a different type of coal. Such a conversion, once made, could not have been easily reversed. At stake was a British monopoly that in 1935 involved millions of tons of coal exports to the Free State per year. Following the implementation of the coal-cattle pact, the Irish Situation Committee, which had met twenty-two times from its inception in 1932 until this point in early 1935, did not convene again until May 1936. This extensive recess on the part of the British ministers serving on the committee was not indicative of any *détente* in Anglo-Irish relations but instead reflected the fact that London's attention was now increasingly preoccupied by other, perhaps more compelling, international concerns.

Throughout the months of May through December 1936, the Irish Situation Committee resumed its meetings in an atmosphere of special urgency. What particularly alarmed committee members were reports that de Valera was at work on a new constitution for the Free State and that he intended in the process to eliminate the Crown entirely from Irish domestic affairs while recognizing the king simply for external purposes. Malcolm MacDonald, who had succeeded J. H. Thomas as Dominions secretary, warned his British colleagues on May 12 that any constitution of this kind would end all hope of keeping the Free State within the empire. In a memorandum titled "Relations with the Irish Free State," MacDonald insisted that a reconciliation between the London and Dublin governments was essential to prevent the further weakening of the moral authority of the British Commonwealth in world affairs. He affirmed, however, that any satisfactory settlement would require strict adherence to two fundamental principles. First, the Dublin government would be obligated to recognize the constitutional position of the king in both the internal and external affairs of the Irish Free State. Second, a united Ireland could not be established without the consent of Northern as well as Southern Ireland. In return, as part of a comprehensive Anglo-Irish agreement, the British government would consent to the abolition of the office of governor general and to the substitution of some other formula, possibly including one in which the king himself might perform the functions of the Crown in the Irish Free State. Other concessions included the promise of ending the economic war and a British declaration affirming that the Free State was responsible for its own destiny.

What MacDonald intended was to remind de Valera that although membership in the Commonwealth was entirely voluntary and not based on compulsion, any departure from that body could make the Free State a foreign country whose citizens would then be aliens anywhere in the empire. But Attorney General Sir Donald Somervell was troubled by some of the language in the MacDonald memorandum, particularly with regard to the imprecision of Irish allegiance to the Crown, and the secretary of state for India, the marquess of Zetland, objected on the ground that any renunciation of force by Britain would make for an unfortunate precedent with regard to the empire. Complicating matters still further was the fact that other committee members, such as Sir Thomas Inskip, minister for the coordination of defense, and Walter Elliot, minister for agriculture, either supported elements of the MacDonald proposal or actually favored still greater concessions. Moreover, it was known that some of the Dominions, notably Canada and South Africa, had no objection whatever to de Valera's suggested plan of external association. Even as the committee wrestled with the problem of how best to respond to any new constitutional challenge from de Valera, events once more overtook the British government.

The abdication crisis of December 1936 caught the committee completely off guard and provided Eamon de Valera with a welcome occasion to implement his particular concept of Commonwealth association. Since Edward VIII had removed himself from the throne before de Valera had had the opportunity to remove him from the Irish constitution, the Irish premier promptly undertook to ensure that the king's successor, George VI, would represent a new reality in Anglo-Irish relations. On December 10, 1936, members of the Dáil were summoned by telegram to meet at 3 P.M. the following day for the purpose of considering, in connection with the proposed Act of Abdication, which would require action by all Dominion legislatures, two specific amendments to the Irish constitution. The two bills that the Irish premier introduced were swiftly characterized by the *Times* of London as a revival of Document No. 2, which de Valera had put forth nearly fifteen years earlier as an alternative to the Anglo-Irish Treaty. The first bill was designed to remove the Crown from the constitution of Saorstát Éireann, while the second recognized the Crown for the purposes of external relations, so long as other nations of the Commonwealth continued to recognize it as "the symbol of their cooperation."

Opposition members in the Dáil denounced the proposed legislation on the grounds that it changed the functions of kingship rather than providing for the abdication of King Edward. De Valera was also attacked for not having consulted with opposition party leaders on an important matter involving constitutional change. John A. Costello, who had served as William Cosgrave's attorney general during the last six years of the preceding Irish government, proclaimed that the new legislation would violate the Free State's pledge to the Dominions that had helped "the Irish people to achieve their freedom in the Imperial Conferences of 1926, 1929 and 1930."

What the debate really involved was a difference over symbolic interpretation between the Cumann na nGaedheal, the Centre party, and the Independents on the one side and Fianna Fáil and its Labour allies on the other. The opposition accused the government of pursuing ambivalent and contradictory policies in its simultaneous embrace of Republicanism and Commonwealth ties. If the state was already sovereign—and both the government and the opposition agreed that it was—the proposed bills could not possibly increase the power of the Saorstát Éireann. They would, however, constitute a clear breach of the 1921 Anglo-Irish Treaty and would also violate the Commonwealth principle of association in which the Crown was explicitly recognized as an integral part of the state. Opposition spokesmen in the Dáil, like Richard Mulcahy and Desmond Fitzgerald, noted that the Constitution Amendment Bill removed the king from the constitution but not from the state and that neither of the two bills dealt with the abdication of King Edward. De Valera conceded the validity of the latter argument, and on December 12 he introduced into the second bill an amendment that did in fact deal with the abdication of King Edward. But another amendment endorsed the interpretive issue on which Cosgrave's and de Valera's followers could not agree: In it the Irish premier described the Crown in the words accepted by the nations of the Commonwealth—"as the symbol of their free association"—rather than in the words employed by the bill—"the symbol of their cooperation."

When the Constitution (Amendment) Bill was moved in the Dáil on December 11, it passed, 79 votes to 54. In reporting these proceedings, the *Times* noted that the governor general's last act was thus to sign the bill that abolished his own office. In point of fact, the bill left the office of governor general in existence for the time being but rendered it functionless. The adoption of a new constitution a few months later formally abolished the office, which de Valera had already reduced to very nominal status. A far more significant measure was the Executive (External Relations) Bill, which the Dáil ratified on December 12 with the amended phrasing intact. Aside from effectively clearing the way for the Constitution of 1937, the bill allotted to the Crown a narrowly defined place and limited functions in the external field. So long as the Free State was associated

> with the following nations, that is to say, Australia, Canada, Great Britain, New Zealand, and South Africa, and so long as the King recognized by those nations as the symbol of their cooperation continues to act on behalf of each of those nations (on the advice of the several governments thereof) for the purposes of the appointment of diplomatic and consular representation and the conclusion of international agreements, the King so recognized may, and is hereby authorized to, act on behalf of Saorstat Éireann for the like purposes as and when advised by the Executive Council so to do.

Throughout the hectic months of 1936 and early 1937, Eamon de Valera devoted a good part of his time and energy to the task of crafting a new constitution for the Irish Free State. And although he did consult with different interest groups within the Irish community, notably with members of the Roman Catholic hierarchy, the Constitution of 1937 was very much de Valera's personal creation. It began with a preamble reasonably suited to a confessional state:

> In the name of the Most Holy Trinity, from Whom is all authority and to Whom, as our final end, all actions, both men and States must be referred, We, the people of Éire, Humbly acknowledging all our obligations to our Divine Lord, Jesus Christ, Who sustained our fathers through centuries of trial, . . . Do hereby adopt, enact, and give to ourselves this Constitution.

But the new constitution also reflected a Republican spirit that dated back to Wolfe Tone, whose enthusiasm for the social contract and for revolutionary France had never been shared by the Irish Catholic hierarchy. Unlike the Constitution of 1922, which embraced the conflicting constitutional doctrines of the British monarchal system and Irish Republicanism, the 1937 document clearly affirmed the concept of popular sovereignty. It was, however, a sovereignty that was to be exercised with a full awareness that ultimate authority derives from God. To this extent, the Irish Constitution of 1937 sought to reconcile the notion of an inalienable popular sovereignty with the medieval concept of a theocratic state.

There was no reference in the new Constitution to either the king or the Commonwealth. Also absent was the term *republic,* since de Valera was of the belief that such a usage could only be employed if the state had jurisdiction over the whole of Ireland. To do otherwise, he thought, would be to dishonor the martyrs of 1916 who had died for an all-Ireland republic. The name of the state was to be Éire or, in the English language, Ireland. The national territory was defined as "the whole island of Ireland, its islands and the territorial seas" but, pending the reintegration of the Six Counties, the laws of the state would apply only to the Irish Free State area. The head of state was to be a popularly elected president whose essential duties were more formal than functional. A *taoiseach,* or prime minister, would head the government, with powers and prerogatives substantially stronger than those of the president of the Executive Council under the old constitution. Despite opposition from the pro-Commonwealth Cumman na nGaedheal party, now called Fine Gael, and from the Labour party, which would have preferred a unequivocally Republican proclamation, the new constitution was approved by the Dáil on June 14, 1937, and then voted on by the electorate in a referendum that was held in conjunction with the general election conducted six weeks later on July 1. The constitution was approved, 685,105 votes to 526,945, and automatically came into force on September 29, 1937.

Even before the endorsement of the constitution by the Irish electorate, the British government had anxiously sought to anticipate the constitutional implications for the Commonwealth relationship. At a meeting of the Irish Situation Committee on June 9, which was chaired by the new prime minister, Neville Chamberlain, Dominions Secretary Malcolm MacDonald advised his colleagues that they were faced with a "choice of evils." It was difficult, MacDonald conceded, to reconcile the language of the Irish constitution with the 1926 Imperial Conference agreement on being "united by common allegiance to the Crown." It would not be inappropriate, therefore, to declare that the Free State had put itself outside the Commonwealth. But to do so, MacDonald warned, would only emphasize the division of Ireland, destroy the hope of all future settlements, leave an unfriendly country at Britain's flank, and strain London's relations with America while at the same time give encouragement to republicans in South Africa and to enemies abroad. The committee reached no agreement that day regarding the proper British response to this latest and most significant constitutional challenge from Dublin, but the general disposition clearly favored the cautious and conciliatory approach recommended by MacDonald.

THE ANGLO-IRISH AGREEMENTS OF 1938

Hence the Irish Free State, renamed Éire in the new Constitution of 1937, became a republic in everything but name. Britain was confronted with the choice of either accepting de Valera's unilateral changes or expelling Éire from the Commonwealth. If Britain chose the latter course, there was a good prospect that some of the Dominions would not follow Britain's lead in rejecting Éire and the unity of the Commonwealth would be shattered, along with much of its influence in the world. A public acceptance of external association, however, could further encourage the already awakened national aspirations of India and other British colonies and create a nightmare for the constitutional theory of the Commonwealth. The British answer was a masterpiece of political pragmatism: London chose to ignore, at least publicly, the implications of the new constitution and to maintain the fiction that Éire was still part of the Commonwealth.

De Valera decided not to challenge this British pretense, and his restraint made possible a negotiated settlement, the following year, of the six-year trade war first caused by Dublin's refusal to pay the land annuities that had been previously promised to the London government. There were, of course, reasons other than de Valera's tempered approach that help explain the ready willingness of the British to seek such an accord. Neville Chamberlain and Malcolm MacDonald, respectively, had replaced Stanley Baldwin and J. A. Thomas in the offices of prime minister and Dominions secretary. London's new leadership clearly placed a higher premium on achieving goodwill with Dublin than it did on enforcing treaty obligations, an attitude no doubt then encouraged by Adolf Hitler's increasing bellicosity. Indeed, even the British military chiefs agreed that it would be better to give up the Irish ports that de Valera wanted than to alienate the Irish at a time of such international uncertainty.

In January 1938, therefore, delegations led by Eamon de Valera and Neville Chamberlain began conferring in London. From the outset, de Valera's objectives were the abolition of partition, the transfer to Irish control of the treaty ports, and the end to duties that were crippling Irish exports. For his part, Chamberlain hoped to extract a defense agreement with the Irish in return for any British concessions.

Negotiations almost reached an impasse, however, when de Valera insisted that London abolish partition in order to end Unionist discrimination against the nationalist minority. The unification of the country, he promised, would give the British the next best thing to a defensive alliance. It would, he said, ensure that the country would not be used as a base of attack against Britain. But Chamberlain was adamant in maintaining that there could be no question of London's putting pressure on Belfast, particularly since His Majesty's government had pledged repeatedly never to allow the status of Northern Ireland to change until such time as a majority of its population so approved. Since de Valera never truly grasped the complexity of the Ulster Unionist issue, either then or later, it is not surprising that he should have acted as though partition were a problem that the British could resolve at will. He did, however, reluctantly conclude that a solution to the Northern Ireland question was not imminent, and he quickly shifted the focus of discussions to goals that were more obtainable.

The Anglo-Irish Agreements were finally signed on April 25, 1938, and were published the following day. Under the provisions of the first of these, Articles 6 and 7 of the Anglo-Irish Treaty of 1921 were abrogated. British control over the dockyard port at Berehaven and the harbor defenses in and aviation facilities near Berehaven, Queenstown (Cobh), and Lough Swilley was terminated. The second agreement effectively ended the economic war: The British dropped their demand for land annuity payments in return for an Irish payment of 10 million pounds against an initial claim of 104 million. And a third agreement provided for a trade pact under which the British market was to be opened again to Irish cattle and foodstuffs. Furthermore, Irish manufacturers were to be able to sell their products in the United Kingdom with few restrictions, while Ireland agreed only to review existing tariffs. Allowance was made for certain British goods to be given duty-free access in the Irish market, and Irish industries not yet "fully established" would continue to be given protection.

When assessing the significance of the 1938 Anglo-Irish Agreements, some historians have given more attention to the return of the so-called treaty ports than they have to the economic implications of the settlement. And that is perhaps entirely understandable. It was, after all, Britain's handing back of the ports that gave Dublin true independence of action and made neutrality achievable. And it was the later implementation of that policy that confirmed the reality of Irish sovereignty.

For Eamon de Valera, the agreements were a personal triumph. His enhanced popularity with the electorate was evident in the 1938 general election, when Fianna Fáil more than recovered the losses it had sustained in the 1937 election and was given an overall majority once more. The political leader of the antitreaty forces had achieved a new respectability in Ireland, where his dismantling of the treaty was widely acclaimed, as well as in Britain, where it was more accepted than applauded.

In 1938, however, it was neither the fear of an invasion from Nazi Germany nor the constitutional evolution from Dominion to sovereign status that most concerned the majority of people in Ireland. It was the continuing state of the national economy, which, in the opinion of some, had been grievously damaged by de Valera's handling of the trade war. What the agreements might ultimately have produced in economic terms is difficult to determine with any certitude since the Second World War intervened before any clear trends could be discerned. The apparent beneficiaries of the new trade pacts included Ireland's livestock producers, who stood to gain greater access to British markets. But London had made this concession in return for the promise that British industrial products would be given better access to the Irish market. There was, therefore, some justification to the taunts by opposition members in the Dáil who accused Fianna Fáil of moving toward free trade and of modifying its proclaimed policy of industrial protection.

To understand how dramatic was this break with the hallowed Fianna Fáil principle of self-sufficiency, it is necessary to recall the almost evangelical zeal of that party's economic nationalism. Ever since first taking office in 1932, de Valera had relentlessly promoted the creation and success of native industries that were to be protected by rigid tariff walls. True freedom, he insisted, was more than political liberty; it also meant independence from foreign economic subjugation. Sean Lemass, de Valera's chief lieutenant in industrial affairs, fought an unequal battle against the ravishes of world depression and a debilitating trade war while attempting to make Fianna Fáil's policy of economic self-sufficiency a reality. Unemployment, however, remained a serious problem, and emigration in the 1930s almost equaled that of the 1920s. But there were also some notable gains. Unemployment benefits were both extended and increased, as were old-age pensions, and beginning in 1934 there were pension provisions for widows and orphans. Perhaps most dramatic of all was the ambitious program of slum clearance and new urban housing construction that the Irish government vigorously pursued.

Why, then, did de Valera depart from his basic economic creed in the 1938 agreements? The fact is that the money needed to finance his social programs was no longer obtainable. Worse yet was the fact that the economy's failure was to some extent due to the government's protectionist policies. Severe quota restrictions on imports, together with high tariff barriers, had permitted many new firms to establish virtual monopolies in the Irish market. The result was that it was not foreign producers but Irish consumers who ended up paying higher prices for poor-quality goods in order to subsidize the new native industries. Pervasive profiteering and rampant inefficiency provoked a sense of public discontent throughout the state. It was for this reason, therefore, that Sean Lemass gave new purpose to the agreements, which were now used to prod Irish industries into becoming efficient and competitive. The Irish-Ireland quest for self-sufficiency was thus slowly but surely discarded from Fianna Fáil's ideological baggage, although no party leader would publicly admit to this for some years to come.

SOCIAL AND POLITICAL UNREST IN THE 1930s

Otherwise, however, there were not many departures from the orthodoxy of Fianna Fáil's often parochial nationalist vision. Gaelic-language promoters and Irish traditional music enthusiasts enjoyed the patronage of official government support, but music and art that reflected any hint of cosmopolitan standards met with suspicion or derision. An almost farcical air of prudery and a repressive spirit of anti-intellectualism characterized the cultural landscape of the 1930s in Ireland under Fianna Fáil. There was, for example, official criticism at this time of certain paintings on exhibit in Dublin's National Gallery because they featured nudes. And more than 1200 books and some 140 periodicals were banned by the Censorship Board in the period between 1930 and 1939. Irish writers like Liam O'Flaherty and Frank O'Connor decried these attacks against artistic expression, to no avail. Sean O'Faoláin expressed his own protest with the 1938 publication of what many believe to be his finest work, *The King of the Beggars*. In it he argued that Gaelic Ireland had died in the eighteenth century because that culture had grown weak by clinging to aristocracy and hierarchy in a world that was gravitating toward democracy. O'Faoláin dismissed the romantic vision of Irish-Irelanders, who thought in terms of ancient Celtic sagas, like Cuchulain, instead of taking their inspiration from a far more relevant model, namely, O'Connell. Modern Ireland, declared O'Faoláin, was conscious of the liberal democratic tradition that it had inherited from the Great Liberator, and it would remain an English-speaking nation in which the differing roles of church and state were subtly but irrevocably defined.

For some Irish intellectuals, like Professor James Hogan of University College, Cork, and Professor Michael Tierney, a former Cumann na nGaedheal TD (deputy member of the Dáil) and professor of Greek at University College, Dublin, such remarks were nothing less than cultural heresy. They rebuked O'Faoláin for characterizing Irish society as mediocre, occasionally neurotic, and generally disenchanted with life in the new state. Nor were such critics any more likely to find other Irish short-story writers of the 1930s and 1940s, like Frank O'Connor or Mary Lavin, any less offensive since these authors also attacked the frugal but virtuous paradise that Gaelic purists evoked as the ideal social reality for Ireland.

Hogan and Tierney were, of course, concerned with issues that went far beyond literary criticism. They were representative of a whole sociopolitical movement in Ireland whose ideological roots were grounded in the vocational ideas on social organization that were first articulated by Pope Leo XIII in his *Rerum Novarum* encyclical of 1891 and subsequently reaffirmed by Pius XI in his *Quadrageismo Anno* encyclical of 1931. Central to the beliefs of these Irish conservative activists of the 1930s was the view that both capitalism and communism were incapable of addressing the crisis then confronting European civilization. What was needed instead, they felt, was a new vocationalist order in which men and women would organize into guilds or corporations that reflected their respective vocations and professions. Government would hence reflect this vocationalist organization of society and would thereby promote social harmony by reducing the conflicts between classes and eventually between states. The idea of a corporate state appealed to right-wing nationalistic movements throughout Europe in the 1930s, and Ireland was no exception. These corporate state supporters were invariably critical of democracy for its leniency and permissiveness and were hostile toward all forms of socialism, especially communism. In Ireland, however, their propensity for conservatism and authoritarianism was further characterized by rigid Catholicism. There were similarities to be found, therefore, but also differences, between the Blueshirts in Ireland, the Blackshirts in Mussolini's Italy, and the Brownshirts in Hitler's Germany.

The Blueshirts were symbolic of the profound tensions that threatened democratic institutions in the Irish state at this time. The group began as a response to the increased activities of the IRA following de Valera's accession to power and were known initially as the Army Comrades Association (ACA). Comprised largely of ex-officers and soldiers of the Free State army, the ACA soon grew to a membership of 20,000. In February 1933 General Eoin O'Duffy was dismissed from his post as commissioner of the Civic Guards (police), and he promptly assumed the leadership of the ACA, which had begun to adopt as its uniform a blue shirt. O'Duffy changed the name of the ACA, calling it the National Guard, although the popular name for his following remained the Blueshirts. Eamon de Valera was quick to restrict parades and public demonstrations by this paramilitary organization, which, though unarmed, was perceived as a public menace. Perhaps the most surprising development in the brief two-year period of Blueshirt militancy was its alliance with W. T. Cosgrave, the leader of Cumann na nGaedheal, which had just reorganized to help form the new Fine Gael party. The Blueshirts were welcomed initially by Fine Gael politicians as protectors against the harassing tactics of IRA hooligans, but O'Duffy's men often broke the law themselves, and they ultimately became a political liability for the Fine Gael party. That fact was brought home most dramatically in 1934 when Fine Gael won only 6 out of 23 local elections, a result that at least partly reflected the disenchantment of farmers over the Blueshirts' failure to alleviate the costs of the economic war as they had promised. By mid-1934, scarcely two years from its inception, the Blueshirt movement was already in eclipse and about to pass from the political scene in Ireland.

Because O'Duffy was sympathetic to the corporatist ideas of the Italian Fascists, there is a temptation to perceive the Blueshirts as indicative of a certain amount of Irish support for that ideology. Indeed, that impression is reinforced by the fact that O'Duffy and 700 of his supporters sailed to Spain in 1936 for the purpose of fighting on the side of General Franco in the Spanish civil war. In point of fact, however, the appeal of the Blueshirt movement had far more to do with local Irish political conditions than it had with any Irish desire to imitate European fascists. Blueshirtism, therefore, was a peculiarly Irish phenomenon that did not espouse the antidemocratic beliefs of continental totalitarian movements.

Eamon de Valera successfully met the challenge to his government from the political right by preventing the Blueshirts from holding uniformed parades and by defeating their candidates at the polls. But the threat from the political left, namely, the IRA, proved to be a good deal more formidable. At first it appeared that Fianna Fáil, upon coming to power in 1932, was about to reconcile its differences with the IRA and form a cordial alliance with it. IRA prisoners were released from the jails, the organization's weekly newspaper, *An Phoblacht,* was permitted to operate once again, and the order outlawing the IRA was allowed to lapse. None of this, of course, converted any of the irreconcilable Republicans to constitutional methods, but the IRA was muted in its criticism of Fianna Fáil so long as there was a more obnoxious enemy, the Blueshirts, with which to contend. By the end of 1934, however, *An Phoblacht* was attacking de Valera with a vehemence that it had once reserved for Fine Gael and the Blueshirts. What angered the IRA was the tendency of Fianna Fáil to represent symbolic changes, such as an end to the oath or the abolition of the post of governor general, as meaningful steps toward an Irish Republic. Radical nationalists demanded instead an immediate break with the British Empire and the quick establishment of a thirty-two-county socialist republic.

IRA violence intensified in 1935, resulting in some bloodshed and death. De Valera was compelled to revive the military tribunal that he had suspended upon first taking office, and he called out against the IRA the special police that he had once used against the Blueshirts. In June 1936 the IRA was again proclaimed an illegal body, and its chief of staff was imprisoned. For a time, at least, it appeared as though de Valera had neutralized yet another paramilitary threat to the Irish state. But events soon proved otherwise.

To Sean MacBride, a former IRA chief of staff, and many of his colleagues, the 1937 constitution was an attempt to legitimize the betrayal of their sacred republic. And the 1938 Anglo-Irish Agreements provoked them still more. If de Valera had hoped that the return of the British-held ports would mollify the militant Republicans, he was wrong. The IRA condemned the agreements for having failed to deal with partition, seeing it as a further proof of the fact that only direct action could reunite the country. Shortly thereafter, British customs stations along the border came under IRA attack, and several were destroyed.

An IRA ultimatum was sent to British Foreign Secretary Lord Halifax on January 12, 1939, demanding the withdrawal within four days of all British forces, civil and military, from Irish soil. Failure to comply would have immediate consequences. The IRA neither expected nor received any response, and it soon implemented an intensive bombing campaign throughout England in the hope that it would reignite an Anglo-Irish conflict and focus world attention on the partition issue. Initially conceived as a careful strategy of sabotage against factories, communications, and power installations, it became in fact an indiscriminate attack on harmless civilian targets, with bombs being placed in mailboxes, public lavatories, and suitcases in railway depots. During the first six months of 1939 there were over 120 such incidents, resulting in the loss of one life and some fifty-five people wounded. Then came the most violent attack, the detonation of a bomb in a crowded street in Coventry, which killed five people and injured seventy others.

The IRA succeeded, if nothing else, in outraging British public opinion. Two men were hanged for their part in the Coventry explosions, and in virtually every instance IRA men were given stiff sentences whenever apprehended and found guilty. Meanwhile, Irishmen living in Britain who had been born in Ireland were compelled to register with the police or, in some cases, were sent back to their native land. No hostility was directed toward Dublin, however, as most English people recognized that de Valera was as much opposed as they were to IRA violence. Indeed, the Dáil passed the Offences against the State Act in June 1939, providing for the internment of prisoners without trial. That was followed by the Treason Act, which authorized the death penalty for acts of treason. And in January 1940 the Emergency Powers Act was passed, under which the Curragh internment camp, just west of Dublin, was opened for IRA detainees. These measures broke the back of the IRA, but they did not completely destroy that organization, which now regarded Fianna Fáil with almost the same loathing as it did the British. The years between 1940 and 1944 were the harshest times ever endured by the IRA, as detainees experienced extended imprisonment, hunger strikes, and even execution. Suppressed by the Irish government and divided by its own factionalism, the IRA was now a small and enfeebled group that had no choice but to go underground for an indefinite duration. So long as the island remained partitioned and the goal of an indivisible republic remained unfulfilled, however, the phoenixlike IRA would rise again if the time came for a new generation to take up the sacred cause.

IRISH NEUTRALITY AND THE SECOND WORLD WAR

It was the prospect of war and not Republican militancy that in 1939 began to erode the new cordiality in Anglo-Irish relations resulting from the agreements of the previous year. Tensions heightened, for example, when it appeared for a time that the British government might include Northern Ireland in a military conscription bill. Parliament's decision in May to exclude the Six Counties from the bill helped to avoid a crisis, since a violent nationalist reaction on both sides of the border would otherwise have ensued. But relations between London and Dublin became strained all the same when the Dáil enacted legislation affirming Ireland's neutrality following the German invasion of Poland on September 1. De Valera had previously and publicly declared that he would never permit the use of Éire as a base for enemy attacks on Great Britain; but he had also affirmed that Éire's cooperation with British military forces was not conceivable while Ireland remained partitioned. Despite frequent pronouncements of this kind by the Irish leader, London reacted with astonishment when de Valera remained firmly committed to neutrality even after Britain entered the war on September 3.

Partition was a real and legitimate concern of the Éire government, but de Valera also manipulated the issue for his own purposes. Throughout the war, for example, he repeatedly complained that England, not Ulster Unionists, occupied a part of Ireland. It was a clever stratagem, particularly when directed toward the significant number of Irish-Americans who, especially after Pearl Harbor, were unreservedly committed to participation on the Allied side. These people often did not fully understand the partition issue, but for many of them it somehow made Irish neutrality seem more justifiable. There was never any likelihood, however, that de Valera would join the British war effort even if London did agree to end the partition of Ireland. When emissaries from the London government offered to negotiate that eventual prospect with Dublin in the summer of 1940, they found de Valera pessimistically resigned to a Nazi victory in the war and resolutely determined not to abandon his policy of neutrality. In point of fact, de Valera had good reason to doubt whether the British were prepared to compel the entry of Irish Protestant Unionists into an Irish state.

Partition may have been a useful pretext for de Valera in propagandizing a rationale for neutrality to people abroad, but there should be no mistaking the fact that neutrality was supported by virtually every constituency in the twenty-six counties. The real reason that the overwhelming majority of Irish citizens favored that policy was that they could see no purpose being served by exposing their defenseless country to the ravages of a war that was not of their making. Moreover, many of them knew that Éire's entering the conflict on the side of Britain would provoke Republican extremists to engage in an unrelenting campaign of sabotage and guerrilla warfare. The real irony of the partition pretext is the fact that it was the availability of Northern ports to Britain that induced the London government to accept the loss of Éire's harbors and thereby respect the claim of Irish neutrality.

Precisely how much the denial of the treaty ports actually cost Britain in terms of vessels sunk by German U-boats is difficult, if not impossible, to estimate. But it should be remembered that the Germans had cracked the Royal Navy's secret code in 1936, a security breach that was not entirely remedied until 1943. Indeed, by that time the British would become far less aggressive in their representations to the Éire government on the subject of the ports, for two reasons. One is that experience in the early and critical years of the war had shown that the Irish ports simply were not as vital as was previously assumed; the other, which underscored the wisdom of de Valera's policy, was that Britain did not have the capability to defend Éire effectively if that country were also to become involved in the war. Later publication of British government records revealed that the cabinet was confidentially informed of these realities by people from the appropriate ministries. London nevertheless continued to make a public issue of the dangers posed by the loss of the Irish ports, all of which suggests that de Valera was not alone in propagandizing for foreign consumption.

Irish neutrality did not prevent individual Irish citizens from contributing to the British war effort. More than 100,000 of them worked in British munitions factories, providing the Irish with needed employment while also compensating for Britain's manpower shortages resulting from wartime conscription. Another 60,000 Irishmen volunteered for the British armed forces, 40,000 of whom crossed the border to enlist in Belfast. If Prime Minister de Valera had wished to prevent Éire citizens from joining the Royal Army, Navy, or Air Force, he might easily have followed the example of other neutral countries by passing a foreign enlistment act making it an offense, punishable by the loss of all civil rights, to join the fighting services of any of the belligerent powers. He did nothing of the kind, and all through the war, Irishmen were at liberty to join the British forces. The fact that they did so in comparatively large numbers caused de Valera no notable concern, although he doubtlessly would have preferred that the enlistments not include men on active duty in the Irish army who deserted in order to fight for Britain. At the end of 1945 it was admitted in the Dáil Éireann that some 4000 of the Irish army, about 10 percent of its total force, had deserted during the war to join British units combating the Axis powers.

There were any number of other ways in which Irish neutrality was decidedly tilted in favor of Britain. Dublin, for example, continued to supply London with crucially important meteorological reports. Two strategically located wireless direction-finding stations at Malin Head on the northern tip of County Donegal cooperated with British ships and aircraft. Irish security authorities informed their English counterparts about the activities of all aliens, particularly Germans, in Éire. The de Valera government also agreed to prohibit commercial lighting in coastal areas north of Dublin that might be used to guide German bombers bound for Belfast. Finally, the Irish permitted the use of their territory for the installation of a British radar station to track German submarines.

None of this mollified Winston Churchill, who had replaced Neville Chamberlain as British prime minister after the fall of France in June 1940. Churchill had helped to negotiate the Anglo-Irish Treaty of 1921, and he took very personally Eamon de Valera's role in unilaterally dismantling it. The personal antipathy between the two men was only compounded by Éire's proclamation of neutrality, which Churchill held to be an illegal act by a Commonwealth nation, and by de Valera's refusal to grant the British access to the treaty ports. Churchill was prepared on more than one occasion to order the seizure of the ports. He was dissuaded by the military chiefs of staff, who warned that Irish resistance would make the cost of such a seizure greater than any gain, and by cabinet colleagues, who predicted that other Dominions would denounce such an act. Even as the tide of war turned against the Germans and the threat to British security substantially diminished, Winston Churchill still fumed about the ignominy of Irish neutrality. In November 1943, for instance, noting that Éire had been excluded from a forthcoming food conference sponsored by the United Nations, Churchill told Foreign Secretary Anthony Eden, "Southern Ireland is a neutral and this is the moment to make her feel her isolation and the shameful position she will occupy at the peace."

By the following year, 1944, as the war was approaching its dramatic climax, both Washington and London became exceedingly anxious about the possibility of the Irish endangering Allied security. The American minister to Éire, David Gray, recommended that the Irish government be asked to close the Axis legations in Dublin lest they somehow compromise the D-day preparations then under way. With Churchill's encouragement and support, therefore, President Franklin Roosevelt sent Prime Minister Eamon de Valera a formal request on February 21, 1944. This communication, which is often referred to as the "American note" in accounts of this period, called for the Irish government to take appropriate steps for the recall of German and Japanese representatives in Ireland because of the opportunity they afforded for highly organized espionage at a critical juncture in the war. De Valera replied that his government had done all it could to prevent espionage against the Allies, and it could not and would not do more.

What de Valera found particularly objectionable about the American note was Roosevelt's contention that the Irish government, in spite of its declaration of friendly neutrality, had in fact pursued a policy that operated in favor of the Axis. It seems reasonable to conclude that the German government would not have shared that view. German airmen who bailed out or were shot down over Éire were interned for the duration of the war, whereas nearly all captured British servicemen were returned to their units. Furthermore, the Irish government compelled the German minister, Dr. Edward Hempel, to surrender his wireless transmitter during the war and denied Berlin's 1940 request to add two additional members to its five-man delegation in Dublin. For its part, the German government refused to accept Éire's newly appointed minister to Berlin without the usual letters of credence, which, in the existing circumstances, still needed to be signed by the British king. His Majesty could hardly be expected to accredit a minister to a power with which he was at war, with the consequence that Éire's Berlin legation was left to the supervision of a chargé d'affaires, William Warnock. And when the legation premises in the Drakestrasse were demolished by an RAF bomb in 1943, Warnock was offered no other facilities, whereupon he transferred the legation's business to a stud farm outside Berlin owned by an Irishman. There was therefore little cordiality, and still less cooperation, between the governments of Dublin and Berlin. And although there was admittedly a certain amount of German espionage, particularly in the early years of the war when some spies did parachute into Éire, it never got very far, thanks largely to an efficient Irish Secret Service and a vigilant Home Defense Force. By any fair standard of judgment, Roosevelt's contention that Irish neutrality operated in favor of the Axis was simply misinformed.

Eamon de Valera provoked another storm of protest in Britain and in the United States when, on May 2, 1945, he called on the German minister to express condolence upon the death of Adolf Hitler. Éire's secretary of the Department of External Affairs, Joseph Walshe, who accompanied de Valera for the ceremonial visit, was apprehensive about the wisdom of that gesture because he anticipated what world reaction would be. But the Irish prime minister had paid a similar visit to the American minister in Dublin upon the death of President Roosevelt a few weeks earlier, and he felt it only correct diplomatic procedure to be consistent in matters such as these.

De Valera's visit to Hempel took place just when the full horror of Buchenwald and other Nazi extermination camps was being revealed, and even those who had otherwise been sympathetic to Éire's neutrality joined in denouncing the Irish prime minister for his diplomatic courtesy on the occasion of Hitler's death. Ironically enough, it was Prime Minister Churchill who helped restore de Valera's popularity, at least among his countrymen in Éire. In his May 13 victory speech, Churchill bitterly attacked his nemesis:

> Had it not been for the loyalty and friendship of Northern Ireland we should have been forced to come to close quarters with Mr. de Valera . . . [and] though at times it would have been quite easy and quite natural, we left the Dublin government to frolic with the Germans . . . and the Japanese . . . to their hearts content.

De Valera waited four days before making a reply, and the moderate, statesmanlike tone of his address gave the Irish prime minister a psychological and moral advantage. Churchill had admitted that he would have justified violating Ireland's neutrality if Britain's necessity had so required. This was an unfortunate remark with the Nazi example so close at hand, and de Valera took full advantage of it by asking if the prime minister intended to say that if Britain's necessity became sufficiently great, other people's rights were not to count. But then de Valera went on to say,

> Mr. Churchill is proud of Britain's stand alone, after France had fallen and before America entered the war. Could he not find in his heart the generosity to acknowledge that there is a small nation that stood alone, not for one year or two, but for several hundred years against aggression . . . a small nation that could never be got to accept defeat and has never surrendered her soul?

The British representative to Éire, Sir John Maffey, advised London of the spontaneous change in the national mood in Ireland. "After de Valera's call on Hempel," Maffey wrote, "the public mind had been too stunned to react quickly, but overnight there came the collapse of the Reich and with the sudden end of censorship there came the atrocity stories and pictures of the concentration camps." To many Irishmen, de Valera's condolences to the Reich had seemed morally reprehensible, and a sense of disgust had emerged amid the growing belief that ideals had been sacrificed for symbols. But Churchill's inflammatory remarks had allowed the Irish prime minister to regain his lost prestige.

Indeed, the truth of Maffey's observation was eloquently demonstrated by R. M. Smyllie a short time later in an article for *Foreign Affairs.* Smyllie was the editor of the *Irish Times,* which was associated with both the diminishing Anglo-Irish ascendancy and ex-servicemen with pro-Unionist sympathies who regarded de Valera's ideal of a rural, frugal, self-sufficient Gaelic Ireland with much distaste. But Smyllie spoke for many Irishmen of different creeds and politics when he wrote:

> Neutrality, almost by definition, is something negative; but Mr. de Valera raised it to the dignity of a national principle, largely because he wanted to be able to prove to the world at large that, after more than seven hundred years of subjection to England, the 26 counties of Southern Ireland at last were really free.

IRISH LIFE AND POLITICS DURING THE EMERGENCY

Behind the edifice of neutrality, life in Ireland from September 1939 to May 1945 was profoundly influenced by what the Irish referred to rather quaintly as "the emergency." An outbreak of foot-and-mouth disease in 1941 decimated livestock throughout the country, and crops suffered from a scarcity of needed fertilizers. The government did sponsor compulsory wheat growing, but it was not sufficient to offset other export losses. Finance ministers also kept a ceiling on salaries in order to check inflation as costs continued to rise and the standard of living fell. Sugar, tea, and fuel were all rationed almost from the outset of hostilities, with bread and other staples being added to that list by 1942. Gas and electricity were nearly always in short supply, and coal was replaced by native peat, or turf, for most home heating. Transportation, particularly the railway system, was hard hit since machinery of all kinds was difficult to obtain and maintain. Compounding the problems of the Irish economy was the fact that the heavy fall in industrial production and the hard times suffered by the farming community contributed to record unemployment and increased emigration, mostly to Britain. It was in these dire circumstances that de Valera tapped Sean Lemass in 1940 to head the newly created Department of Supplies. Though successful in planning and providing for the country's most essential needs, efforts of this kind never did raise the economy above the subsistence level.

Ireland in the early 1940s is sometimes described as having been culturally isolated and economically destitute. But these were not new dimensions of Irish life; they had been central to the country's experience since independence in 1922. If anything, the period of the emergency provided an opportunity for national introspection and self-evaluation. The Gaelic revival movement, for instance, was called into question by teachers who saw it as an irrelevancy in the face of the unabated emigration from rural areas. The future of the Gaelic revival, therefore, would not be found in the Gaeltacht (Irish-speaking regions, principally in the south and west) but rather in urban settings, where the philosophical underpinnings of the movement could be explored by sophisticated intellectuals. It was, indeed, an evolution different from the one Douglas Hyde projected when he founded the Gaelic League.

Sean O'Faoláin remained throughout the emergency a vocal critic of Irish laws and institutions. He said of wartime Ireland, "Life is so isolated now that it is no longer being pollinated by germinating ideas windborne from anywhere." But it was O'Faoláin's remarkable periodical, *The Bell,* which he founded in 1940 and edited until 1946, that contributed so richly to the literary landscape of this era. *The Bell* was published each month in an edition of 3000 copies and contained the writings of both new and established authors. Moreover, O'Faoláin used the journal to editorialize against some of his old adversaries, including the Censorship Board and the Gaelic revival. Again and again, he condemned the provincialism and prudery that he saw in the cultural and aesthetic standards of Irish society. *The Bell* helped to promote the ideals of rational reflection and social analysis without which postwar Ireland would have been less well prepared to meet the challenge of social modernization.

There were changes too in the fortunes of the respective Irish political parties during the period of the emergency. Fianna Fáil, for example, succeeded in greatly expanding its base of support by attracting business and property interests, which

SEAN O'FAOLAIN
1900–

Sean O'Faolain has been the most important intellectual force in post-Treaty Ireland. As novelist, short story writer, literary critic, biographer, political commentator, and editor he has served as the liberal conscience of Irish nationalism. (Courtesy of the Irish Tourist Board)

had heretofore been alienated by the party's populist focus. But de Valera's repression of Republican extremists, together with the modification of his more radical policies, won him supporters from some merchants, strong farmers, and Anglo-Irish families. He was also able to use the almost universally popular policy of neutrality to good party advantage in the election of 1943, when Fianna Fáil's slogan was "Don't change horses when crossing the stream."

The war years, however, were disastrous for Fine Gael. Its brief flirtation in the early 1930s with the quasi-fascist Blueshirt movement continued to haunt the party well into the 1940s. And the popular response to de Valera's role in the Anglo-Irish Agreements of 1938 did not help either. Fine Gael was confronted with a major dilemma upon the outbreak of war. A decision to support neutrality would effectively repudiate the party's pro-Commonwealth position, but to do otherwise would go contrary to the wish of the vast majority of the Irish people. Fine Gael elected to support the national policy, resulting in the resignation of its deputy leader, James Dillon. The 1943 election represented a serious defeat in which the party lost thirteen seats and, in 1944, the Fine Gael leader, W. T. Cosgrave, retired from political life.

While Fine Gael appeared to be in serious decline, the parliamentary Labour party made a surprising advance in the election of 1943. Labour, benefiting from public disaffection with wartime shortages, increased its strength in the Dáil from nine to seventeen seats. In an election the following year, however, Labour was badly split by an internecine struggle between the moderate followers of William O'Brien and the militants led by James Larkin. As a result, Labour won only twelve seats in 1944, and even these were divided between rival factions.

A new party, Clann na Talmhan (Children of the Land), which represented essentially a farming constituency, emerged in the election of 1943. It was reflective of the general unhappiness among small farmers with Fianna Fáil's lack of farming progress, particularly in the western counties. The party won ten seats in the 1943 election but never exercised much influence in the Dáil owing to its political inexperience and to programs that had only regional interest. Clann na Talmhan had only seven seats after the election of 1948, but those were enough to win representation that year in the first interparty government. Thereafter, the party fell into permanent obscurity, but its very presence in the mid-1940s was a signal of Fianna Fáil's vulnerability.

That was not, however, the popular image of the governing party. De Valera won a strong overall majority in the election of May 1944 thanks to the split in the Labour party, the weakening of Fine Gael following Cosgrave's retirement, and the public outcry against the American note and the challenge that it represented to Irish neutrality. Indeed, Fianna Fáil appeared to be solidly entrenched as the governing party for many years to come when the war ended in 1945. Even the party's 1945 candidate for the largely ceremonial post of president, Seán T. O'Ceallaigh, won a decisive victory at the polls. Yet for a party in power, the outlook in the immediate postwar years was not promising. Imports were up, exports were down, and wages continued to be repressed by government action. Not only was there no end to the wartime restrictions and shortages, but the weather also contrived to deal the Irish economy a devastating blow. The summer of 1946 was exceptionally wet, reducing grain production and leading to bread rationing, and the severe winter of 1947, which crippled much of western Europe, caused major dislocations in Irish industry and transport. Fianna Fáil responded in 1947 with increased taxation in order to finance higher food subsidies, and that legislation contributed to a growing sentiment of discontent and frustration.

These increasingly depressed circumstances produced a political reaction that found expression in the emergence of yet another new party, Clann na Poblachta (Children of the Republic). The thrust of this movement was in the direction of social and economic reform, with a special emphasis on the Republican ambitions that Fianna Fáil had first articulated upon coming to power in 1932. The Clann na Poblachta also had a popular leader in Seán MacBride, the son of Irish actress Maud Gonne and John MacBride, an executed martyr of the Easter Rising. Many contemporary observers believed that this new party was destined to dethrone Fianna Fáil, particularly after a few by-election triumphs in 1947. De Valera decided not to allow MacBride's followers an opportunity to consolidate a national organization and hence called for an early election in February 1948.

THE IRISH REPUBLIC, 1948–1959

Fianna Fáil won the battle but lost the war with this strategy. Clann candidates gained only ten seats while Fianna Fáil, although losing its overall majority, was still by far the largest single party (68 seats out of 147). Fine Gael increased its strength but marginally, from 30 to 31 seats, with the remaining Dáil contests being won by Labour, Clann na Talmhan, and Independent candidates. So profound was the desire to oust Fianna Fáil after its sixteen years in power that these ideologically disparate parties actually succeeded in forming the coalition needed to drive de Valera from office. The post of prime minister (taoiseach) went to a distinguished Fine Gael lawyer, John A. Costello, who had served as attorney general in the Cumann na nGaedheal government of yesteryear. The Fine Gael party also claimed the ministries of finance, defense, justice, agriculture, and industry and commerce. Labour ministers were given the posts of tánaiste (deputy premier), local government, and posts and telegraphs. The ministry of lands and fisheries went to Clann na Talmhan. Finally, the new party, Clann na Poblachta, was given the respective ministries of external affairs and health. It was an improbable alliance that nonetheless managed to remain in office for three years, around the average length of time for most Irish governments since independence. Numerous reasons account for the unexpected success of the coalition, not least among them being Costello's skill as a chairman and the concern shared by all parties that de Valera might return to power.

Innovative programs were begun, including a land rehabilitation project to bring some 4 million acres back into production and an industrial development authority for the purpose of promoting and coordinating industrial expansion. New housing construction was vigorously undertaken, and national health programs were improved. Critical to the success of most of these programs, however, were the funds received from the European Recovery Program (the Marshall Plan), which Ireland had begun participation in under Fianna Fáil in 1947. The ERP provided grants and loans totaling 150 million dollars by 1950, all of which represented desperately needed capital investment even if it did cause subsequent problems with inflation.

It was perhaps inevitable that some action favoring the declaration of a republic would be forthcoming, given Clann na Poblachta's preoccupation with that subject and the coalition's dependence on Clann's ten votes in the Dáil. The initiative to repeal the 1936 External Relations Act, which had defined an ambiguous relationship with Britain and the Commonwealth, came quite naturally from Sean MacBride. But the proposal was genuinely supported by Taoiseach Costello. Costello was aware that the idea of a republic had divided Irishmen ever since the Civil War, and he believed that a resolution of the question would help to take the gun out of Irish politics. For the leader of Fine Gael, which was popularly seen as the pro-Commonwealth party, this was a statesmanlike view. There has been some controversy among historians over whether or not the Irish cabinet had agreed to repeal the External Relations Act prior to Costello's announcement to that effect while on a tour of Canada in September 1948. It now seems reasonably clear that this was a deliberative decision reached collectively beforehand. The taoiseach, however, astounded the London government when he replied in the affirmative to a news reporter who asked if the proposed act required Dublin's secession from the Commonwealth.

In November 1948 the Republic of Ireland Bill was introduced in the Dáil. The preamble explained that the status of a republic would permit the Irish president, rather than the British sovereign, to exercise executive powers or functions in connection with the state's external relations. Costello said, in the course of the debate on the bill, that the republic would put an end to the generations of alienation in Irish politics and that it would strengthen, not weaken, relations with Britain and the Commonwealth. In reply to the objection that this step would make the goal of ending partition more difficult than before, Costello held that Northern Ireland had seemed unmoved in any case by Éire's earlier restraint. The bill ultimately passed through all the stages, and it was agreed that the republic would be formally implemented on the symbolic date of Easter Monday 1949.

British Prime Minister Clement Attlee complained that he had not been given notice of the Irish government's intentions, and indeed he had not. But Attlee reciprocated the discourtesy later in 1949 at the time when the imperial parliament passed the Ireland Act, recognizing the change in Ireland's constitutional status. Without consulting Dublin, the British added a proviso that Northern Ireland would never be detached from the United Kingdom without the consent of the Northern Ireland legislature. That, of course, angered the Irish government, but this so-called guarantee to the Unionist majority in Ulster was destined to cause much regret also for future British ministers. Meanwhile, however, the most remarkable development in these events of 1949 is that the Irish demanded, and the British conceded, all the privileges that Commonwealth membership had previously afforded. Indeed, the arrangement gave new meaning to the phrase "special relationship," which is sometimes used to describe Anglo-American ties but in fact is a more appropriate description for Anglo-Irish relations since 1949.

Clement Attlee's government was no less keen than its predecessor had been about preserving the essential links of Commonwealth, but Labour ministers were perhaps more pragmatic and less sentimental when pursuing that objective. Attempts by London to draw Éire back into a closer Commonwealth relationship were unavailing precisely because the trend in Irish politics was clearly in the other direction. Nevertheless, postwar shortages and rationing in Britain prompted the Labour government to appreciate the value of Éire as a source of food and labor and as a market for British goods. It was becoming painfully apparent that the continuation of Commonwealth trade preferences to Éire were very likely to be at least as beneficial to Britain as they were to Éire.

British cabinet minutes and other documents on London's policy toward Éire between 1945 and 1949 further reveal sharp differences of opinion within the Labour leadership. Herbert Morrison, Ernest Bevin, and Harold Wilson, among others, deeply resented Dublin's repeal of the External Relations Act and believed that the end of Éire's membership in the Commonwealth must also end reciprocal citizenship rights and imperial preferences. Unlike Churchill, their objections did not relate to any romantic concerns about the sanctity of the empire but to the more materialistic issue of Britain's trade relations with other nations. Even ministers who sought accommodation with the Irish, like Lord Addison and Philip Noel-Baker, did so without any apparent affection for the Irish or for the merits of the Irish viewpoint.

London's response to the 1948 Republic of Ireland Act was initially hostile. Realizing that it was no longer possible to perpetuate the fiction that Éire had not left the Commonwealth in 1937, the British suggested to Dublin that there would be serious implications involving nationality questions and trade preferences if Ireland were to become a foreign country in relation to the Commonwealth. The Dominions, however, already worried about the negative impact that punitive measures of any kind might have on their own constituents of Irish descent, demanded that London find some way of protecting the Irish from the consequences of their own action. Even members of Prime Minister Attlee's own Labour party who represented urban constituencies with a large Irish vote spoke openly of the need for Britain to do something. London's response was decidedly innovative. Under the terms of the Ireland Act of 1949, the Westminster Parliament accorded the Republic of Ireland a "nonforeign" status that insulated the Irish in the two areas where they were most vulnerable—citizenship and trade.

The retention of Commonwealth trade preferences for Ireland was important, but so was the question of Irish citizenship, which de Valera had attempted to resolve sometime earlier with the Irish Nationality Act of 1935. But London and Dublin had never shared a common interpretation of that particular law—and not until the British Nationality Act of 1948, which was mutually agreed on by both countries, was the question put to rest. The effect of the 1948 law was that citizens of Éire, though no longer British subjects, would, when in Britain, be treated as if they were British subjects—a concession of enormous importance for the many Irish men and women living and working in Britain. Reciprocity was accorded to British subjects who, when in Ireland, would be accorded the same treatment as Irish citizens. What is sometimes overlooked, however, is the fact that there was a very real distinction in the way each country perceived this nonalien status. British subjects in Éire could not vote, hold public office, or work in the government service of Éire, whereas Éire citizens in Britain could do all of these.

Hence the British Nationality Act acknowledged Éire's symbolic need for a separate citizenship without changing its practical effects on individuals. The Republic of Ireland Act created in law what had been in fact true since the External Relations Act was passed in 1936: Éire had been a sovereign independent republic and not really a participating member of the Commonwealth since that date.

Finally, the Ireland Act also recognized the desire of the Éire government to manifest its independence from the United Kingdom and that of the Northern Ireland government to maintain its independence from Éire. British policy toward partition never changed: If the Northern and Southern Irish wished to unite into a single political entity, no obstacle would be put in their way; but no British government, not even a Labour government with a large parliamentary majority, could surrender a part of the United Kingdom against its wishes.

Domestically, the pivotal event in the history of the Costello coalition government was the ''mother-and-child scheme'' crisis. Dr. Noel Browne, Clann na Poblachta minister of health, had made impressive strides toward improving the quantity and quality of Irish health care. A former tuberculosis victim himself, Browne labored diligently to institute a comprehensive program of X-ray diagnosis, increased and improved sanitarium facilities, and routine vaccinations for schoolchildren in what proved to be a highly successful war on that disease. He was also interested in lowering the high infant mortality rate in Ireland.

In 1951 the coalition presented to the Dáil a bill sponsored by Browne that called for a national prenatal and postnatal health program. It specifically provided for, among other things, maternity treatment and medical attention for children up to the age of 16 free of charge and without a means test. The Irish Medical Association quickly denounced the scheme as a step toward socialized medicine and further objected that it would interfere with the doctor-patient relationship. Catholic bishops joined in the attack, claiming that the right to provide for the health of children belongs to the parents, not the state. These clerics were especially opposed to the proposal that local medical officers should instruct women and girls in sex education, a proposal that might well lead to birth control and abortion. Browne then went to considerable lengths to ensure that the program would in no way be in conflict with Catholic teaching. The bishops were unmoved, however, and Costello informed Browne that the government could not endorse a program that the bishops found objectionable. But Browne stood his ground until he was told to resign by his own party chief, Sean MacBride. The controversy became a national scandal when Browne then released the correspondence on the affair to the press. Lamenting the loss of the talented and dedicated cabinet minister and physician, *The Irish Times* remarked: ''The most serious revelation however is that the Roman Catholic Church would seem to be the effective government of this country.''

Browne's removal from office and the abandonment of his proposed scheme were no more the exclusive consequence of episcopal politics than was Parnell's repudiation in 1891. Some members of the hierarchy, particularly Archbishop John McQuaid of Dublin, admittedly did engage in questionable pressure tactics. But there were other reasons for Browne's defeat, such as the opposition of the Irish Medical Association and the growing estrangement between Browne and some of his colleagues who doubted that the scheme was financially viable. Nevertheless, people resented the intrusion of the bishops and priests in what they considered essentially a secular matter. The coalition government fell because of defections resulting from Browne's departure from office. Fianna Fáil then returned to power, and after negotiating mutually acceptable terms with the hierarchy, de Valera won passage of a health act that retained much of Browne's original proposal. Perhaps the most salutary effect of this first church-state crisis since independence was that it was also the last one. The bishops were quick to realize that although the populace respected their moral authority in what were truly episcopal affairs, the Irish would not permit a clerical veto over the proper functioning of liberal democracy.

Fianna Fáil floundered as a minority government from 1951 to 1954, whereupon de Valera was forced to call another general election. The balloting resulted in Costello heading a second coalition administration. But the 1950s were a dismal economic period irrespective of which party was in power as inflation, increased taxation, and trade imbalances continued to hound Costello as they had de Valera. Perhaps the most noteworthy event came in 1955, when the Soviet Union, in a compensatory deal worked out with the West, agreed not to veto again Ireland's admission to the United Nations. The Dublin government, which had previously refused to join the North Atlantic Treaty Organization so long as partition existed and the British remained a NATO member, made clear that UN membership represented no departure from the Irish policy of neutrality.

This was also a time of IRA resurgence. A new generation of young nationalists had grown up in a country that had been insulated not only from war but also from prosperity and hope. The 1949 declaration of the Republic had still left a truncated country, and the boredom and frustration of a stagnant economy caused much discontent. The IRA leadership, strengthened with fresh recruits, began a Northern campaign in the closing months of 1956. When raids were subsequently conducted against police barracks across the border in the Six Counties, Taoiseach John Costello responded by pledging the full resources of the state to halt the campaign of violence. That provoked Sean MacBride to renounce the government and to take the tiny Clann na Poblachta party out of the ruling coalition on the argument that Costello offered no alternative of his own for ending partition. Beset by political defections and economic decline, the government fell only to be replaced by a resurgent Fianna Fáil, which won seventy-eight seats and thereby held a comfortable overall majority of ten. This 1957 election was to inaugurate yet another sixteen-year reign for Fianna Fáil. And although de Valera had been returned once more as taoiseach, he stepped down two years later, in 1959, to become his party's successful candidate for president of the Republic.

This marked the end of a remarkable era in Irish politics. De Valera was now 77 years old and almost totally blind, but he was destined to have two presidential terms. He was reelected in 1966 and served with distinction in his nonpolitical and ceremonial post until 1973 when, at the age of 91, he retired to private life. Although he lived another two years, into his ninety-third year, and died on August 29, 1975, the age of de Valera in Irish politics effectively ended in 1959.

CHAPTER 14

Modern Ireland, 1959–1988: Adjusting to a European Future

ABANDONING ECONOMIC SELF-SUFFICIENCY

Sean Lemass succeeded de Valera as the new parliamentary leader of Fianna Fáil and taoiseach. He came to power at a time when a new generation of voters were obviously bored with the old quarrels between the veterans of the treaty debate and the Civil War. These people aspired to the lifestyle then being enjoyed by an increasing number of Americans and Europeans. They wanted to join the mainstream of Western culture and to enjoy the comforts and luxuries that derive from modern technology.

Lemass responded to these new aspirations. Abandoning the self-reliance of Sinn Fein economic nationalism and de Valera's frugal-comfort idealism, T. K. Whitaker, the secretary of the department of finance, began a campaign to lure foreign investments into the Irish economy. Some of the strategies employed were offers of tax exemption, land and financial grants for factory location and construction, and an emphasis on the availability of cheap labor. Companies from all over the Western world and Japan accepted the advantageous Irish offer and set up factories and plants, which, in time, diminished unemployment and drastically reduced the tide of emigration.

Between 1959 and 1966, therefore, Sean Lemass presided over a miniature industrial revolution as foreign investment increased substantially and Irish exports expanded dramatically. In 1961 the Dublin government sought to obtain membership in the European Economic Community (Common Market) but allowed the application to lapse when French President Charles de Gaulle vetoed British entry in 1963. So dependent were Irish producers on the British market that it made no sense for Ireland to join the EEC if Britain were to be kept out. By 1971, however, the British and Irish were again debating the merits of Common Market membership in terms of what was now seen as their "European destiny." In Ireland, that resurrected the old arguments regarding Irish Ireland and Irish economic self-sufficiency, but since British entry was now assured, proponents of membership warned against the dangers of being excluded from the powerful and prosperous European trading bloc. A national referendum was held in 1972 during which no fewer than four out of every five voters favored joining the EEC. Ireland subsequently became a member on January 1, 1973.

Dublin, of course, had begun moving away from the shelter of tariff walls into wider trade structures almost a decade earlier. The Irish had participated in the Kennedy Round of general tariff reductions and had in December 1965 entered into a free trade agreement with Britain. This pact represented a major breakthrough whereby London abolished virtually all restrictions on Irish imports in return for a dismantling of tariff barriers on British goods and an end to tax incentives and subsidies for foreign investors over a period of fifteen years. Membership in the EEC, however, did not bring the immediate profits expected earlier by the farming community. The Irish economic boom, like that of the rest of the West in the 1970s, broke on the rock of inflation. Hardest hit were the poor, whose wages simply did not keep pace with price increases. Even tourism, which had emerged in the 1960s as Ireland's most important economic activity after agriculture, suffered from the OPEC oil boycotts and the general decline in the world economy. Without the generous incentives of earlier years, and disenchanted by the lack of energy and initiative among some members of the Irish labor force, foreign industries began shutting plants down by the late 1970s and early 1980s. Ireland, a society that already had the fastest-growing population under the age of 30 in western Europe, witnessed once again the frustration of high unemployment and the sorrow of involuntary emigration. Making matters more difficult was the fact that one popular option for earlier emigrants, settling in America, was no longer readily available because of the quotas established by Congress in the 1960s for all foreign nationals seeking admission to the United States. Many Irish citizens came to America anyway, ostensibly as visitors, and have remained as illegal aliens. The plight of these people in the late 1980s, and the prospect of many more to come during the 1990s, poses a serious obstacle to harmonious relations in the future between Dublin and Washington.

Irish foreign policy has always accommodated itself to shifting economic, cultural, and social climates. After being admitted to the United Nations in 1955, Ireland was capably represented by articulate diplomats who condemned imperialism and who often acted as spokesmen for Third World victims of Western colonialism. Irish envoys, like Conor Cruise O'Brien, felt that the history of their own country made them the natural allies of oppressed and disenfranchised people. Their conduct at the UN often infuriated Catholic bishops in Ireland and in the United States, as in the instance of Ireland's initial willingness to discuss the entry of Communist China into that world organization. But the increasing interdependence of Irish trade with that of the West led inevitably to more cautious positions, as was evidenced by the Irish vote against the admission of mainland China to the UN in 1962. Indeed, Minister for External Affairs Liam Cosgrave made it abundantly clear that Ireland's opposition to imperialism did not extend to national liberation movements that were either Soviet-inspired or otherwise incompatible with progressive Western positions. Indicative of that sentiment is the fact that of the forty-four roll call votes taken in the eleventh plenary session of the General Assembly, a period during which Cosgrave headed external affairs, thirty-nine of those cast by Ireland coincided directly with those of Britain and the United States. What was often insufficiently appreciated by some officials in London and Washington, of course, was the fact that Western interests could be better served by an Ireland that had influence with Third World countries precisely because of its nonalignment in the world arena. Surely this can be seen in the popularity and effectiveness of Irish soldiers on UN peacekeeping missions for three decades in the Middle East, the Congo, Cyprus, and elsewhere.

NEW CHALLENGES AND OPPORTUNITIES

Perhaps the boldest initiatives undertaken by Fianna Fáil Taoiseach Sean Lemass were his meetings with the reformist Prime Minister Terence O'Neill of Northern Ireland, first in Belfast and then in Dublin, during January and February 1965. It marked the first time that any head of government from the South had had official talks with his Northern counterpart on Irish soil. For a time it appeared as though the meetings might help to normalize relations between the two governments and lead to increased cross-border cooperation. But in 1966 the celebrations to mark the fiftieth anniversary of the 1916 uprising were used in the North by nationalist and Unionist extremists alike as an occasion for resuming intercommunal tensions. Lemass retired from office later that year and was succeeded by Jack Lynch, who also met with O'Neill in a second round of shuttle summitry between Belfast and Dublin during December 1967 and January 1968. By that time, however, the civil rights agitation in Northern Ireland had begun to imperil Terence O'Neill's political fate and to lessen the prospects for any further progress in North-South discussions.

Jack Lynch led Fianna Fáil to a triumphant victory in the general election of 1969. Yet gaining a majority of seats in the Dáil did not mean that the party was spared serious challenges. A somewhat self-inflicted Fianna Fáil crisis was Lynch's May 1970 firing of two of his senior ministers, Charles Haughey and Neal Blaney, who were later arrested on charges of conspiring to import arms and ammunition for the IRA into Northern Ireland. A third minister, Kevin Boland, resigned in sympathy. Haughey and Blaney were later acquitted of the charges, and Haughey went on to become leader of the Fianna Fáil party and taoiseach of the Republic in the 1980s. But the incident illustrates all the same how corrosive the Ulster question had become for the political environment in the Irish state.

Dissatisfaction over the government's Northern Ireland policy, or lack thereof, may have been part of the reason why the electorate turned against the Fianna Fáil party in the general election of March 1973, but inflation and rising prices were also the cause of much unhappiness. After sixteen years in power, there was against Fianna Fáil the same sentiment as had been evident in the 1948 election: the desire for change simply for its own sake. In any event, Fine Gael and Labour were able to agree on a fourteen-point program that carried them to power. Fine Gael leader Liam Cosgrave and Labour leader Brendan Corish then became taoiseach and tánaiste in yet another attempt at coalition government.

Despite the failure of various British attempts to devise a power-sharing plan for Unionists and nationalists in Ulster, the tenor of Anglo-Irish relations improved during the early years of Prime Minister Liam Cosgrave's term in office. Indicative of the ecumenical spirit of the time was the popularity of President Erskine Hamilton Childers, a Protestant, whose appeal for sectarian harmony and moderation struck a responsive chord within the Republic. Childers, a peace-loving man who died in November 1974, would have been appalled and dismayed by the July 21, 1976, assassination in Dublin of British ambassador Christopher Ewart-Biggs and by the bombing of a Dublin courthouse a few weeks later. Despite denials of responsibility by the "official" and "provisional" branches of the IRA, the government of the Irish Republic promptly declared a state of emergency. The Dáil then introduced two bills that increased the powers of the police in combating IRA activities and provided more severe penalties for membership in the IRA and other subversive organizations.

The coalition government of Fine Gael and Labour had been in office for over four years when Taoiseach Liam Cosgrave called for an election in 1977. Fianna Fáil, led by former taoiseach Jack Lynch, campaigned against taxation programs, poor employment prospects, and the growing crime rate. The party also promised to abolish the motor tax and to increase the level of tax-free earnings. It was a platform that appealed to the electorate; Fianna Fáil won 84 of the 148 seats in the Dáil, and Lynch's new government took office in July 1977.

The February 1978 budget completed the implementation of the campaign promises that Fianna Fáil had made prior to the election, and the Republic, for a short time anyway, appeared to be enjoying an economic boom. But soon the spiraling cost of housing and trade union demands for substantial wage increases prompted the Lynch government to issue a green paper calling for a curb to public expenditure and greater restraint in wage demands. The Irish Congress of Trade Unions and the government took to issuing charges against each other as the economy began progressively to deteriorate.

An economic challenge of another kind confronted Dublin when pressure mounted within the Irish Republic to join the European Monetary System. Mindful that bank interest charges and the earnings from Irish trade with the continent were affected by British industrial difficulties and, occasionally, by the political needs of the British government, Irish public opinion strongly favored entry into the EMS. After five years of beneficial EEC membership, many Irish nationals could see little reason why their agriculture-based economy should be conditioned by the notably different problems and interests of the United Kingdom. In the closing weeks of 1978, therefore, the Republic made its historic bid to "break with sterling." The actual transition, however, was delayed when the EMS members failed to produce the 650 million pounds in grants over five years that Ireland required. In March 1979 the long-awaited break between the Irish and British currencies was accompanied by a decline in the Irish pound to an exchange rate of 88 pence sterling by midsummer. A strike by postal workers also deprived the country of mail collections and deliveries for five months, and the international oil crisis caused severe gasoline shortages throughout the Republic. Contrasting strongly with the problems and tensions of the year was the national euphoria that greeted Pope John Paul II at the end of September. At least 300,000 people attended the appearances of His Holiness at Drogheda, Galway, Limerick, and the Marian shrine at Knock in County Mayo. And an estimated congregation of 1.3 million attended a mass celebrated by the pontiff in Dublin's Phoenix Park.

Virtually everyone was surprised by Prime Minister Jack Lynch's sudden resignation on December 5, 1979, and the quick succession of Charles Haughey as taoiseach and leader of the Fianna Fáil party. Haughey began his term in office by appealing for national understanding of the country's economic ills. An agreement was reached in October between the government, the unions, and the employers for a 15 percent pay increase over a fifteen-month term. Meanwhile, Haughey and British Prime Minister Margaret Thatcher paid each other official visits in London and Dublin, and relations between the two countries became unexpectedly cordial in the first year of the new taoiseach's term. In the autumn of 1980, Brian Friel's play *Translations* began its Dublin run and was hailed by some critics as the finest Irish drama in a generation. The theme of the play, a culture clash between Irish and English attitudes in nineteenth-century Donegal, had a special significance for everyone who had endured the Northern Ireland tensions of the 1970s.

Unionist alarm in Ulster over the undisclosed discussions between London and Dublin induced Prime Minister Thatcher to affirm again Britain's resolve that the people of Northern Ireland would never be compelled to join the Republic against their will. The reaction in the South to that affirmation, combined with Dublin's deteriorating economy, did not favor Charles Haughey, who chose the spring of 1981 to call for a general election. Fianna Fáil's substantial majority was converted into a minority of 78 seats in the new 166-seat Dáil (which had been expanded to reflect the population increase of the 1970s), and Fine Gael won 65 seats in that balloting. That was far short of a majority, but Fine Gael was able to forge a coalition with the Labour party and four independent deputies. Fine Gael leader Dr. Garret FitzGerald, who took office on June 30, brought to the premiership a reputation for integrity and competence as one of the country's leading economists. FitzGerald soon embarked on a crusade for constitutional reform within the Republic, the purpose of which was to delete the elements of the Republic's constitution that Northern Protestants found distressing. At issue were factors encompassing family law, especially the prohibition against divorce in the Republic, and nationalist aspirations, such as the constitution's claim to jurisdiction over "the whole island of Ireland." Opposition in the Dáil to these initiatives was vocal and spontaneous, but that did not prevent FitzGerald from paying a call to No. 10 Downing Street in November. Following their meeting, the British and Irish prime ministers announced the creation of an intergovernmental council to advise both governments on matters of common concern.

By any standard, 1982 was a momentous year in the political life of the Irish Republic. On January 27 the Fine Gael coalition government fell when an independent deputy refused to support a budget proposal to tax clothing and footwear. In the general election that followed, neither major party gained a majority, but Fianna Fáil was able to come to power when smaller groups, such as the Socialist Workers' party, gave it their support. Accordingly, Charles Haughey was returned to office as taoiseach on March 9. Haughey was soon involved in a dispute with the United Kingdom over EEC agricultural policy, and he later rejected a London proposal for a new assembly in Northern Ireland. What outraged the British most, however, was the Irish government's response to what London regarded as Argentinian aggression in the Falkland Islands (called the Malvinas by Argentina). Dublin called on the UN Security Council to end hostilities in the South Atlantic and, together with Italy, subsequently refused to renew EEC sanctions against Argentina.

Anglo-Irish relations, which earlier had been strained by London's tough stance toward the hunger strikers in Northern Ireland, were aggravated still further by the occasion of Prime Minister Haughey's visit with President Ronald Reagan at the White House on St. Patrick's Day. After inviting the president to pay an official visit to Ireland, Haughey publicly called on the United States to encourage Britain to take a more positive attitude toward Irish unity. Reagan remained diplomatically noncommittal while Margaret Thatcher silently fumed in London.

But 1982 was also the year in which Ireland celebrated the centenaries of the birth of its most of distinguished writer, James Joyce, and statesman, Eamon de Valera. There was also much jubliation throughout the country when the Irish rugby team won the Triple Crown for the first time since 1949 by defeating Scotland 21–12. And late in November, RTE (Irish television) and FR3 (a French channel) began transmitting the first episodes of the jointly produced television version of Thomas Flanagan's novel *The Year of the French*.

Economic woes and a ministerial scandal involving the resignation of the attorney general led to a vote of no confidence in the Haughey government on

November 4, thus requiring a third general election in less than eighteen months. In the subsequent balloting, Fianna Fáil won 75 seats in the Dáil, but Fine Gael picked up 70 and, together with Labour's 16, was able to form a coalition on a program of national recovery. It was not the economy, however, but the issue of abortion that now challenged Taoiseach Garret FitzGerald. Mother Teresa of Calcutta had addressed a capacity crowd in Dublin's national stadium during the month of August, lending her support to those opposed to abortion. Both the Fine Gael and Fianna Fáil parties were strongly pressured into supporting a constitutional amendment that would outlaw abortion in the Republic, but FitzGerald wished to have it worded in such a way as not to give offense to the Protestant community. Fianna Fáil insisted on more categorical language, and thanks to some Fine Gael defections, the Fianna Fáil version prevailed in the Dáil and was subsequently put to the people in a referendum. Meanwhile, the Irish Labour party condemned the amendment, and many academics, professional people, feminist leaders, and various other groups, including some who opposed abortion but saw no virtue in prohibiting it in the constitution, formed a vocal opposition. It was all to no avail, however, for the eighth amendment to the Irish constitution carried the referendum, held on September 7, 1983, by a wide margin (841,233 votes to 416,136). It reads:

> The state acknowledges the right to life of the unborn, and with due regard to the equal right to life of the mother, guarantees in its laws to respect, and as far as practicable, by its laws to defend and vindicate that right.

This was a personal rebuff for Taoiseach FitzGerald, who had previously announced that he would vote against the amendment. Reaction among Ulster Protestant leaders, as he had expected, was sharply critical. Yet for a year that began with a January scandal involving the unauthorized telephone bugging of certain journalists and politicians, leading to the resignation of the Garda commissioner, even the divisive issue of Northern Ireland might have been a welcome distraction from the taoiseach's domestic woes. In March 1983 the Irish government, for the first time in its history, boycotted New York's St. Patrick's Day parade to protest the appointment of a pro-IRA activist as grand marshal of that event.

SOCIAL AND POLITICAL ADJUSTMENTS TO THE NEW REALITIES

This was also a time of profound social change in the Republic, and the new militancy toward the Northern question and the debate over abortion and other moral issues were indicative of that fact. Still, for all its problems, life in Ireland had become notably better than it had been for generations. To be sure, the changes in Irish society over the past twenty to thirty years have been nothing less than revolutionary. Television has clearly been a catalyst in this transformation. Viewers in Dublin were receiving BBC transmissions as early as 1953, and Irish newspapers soon began publishing that network's program schedule for the convenience of subscribers. Telefís Éireann, which began broadcasting in 1962, gave further impetus to the interest in the new medium, and by the mid-1960s there were no fewer than 350,000 sets in the slightly less than 700,000 households in the Republic. By that time a good number of viewers could get the two principal British channels, ITV and BBC, in addition to the Irish station, RTE. Anglo-American values and lifestyles, wholly alien to the traditional values fostered heretofore by both church and state in Ireland, began to have an effect on Irish viewers.

Cinema censorship was made considerably more liberal after the establishment of the Films Appeal Board in 1964. Three years later the Censorship of Publications Act limited to twelve years the period for which a book might be banned, and although the prohibition could be renewed at the end of that time, the effect of the act was to release 5000 suppressed titles at a single stroke. Nudity in magazines or on the stage encountered greater difficulty, but there, too, the earlier restraints gave way by the late 1970s and 1980s. Contraception and other issues of sexual morality were now as likely to be discussed on talk shows in Dublin as they were in London. The inhibitions of a more parochial era were gradually being shorn away.

The 1960s, 1970s, and 1980s also witnessed sweeping changes in the Roman Catholic church in Ireland. Pope John XXIII and the Second Vatican Council set in motion a revolution of change no less significant than the one that accompanied the changes in Irish cultural and social mores. Some of the changes were liturgical, as in the instance of Latin being replaced by the vernacular and in the discontinuance of lenten and eucharistic fasts and abstention from meat on Fridays. Other changes were ecumenical, allowing for joint religious services with Protestants and for attendance at non-Catholic weddings and funerals. The surrender of so much traditional authority may have been consistent with the societal changes of the day, but it also had an impact on new religious vocations in Ireland. Despite the growth in overall population during this period, the number of seminarians studying for the priesthood fell more than 50 percent between 1959 and 1972. Some of this, of course, may have been due more to increased socioeconomic mobility than to uncertainty over changes in the church, but the effect was to diminish religious vocations in a nation that had once sent missionaries to virtually every part of the world. A Catholic ethos still pervades the country, however, despite the appearance of greater secularization in Ireland; as in the hierarchy's removal in 1970 of the ban prohibiting Catholics from sending their children to Trinity College, Dublin under pain of excommunication, or the 1972 national referendum which removed the special status of the Church (article 44) from the constitution.

The year 1984 witnessed the June visit to Ireland by U.S. President Ronald Reagan. Reagan was only the second foreign guest ever (President John Kennedy was the first, in 1963) to be given the honor of addressing a joint session of the Irish Parliament (Oireachtas). In his remarks, Reagan reviewed East-West relations but also took note of the violence in Northern Ireland and condemned terrorism. There was little comparison between the Kennedy and Reagan visits, however, other than the parliamentary address. While Kennedy, who was universally popular throughout Ireland, had generated a devotional fervor approaching that of a religious pilgrimage, Reagan's visit was marred by public protests against American foreign policy and a boycott by some faculty and students on the occasion of the president's receiving an honorary degree at University College, Galway.

With the advent of 1985, inflation in Ireland was brought down to one of the lowest levels in Europe, but the means by which that was accomplished—the stabilization of prices—resulted in record unemployment. FitzGerald's efforts to guide the Irish economy away from the shoals of recession was further handicapped by declining international demand for microchips, which prompted several foreign manufacturers to leave Ireland. Equally debilitating was the cost of foreign borrowing, which continued to expend resources that might otherwise have funded investment in the Republic. This was also the year in which social activists confronted the Roman Catholic Church once more, this time in support of a limited liberalization of the law relating to the availability of contraceptives. Archbishop of Dublin, Dr. Kevin McNamara, denounced this move, as well as the attempt by activists to remove the constitutional ban on divorce. African famine relief, however, was a cause that engendered little dissent in Ireland, and Dublin rock star Bob Geldof conceived and led the Live Aid effort in which the Republic made the biggest financial contribution proportionate to population (8 million Irish pounds from a population of 3.5 million) of any country in the world.

Perhaps the greatest accomplishment of this particular FitzGerald administration was the Anglo-Irish Agreement of November 1985, which will be discussed in Chapter 15. The popularity of the Fine Gael government, together with the difficulties then being encountered by Fianna Fáil, gave the impression that FitzGerald would be reelected easily in the next balloting, which could be held no later than in the autumn of 1987. The defection of Fianna Fáil members of the Dáil to the newly founded right-wing party, the Progressive Democrats, seemed to suggest the imminent decline of Charles Haughey's political party. Garret FitzGerald, however, was the unlikely savior of Fianna Fáil owing to his persistent attempts to liberalize the laws and the constitution to make them more suitable to a modern pluralist society.

It was FitzGerald's coalition partner, the Labour party, that actually precipitated the sudden change in political climate. Labour had been urging the removal of the constitutional ban on divorce for some time, and FitzGerald thought the moment propitious because he mistakenly read public opinion as having swung in favor of the reform. The government therefore brought forward a proposed amendment to the constitution that provided for divorce in cases where a marriage had irretrievably failed for at least five years. Protestant churches endorsed the proposed bill, but Roman Catholic bishops said that the experience of divorce laws in other countries counseled against emulating that example. Some priests and conservative laymen went still further and warned that divorce would subvert the rights of the spouse and children of the first marriage, in addition to complicating the operation of traditional inheritance laws. A referendum was held on June 6, 1986 in which nearly 60 percent of the electorate voted, and of them, 64 percent rejected the amendment. It was another setback for Garret FitzGerald and another cause for concern throughout the Protestant community on both sides of the border.

Charles Haughey and Fianna Fáil captured control of the twenty-fifth Dáil in a general election on February 17, 1987, in which 76 percent of the electorate voted. Fianna Fáil won a commanding 81 seats, Fine Gael captured only 51, and the remaining seats were divided among the Progressive Democrats (14), Labour (12), the Worker's party (4), Independents (3), and the Democratic Socialist party (1). On October 9, 1987, Haughey announced the most dramatic domestic initiative in many years: the Program for National Recovery. Designed to put Ireland's economy back on a path of long-term and sustained growth, the plan was a product of several months of negotiation among the Dublin government, the Irish Congress of Trade Unions, the Confederation of Irish Industry, the Construction Industry Federation, and the farming organizations. One major objective of the plan is the creation of no fewer than 20,000 extra jobs by 1998.

Haughey's blueprint for an economic miracle also involves the toughest program of cuts in public expenditures that Ireland has had in thirty years. Indeed, the government's retrenchment has been harsher than anything imagined in the proposals that drove Fine Gael from power in early 1987. Some of Fianna Fáil's traditional constituencies, such as health, education, and the construction industry, have been among the areas hardest hit. The taoiseach's nonpartisan approach left Alan Dukes, who succeeded to the leadership of Fine Gael following FitzGerald's resignation, with no choice but to support the government. To do otherwise would have made the opposition party appear uncommitted to solving the nation's financial problems.

No Irish government in recent times, however, has been able to afford the luxury of ignoring the Northern issue for very long. The savage kidnap of Dublin dentist John O'Grady and the escapades of the self-styled "Border Fox" Dessie O'Harie were but two of many stories in the Irish press during 1987 that focused on the activities of Republican terrorists. And the mindless bombing deaths of eleven civilians at a November Remembrance Day service in Enniskillen provoked such intense feelings of guilt and disgust that few protested the infringement on civil liberties when some 50,000 homes in the Republic were searched. Moreover, what had begun as a cautious attempt at Anglo-Irish *glasnost* following the Hillsborough Accord of 1985 suddenly became unhinged in 1988. A succession of British missteps on Northern Ireland contributed to the impression in the Republic that Prime Minister Margaret Thatcher was not, after all, truly serious about her pledge to work with Dublin for justice in the Six Counties. If that suspicion on the part of some should become a conviction on the part of many, people in the Irish Republic may find themselves caught up in events that lead not to the heights of economic recovery but rather to the depths of the Northern quagmire.

CHAPTER 15

The Northern Specter, 1920–1988: A Continuing Crisis in the Conflict of Cultures

BACKGROUND

From its inception, Northern Ireland made little sense as a geographic entity (it covers an area of 5276 square miles, only slightly more than the state of Connecticut's 4899 square miles) or as a cultural community. During the 1912–1914 Home Rule crisis, British politicians decided that their most feasible option was to partition Ireland if nationalist demands and Unionist anxieties were to be mollified. These ministers concluded that it would be unjust to place a 25 percent Protestant minority in an Ireland controlled by a 75 percent Catholic majority. So they passed the 1920 Government of Ireland Act, which not only partitioned the country but also left a Six County northern state in which a 33 percent Catholic minority was placed under the domination of a 66 percent Protestant majority.

London had never intended to include only counties with Unionist majorities. Tyrone and Fermanagh were made a part of the new state of Northern Ireland despite their nationalist majorities for two reasons: It was hoped that an area large enough to make the North economically and politically viable would help to pacify the Protestant Unionists and that the security provided by the latter's two-to-one majority over the Catholic nationalists would produce a tolerant government that would seek to conciliate and integrate the minority. Both hopes proved ill-founded. Ulster Unionists had never asked for Home Rule and ultimately accepted it only because it was preferable to a united Ireland. For their part, the Catholic minority in Northern Ireland was committed to the values and destiny of Irish nationalism.

Both sides are therefore to blame for the early failure of the Ulster experiment. Catholics simply did not reconcile themselves to permanent inclusion in a remnant of the United Kingdom and felt betrayed by their exclusion from the long-awaited Irish nation. Their militancy against the local parliament at Stormont, just outside Belfast, gave even moderate Unionists little encouragement for believing that cooperation with Catholic nationalists was at all possible. The schism between the two communities was not helped by Sir James Craig, the first prime minister of Northern Ireland, who then proceeded to announce that the Six Counties would be a Protestant nation for a Protestant people. Whether or not the outcome might have been different had the Catholic minority shown itself capable of functioning as a loyal parliamentary opposition is difficult to say, but there is no denying the fact that Northern Ireland adopted statutes and policies that quickly relegated Catholics to second-class citizenship.

Prime Minister Craig, for example, sought and obtained British permission to scrap the proportional representation features of the Better Government of Ireland Bill. And his successor, Sir Basil Brooke, once advised Protestants not to employ Catholics as a way of driving them out of the Six Counties. Moreover, while the Westminster and Stormont franchises were both based on democratic British election practices, Catholics in Northern Ireland were routinely denied fair representation in local government through gerrymandering, household suffrage, and plural votes for business property. The consequence was that even in places where they were a majority, Catholics did not control county, town, or urban councils. In Londonderry, for instance, Catholics constituted a two-thirds majority of the population, but there were twelve Protestants and eight Catholics on the city council. This absence of local influence was even more damaging to Catholic interests than was their minority position at Stormont because it was local government authorities who allocated jobs, housing, and social welfare.

Because politics in Northern Ireland has been rooted in sectarian distinctions rather than in attitudes toward social and economic issues, democracy as majority rule cannot work there. Since 1920, Northern Ireland has functioned as a one-party state. The vast majority of Protestants have been uncritically and unreservedly loyal to a Unionist party under the dictation of the Orange Lodges. In its economic development programs, the Stormont government ignored the Catholic districts west of the Bann River, resulting in chronic Catholic unemployment of close to 40 percent in that area.

Six County Catholics have had good reason to believe that they are victims of an authoritarian system. In addition to the overwhelmingly Protestant Royal Ulster Constabulary, the Stormont government created the armed and exclusively Protestant B-Special force to supplement the regular police. To Catholics, oppressed by B-Special arrogance, brutality, and bigotry, these sectarian paramilitary enforcers of law and order were the gestapo of the Orange police state. The work of the RUC and the B-Specials was made easier by the Special Powers Act, which permitted authorities to arrest and imprison suspected nationalist enemies of the state without ordinary legal procedures and to detain them in jail for an indefinite period without trial.

Inferior educational opportunities plus government and employer discrimination policies have meant that Catholics carry the largest burden of poverty in the Six Counties, but it is not an exclusively Catholic condition. In rural Northern Ireland, Protestants own most of the best lowland farms while Catholics grub out a hazardous existence in rocky hill country, but most Protestant farmers are by no means affluent. And a post–World War II decline in the shipbuilding and linen industries has made Northern Ireland the most economically depressed portion of the United Kingdom, with an unemployment rate that victimizes Catholics and Protestants alike.

Irish Republicans with socialist leanings have explained Northern Ireland as an example of capitalist divide-and-conquer tactics. They say that men of wealth and property have encouraged and manipulated sectarian rivalries to prevent working-class solidarity, leaving them in control of the economic and political structures. This is a plausible interpretation of the situation. Sectarian conflict has helped preserve poverty-ridden Northern Ireland as the most conservative portion of the United Kingdom. Protestant farmers and urban workers follow and support the leadership of the ultraright Unionist party, and no-popery has made it possible for politicians to distract the Protestant proletariat from pressing economic and social problems. It is an interesting paradox: British welfare state policies have eased the political burdens of reactionary Ulster Unionism.

Despite the rationalism of the socialist perspective, bigotry in the North defies reasonable explanations. The loyalty of the Protestant masses is more than the product of capitalist manipulation. Like poor whites who despise poor blacks in the United States, Ulster Protestants receive a psychological lift in believing that they are a more superior breed than Catholics. And poor Protestants appear to be much more bigoted than their upper- and middle-class coreligionists.

Protestant xenophobia is often expressed in racist rhetoric. They refer to Catholics as "Pope heads," "Teagues," "bloody Micks," and "Fenians." Many Protestants warn their children against associating with Catholics because they are inherently treacherous, violent, dirty, and lazy. They say that Catholics breed like rabbits on orders from their priests so that they will outnumber Protestants at the polls. It is a claim that strikes some Protestants as credible, especially since the 1981 census reported that the population ratio between the two communities was roughly 60 percent to 40 rather than the 66 to 34 percent of six decades earlier.

Anti-Catholicism in Ulster reflects fear as much as ignorance, a function of the old siege mentality. After almost four centuries in Ireland, Protestants still feel like strangers in the land, convinced that the native Catholic Irish are determined on revenge. They really have little confidence in the staying power of the British when things get tough. They have translated their fear of Catholic vengeance and doubts about British fortitude into years of brutal oppression, which Catholics have recently answered in determined resistance.

Protestant anxieties are not entirely without merit. The reality of Catholic power in the South and the institutionalization of Irish-Ireland nationalism in the constitutions of both the Free State and the Republic have contributed to the cultural and religious dimensions of partition. And World War II played a significant part in defining the separate identities of North and South. To nationalists in the twenty-six counties of the Irish Free State, the neutrality of their country was a statement of sovereignty. Going it alone from 1939 to 1945 gave Irish nationalists a psychological lift and confidence in the durability of the state they had created. To Ulster Unionists, the neutrality of nationalists was an unconscionable tribute to the forces of totalitarianism that threatened the survival of the United Kingdom. World War II divided the historical experiences of the two Irelands, emphasizing the Irishness of

SEAMUS HEANEY

Seamus Heaney is the most renowned of the Northern Ireland Catholic poets. (*The Pacemaker Press,* Belfast.)

the South while accentuating the Britishness of the North. Northern Ireland Protestants today are attracted by a no-popery nativism that is no longer fashionable in Britain, and the nationalism of Northern Catholics is more intense than in the South. Ulster Catholics cling to myths, legends, and memories of revolutionary heroes that are fading in Common Market, European Ireland. Since there always has been a close connection between Irish nationalism and the literary muse, the Northern troubles have inspired much literary talent, energy, and production in the Ulster Catholic community, perhaps even more than in the Republic. Seamus Heaney, John Montague, Brian Moore, Patrick Boyle, Benedict Kiely, Seamus Deane, and Brian Friel are some outstanding examples of the Northern Catholic genius. Surprisingly, for all its advantages in education, wealth, and opportunity, the Northern Ireland Protestant community has not come close to matching the literary contribution of a people it considers inferior. One Protestant writer, Maurice Leitch, describes his own kind as "An ugly race . . . No poet will ever sing for them—of them."

More Catholics have expressed frustration in violence than in literature. Many of them have joined the Irish Republican Army in terrorist attacks on symbols of British authority. Some Northern Ireland Catholics were so bitter about their condition and partition that they hoped and prayed for a German victory in World War II as a prelude to a united Ireland. In Brian Moore's novel *The Emperor of Ice Cream,* Burke, a middle-class Catholic solicitor in Belfast, tells his son, "When it comes to grinding down minorities, the German jackboot isn't half as hard as the heel of John Bull." And there was Gallagher, the working-class Catholic from the Falls Road. He and his neighbor "considered it a point of honor to leave a light shining in the upstairs window at night in case any German bombers might come over the city." Gallagher had once been a member of the IRA but lost confidence in it: "He put his money on Hitler. When Hitler won the war Ireland would be whole again, thirty-two counties, free and clear." Burke and Gallagher did not change their minds about the Nazis until a bombing raid on Belfast destroyed the home of the former and the family of the latter.

After World War II, many Catholics realized that neither the oratory of politicians in the Republic nor IRA terrorism would unite the two Irelands. They also understood that the British Labour government's welfare state program could improve the condition of their existence. A 1944 British education act provided scholarships for Northern Ireland Catholics to attend university. An increasing segment of Catholic opinion, particularly among the expanding middle class, decided that first-class citizenship in Northern Ireland was a more practical objective than a united Ireland. This shift in attitude, and the work of police forces on both sides of the border, resulted in the failure of the IRA 1956–1962 terrorist campaign, forcing militant Republicans to reevaluate their strategy. For all practical purposes, the IRA ceased functioning for a time in the Six Counties after 1962.

Friendly contacts in 1965 between the prime ministers of Northern Ireland and the Irish Free State suggested that the Ulster question was moving from hate-provoking rhetoric and violence toward negotiation and conciliation. In *Ireland since the Rising,* Timothy Patrick Coogan, an influential Irish journalist, predicted that while there were still serious problems of sectarian discrimination in the Six Counties, conversations between Northern and Southern leaders would

> have healthy repercussions on the relationships between Protestants and Catholics on both sides of the borders. . . . The new spirit discernible in so many quarters is more representative of the future character of the North than the present evidence of gerrymandering and discrimination.

NORTHERN IRELAND CIVIL RIGHTS MOVEMENT

The process of slow but gradual change in Northern Ireland came to an abrupt halt in 1968. Civil rights agitation in other parts of the world, particularly in the United States, inspired Northern Ireland Catholics. In 1967 the Northern Ireland Civil Rights Association started as a coalition effort to achieve equal citizenship, rights, and opportunities for all residents of the Six Counties. Catholic middle-class moderates joined with socialists, Republicans, Protestant liberals, and the People's Democracy, a group seeking an Irish Workers's Republic that included Bernadette Devlin and Eamon McCann. They marched through the streets singing the song of the American civil rights movement, "We Shall Overcome." The Royal Ulster Constabulary, B-Specials, and Protestant mobs harassed them and beat them up. Television cameras brought life behind the "Orange curtain" to the attention of British and world opinion, creating a wave of international sympathy for the oppressed Catholic minority in Northern Ireland.

Encouraged by Prime Minister Harold Wilson's Labour government in Britain, Northern Ireland Prime Minister Terence O'Neill cautiously weighed the situation and decided to take a few small steps in the direction of civil rights and social justice. But fanatics in the Orange Order, including Reverend Ian Paisley, the leading no-popery demagogue, and ambitious politicians like William Craig, shouted, "No surrender!" Frightened by the frenzy of majority Protestant opinion, O'Neill lost his nerve, equivocated, procrastinated, and finally resigned from office. His successor, James Chichester-Clark, promised early reform. After moving too slowly for the Green and too fast for the Orange, he also resigned, turning power over to Brian Faulkner, a somewhat flexible Unionist.

Since 1969 the older issues of partition and a united Ireland have emerged from the shadows to reduce the importance of civil rights. Orange extremists with their hate rhetoric and taunting sectarian parades; the Royal Ulster Constabulary and B-Specials (the latter were abolished in October 1969), acting as partisan Protestant armies rather than as police forces; timid Stormont and Westminster politicians; and impatient Catholic radicals, socialists, and Republicans combined to transform confrontational protest tactics into a condition of civil war. Encouraged by police apathy, and sometimes support, Protestant mobs forced Derry and Belfast Catholics to retreat into barricaded ghettos. During the civil rights phase of the Ulster crisis, the IRA kept a low profile, promoting civil liberties as a strategy to mobilize and radicalize Catholic ghetto communities. In 1969 Protestant violence revived the

IRA as a Catholic defense force, and Catholics welcomed IRA protection. The Irish in Britain and America supplied the Republicans with money to purchase weapons.

At the same time that the IRA revived, it split into "official" and "provisional" wings. Members of the official wing interpret the Northern Ireland situation in a Marxist context. They aspire to an all-Ireland socialist republic as the ultimate solution to conflict. Until a truce with the British army in 1974, officials directed their violence against British authority, carefully avoiding attacks on Irish Protestants. Members of the provisional wing, indiscriminate in their terrorism, killing Protestant civilians as well as British soldiers, also claim to be socialists but not Marxists. Despite their proletarian slogans, provisionals represent the traditional Republican thesis that the British presence is the essence of the Ulster question and that violence is the only way to convince the British to evacuate Northern Ireland and unite the country. They propose a nine-county Ulster regional legislature subordinate to an all-Ireland Parliament, which, they contend, would satisfactorily fulfill Ulster Catholic nationalist hopes for a united Ireland and also accommodate Ulster Protestant Unionist demands for regional autonomy. Those early objectives are not articulated so frequently today as Marxists have come to dominate both the provo leadership and the Irish National Liberation Army, a militant group that broke away from the officials.

In August 1969, after weeks of violence in Derry and Belfast, the British government sent troops to Northern Ireland to keep the peace. At first Catholics welcomed them as protectors, but within a few months the IRA and the soldiers were at war. Permanent good relations between the Catholic community and the British army were almost impossible to sustain. Since the army was a law-and-order extension of the Protestant Unionist state, it could not function as a neutral agency. Soldiers disarmed Catholics but permitted Protestant extremists to keep their weapons. The presence and the conduct of the army supported IRA propaganda that the conflict in the North was a renewal of the Anglo-Irish War.

On August 9, 1971, acting on the orders of the Faulkner regime, the army aided the police in seizing and interning 342 people who were alleged to be members of or sympathizers with the provisional and official IRA groups. Yet Protestant extremists who were the first to instigate violence in the Six Counties were spared internment. By mid-December the authorities had apprehended over 1500 suspects (934 were quickly released), virtually all of them Catholic. Instead of calming the situation, internment intensified minority bitterness, consolidating the ghettos behind the IRA. While Republicans vigorously protested the existence of Long Kesh and other internment camps and the torture that went on in them, they were a blessing to the IRA cause, providing evidence of British injustice and cruelty in Ireland. After internment, Catholic opinion lost all interest in coming to terms with Stormont: Extremists demanded a united Ireland; moderates would accept nothing less than the end of the Northern Ireland state as established in 1920.

On January 30, 1972, British paratroopers gunned down thirteen Derry Catholics who were participating in a protest demonstration. "Bloody Sunday" further fanaticized Catholic nationalist opinion and dealt a death blow to Stormont.

In March 1972 the British Conservative government suspended the authority of the Northern Ireland government for a year and placed the Six Counties under direct Westminster rule. It promised a quick and satisfactory solution to the Northern Ireland crisis. William Whitelaw, who went to Belfast as secretary of state for Northern Ireland, appeared to have a feel for the Irish milieu and was able to communicate with both Protestant and Catholic camps.

When the blood-soaked streets of Derry and Belfast shattered Southern optimism concerning the situation in Northern Ireland, politicians in the Republic expressed sympathy and concern for Six-County Catholics and pledged traditional nationalist commitments to a united Ireland. The Fianna Fáil government sent frequent protests to Westminster concerning the harsh treatment of Northern Ireland Catholics, unsuccessfully tried to get the United Nations to mediate the crisis, and established refugee camps and hostels for Catholic refugees who had fled Protestant violence in the North. Official Irish government response to the Northern situation went beyond protest when it said that the Republic could not stand by idly if the Stormont regime or Protestant mobs continued to menace the Catholic minority with acts of brutality.

When people discussed Northern Ireland in their homes or pubs in the Irish Republic, they often expressed empathy for the IRA as the heirs of Easter Week and the Anglo-Irish War. Except for spontaneous reactions to Bloody Sunday, however, Irish opinion has remained generally calm and often ambiguous on the subject of events in the Six Counties. Even today only about 3 percent of the voters support Sinn Fein candidates in elections. And as Conor Cruise O'Brien affirmed in *States of Ireland* (1973), there is a deep concern that the virus of Northern violence could destroy liberal democracy in the Republic. Many members of the business community are frightened that the turbulence in Northern Ireland could discourage potential investors in Irish industry, and they feel certain that it has scared off likely tourists from Britain and the United States. And frequently citizens of the Republic will frankly admit that they do not understand or even like Ulster people, Protestant or Catholic. They consider them a separate breed with their own regional personality, presenting difficult if not insurmountable religious, economic, and cultural problems of assimilation for a united Ireland.

ATTEMPTS AT POWER SHARING AND DEVOLUTION

In March 1973 the British government presented its solution to the Northern Irish problems in a white paper, *Northern Ireland Constitutional Proposals*. The white paper rejected majority rule and proposed power sharing as the alternative. It also proposed an eighty-member Assembly elected by proportional representation and an Executive Committee with Catholic representation. Britain refused to give the new government the authority or stature that had been accorded earlier to Stormont [the Northern Ireland Parliament] and specifically reserved police and judicial powers for Westminster. In addition to establishing new power-sharing political institu-

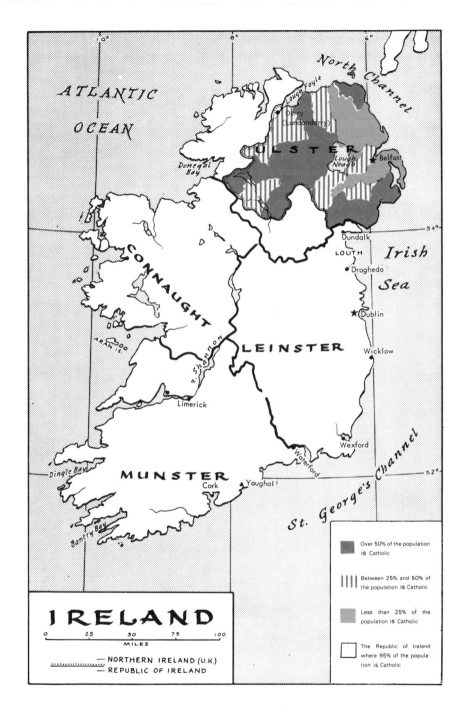

CATHOLIC POPULATION CENTERS IN NORTHERN IRELAND

tions, the white paper guaranteed Catholic civil rights in voting, local government, jobs, housing, and education. It also constructed a bridge to Irish unity by suggesting a Council of Ireland composed of British, Irish, and Northern Irish representatives to discuss problems of mutual interest and concern. Britain thereby gave notice of its acquiescence to the principle of a united Ireland if accomplished through negotiations and with the consent of public opinion on both sides of the border.

Led by Ian Paisley and James Craig, extreme Unionists denounced the white paper as a betrayal of Ulster Protestants and a major step in the direction of a united Catholic Ireland. Paisley said that he would prefer complete integration into the United Kingdom to the existence of a power-sharing puppet legislature. The IRA also rejected the white paper, arguing that it perpetuated the British presence in Ulster. Ignoring these dissenting expressions, Whitelaw began implementing the white paper. In this he had the support of Faulkner's moderate Unionists and the Social Democratic and Labour party (SDLP), a socialist, nationalist parliamentary movement with more support in the Catholic community than the IRA. The Alliance party, a nonsectarian coalition of moderates, also agreed to give the British proposal an opportunity to work.

June 1973 elections for the Northern Ireland Assembly gave Faulkner's Unionists 23 seats; SDLP, 19; Unofficial Unionists, 10; Democratic Unionists, 9; Alliance, 8; Vanguard, 6; West Belfast Loyalists, 2; and Northern Ireland Labour, 1. Five months later a Coalition formed an Executive Committee of six Faulkner Unionists, four SDLP, and one Alliance. Faulkner was chairman and Gerry Fitt, the SDLP leader, his deputy.

In December 1973 representatives of the British, Irish, and Northern Ireland governments met at Sunningdale, England. After four days of discussion they agreed to establish a Council of Ireland with a fourteen-member Ministry, equally divided between representatives of the Irish Republic and Northern Ireland, and a Consultative Assembly to which citizens of both Irelands would be elected proportionately. The Sunningdale conference also recommended that the Irish Republic recognize British sovereignty over Northern Ireland as long as a Six-County majority preferred to remain in the United Kingdom and urged the British government to agree to implement Irish unity as soon as that objective represented a Northern Ireland consensus. In March 1974 the taoiseach of the Republic, Liam Cosgrave, responded to the Sunningdale recommendation by recognizing Northern Ireland as British territory until its citizens, in a democratic election, indicated another preference.

Public opinion in Britain and in the Irish Republic was confident that the white paper and Sunningdale would pacify Northern Ireland and bring Ireland closer to national unity. But the new arrangement was doomed from the start. Consensus, not documents, produces stability, and the white paper and the Sunningdale agreements did not represent the will of the Six-County majority. While many Ulster Catholics were ready to compromise on their grievances and aspirations, the vast majority of Protestants disliked power sharing and hated the Council of Ireland.

While politicians talked in the Assembly, terrorist bombings, murders, assassinations, and burnings convulsed Northern Ireland, with a variety of Protestant paramilitary organizations competing with the provisional IRA as instruments of violence. By the spring of 1974, over 1000 people had died from shootings, bombings, and fires in the Six Counties; three years later the figure approached 1500. Protestant terror gangs assassinated Catholics in all parts of Northern Ireland and carried their campaign of intimidation into the South. On Friday, May 17, 1974, bombs killed five people in Monaghan and twenty-three in Dublin and wounded hundreds of others. And during 1975 the IRA transported terror to Britain in the forms of arson, bombing, and assassination in an effort to coerce British withdrawal from Ulster.

Beginning in the spring of 1974, Protestant extremists opened a determined and coordinated offensive against the white paper program, concentrating primarily on the Council of Ireland. On May 15 the Protestant Ulster Workers Council, with the support of ultra-Unionist politicians and paramilitary terrorist groups like Vanguard and the Ulster Defense Association, began a general strike, insisting on the termination of the Council of Ireland. Merlyn Rees, the British Labour party secretary of state for Northern Ireland, refused to negotiate with strike leaders. Within a few days Northern Ireland experienced a severe economic crisis involving shortages of food, electrical power, and other basic necessities. Responding to strike coercion and to the urgent requests of its moderate Unionist ally in the coalition, the SDLP reluctantly agreed to the suspension of the Council of Ireland for four years. Sensing complete victory, Protestant extremists escalated their demands. They insisted on the resignation of the Executive Committee and the Assembly and called for new elections, obviously expecting the restoration of Protestant ascendancy.

The nationalist SDLP responded by demanding that the British government take action to preserve power sharing. On Friday, May 24, after insisting that he would preserve law, order, and the constitution in Northern Ireland, Prime Minister Harold Wilson sent 500 more soldiers into the Six Counties, bringing British troop strength there to a total of 16,500. In the early morning hours of Sunday, May 26, the military occupied electrical power plants and some gasoline stations, but the British Labour government had moved too late. Soldiers lacked the competence to operate the power plants, and the British show of strength only solidified Protestant opinion—urban and rural—against the Faulknerite-SDLP-Alliance coalition. Finally Faulkner and his moderate Unionist colleagues resigned from the Executive Committee, destroying the power-sharing experiment. Britain then suspended the Executive Committee and the Assembly for a period of four years and returned Northern Ireland to the jurisdiction of Westminster.

In July 1974 the British government offered another white paper solution to the Northern Ireland problem. It called for a convention to meet for the purpose of producing a consensus constitution based on the principle of power sharing. Elections for the convention gave the ultra-Unionist factions 40 out of 78 seats. During the summer of 1975 the convention prepared recommendations for presentation to the British government. Although there was a split in the ultra-Unionist camp between Paisley and Craig—the latter was willing to make some concessions to power sharing—the convention submitted a report in November that insisted on a return to majority rule and an end to British government interference with the right of Protestant Unionists to control the destiny of Northern Ireland. Britain rejected Protestant ascendancy, Northern Ireland remained under the authority of Westminster, and the violence continued as before.

On August 10, 1976, three young children walking with their mother were killed by an IRA car that crashed after the driver was shot dead in a gun battle. There were thirty-seven different shooting incidents in Ulster that day, in addition to twenty bomb attacks and nineteen car hijackings. But it was the deaths of these innocent children that inspired a group of Protestant and Catholic women, led by Mrs. Betty Williams and Miss Mairead Corrigan, the children's aunt, to form a movement they called the Peace People and to invite women everywhere to join in a campaign against violence. Ten thousand women, including a good number of Protestants, attended a peace rally in Andersontown on August 14 despite death threats from the IRA. That demonstration served notice to the world that the perpetrators of violence in Northern Ireland were a small minority and that most people there yearned for peace. A little more than a year later, on December 10, 1977, the Nobel Peace Prize of 80,000 pounds was awarded to the peace movement's cofounders, Williams and Corrigan.

The highlight of the year for Ulster in 1977, however, proved to be the queen's Silver Jubilee visit in August. The IRA made a concerted effort to have the visit canceled by threats of bombing and civil disorder, but the queen succeeded in following her appointed schedule, under heavy security, without hindrance. In September, U.S. President Jimmy Carter responded to pressure from Irish-Americans by making a guarded statement on Northern Ireland in which he endorsed power sharing as a solution and offered industrial investments as an incentive for peace. Neither the Unionist leaders nor the British leaders in London evinced much interest in Carter's cautiously phrased remarks.

During 1978, as the level of violence in Northern Ireland began to decline for a time, the IRA began a propaganda campaign for the restoration of "special category" status to terrorists serving prison sentences. More than 300 IRA prisoners declined to wear prison clothes and thus naked, except for their blankets, proceeded to deface their cells with urine and feces, creating a health hazard for themselves and the prison staff. IRA propagandists attempted to represent the outrageous conditions in the H Block of the Maze Prison as the deliberate policy of the state authorities, but the London government rejected such claims as nonsense and sternly warned that there would be no compromise with the men who had gone "on the blanket" and defied prison regulations. Later, on November 26, the deputy governor of the Maze, in charge of the H Block, was shot dead at his home in Belfast.

Failing to move London by its propaganda efforts, the IRA turned in 1979 to violence against British dignitaries. On March 22 the British ambassador to the Netherlands, Sir Richard Sykes, was shot dead at the Hague and, on March 30,

Airey Neave, M.P., was killed by a bomb in the members' parking lot at the House of Commons. Public outrage in Britain was almost unrestrained when, on August 27, the earl of Mountbatten, a member of the royal family, was killed in a boat by an IRA bomb while on holiday at his home near Mullaghmore in the Irish Republic. Moreover, eighteen British soldiers were killed at Narrow Water Castle, County Down, that same day by land mines detonated from across the border. Prime Minister Margaret Thatcher flew to Belfast and visited troops on the border. At a meeting with Thatcher after the Mountbatten funeral, Irish Prime Minister Jack Lynch pledged Dublin's cooperation in future border security.

Throughout much of 1980 a good deal of time and attention were given to a British-sponsored interparty conference on Northern Ireland that included the Reverend Ian Paisley's Democratic Unionist party, the largely Roman Catholic SDLP, and the moderate, largely Protestant Alliance party. The purpose of the conference was to explore possible common ground for a future constitution. On July 2 the London government published a "discussion paper" that ruled out any return to a simple majority administration for Ulster and recommended instead an Assembly of eighty members elected by proportional representation. The proposal also included a power-sharing formula, which was viewed suspiciously by Protestants and Catholics alike. British patience was growing thin, as evidenced by a December poll published in the *Sunday Times* showing that substantially more than half the people questioned would welcome an end to the union.

On March 1, 1981, IRA prisoner Bobby Sands began a fast to protest British rule in Northern Ireland and the nonpolitical status of nationalist prisoners in the H Block. The fast became an IRA publicity coup when Sands was put forward as a candidate for Parliament following the March 5 death of Frank Maguire, Independent M.P. for Fermanagh and South Tyrone. The Catholic SDLP was afraid to contest the seat, and Sands defeated former Unionist cabinet minister Harry West in a vote of 30,492 to 29,046. It was a stunning propaganda victory for the IRA, which promptly claimed that the victory of Bobby Sands destroyed the British myth that the Irish "freedom fighters" were not supported by the majority of Catholics. After Sands died on May 5, following a sixty-six-day fast, serious disorders broke out in the nationalist areas of Belfast as the polarization between Catholics and Protestants became still more intense. Ten other prisoners subsequently died on hunger strikes, the last on August 20, and each death was followed by outbreaks of violence.

THE NEW IRELAND FORUM AND THE ANGLO-IRISH AGREEMENT

Renewed efforts to find an acceptable form of devolved government for Northern Ireland began again in 1982. On February 17 the British government proposed a seventy-eight-member Assembly, elected by proportional representation. A Northern Ireland assembly bill was given royal assent on July 23, and elections were duly held on October 20. All of the major parties in the province contested the election.

JOHN HUME

John Hume is head of the Social Democratic Labour Party and is the leading spokesman of constitutional nationalism in Northern Ireland. (*Irish News*, Belfast.)

The SDLP did so, however, on the basis that it was not prepared to take any seats that it won. Only the Ulster Unionists, the Democratic Unionist party, the Alliance party, and two other independent Unionists, totaling 58 of the 78 members elected, took their seats when the Assembly met for the first time on November 11. The SDLP, which had only won 14 seats, due partly to an unusually heavy Sinn Fein turnout at the polls, argued that there was no point in its participation since the main Assembly parties had excluded the prospect of power sharing. Instead, the SDLP called for the government of the Irish Republic to set up a Council for a New Ireland that might study acceptable forms of government for the whole island and prepare the way for all-Ireland institutions. The New Ireland Forum, which first met in Dublin in May 1983, was a response to that appeal. The Forum suggested, for example, three different possible options: first, a unitary state with pluralist constitutional guarantees for all; second, a federal solution in which North and South would be separate units under one central government, but each with rigid guarantees of religious liberty and each with its own laws on such matters as contraception and divorce; and last, dual sovereignty, with Dublin and London sharing authority in the North. Altogether, the Forum received over 300 submissions and heard oral presentations from thirty-one individuals and groups. Despite the fact that British

Prime Minister Margaret Thatcher rejected the alternatives for Northern Ireland that were proposed by the Forum, SDLP leader John Hume hailed the event as ''an extraordinary day in the history of our island. . . . Things cannot be the same again.''

There was cause for concern too, however, as the Sinn Fein electoral victories following the hunger strikes had illustrated. And it was indeed the fear that the Catholic minority in the North might be won over by the IRA that prompted the British and Irish governments to join in a bold 1985 plan for breaking the cycle of violence and despair in the Six Counties. Meeting at Hillsborough in Northern Ireland, Prime Minister Margaret Thatcher and Taoiseach Garret FitzGerald signed, on November 15, what has come to be known alternately as the Hillsborough Agreement or the Anglo-Irish Accord. With that document the Irish Republic formally recognized the right of the Northern province to remain within the United Kingdom for as long as a majority of its citizens so desired. The agreement also provided for an intergovernmental conference, serviced by a secretariat located at Maryfield outside Belfast, to provide a framework for regular meetings between the two governments at both the ministerial and official levels. This conference was to enable the Irish government to advance views and proposals on a range of political, security, and legal matters, thus reflecting and representing the concerns of the minority in the north. Finally, the agreement endorsed the Westminster policy of seeking devolution on a basis that would secure widespread acceptance throughout the community.

The SDLP enthusiastically backed the agreement and expressed the hope that various social and political reforms would follow. A more cautious note was struck by the Alliance party, which expressed reservations about the new arrangements, especially with respect to the lack of consultation with local parties. But the party said it would suspend judgment in order to allow time to see if the agreement would bring benefits to the community. Nationalist and Unionist militants were more judgmental. Sinn Fein opposed the new understanding because it accepted partition and promised valueless reforms. Almost as predictably, the Official Unionist party and the Democratic Unionist party both opposed it for the very reason that it permitted a foreign state, the Irish Republic, to have a voice in the affairs of Northern Ireland.

It was, to be sure, a remarkably subtle and sophisticated agreement, and the Unionists were correct in their assumption that it could eventually compromise the position of Northern Ireland within the United Kingdom. Specifically, the amount of power that the Irish government might be able to exercise in Northern Ireland was, by definition, to be in inverse ratio to the amount of power conferred on a devolved government in Belfast. Yet the condition that Britain had set for the reestablishment of any devolved government in Northern Ireland was, quite simply, the power-sharing formula that Unionist politicians have consistently rejected since 1974.

The impact of the accord on the Unionist majority in Northern Ireland was nothing less than traumatic. There were public demonstrations, confrontations with the police, and sporadic violence as outraged loyalists expressed their sense of shock and fury over what they perceived as Thatcher's "treachery." Then, on December 17, 1985 all fifteen Unionist M.P.'s resigned their seats at Westminster in protest over the Hillsborough Agreement.

Not to be deterred, Dublin and London proceeded to implement the November 15 understanding in timely fashion. The measure was ratified in the Dáil, 88 votes to 75, and, interestingly, it passed the House of Commons by an over-whelming majority of 473 to 47. The agreement then automatically came into force on November 29, and the first meeting of the Anglo-Irish Intergovernmental Con-ference took place subsequently at Stormont Castle on December 11. As the year 1985 drew to a close, the number of people killed in the province as a result of political violence came to fifty-five, down from sixty-four the previous year. But the IRA and the splinter Irish National Liberation Army (INLA) had begun to focus on members of the security forces, resulting in the deaths of no fewer than twenty-three members of the Royal Ulster Constabulary. Another notable feature of deaths during 1985 was the high number of Catholics who were killed by IRA or INLA terrorists because of even casual or benign contact with security forces, as in instances of craftsmen involved in the construction of police stations.

There are any number of obvious parallels between the Northern Irish cultural, national, and sectarian conflict and the Israeli-Palestinian confrontations and guerrilla escapades that were, and are, concurrent to the Ulster crisis. But there are also many differences. One cannot, for example, imagine an Israeli or a Palesti-nian becoming a hero, however briefly, to most of the population among both of those warring communities. Yet that is exactly what happened in Northern Ireland, where sports can, and occasionally does, eclipse politics. Barry McGuigan, the "Clones Cyclone," won the world featherweight boxing championship in June 1985, just as Dennis Taylor had won the world snooker championship a few weeks earlier, in April. Their respective achievements were a source of great pride to nearly all Ulster inhabitants, irrespective of denominational affiliation. Music was yet another shared experience, particularly among Northern Ireland teenagers, Prot-estant and Catholic alike, who often wore the same sweatshirts featuring Irish rock musicians, like Bob Geldof, or Irish rock bands, like U2.

But at the outset of 1986, the spirit in Northern Ireland was anything but ecumenical. The IRA's response to Sinn Fein reversals at the polls was to intensify the terror. Radicalism was increasingly more evident among Unionists too, where-upon newly emergent leaders, like Peter Robinson, made even the Reverend Ian Paisley appear moderate by comparison. In June 1986, however, the Assembly was dissolved, and London made it clear that the future of Northern Ireland self-gover-nance was directly linked to the intergovernmental conference. The joint British and Irish staffs met regularly at the secretariat outside Belfast even as the destructive conflict continued unabated. Sixty-two deaths resulted from political violence, seven more than during the previous year. And there were new categories among the targets: For instance, there were an unusually high number of loyalist assaults against both Catholic homes and the homes of policemen of either faith who were seen as upholding government policies resulting from the agreement.

In the general election of 1987, thirteen of Northern Ireland's seventeen seats in the Westminster Parliament were won by Unionist parties, three by the SDLP, and one seat, West Belfast, by Sinn Fein. The so-called McBride Principles, a strategy advanced by the Irish statesman Sean McBride for a boycott of all commercial investment in the Six Counties because of discrimination against the minority population, was a particularly divisive issue given the 17.6 percent unemployment in the province compared with 9.5 in the rest of the United Kingdom. London responded in September 1987 with a revised guide to religious equality of opportunity in employment for the government's frankly ineffective Fair Employment Agency.

Anglo-Irish relations began to wear thin in January 1988, when the Thatcher government announced that it would not, for reasons of national security, prosecute a group of officers in the Royal Ulster Constabulary who were involved in a shoot-to-kill policy in 1982 and 1983. That drew loud protests from Dublin, and it angered Irish taoiseach Charles Haughey. The official inquiry into the case has never been published, and Haughey met with Thatcher in mid-February to demand that the report be made public and that the implicated officers be brought to trial. Thatcher's rejection of Haughey's request appeared all the more callous when, in that same month, an explosive new book, entitled *Stalker,* appeared. It was written by now-retired Deputy Chief Constable John Stalker of the Greater Manchester police force, who was placed in charge of the RUC probe in 1984 but was dismissed two years later. Stalker writes that he was fired because he had implicated RUC officers and had found that at least eleven policemen were involved in a conspiracy to subvert justice.

Dublin was also shocked in late January 1988 by a British appeals court's decision to uphold the convictions of six men, all Ulster Catholics, who had previously been sentenced to life imprisonment for two terrorist bombings in Birmingham in 1974. The defendants had argued that their confessions had been compelled under duress. Moreover, new evidence had emerged casting doubt on their guilt. Then, in February, a Roman Catholic Ulsterman, Aidan McAnespie, was mistakenly shot and fatally wounded as he passed through a security checkpoint in Northern Ireland. Haughey ordered an independent investigation of the case on Dublin's side of the border when it was learned that McAnespie, who had done low-level electioneering for Sinn Fein, had been harassed at the same checkpoint on earlier occasions. An infuriated Thatcher then publicly declared that Dublin had no right to inquire into ''matters north of the border.'' Her response was cheered by Unionists, and it placed in some doubt the future effectiveness of the Hillsborough Agreement.

What must be remembered, of course, is the fact that the agreement is critically dependent on a successful improvement of relations between not only the security forces and Catholics in Northern Ireland but also between the Republic and the Six Counties in cross-border monitoring of the IRA. The full implications of this pact are perhaps only dimly understood by some British and Irish citizens, for the arrangements that it contains are virtually unprecedented. Northern Ireland is presently unique in international law, for although it remains a part of the United Kingdom, the agreement confers on two distinctly separate governments the legal right, underscored by a treaty registered with the United Nations, to determine jointly specific issues that touch on the essence of sovereignty in Northern Ireland. These are the kinds of distinctions that often escape either the attention or the interest of many Irish-Americans.

CHAPTER 16

Irish America and the Contemporary Conflict in Northern Ireland

CHARACTER OF THE IRISH-AMERICAN COMMUNITY TODAY

Irish America has been far less responsive to the strife in Northern Ireland over the past two decades than it was to the cause of nationalist Ireland only fifty years before. One reason is that a large part of this American community is now two generations or more away from any direct experience with Irish life. Another is that most Irish-Americans are the descendants of immigrants from the west or south of Ireland and have little familiarity with the tradition of Ulster's communal schism. It may even be argued that Irish-Americans have, as a group, become too assimilated in the United States to think much about events in Ireland, despite the interest today in ethnic identity. As Oscar Handlin and other immigration historians have observed, organizations like the Sons of St. Patrick or the Sons of Italy have no counterpart in Europe. Nationalist sentiment may be the force that holds such groups together, but their real purpose is to ease the transition of immigrants into

American life. They help compensate for a sense of individual weakness by asserting group strength. Contrary to the charge of their critics, such organizations do not create "hyphenated Americans"; they serve to smooth away the hyphen. They promote adjustment to American ways and adoption of American ideals, rather than retard them. Millions of second- and third-generation Irish-Americans had, by the 1970s, moved well away from the initial period of immigrant anxiety and adjustment. As Americans, they had the security to view the Ulster problem from an emotional distance. Former U.S. Ambassador to Ireland William V. Shannon believes that for Irish Americans "to enter fully into the passions that convulse Northern Ireland would require a journey into the past they are reluctant to make. They are too involved with the American present and future."

There is, however, another constituency within the Irish-American community that perceives the Ulster crisis in an entirely different way. These are, for the most part, the recent Irish immigrants who provide the hard core support for the IRA in the United States. As with past Irish-American nationalism, the response of Irish immigrants to the events in Northern Ireland communicates the bitterness they feel about the impoverished Ireland they left and their sense of insecurity in America. And because IRA supporters hold the Irish government responsible for the economic conditions that forced them to emigrate and denounce it as a puppet of British imperialism, these immigrants are unmoved when Irish officials plead with Americans not to aid IRA activities. Indeed, Irish immigrant support for the IRA reflects a dissatisfaction with their position in the United States. They do not share the values and attitudes of the American-born Irish or participate in their middle-class standing or respectability. The situation in Northern Ireland has afforded them the means of expressing their own identity in an increasingly ethnic-conscious America. Yet their attitude is strangely incompatible with their strong law-and-order stance on other American issues. They refuse, for example, to recognize the obvious similarities between black America and Catholic Northern Ireland. They deliberately ignore the socialist pronunciations of the contemporary IRA. And they purport not to see any obvious comparison between the IRA and political terrorist organizations in other parts of the world.

Irish-born Irish-Americans are not nearly as numerous today as they were at the time of the Irish war for independence. There were, for example, some 4 million such immigrants in 1919, compared with fewer than 300,000 in 1969. Yet this immigrant community, particularly in the Eastern states of Massachusetts, New York, New Jersey, and Pennsylvania, provides much of the militant thrust behind Irish America's support for the IRA. These people are often driven by blind hatred and have no faith in British power-sharing proposals or in any rational political compromise. They have no interest in any minority rights guarantee on the part of the United Kingdom, the United States, or the United Nations. They believe that the IRA claim to full sovereignty over Northern Ireland is historically justified and must be accomplished by force of arms. Their perception of Ireland is often simplistic and uninformed.

IRA PROPAGANDA IN AMERICA AND THE PROBLEM
OF PERCEPTION FOR BRITAIN

But Irish Republicanism is often given a wider and more sympathetic hearing in the United States than the relative size or illiberal views of the Irish immigrant community would seem to warrant. One reason for this has been the carefully calculated tone of the Irish Republican campaign in America. As Maria McGuire tells us in her book *To Take Arms,* provisional IRA fund-raisers were instructed to make copious references to the martyrs of 1916 and 1919–1922. They were also advised to promote anti-British sentiment by recalling the potato famine and the Black and Tans but were cautioned against saying anything praiseworthy about socialism or anything critical about the Catholic church. American television is another reason for the notable attention given to the Northern Ireland issue in the United States. At the 1981 funeral of hunger striker Bobby Sands, correspondent Neil Hickey reported that the IRA ensured that American television crews were afforded fully equipped scaffolding on which to mount their cameras. Viewers in the United States were thereby treated to the dramatic spectacle of hooded Provos at the gravesite firing volleys of salute toward an overcast sky. The image conveyed to the television screen was that of a noble tribute to an honored martyr and a rightful cause.

This problem of perception is, of course, a major obstacle for the British to overcome in explaining their own position on Northern Ireland to American audiences. In condemning the atrocities and in suppressing the terrorism of the provisional IRA, London has failed to capitalize on the fact that the IRA political platform calls for the overthrow of government authorities on both sides of the border and for a socialist program involving the nationalization of banks and industries throughout Ireland. Instead, the Provos have been permitted to characterize the IRA campaign as a holy war, perhaps even the final chapter in the age-old struggle between Celt and Anglo-Saxon. The frequently conservative social thinking of many Irish-Americans has, as a result, given way to the romantic idealism deliberately and effectively cultivated by IRA disinformation. Once again, as happened during the 1919–1921 war for Irish independence, Irish Republicanism has bested Britain in the propaganda war for American public opinion. Only in very recent times have people outside Ireland become more discriminating in their assessment of IRA claims.

Indeed, the terrorist image that has become synonymous with the IRA Provo since the late 1970s is the single most important reason for the modest success the IRA has had in winning widespread American support for its cause. Neither the IRA's stridently Anglophobic rhetoric nor its patently socialist manifestos have alienated people in the United States as much as that organization's identification with violence and killing. And that general sense of revulsion was also shared by some Irish-Americans. Appearing before a 1972 Congressional subcommittee hearing on conditions in Northern Ireland, New York City resident and writer Jimmy Breslin recounted his own experiences in Ulster and condemned people who collected funds in Manhattan taverns for the purpose of purchasing weapons for the IRA. Breslin remarked:

> The idea of raising money on Second Avenue to buy guns so that an 18-year-old in Derry can kill an 18-year-old British soldier, a soldier from Manchester who knows nothing of the reasons for the fight he is in, this notion to me is sickening.

NORAID AND THE AMERICAN CONNECTION WITH ULSTER

One of the major conduits for smuggling arms from the United States to Northern Ireland in recent times has been the Northern Aid Committee. Popularly known as NORAID, the organization was founded in 1970 by Michael Flannery and two other IRA veterans of the 1919–1922 period. NORAID publicity director Martin Galvin, an attorney with the New York Sanitation Department, has claimed that the organization has ninety-two chapters in seventy American cities and that the total membership numbers about 5000. Headquartered in a drab second-floor Broadway office in upper Manhattan, sandwiched between a funeral parlor and a branch bank, NORAID does not give the appearance of being an ominous organization that is supplying illicit weapons to terrorists abroad. Moreover, NORAID officials have always insisted that the funds raised by their organization, estimated by Martin Galvin to be 300,000 dollars a year, have been used mostly to support the families of IRA members interned by British authorities. But American intelligence sources estimated in 1975 that only 25 percent of the money was spent for such purposes while fully 75 percent was used for the purchase of weapons and munitions.

United States citizens, including Irish-Americans, did not have to depend on the judgment of their government alone in evaluating NORAID's complicity in providing weapons for the IRA. Indeed, four successive Irish prime ministers have made the same charge. Liam Cosgrave told a joint session of Congress that aid to "relief" organizations like NORAID did not help to resolve the problem of Ulster. Jack Lynch warned American contributors to NORAID that their money, rather than going for the support of widows and orphans, was in fact used to *make* widows and orphans. Garret FitzGerald similarly condemned such American aid to the IRA, and Charles Haughey went still further and declared, "There is clear and conclusive evidence available to the government here from security and other sources that NORAID has provided support for the campaign of violence."

Remarks such as these prompted former New York Council President Paul O'Dwyer, a NORAID attorney, to decry the growing rift between the Irish and Irish-Americans. O'Dwyer, a distinguished member of the Democratic party in New York, is a native of County Mayo and is representative of that community of Irish-born Americans who identify with the Democratic tradition in American politics but with the Republican tradition in Irish politics. Yet as Irish cabinet minister Conor Cruise O'Brien observed in a 1976 speech before an American Chamber of Commerce meeting in Dublin, the Republican tradition in Ireland has set itself above democracy. And in direct response to O'Dwyer, O'Brien denied that any rift existed between the Irish and Irish-Americans. "I do believe," he added, "that a minority of Irish Republicans are interested in trying to produce such a rift, and to intimidate Irish people with the idea that they cannot afford such a rift."

Throughout the 1970s and early 1980s, courts in the United States and Canada tried a number of NORAID officials for arms offenses. Some received suspended sentences; others were jailed. Michael Flannery and four codefendants, however, were acquitted by a New York court in November 1982 when the government failed to prove that they had deliberately sought to export arms without the necessary official permit. Organizers of the 1983 St. Patrick's Day parade in New York then selected Flannery as the parade's grand marshal, which resulted in public denunciations of that decision by leading Irish-American politicians. NORAID was also condemned by the U.S. Bureau of Alcohol, Tobacco and Firearms, which, together with other federal agencies, helped to secure the indictments of people who were transporting guns into Northern Ireland.

As more NORAID members were jailed on weapons offenses and as that organization became publicly linked with the provisional IRA, another group, calling itself the Irish National Caucus, assumed a more prominent role among Americans concerned with the course of events in Ulster. The Caucus was first formed in 1974 and had as its purpose to make the violations of human rights in Ulster a moral issue for all Americans. By 1979 no fewer than 130 congressmen had signed on with the Caucus-sponsored Ad Hoc Committee for Irish Affairs under the chairmanship of New York Representative Mario Biaggi. An open schism developed between Irish National Caucus director Father Sean McManus and NORAID leader Michael Flannery when the Caucus proposed hosting a "peace forum" in Washington to which members of both the Ulster Defense Association and the Irish Republican Army would be invited. Nothing came of the plan, and aside from providing further evidence of the divisions within the Irish-American community over the subject of Northern Ireland, the Irish question remained as much on the periphery of American politics as it had been for more than fifty years.

CONCERN AND CONSTRAINT IN CONFRONTING THE ULSTER CRISIS

Irish-American politicians have come to appreciate the complexity of the Northern Ireland problem after making a few missteps while promoting the ever-controversial aspirations of Irish nationalism. In 1971, for example, Senator Edward Kennedy somewhat impulsively called for Britain's immediate withdrawal from Ireland and declared that those Protestants who could not accept a united Ireland "should be given a decent opportunity to go back to Britain." By 1973 Kennedy was affirming that Protestants must have an equal role with Catholics, but he continued to insist that the unification of Ireland under the jurisdiction of Dublin was the only sensible solution to the Ulster crisis. Finally, in 1977, in response to appeals from Garret

FitzGerald and other prominent Dublin politicians, Senators Edward Kennedy and Daniel Patrick Moynihan, together with Governor Hugh Carey and House Speaker Thomas "Tip" O'Neill, issued a St. Patrick's Day statement that condemned the IRA as the real obstacle to peace in Northern Ireland. It was these same Irish-American leaders, popularly referred to as the "Four Horsemen," who persuaded President Jimmy Carter to make his August 1977 offer of United States help toward a solution for Ulster. Specifically, the President promised to encourage substantial American investment in Northern Ireland provided a settlement could be reached between the Protestant and Catholic communities.

Kennedy and his colleagues became increasingly frustrated over the next two years when none of the principal parties took any real initiative toward a reconciliation in Ulster. Meanwhile, successive human rights investigations continued to condemn police brutality in Northern Ireland. The Four Horsemen accordingly issued another St. Patrick's Day statement in 1979, which, reflecting their keen sense of betrayal, blamed British insensitivity rather than IRA terrorism as the principal cause for the continuing strife in Northern Ireland. That contention was promptly dismissed as naive by British Labour leader Shirley Williams, while a subsequent statement by these Irish-American leaders calling for British withdrawal from Northern Ireland was ridiculed as reckless and irresponsible by Irish Labour leader Conor Cruise O'Brien. Nevertheless, the Four Horsemen, together with President Carter, did succeed in impressing upon London the importance of the American dimension to the Irish problem when considering any future resolution to the Northern Ireland conflict. British Prime Minister Margaret Thatcher reflected this new disposition when she gave the *New York Times,* but not a single British newspaper, an exclusive interview on her proposal for devolution of political power in Ulster one week before announcing it publicly.

But while the power-sharing proposals advanced by the British government in recent times have tempered the criticism of some congressmen and governors who, since 1981, have acted as a group known as the "Friends of Ireland", these schemes have been sharply rejected by militant Irish-American Republican groups. The latter are not interested in the achievement of civil rights for all citizens of a Northern Ireland that remains within the United Kingdom. Rather, they support the call of the IRA for the overthrow of British authority in Ulster and for the unification of Ireland. The majority of Irish-Americans today, however, are disinclined to heed appeals from the IRA as that organization's true character becomes better known. On March 1, 1981, for instance, the *New York Times Magazine* featured a story on international terrorism, and its depiction of the Irish Republican Army is representative of the kind of information regarding Northern Ireland that is presently gaining wider currency among American readers. One excerpt reads:

> The IRA has come a long way since its early days of dependence upon the United States. Fund raising is mostly done at home nowadays, by means of protection rackets, brothels, massage parlors and bank stickups. And the incoming hardware is largely Soviet-made. It took only a few years to make the transformation with the help of the international terror network.

On March 1, 1988, exactly seven years from the date of the *New York Times* article, the Associated Press carried a story that addressed this same reality. According to the AP, more than 100 tons of weaponry had been clandestinely shipped to Ireland from Libya. What worried the authorities in both London and Dublin about this most recent instance of arms smuggling from terrorist suppliers were reports that the shipments contained Soviet-made SAM-7 antiaircraft missles. If true, the IRA now possessed a fearsome potential for escalating the violence in Northern Ireland.

Perhaps, therefore, it is not only their assimilation into the mainstream of American society that has distanced most Irish-Americans from the cause of Irish Republicanism. Disillusionment with the nature and methods of the contemporary IRA has almost certainly been an equally restraining factor for these well-educated and sophisticated ethnics. John Brecher, a correspondent for *Newsweek* magazine, made this generational difference rather poignantly in a May 1981 article. Brecher recalled that when three Irish nationalists in British custody starved themselves to death in 1920, fully 100,000 angry Irish-Americans poured onto the Boston Common. In May 1981, when IRA hunger striker Bobby Sands died in yet another act of protest, barely 100 people demonstrated outside the home of the British consul general in Boston. Although the disparity between these figures does not necessarily represent the true measure of Irish-American concern for the Northern Ireland problem today, it does serve to underscore an essential difficulty for this ethnic community. Irish-Americans have discovered that they support an ideal, the unification of Ireland, which is the professed goal of an organization that they increasingly feel to be morally abhorrent. This is the dilemma that confronts thoughtful Irish-Americans and accounts to a large extent for the notable absence of their traditional enthusiasm for the romantic aspirations of nationalist Ireland.

CHAPTER 17
Ireland in the 1990s

THE REPUBLIC OF IRELAND

The 1980s and 1990s have proven to be a period of enormous change for residents of both Northern Ireland and the Republic of Ireland. Perhaps the most significant areas of change have occurred less in a political or diplomatic context than in the Irish definition and understanding of themselves as a people and nation.

In 1988 a decidedly sober mood seemed to pervade the country. Ireland was troubled by violence, poverty, and fading confidence in the future. None of this, of course, was new to the Irish experience, but rapidly increasing urbanization was altering the nation's economic and social landscape and changing the nature of traditional problems. The poverty Ireland experienced was no longer primarily a result of its traditional rural setting. Nor was Ireland experiencing the same urban poverty that had given rise to the movement of Jim Larkin, and others like him, in the earlier part of the century. Instead, Ireland was now confronted with the experience of urban unemployment, with drug-related crime, and with the attendant consequences that have long plagued modern European and American societies.

By the late 1980s, fully 50 percent of the Irish population resided in Dublin and its environs. The traditional landscape of "dear, dirty Dublin" became nearly unrecognizable as gentrification transformed much of the city center, while working-class suburbs, which possessed all the charm of American public housing projects, grew up around the city's edges, particularly to the north. Typical examples are the tower blocks and terrace houses of Ballymun which have been immortalized in the novels of Roddy Doyle, and in such films as *The Commitments* and *The Snapper.*

The north side of the Liffey remains home to Dublin's working classes. Although this area is generally regarded as more down-to-earth than the more bourgeois south side, the fact remains that the north side and the ever-expanding suburbs are coping with growing social and economic problems and are the scenes of increasing crime and violence. Overcrowding and unemployment have produced crime, family instability, and drug dependence on a scale quite unexpected for many who thought that Irish life would somehow escape these contemporary phenomena. In fact, a good part of Dublin's disorder is related to heroin and cocaine use.

Urbanization contributed much to the sense of doubt and uncertainty that fell upon Ireland in the late 1980s. With a majority of the country's population born after 1960, some social and economic dislocation was perhaps inevitable as that generation came of age. What compounded the problem in Ireland, however, was that the maturing of this generation coincided with the negative consequences of unemployment, a fading economy, and urbanization, all of which contributed to a growing crisis of confidence, especially among the young, over the future of the country.

Meanwhile, the absence of appropriate economic opportunities in the rural areas of Ireland helped to spark a migration to the cities. Ireland's embrace of the economic policies and opportunities afforded by its membership in the European Community (EC) had, at least initially, positively influenced the modernization of agriculture and the improvement of the general standard of rural living. Indeed, in the 1980s, the revered Irish family farm appeared to be a stronger institution than it had been before the coming of the EC. While modernization had improved the economic prospects of rural Ireland during the 1970s, it had also created an economic situation in which the country's agricultural base could no longer provide employment for the bulk of the rural population. In and of itself, that situation hardly represented anything new. Rural areas had long been the country's principal source of emigration. The difference in the current era lies in the fact that the young generation which can find no place for itself in rural Ireland is better-educated and more able to adjust to life away from the farm. It is also true that the young are not as willing to desert their native land as were earlier generations. Thus, the migration of rural school leavers to the urban areas of Dublin, Cork, Galway, and other cities reveals a desire to find an economic niche without following the traditional path of overseas emigration.

Because these young people recognize that rural Ireland cannot provide a livelihood for them, they have sought refuge in the cities. Unfortunately, the arrival of these young people in the urban centers has coincided with a period of severe economic recession. Thus, while many of these men and women have sought their fortune in their own country, even the best-educated among them have discovered that there is little need for their skills. Meanwhile, those with few qualifications soon learn that Dublin and other urban areas offer little more opportunity than do their native villages. For them, life in the city generally means a life on the dole in a bleak suburb, or in a crumbling working-class neighborhood.

The chronic unemployment that has plagued Ireland ever since independence in 1922 reached particularly high levels in the late 1980s. Cuts in government spending decreased the size of the public work force at a time when a global recession was leading to job losses in the private sector as well.

Nor, as previously noted, was emigration as attractive or as feasible an option as in earlier days. Britain, the United States, and Australia—Ireland's traditional outlets for those seeking a better life—were experiencing economic difficulties of their own. Moreover, the U.S. policy of limiting immigration further exacerbated the problem. Both Britain and the United States still attracted sizable communities of Irish immigrants. Although as many as 50,000 illegal Irish immigrants were to be found in New England alone during the late 1980s, the days when the United States could or would absorb the greater part of Ireland's excess population appeared to be over.

If the Irish urban scene seemed especially bleak during the late 1980s, the decade of the 1990s has witnessed a concerted attempt by the Irish to address their fiscal problems. While the unemployment rate remains high in both rural and urban areas, efforts to improve the cities themselves have proceeded apace. In 1991, for example, Dublin celebrated its one-thousandth anniversary, and the major renovations that accompanied that celebration helped to transform a part of the central city for its many visitors. Employment schemes have also lessened somewhat the despair of working-class youth, while the government, albeit belatedly, has recognized the severity of the drug problem in urban Ireland and has endeavored to address it.

Perhaps even more important, however, is the sense that the Irish people's view of themselves has changed over the last decade, as the urbanization of the country has led to differing views on society, religion, and politics.

There is little semblance in modern Ireland to the monolithic conservatism and economic self-sufficiency to which de Valera aspired. Rather, the combination of the relative prosperity of the 1960s and 1970s with the increased population of those years has created a young generation that is demographically large and well-educated, and that is also far more modern than their parents' generation. With so substantial a number of them living in urban areas, these youths have tended to drift away from the traditional emphasis on hearth and home. More open to differing lifestyles, they find the lack of "progress" in traditional Ireland frustrating and backward. Many of them tend to support politicians and social developments that reflect their own attitudes and, indeed, often disparage the traditional Ireland from which they have sprung.

These changing social attitudes have been very evident in political developments in the 1990s. While the Irish have had to contend with a political system dogged by scandal and reactionary politicians, there have been positive signs of change. Perhaps most important was the election in 1991 of Mary Robinson as president of the Republic. The presidency had traditionally been a largely ceremonial office and had usually been seen as a sinecure for politicians well past their prime. Mrs. Robinson, a Labour party member and barrister who made her reputation as an advocate for women's rights, was never expected to win the office. Indeed, her election can be attributed to the opportunity provided by the bickering that transpired between the two major political parties during the campaign. Having won the presidency, however, Mrs. Robinson has remade it in her own image. Although constitutionally barred from speaking out or participating in political matters, she has established herself as the most respected and trusted figure in Irish government. In her travels throughout the country, she has reached out to the dispossessed among Ireland's citizens, and given them hope of a better day. She is especially appealing to the young who see in her the embodiment of the change they believe is necessary for their nation. In a nonpolitical but highly effective manner, she has established a dialogue with women in Northern Ireland and has been effective in supporting peacemaking efforts in that province. On the international stage, President Robinson has assumed a role as the representative of all that is positive and good about Ireland. Irish-Americans in particular have developed a genuine respect and affection for her. It is perhaps one of the most encouraging indications of Ireland's changing sense of itself that Mary Robinson is the most popular figure in the country today.

Yet, on the political front, change has not come as easily. Politics remains the province of a "good-old-boy" system of government. From 1987 to 1992, Charles Haughey of Fianna Fáil served as *taoiseach* (prime minister). Haughey represented old-style Irish politics in the extreme. With a career often highlighted by controversy and scandal, Haughey had the effect of dividing the country along personal lines. People tended to be for or against him rather than for or against his party's positions. Haughey's business dealings, as well as his involvement in nationalist activities in Northern Ireland, contributed to the perception, at least on the part of some, that he was not an entirely trustworthy figure.

Nonetheless, his term as *taoiseach* did contribute economic benefits to the country. Haughey made large-scale cuts in public spending in an effort to reduce the public debt, a courageous if highly unpopular move. He managed to win the support of organized labor, and, to almost everyone's surprise, he succeeded in reversing the downward slide of the Irish economy.

Before long, however, Haughey was once again engulfed in scandal. A series of business deals in 1991 had taxed the patience of the country with its flamboyant leader. Then, in 1992, his own colleagues in Fianna Fáil turned on him. His party's coalition partners, the Progressive Democrats, threatened to bring down the government if Haughey did not resign. Finally, when it became clear to him that his support in Fianna Fáil was diminishing, Haughey did just that.

The period that followed illustrated the extent of Ireland's new mood. Emboldened by the election of Mary Robinson, people appeared anxious for change. Although Haughey was succeeded by his former finance minister, Albert Reynolds, similarities between the two were relatively few. A businessman who had made a fortune, Reynolds was nonetheless a simple, decent man, quite unlike the flashy Haughey. The early days of the Reynolds administration continued many of Haughey's economic policies, but they were also devoted to restoring faith in the integrity of government.

By autumn, Reynolds too was in the glare of unpleasant political wrangling, and, in November, his government fell and he called a general election. Both of the traditional political parties lost between 10 and 20 percent of their seats in the Dáil Éireann, while the Labour party doubled its representation. Fianna Fáil and Fine Gael each retained large blocs of seats, but not enough for either to form a government without Labour's assistance.

The election also brought into greater prominence the popular Labour leader Dick Spring. Born in 1950, Spring enjoyed popular support among younger voters. He had served as deputy prime minister *(taniste)* and had been an active opponent of Haughey, especially during the final days of the latter's term as *taoiseach*. Now Spring found himself in a position in which he could determine the shape of the next government. After long negotiations, Labour finally agreed to form a coalition government with Fianna Fáil. In exchange, Albert Reynolds stayed on as prime minister, while Spring himself became deputy prime minister and foreign minister.

For two years, Spring and the policies of the coalition drew praise from all sides. In particular, Spring was given major credit for advances in the Northern Ireland peace process, including the cease-fire of August 1994. The coalition government's proposed reform program, which was popular with the people but not with the Dáil, floundered. Several of the more substantial elements of the program, including better housing, an ethics in government bill, and fairer taxation, failed to be enacted into law.

Issues of Church-state separation continued to plague the new government as they had the old. In 1992, Ireland faced one of its most difficult political/religious controversies. The nation as a whole has always maintained a solid opposition to abortion. Legislation even forbids the dispensing of information about abortion availability in other countries. While some feminist groups have tried to overturn the ban on information about abortion, and while hundreds of women each year cross the Irish Sea to obtain abortions in Britain, the nation's leaders and the population in general have taken an unyielding antiabortion stance. Despite criticism from feminists and others, Ireland has even gone so far as to enshrine its opposition to abortion in its constitution.

It was also in 1992 that a controversy arose that no one had anticipated—a controversy that forced the Irish to ask themselves some hard questions about their position on abortion. A fourteen-year-old girl was raped by a family friend and found herself pregnant. She could have done as thousands of Irish women do each year and gone quietly to England for an abortion. Instead, her parents, who wished to see her rapist prosecuted, asked permission to bring tissue from the fetus back from England in order to establish paternity and thus identify the rapist. When the news of the request became public, the girl and her plight became a cause célèbre.

Identifying or prosecuting the rapist became a minor concern. Instead, the Irish courts, media, and people seemed to focus their attention on preventing the abortion. In order to do so, the courts ruled that the girl could not leave Ireland. An international outrage erupted. The European Community argued that the Irish courts could not impede Irish citizens' right to travel freely. Feminists expressed their horror. The Church came down squarely on the side of those who wished simply to prevent the evil of an abortion by whatever means. The girl herself, largely lost in the tumult, threatened suicide. Ultimately, the Irish High Court ruled that the girl could travel to England but evaded the issue of freedom of travel in general; instead, it used the girl's mental instability and threats of suicide as a rationale for allowing her to go to England. It never addressed the issue of the rape or the abortion. For most people in Ireland, irrespective of their position on the abortion issue, the decision was no decision at all. To the more progressive elements of the Irish voting population, it seemed once again that the Church had dictated to the state.

The always potentially troublesome issue of the relationship between Church and state arose again, even if indirectly, in the political crisis of 1994. The coalition government, led by Albert Reynolds of Fianna Fáil, was generally admired for its efforts at political reform and its contribution to the cessation of hostilities in Northern Ireland, but it faced a serious scandal at home. In spite of accusations that the attorney general had delayed for many months the extradition to Northern Ireland of a Catholic priest charged with sexual abuse of minors, Reynolds named the attorney general to the High Court. Furthermore, he did so in full knowledge of the attorney general's equivocation with regard to the extradition issue. Once again it seemed that a member of the government had placed protection of the image of the Church above the public good. Eventually, the priest was extradited, but Reynolds had made a serious blunder. In November 1994 he was forced to resign. Many worried that without his leadership the peace process in the North might unravel. That has not happened, and Reynolds' successor, John Bruton of Fine Gael, has shown himself to be both willing and able to continue the work of peacemaking.

The Church's considerable influence within the Irish state persists, and it is a source of no little frustration to those who wish the Irish nation to modernize. In mid-1995, the Irish government threw the full weight of its support behind a referendum that would end Ireland's status as the only member of the European Community to forbid civil divorce. A similar referendum had failed to achieve a majority of the vote in the late 1980s. In the hope of avoiding a repeat of that outcome, the government sought to anticipate and to respond to concerns related to the proposed legislation. Such concerns as inheritance, child support, and spousal support were addressed in the referendum. The Church itself took no stand, though private organizations arose to speak for the Church and for Irish conservatives. The proposed solution was hardly radical. Four years of separation would be necessary before a divorce could be granted.

Initially, it appeared that the referendum would pass handily. As many as 70 percent of the voters at one time expressed support for it. As referendum day grew closer, however, opposition to the divorce bill intensified. When the polling was finally conducted in November 1995, the referendum passed by less than 1 percent of the vote. Indeed, the vote was so close that opponents have filed appeals to stop its implementation. Even in early 1996, it remains uncertain whether divorce will actually come to Ireland in the near future.

Clearly the Roman Catholic Church continues to exert a force in the politics of Ireland, but does it still dominate the social and private lives of the Irish people? Although more than 90 percent of Irish citizens still identify themselves as Roman Catholic, and about 80 percent of them attend Mass regularly, an authoritative study in the *International Social Science Journal* (September 1995) contains a 1990–1991 survey in which only 50 percent of religious believers in Ireland identified God as important in their lives. Irish society in general has grown more secular, and the notion of the parish priest laying down the law on every matter is no longer acceptable to most Irish. The Church tries to address the problems of young people in a changing society, but such exhortations most often fall on deaf ears. Even the efforts undertaken by the Church to address the serious social ills of poverty and unemployment have lost much of their credibility. The Church as an institution has forfeited its once unquestioned place in Irish society by its harsh stance and its overinvolvement in political issues. Nor have the Church's interests been well served by the serious decline in the quantity and quality of the clergy. The retreating influence of Catholicism in people's lives in Ireland can be partly attributed, of course, to the successive and highly publicized sexual scandals involving pedophile priests and clerical mistresses, even at the episcopal level, in recent years. Many practicing Catholics now often ignore Church teachings on questions of sexual morality and follow their own consciences in such matters. Moreover, the Church's hard-line stance on issues such as contraception and divorce, as well as its unyielding authoritarian approach to the Irish people, has damaged its authority and credibility.

The hierarchy, however, remains staunchly conservative and seems almost blind to the realities of Irish life in the 1990s. Positions taken by the Church and the lack of appreciation of the lives of ordinary people displayed by the bishops have only worsened the crisis of confidence among the Irish regarding their Catholicism.

One must recognize, of course, that a crisis in confidence with respect to the Church is for many people a crisis of identity as well. For most Irish, to be Irish means to be Catholic. Since the days of Daniel O'Connell in the nineteenth century, Catholicism has been linked inextricably with Irish nationalism. To lose that dimension of their Irish identity as a price for joining the modern world would be a great sacrifice indeed for the Irish to make.

Along with the complicated state of Irish politics and its tangled relationship with the Roman Catholic Church, change is also evident in the Irish economy. Since independence in 1922, Ireland's economy has consistently lagged behind that of virtually every other Western European nation. However, since Ireland's admission into the European Community in the 1970s, the country has made a concerted, if sporadic, effort to improve the economic picture. Even the recession of the late 1980s and early 1990s has not entirely halted Ireland's improving economic performance. Nonetheless, this relatively better performance needs to be viewed against Ireland's backward starting point. Until the late 1950s, Ireland had made little effort to modernize its economy. Not until the era of Sean Lemass did the Irish begin to respond to the economic realities of the modern European world. In addition, the Irish continue to face serious fiscal difficulties. Periodic worldwide recessions have not helped, of course, but several problems unique to Ireland have also been detrimental to Irish economic growth and they continue to be so today.

Government encouragement of foreign investment in Ireland has developed into a somewhat mixed blessing. The increase in exports created by these firms is a deceptive feature. Because the profits from these investments tend to return to the investors' home countries, their benefit to the Irish economy has been limited. Moreover, while such investment has certainly been responsible for the creation of a significant number of jobs, foreign investors are far too likely to pull up stakes and move elsewhere if Irish investments become too costly, or if the investors experience a period of financial difficulty. Thus, foreign investment has tended to impact erratically upon Ireland's employment picture.

Secondly, Ireland has long suffered, and continues to suffer, from a high level of government spending. The 1980s were a period of excessive expenditures by Fianna Fáil and Fine Gael governments alike. Beginning in 1987, the government began a conscious effort to reduce spending and to lessen the size of the national debt. But Ireland faces some extraordinary problems in attempting to lessen public expenditures. Because the country's population is so young, large sums must be spent on both social welfare and education. In addition, Ireland's consistently high levels of unemployment create the need to spend large sums for unemployment benefits. Moreover, many Irish people look at the levels of spending on social benefits in other European countries and are unwilling to settle for much less, despite their much weaker economy. Consequently, politicians are under constant pressure to keep the benefits at high levels. Various governments have developed reform programs designed to curb spending, but development is not implementation. Although the Irish complain constantly about their high level of taxation, they remain ambivalent about supporting serious cuts in public spending, even if such cuts might make a tax reduction possible.

In a related issue, Ireland's persistently high levels of unemployment contribute to the weakness of the Irish economy in many ways. As we have seen, unemployment fuels the machine that leads to excessive government spending. Job creation schemes have not proven their worth. Moreover, the demographics of Ireland's young population certainly worsen the employment prospects, while the country's agricultural economic base seems to exacerbate the situation still further.

The problem seems to lie in a distinctly Irish situation. First, the continuing migration of young people from farm to city places additional pressures on both the economic resources and the availability of jobs in urban areas. Second, even though the government's efforts to cut spending have helped the overall economy, they have reduced the availability of public-sector jobs, thus increasing the unemployment problem. Moreover, as young people choose to remain in the country rather than emigrate, they increase the unemployment rolls. The Irish have also faced the consequences of periodic recession throughout the 1980s and 1990s. During such periods, job creation tends to draw to a halt.

These factors and others, such as labor-management disputes and strikes, as well as Ireland's transportation and communication backwardness, have tended to increase the problem of unemployment. The government currently regards the improvement of the employment picture as its most serious challenge, but so far its efforts have had limited success.

The Irish do have a source of hope, however. In recent years, Ireland has seen its birth rate fall dramatically. The Irish at last have followed the European trend toward small families. By about the year 2000 this downturn in family size should begin to produce a smaller number of young people entering the work force. The hope is that unemployment will decrease as well.

Despite all the emphasis we have placed on Ireland's increasing urbanization, it is important to keep in mind that agriculture is still Ireland's most important industry. The Irish cherish—indeed, almost worship—the family farm. Their history certainly explains their attitude. Because their ancestors were unable to own their own farms until the enactment of land legislation in the late nineteenth and early twentieth centuries, most Irish farmers view the right to possess land as their most important treasure. Though their holdings may be too small to be productive in a modern economy, they cling to them all the same and insist that the government should help them even if such assistance is not in the interest of the country as a whole. European Community policies have both helped and damaged the rural economy. They have encouraged expansion and modernization but until recently have not addressed the issue of the very small farmer who cannot afford the equipment needed to operate efficiently. Continued migration to the cities as well as emigration have left many farming communities half deserted, yet most people in rural areas recognize that leaving is the best option for their children. The stories of rural school leavers whose gifts on finishing secondary school are plane tickets to London or New York, or bus tickets to Dublin or Cork, are no myth. The depopulation of western Ireland is a serious problem which the nation as a whole must address.

And this problem brings us full circle to the question of Ireland's sense of identity. Life in rural areas has contributed mightily to the Irish identity and imagination. Irish literature from the Anglo-Irish writings of Maria Edgeworth in the eighteenth century to the poetry of Seamus Heaney today has the experience of rural Ireland stamped upon it. If the Irish lose this aspect of their identity, they will have lost something vital and essential. Thus, the politicians and economists face a problem that cannot be solved in the halls of the Dáil or in the formulas of the budget theoreticians. Rather, to determine whether Ireland will remain a unique people or just become a poor European nation, the Irish must look into their very souls and decide who and what they want to be.

THE SIX COUNTIES

Northern Ireland in early 1996 is also experiencing the desire for change which has characterized the Republic during the 1990s. While the terrorists on both sides remain wary of each other, a cease-fire proclaimed by the Irish Republican Army (IRA) in August 1994 was still tentatively in place in 1996. Peacemaking has become a respectable activity among moderate politicians on both sides of the sectarian divide. By and large, the cease-fire has been effective in eliminating political violence in Northern Ireland. For the first time in a generation, people there have begun to experience and enjoy a measure of normal living. Despite the harsh rhetoric of some of their leaders, in particular the more radical Unionists, the people of Northern Ireland appreciate and aspire to the benefits of an environment without random violence.

People also appreciate the prosperity that even this tenuous peace has brought them. In 1995, tourism in the Six Counties increased substantially. Many tourists who once would have consciously excluded Northern Ireland from a visit now just as deliberately include visits to Belfast, Derry, and other Northern Ireland tourist sites.

Foreign investment in Northern Ireland has also grown, although not nearly as much as might be hoped. Such as it is, the growth has had a positive impact on improving relations between the two communities. Foreign investors have little interest in encouraging or permitting ancient hatreds to divert their workplaces from productivity. Even if some investors had to be prodded into taking a proactive role in guaranteeing equal and fair employment, they have undertaken such efforts. Most new industries employ, and thus integrate, both communities.

The U.S. government, under the Clinton administration, has engaged in an active effort to encourage American investment on both sides of the border. Indeed, its example and encouragement have helped to develop a new confidence in the future that has come to characterize many Irish businesses.

Nonetheless, the effort to effect change has been just as sporadic and uneven in Northern Ireland as in the Republic. Political events in particular demonstrate how fragile the peacemaking process really is. In November 1994, for example, the resignation of Albert Reynolds as *taoiseach* in the Republic placed the peacemaking negotiations at risk because it was uncertain whether British Prime Minister John Major would have the same good working relationship with the new *taoiseach,* John Bruton. As it happens, the change in the Irish government, from Fianna Fáil to Fine Gael, did not result in any diminution in Anglo-Irish cooperation. Bruton has continued the initiatives taken by Reynolds in working with Major.

Prime Minister Major, however, faces an even more daunting problem in his efforts to achieve peace. His Conservative party has long promised the Unionists of Northern Ireland that the British will never force them into a united Ireland against their will. Many Unionists view this promise as a virtual covenant guaranteeing that the British will never alter conditions in Northern Ireland in any way. Thus, for many Unionists, any conciliatory action taken by the British government toward the Nationalist community, or any involvement in talks by the British with representatives of the Republic, represents a betrayal of Britain's promises to them.

Major is thus placed in an extremely difficult position. He genuinely wishes to bring about peace. Unlike his predecessor, Margaret Thatcher, who viewed her Northern Ireland policy largely in terms of suppressing violence even as she developed the Anglo-Irish Agreement of 1985, Major is willing to sit down and talk about alterations in the Northern Ireland picture. But he is handicapped by an insurmountable obstacle in his own fragile political position. The 1992 general election confirmed Major and his party in power for five years, but with only a very slim majority. Since that time he has seen this small Conservative majority in Parliament dwindle away. By January 1996, it was down to just two Members. In such circumstances, Northern Irish Unionists are in a position to name their price for keeping the Conservatives in power through the end of their term in April 1997. Although they usually vote with the Conservatives, the Unionists are far more interested in their own agenda than they are in preserving John Major in power.

Nor is Major's political survival the only development likely to affect the course of peacemaking in Northern Ireland. President Bill Clinton has taken a far more active stand in efforts to bring about peace than had most previous American presidents. Clinton's recent appointment of former Senator George Mitchell as chairman of a commission to set up the framework for a surrender of weapons, as well as his administration's financial assistance to economic development in the border areas between Northern Ireland and the Republic of Ireland, illustrate his administration's interest in and commitment to Ireland. Both the northern and southern Irish tend to view Clinton positively but the policies he represents are at some risk. Americans at the present time are far more concerned with their own economic well-being than they are with any foreign policy issue, and a new president may not regard bringing peace to Northern Ireland as a high priority. Thus, the American role in the peace process remains in doubt in 1996.

Nor are the leaders on all sides anxious to make peace. Ian Paisley (discussed in previous chapters) continues to rant against movement in the direction of peace on any but his own terms. More worrisome was the selection in 1995 of hard-line politicians as the leadership of the official Unionist party in Northern Ireland. Such staunch Unionists have little interest in negotiating peace, or anything else, with either Major or Bruton. Indeed, they consider the very involvement of representatives from the Republic as an insult to them and their position.

It must also be remembered that the cease-fire and the cessation of hostilities in Northern Ireland have ended only political violence. In both religious communities, organized crime remains an important problem and every bit as serious a source of violence as were The Troubles themselves. The people of Northern Ireland, with the help of the British government, must solve their own crime problem, but the power that these gangs have developed throughout the Six Counties will present a daunting challenge to the local police forces. Since these gangs exploit old divisions, they find the coming of peace to be a problem and probably will continue in activities that are likely to prevent peace for a very long time. They already control whole areas of Belfast, and they will not give up easily.

Even so, the people of Northern Ireland cling to any hope of peace they see. On a symbolic level, during 1995 there were two events that indicated how far the people—if not their politicians—have come in their hopes for reconciliation. In the summer of 1995, the Prince of Wales became the first member of his family to visit Dublin since independence in 1922. The Prince shared with his hosts his longstanding desire to visit the city and to meet the Irish people. While he said nothing of political significance during his visit, his very presence symbolized a new period of reconciliation between Ireland and England. To reemphasize this point, later in 1995, Mary Robinson, president of the Republic, visited with Queen Elizabeth at Buckingham Palace.

In November-December 1995, President Clinton visited both Northern Ireland and the Republic of Ireland. His tumultuous welcome in Dublin reminded observers of the visit of President John F. Kennedy in 1963. There was a significant difference, though. Kennedy had been welcomed home as the son of emigrants, as a member of the Irish diaspora. Clinton, on the other hand, who has meager Irish roots (though a few were dug up for the occasion), was being recognized for his actions on behalf of the Irish people. Moreover, while Kennedy never set foot in Northern Ireland, Clinton's activities were primarily directed to the people of the Six Counties where his welcome was less certain. Indeed, some Unionist leaders had called upon Protestants to boycott the events surrounding his visit. Instead, the people of Belfast and Londonderry opened their arms to him. Most events were carefully staged, but the people who thronged the streets seemed to offer him a genuinely sincere welcome. For Protestant and Catholic alike, Clinton's arrival as the first American president ever to visit Northern Ireland appeared to symbolize their own commitment to reconciliation and hope in their homeland. The politicians on all sides will do well to listen to these people and to their cheers at every mention of a world at peace.

Just how difficult such a peace will be to achieve was poignantly demonstrated, of course, when an Irish Republican Army bomb exploded in the Docklands area of East London on February 9, 1996, killing two people and wounding thirty-nine in an act of terrorism that seriously compromised the credibility of the seventeen-month cease-fire. Although there might have been still greater loss of life had the IRA not notified a Dublin newsroom about the intended target less than two hours before the blast, the half-ton bomb, which caused property damage in the tens of millions of dollars and came close to engulfing Canary Wharf, home of Europe's tallest office building, nevertheless had the effect of calling into question the future of the peace process.

An early analysis by seasoned observers was that British Prime Minister John

Major may have provoked the IRA by appearing to side with Unionists in calling for elections to create negotiating teams rather than accepting Senator George Mitchell's recommendation that both the Protestant paramilitaries and the IRA turn in their weapons before the start of formal peace negotiations. On February 14, the London Government ordered 500 soldiers back to Northern Ireland to bolster the 16,000 troops already stationed there, and the Belfast police force began issuing rifles once again to some of its members. If nothing else, the IRA bombing had recalled for everyone just how fragile was the understanding that had led to the cessation of hostilities. Like the minefields of Bosnia, the hidden hazards to peace in Northern Ireland pervade the landscape. Yet, for a people who have endured a generation of unrelenting horror, there is really no choice but to go forward. This bombing is, after all, only the latest installment of the ongoing Irish experience.

Recommended Reading

GENERAL STUDIES AND INTERPRETATIONS

BECKETT, J. C., *The Making of Modern Ireland, 1603–1923*. New York: Knopf, 1966.

BOTTIGHEIMER, KARL S., *Ireland and the Irish: A Short History*. New York: Columbia University Press, 1982.

BOYCE, D. GEORGE, *Nationalism in Ireland*. Baltimore: Johns Hopkins University Press, 1982.

COSTIGAN, GIOVANNI, *A History of Modern Ireland*. New York: Pegasus, 1969.

CULLEN, L. M., *An Economic History of Ireland since 1660*. London: Batsford, 1972.

DEPAOR, LIAM, *The Peoples of Ireland: From Prehistory to Modern Times*. South Bend: University of Notre Dame Press, 1986.

EDWARDS, OWEN DUDLEY, "Ireland," in *Celtic Nationalism*, ed. Owen Dudley Edwards. New York: Barnes & Noble Books, 1968.

EDWARDS, RUTH DUDLEY, *An Atlas of Irish History*. London: Methuen, 1973.

EVANS, E. ESTYN, *The Personality of Ireland: Habitat, Heritage and History*. Cambridge, England: Cambridge University Press, 1973.

FOSTER, RAY, *Modern Ireland, 1600–1972*. New York: Viking, 1989.

FREEMAN, T. W., *Ireland: A General and Regional Geography*. London: Methuen, 1960.

GARVIN, TOM, *The Evolution of Irish Nationalist Politics*. Dublin: Gill and Macmillan, 1981.

HACHEY, THOMAS E., *Britain and Irish Separatism: From the Fenians to the Free State, 1867–1922.* Skokie, ILL.: Rand McNally, 1977.

HERNON, JOSEPH M., JR., "The Last Whig Historian and Consensus History: George Macaulay Trevelyan, 1876–1962," *American Historical Review,* 81:1 (February, 1976), 66–97.

HOPPEN, THEODORE, *Elections, Politics and Society in Ireland, 1832–1885.* Oxford: Clarendon Press, 1984.

LYONS, F. S. L., *Ireland since the Famine.* New York: Scribner, 1971.

MACDONAGH, OLIVER, *Ireland.* Englewood Cliffs, N.J.: Prentice-Hall, 1968.

————, *States of Mind: A Study of Anglo-Irish Conflict, 1780–1980.* Boston: George Allen & Unwin, 1983.

MANSERGH, NICHOLAS, *The Irish Question, 1840–1920* (rev. ed.). Toronto: University of Toronto Press, 1964.

MCCAFFREY, LAWRENCE J., *The Irish Question, 1800–1922.* Lexington: University Press of Kentucky, 1968.

MCCARTNEY, DONAL, *The Dawning of Democracy: Ireland, 1800–1870.* Dublin: Helicon, 1987.

MCDOWELL, R. B., *The Irish Administration, 1801–1914.* Toronto: University of Toronto Press, 1964.

MOODY, T. W., AND F. X. MARTIN (EDS.), *The Course of Irish History.* Cork: Mercier Press, 1978.

MOODY, T. W., AND F. X. MARTIN, AND F. J. BYRNE (EDS.), *A Chronology of Irish History to 1976.* A New History of Ireland Series, vol. 8, part 1, New York: Oxford University Press, 1982.

O'FAOLAIN, SEAN, *The Irish.* Harmondsworth, England: Pelican, 1969.

O'FARRELL, PATRICK, *Ireland's English Question.* New York: Schocken Books, 1972.

————, *England and Ireland since 1800.* New York: Oxford University Press, 1975.

OREL, HAROLD (ED.), *Irish History and Culture: Aspects of a People's Heritage.* Lawrence: University of Kansas Press, 1976.

STRAUSS, ERIC, *Irish Nationalism and British Democracy.* New York: Columbia University Press, 1961.

TIERNEY, MARK, *Modern Ireland Since 1850.* Dublin: Gill and Macmillan, 1978.

IRELAND: 200 B.C.–A.D. 1800

BOLTON, G. C., *The Passing of the Act of Union.* London: Oxford University Press, 1966.

CONNELL, KENNETH, *The Population of Ireland, 1750–1845.* London: Oxford University Press, 1950.

CORISH, PATRICK, *The Catholic Community in the Seventeenth and Eighteenth Centuries* (Helicon History of Ireland, vol. 5). Dublin: Helicon, 1981.

DOLLEY, MICHAEL, *Anglo-Norman Ireland* (Gill History of Ireland, vol. 3). Dublin: Gill and Macmillan, 1972.

EDWARDS, R. DUDLEY, *Ireland in the Age of the Tudors: The Destruction of Hiberno-Norman Civilization.* London: Croom Helm, 1977.

ELLIOTT, MARIANNE, *Partners in Revolution: The United Irishmen and France.* New Haven, CT: Yale University Press, 1982.

ELLIS, STEPHEN G., *Tudor Ireland, 1470–1603.* White Plains, N.Y.: Longman, 1985.

FERGUSON, O., *Jonathan Swift and Ireland.* Urbana: University of Illinois Press, 1962.

HENRY, FRANÇOIS (ED.), *Irish Art in the Early Christian Period.* Ithaca, N.Y.: Cornell University Press, 1965.

JAMES, FRANCIS GODWIN, *Ireland in the Empire, 1688–1770.* Cambridge, MA: Harvard University Press, 1973.

JOHNSTON, EDITH MARY, *Ireland in the Eighteenth Century* (Gill History of Ireland, vol. 8). Dublin: Gill and Macmillan, 1974.

LECKY, W. E. H., *A History of Ireland in the Eighteenth Century,* abridged by L. P. Curtis, Jr. Chicago: University of Chicago Press, 1972.

———, *The Leaders of Public Opinion in Ireland.* London: Longmans Greene, 1871, 1883, 1903.

LYDON, JAMES, *Ireland in the Later Middle Ages* (Gill History of Ireland, vol. 6). Dublin: Gill and Macmillan, 1972.

MACCURTAIN, MARGARET, *Tudor and Stuart Ireland* (Gill History of Ireland, vol. 7). Dublin: Gill and Macmillan, 1972.

MAHONEY, THOMAS H. D., *Edmund Burke and Ireland.* Cambridge, MA: Harvard University Press, 1960.

MACNIOCAILL, GEARÓID, *Ireland before the Vikings* (Gill History of Ireland, vol. 1). Dublin: Gill and Macmillan, 1972.

MCDOWELL, R. B., *Irish Public Opinion, 1750–1800.* London: Faber and Faber, 1944.

MOODY, T. W., AND F. X. MARTIN (EDS.), *Early Modern Ireland, 1534–1691* (New History of Ireland Series, vol. 3). New York: Oxford University Press, 1984.

MOODY, T. W., AND W. E. VAUGHN (EDS.), *Eighteenth Century Ireland, 1691–1800* (New History of Ireland Series, vol. 4). New York: Clarendon Press/Oxford University Press, 1986.

NICHOLLS, KENNETH, *Gaelic and Gaelicized Ireland in the Middle Ages* (Gill History of Ireland, vol. 4). Dublin: Gill and Macmillan, 1972.

O'CONNELL, MAURICE, *Irish Politics and Social Conflict in the Age of the American Revolution.* Philadelphia: University of Pennsylvania Press, 1965.

O'CORRÁIN, DONNCHA, *Ireland before the Normans* (Gill History of Ireland, vol. 2). Dublin: Gill and Macmillan, 1972.

OTWAY-RUTHVEN, J. *A History of Medieval Ireland,* 2nd ed., New York: St. Martin's Press, 1980.

PAKENHAM, THOMAS, *The Year of Liberty: The Great Irish Rebellion of 1798.* London: Hodden and Stoughton, 1966.

SENIOR, HEREWARD, *Orangeism in Ireland and Britain, 1795–1836.* New York: Hilary House Distribution Ltd., 1966.

WALL, MAUREEN, *The Penal Laws, 1691–1760* (Irish History Series, No. 1). Dundalk: Dundalgen Press for the Dublin Historical Association, 1961.

———, "The Rise of the Catholic Middle Class in Eighteenth Century Ireland," *Irish Historical Studies,* 11 (September 1958), 91–115.

WATT, JAMES, *The Church in Medieval Ireland* (Gill History of Ireland, vol. 5). Dublin: Gill and Macmillan, 1972.

FROM THE UNION THROUGH THE FAMINE

AKENSON, DONALD H., *The Irish Educational Experiment.* Toronto: University of Toronto Press, 1970.

BLACK, R. D. COLLISON, *Economic Thought and the Irish Question, 1817–1870.* Cambridge, England: Cambridge University Press, 1960.

BRODERICK, JOHN F., S.J., *The Holy See and the Irish Movement for the Repeal of the Union with England, 1829–1847.* Rome: Universitatis Gregorianne Press, 1951.

BROEKER, GALEN, *Rural Disorder and Police Reform in Ireland, 1812–1836.* Toronto: University of Toronto Press, 1970.

BROWN, THOMAS N., *Nationalism and the Irish Peasant* (American Committee for Irish Studies Reprint Series, ed. Emmet Larkin and Lawrence J. McCaffrey). Chicago:

University of Chicago Press, 1971. Originally published in *The Review of Politics,* 15 (October 1953), 403–445, and has been reprinted in Lawrence J. McCaffrey (ed.), *Irish Nationalism and the American Contribution.* New York: Arno Press, 1976.

CAHILL, GILBERT, "Irish Catholicism and English Toryism, *Review of Politics,* 19 (January 1957), 62–76.

———, "Irish Popery and British Nativism: 1800–1848," *Cithra,* 13 (May 1974), 3–18.

———, "The Protestant Association and the Anti-Maynooth Agitation of 1845," *Catholic Historical Review,* 43 (October 1957), 273–308.

DALY, MARY E., *The Famine in Ireland.* Dundalk: Dundalgen Press for the Dublin Historical Association, 1986.

DUFFY, CHARLES GAVAN, *Young Ireland.* London: T. Fisher Unwin, 1896.

EDWARDS, R. DUDLEY, AND WILLIAMS, T. DESMOND (EDS.), *The Great Famine: Studies in Irish History, 1845–1852.* Dublin: Browne and Nolan for the Irish Committee for Historical Studies, 1956.

GALLAGHER, THOMAS, *Paddy's Lament: Ireland 1846–1847, Prelude to Hatred.* Orlando, FL.: Harcourt Brace Jovanovich, 1987.

GASH, NORMAN, *Mr. Secretary Peel.* Cambridge, MA.: Harvard University Press, 1961.

GWYNN, DENIS, *Daniel O'Connell: The Irish Liberator.* Cork: Cork University Press, 1947.

———, *O'Connell, Davis, and the Colleges Bill.* Cork: Cork University Press, 1948.

———, *Young Ireland and 1848.* Cork: Cork University Press, 1949.

HERNON, JOSEPH M., JR., "A Victorian Cromwell: Sir Charles Trevelyan, The Famine and the Age of Improvement," *Eire-Ireland,* 22:3 (Fall, 1987), 15–29.

JENKINS, BRIAN, *Era of Emancipation: The British Government of Ireland, 1812–1830.* Montreal: McGill–Queen's University Press, 1988.

LARKIN, EMMETT, "The Quarrel among the Roman Catholic Hierarchy over the National System of Education in Ireland, 1838–1841," in *The Celtic Cross,* ed. Ray B. Browne, William Roscelli, and Richard J. Loftus. Lafayette, IN.: Purdue University Press, 1964.

LECKY, W. E. H., "Daniel O'Connell," in *The Leaders of Public Opinion in Ireland.* London: Longmans Greene, 1871, 1883, 1903.

MACDONAGH, OLIVER, *The Hereditary Bondsman: Daniel O'Connell, 1775–1829.* London: Weidenfeld and Nicolson, 1988.

MACHIN, G. I. T., *The Catholic Question in English Politics.* London: Oxford University Press, 1964.

MACINTYRE, ANGUS, *The Liberator: Daniel O'Connell and the Irish Party, 1830–1847.* London: Hamish and Hamilton, 1965.

MACLOCHLAINN, AILFRID, "The Racialism of Thomas Davis: Root and Branch," *Journal of Irish Literature,* 5 (May 1976), 112–122.

McCAFFREY, LAWRENCE J., *Daniel O'Connell and the Repeal Year.* Lexington: University Press of Kentucky, 1966.

McCARTNEY, DONAL (ED.), *The World of Daniel O'Connell.* Cork: Mercier Press, 1980.

McDOWELL, R. B., *Public Opinion and Government Policy in Ireland.* London: Faber and Faber, 1952.

MILLER, DAVID W., "Irish Catholicism and the Great Famine," *Journal of Social History,* 9 (September 1975), 81–98.

MOLKYR, JOEL, *Why Ireland Starved: A Quantitative and Analytical History of the Irish Economy, 1800–1852.* Boston: George Allen & Unwin, 1983.

NOWLAN, KEVIN, *The Politics of Repeal.* Toronto: University of Toronto Press, 1965.

NOWLAN, KEVIN, AND MAURICE O'CONNELL (EDS.), *Daniel O'Connell: Portrait of a Radical.* Belfast: Appletree Press, 1984.

O'CONNELL, MAURICE R. (ED.), *The Correspondence of Daniel O'Connell,* 8 vols. New York: Barnes & Noble Books, 1973–1980.

O'FAOLAIN, SEAN, *King of the Beggars: A Life of Daniel O'Connell.* Dublin: Poolbeg Press, 1986.

O'FERRALL, FERGUS, *Catholic Emancipation: Daniel O'Connell and the Birth of Irish Democracy, 1820–1830.* Dublin: Gill and MacMillan, 1985.

———, *Daniel O'Connell.* Dublin: Gill and Macmillan, 1981.

O'NEILL, THOMAS P., "The Economic and Political Ideas of James Fintan Lalor," *Irish Ecclesiastical Record,* 74 (November 1950), 398–409.

'O TUATHAIGH, GEARÓID, *Ireland before the Famine, 1798–1848.* Dublin: Gill and Macmillan, 1972.

REYNOLDS, JAMES A., *The Catholic Emancipation Crisis in Ireland, 1823–1829.* New Haven, Conn.: Yale University Press, 1954.

SALAMAN, R. N., *The History and Social Influence of the Potato.* Cambridge, MA.: Harvard University Press, 1949.

TIERNEY, MICHAEL (ED.), *Daniel O'Connell.* Dublin: Browne and Nolan, 1949.

WHYTE, JOHN H., "The Appointment of Catholic Bishops in Nineteenth-Century Ireland," *Catholic Historical Review,* 48 (April 1962), 12–32.

———, "Daniel O'Connell and the Repeal Party," *Irish Historical Studies,* 11 (September 1959), 297–316.

———, "The Influence of the Catholic Clergy on Elections in Nineteenth-Century Ireland," *English Historical Review,* 75 (April 1960), 239–259.

WILLIAMS, T. DESMOND, *Secret Societies in Ireland.* New York: Barnes & Noble Books, 1973.

WOODHAM-SMITH, CECIL, *The Great Hunger: Ireland, 1845–1849.* New York: Harper & Row, 1962.

FROM THE FAMINE TO THE FALL OF PARNELL

ARNSTEIN, W. L., "Parnell and the Bradlaugh Case," *Irish Historical Studies,* 13 (March 1963), 215–235.

BEW, PAUL, *C. S. Parnell.* Dublin: Gill and Macmillan, 1981.

CORFE, THOMAS, *The Phoenix Park Murders: Conflict, Compromise and Tragedy in Ireland, 1879–1882.* London: Hodder and Stoughton, 1968.

COMERFORD, R. V., *The Fenians in Context: Irish Politics and Society, 1848–1882.* Atlantic Highlands, N.J.: Humanities Press, 1985.

CURTIS, L. P., JR., *Coercion and Conciliation in Ireland, 1880–1892.* Princeton, N.J.: Princeton University Press, 1963.

DAVITT, MICHAEL, *The Fall of Feudalism in Ireland.* New York: Harper & Row, 1904.

DUFFY, CHARLES GAVAN, *The League of the North and South.* London: Chapman and Hall, 1886.

FEINGOLD, WILLIAM, *Revolt of the Tenants: The Transfer of Local Government in Ireland, 1872–1886.* Boston: Northeastern University Press, 1984.

GLASER, JOHN A., "Parnell's Fall and the Nonconformist Conscience," *Irish Historical Studies,* 12 (September 1960), 119–138.

GRIFFIN, BRIAN, "Social Aspects of Fenianism in Connacht and Leinster, 1858–1870," *Éire-Ireland,* 12 (Spring 1986), 16–38.

HAMMOND, J. L., *Gladstone and the Irish Nation* (2nd ed.). Hamden, Conn.: Shoe String Press, 1964.

HARMON, MAURICE (ED.), *Fenians and Fenianism.* Seattle: University of Washington Press, 1970.

HERNON, JOSEPH M. JR., "The Historian as Politician; G. O. Trevelyan as Irish Chief Secretary," *Eire-Ireland,* 8:3 (Fall, 1973), 3–15.

HEYCK, THOMAS WILLIAM,   *The Dimensions of British Radicalism: The Case of Ireland, 1874–1895*. Urbana: University of Illinois Press, 1974.

HURST, MICHAEL,   *Parnell and Irish Nationalism*. Toronto: University of Toronto Press, 1968.

LEE, JOSEPH,   *The Modernization of Irish Society, 1848–1918*. Dublin: Gill and Macmillan, 1973.

LOUGHLIN, JAMES,   *Gladstone, Home Rule, and the Ulster Question, 1882–93*. Atlantic Highlands, N.J.: Humanities Press, 1987.

LYONS, F. S. L.,   *Charles Stewart Parnell*. London: Oxford University Press, 1977.

———,   *The Fall of Parnell, 1890–1891*. Toronto: University of Toronto Press, 1960.

MAGNUS, PHILIP,   *Gladstone*. New York: Dutton, 1964.

MARLOW, JOYCE,   *Captain Boycott and the Irish*. New York: Dutton, 1973.

McCAFFREY, LAWRENCE J.,   *Irish Federalism in the 1870s: A Study in Conservative Nationalism*. Philadelphia: American Philosophical Society, 1962.

McCREADY, H. W.,   "Home Rule and the Liberal Party, 1880–1901," *Irish Historical Studies*, 13 (September 1963), 316–348.

MOODY, T. W.,   *Davitt and Irish Revolution, 1846–1882*, New York: Oxford University Press, 1982.

——— (ED.),   *The Fenian Movement*. Cork: Mercier Press, 1968.

NORMAN, E. R.,   *The Catholic Church and Ireland in the Age of Rebellion, 1859–1873*. Ithaca, N.Y.: Cornell University Press, 1965.

O'BRIEN, CONOR CRUISE,   *Parnell and His Party, 1880–1890*. Oxford: Clarendon Press, 1960.

O'BRIEN, WILLIAM, AND DESMOND RYAN (EDS.),   *Devoy's Post Bag, 1871–1928*, 2 vols. Dublin: Fallon, 1948, 1953.

Ó BROIN, LEON,   *Fenian Fever: An Anglo-American Dilemma*. New York: New York University Press, 1971.

RYAN, DESMOND,   *The Fenian Chief*. Dublin: Gill and Macmillan, 1967. A biography of James Stephens.

THORNLEY, DAVID,   *Isaac Butt and Home Rule*. London: Ambassador Press, 1964.

WHITE, TERENCE DE VERE,   *The Road of Excess*. Dublin: Browne and Nolan, 1946. A biography of Isaac Butt.

WHYTE, JOHN,   *The Independent Irish Party, 1850–1859*. London: Oxford University Press, 1958.

FROM THE FALL OF PARNELL TO THE TREATY

BEASLAI, P.,   *Michael Collins, Soldier and Statesman*. Dublin: Talbot Press, 1937.

BENNETT, RICHARD,   *The Black and Tans*. Boston: Houghton Mifflin, 1959.

BEW, PAUL,   *Conflict and Conciliation in Ireland, 1890–1910: Parnellites and Agrarian Radicals*. Oxford: Clarendon Press, 1987.

BOYCE, D. G.,   *Englishmen and Irish Troubles: British Public Opinion and the Making of Irish Policy, 1918–1922*. Cambridge, MA.: M.I.T. Press, 1972.

BOYLE, JOHN,   "Irish Labour and the Rising," *Éire-Ireland*, 2 (Autumn 1967), 122–131.

BROMAGE, MARY,   *De Valera and the March of a Nation*. New York: Noonday Press, 1956.

BUCKLAND, PATRICK,   *Irish Unionism, Vol. 1: The Anglo-Irish and the New Ireland, 1885–1922*. Dublin: Gill and Macmillan, 1972.

———,   *Irish Unionism, Vol. 2: Ulster Unionism and the Origins of Northern Ireland, 1886–1922*. Dublin: Gill and Macmillan, 1973.

———,   *James Craig*. Dublin: Gill and Macmillan, 1981.

CLARKSON, J. DUNSMORE,   *Labour and Nationalism in Ireland*. New York: Columbia University Press, 1925.

COFFEY, THOMAS,   *Agony at Easter*. Baltimore: Penguin, 1969.

COSTIGAN, GIOVANNI,   "The Anglo-Irish Conflict, 1919–1922: A War of Independence or Systemized Murder?" *University Review*, 5 (Spring 1968).

CURRAN, JOSEPH,   *The Birth of the Irish Free State, 1921–1923*. University, Ala.: University of Alabama Press, 1980.

CURTIS, L. P., JR.,   *Anglo-Saxons and Celts: A Study in Anti-Irish Prejudice in Victorian England*. Bridgeport, Conn.; Conference on British Studies, 1968.

————,   *Apes and Angels: The Irishman in Victorian Caricature*. Newton Abbot, England: David and Charles, 1971.

DANGERFIELD, GEORGE,   *The Damnable Question*. Boston: Little, Brown, 1976.

————,   *The Strange Death of Liberal England*. New York: Capricorn Books, 1961.

DAVIS, RICHARD,   *Arthur Griffith and Non-violent Sinn Fein*. Dublin: Anvil Books, 1974.

DUNLEAVY, GARETH,   *Douglas Hyde* (Irish Writers Series). Lewisburg, PA.: Bucknell University Press, 1974.

EDWARDS, RUTH DUDLEY,   *James Connolly*. Dublin: Gill and Macmillan, 1981.

————,   *Patrick Pearse: The Triumph of Failure*. Boston: Faber and Faber, 1979.

ELLIS, P. BERESFORD,   *A History of the Irish Working Class*. New York: George Braziller, 1973.

FARRELL, BRIAN,   *The Founding of Dáil Éireann*. Dublin: Gill and Macmillan, 1971.

FERGUSON, SIR JAMES,   *The Curragh Incident*. London: Faber and Faber, 1964.

GAILEY, ANDREW,   *Ireland and the Death of Kindness: The Experience of Constructive Unionism, 1890–1905*. Cork: Cork University Press, 1987.

GOLDRING, MAURICE,   *Faith of Our Fathers: The Formation of Irish Nationalist Ideology, 1890–1920*. Dublin: Repsol Publishing, 1987.

GWYNN, DENIS,   *The Life of John Redmond*. London: Harrap, 1932.

HOLT, EDGAR,   *Protest in Arms: The Irish Troubles, 1916–1923*. London: McClelland, 1960.

HYDE, H. MONTGOMERY,   *Carson*. London: Heinemann, 1953.

JENKINS, ROY,   *Asquith*. London: Collins, 1965.

LARKIN, EMMET,   *James Larkin, Irish Labour Leader, 1876–1947*. Cambridge, MA.: M.I.T. Press, 1965.

LYONS, F. S. L.,   *The Irish Parliamentary Party, 1890–1910*. London: Faber and Faber, 1951.

————,   *John Dillon*. Chicago: University of Chicago Press, 1968.

MACARDLE, DOROTHY,   *The Irish Republic*. London: Farrar, Straus, 1965.

MARTIN, F. X., AND F. J. BYRNE (EDS.),   *The Scholar Revolutionary: Eoin MacNeill, 1867–1945, and the Making of the New Ireland*. New York: Barnes & Noble Books, 1973.

MCDOWELL, ROBERT,   *The Irish Convention, 1917–1918*. Toronto: University of Toronto Press, 1970.

MCHUGH, ROGER (ED.),   *Dublin, 1916*. London: Arlington Books, 1966.

MITCHEL, ARTHUR,   *Labour in Irish Politics, 1890–1930*. Shannon, Ireland: Irish University Press, 1974.

MORRISSEY, THOMAS J., S.J.,   *Toward a National University: William Delany, S.J. (1835–1924)*. Atlantic Highlands, N.J.: Humanities Press, 1985.

NOWLAN, KEVIN B. (ED.),   *The Making of 1916*. Dublin: Stationery Office, 1969.

O'BRIEN, CONOR CRUISE (ED.),   *The Shaping of Modern Ireland*. Toronto: Toronto University Press, 1960.

O'BRIEN, JOSEPH V.,   *Dear Dirty Dublin: A City in Distress, 1899–1916*. Berkeley: University of California Press, 1982.

————, *William O'Brien and the Course of Irish Politics, 1881–1918*. Berkeley: University of California Press, 1976.

Ó BROIN, LEON, *The Chief Secretary: Augustin Birrell in Ireland*. London: Chatto & Windus, 1969.

————, *Dublin Castle and the 1916 Rising*. New York: New York University Press, 1971.

O'CONNOR, FRANK, *The Big Fellow: A Life of Michael Collins*. London: Corgi Books, 1961.

O'DAY, ALAN, *The English Face of Irish Nationalism: Parnellite Involvement in British Politics, 1880–1886*. Dublin: Gill and Macmillan, 1977.

O'FAOLAIN, SEAN, *De Valera*. Harmondsworth, England: Penguin, 1939.

RYAN, A. P., *Mutiny at the Curragh*. New York: St. Martin's Press, 1956.

SHANNON, CATHERINE, *Arthur Balfour and Ireland (1874–1922)*. Washington, D.C.: Catholic University of America Press, 1988.

STEWART, A. T. Q., *Edward Carson*. Dublin: Gill and Macmillan, 1981.

————, *The Ulster Crisis*. London: Faber and Faber, 1967.

TAYLOR, R., *Michael Collins*. London: Four Square Books, 1958.

WARD, ALAN J., *The Easter Rising: Revolution and Irish Nationalism*. Arlington Heights, IL.: AHM Publishing, 1980.

POSTTREATY IRELAND

ARMOUR, WILLIAM STAVELY, *Ulster, Ireland, Britain: A Forgotten Trust*. London: Duckworth, 1938.

ARTHUR, PAUL, *Government and Politics of Northern Ireland*. Essex: Longman, 1980.

BAMBERG, CHRIS, *Ireland's Permanent Revolution*. London: Bookmarks, 1986.

BARRITT, DENIS P., AND CHARLES F. CARTER, *The Northern Ireland Problem: A Study in Group Relations* (2nd ed.). London: Oxford University Press, 1972.

BELL, J. BOWYER, *The Secret Army: A History of the IRA, 1916–1970*. London: Sphere Books, 1972.

BEW, PAUL, AND HENRY PATTERSON, *Sean Lemass and the Making of Modern Ireland, 1945–66*. Dublin: Gill and Macmillan, 1982.

BISHOP, PATRICK, AND EAMON MALLIE, *The Provisional IRA*. London: Heinemann, 1987.

BOLAND, KEVIN, *The Decline and Fall of Fianna Fáil*. Dublin: Mercier Press, 1982.

————, *Fine Gael: British or Irish?* Dublin: Mercier Press, 1984.

BOULTON, DAVID, *The UVF, 1966–73: An Anatomy of Loyalist Rebellion*. Dublin: Gill and Macmillan, 1973.

BOWMAN, JOHN, *De Valera and the Ulster Question, 1917–1973*. Oxford: Clarendon Press, 1982.

BOYLE, KEVIN, TOM HADDEN, AND PADDY HILLYARD, *Law and State: The Case of Northern Ireland*. London: Martin Robertson, 1975.

BROMAGE, MARY, *Churchill and Ireland*. Notre Dame, IN.: Notre Dame Press, 1964.

BUCKLAND, PATRICK, *A History of Northern Ireland*. Dublin: Gill and Macmillan, 1981.

BUDGE, IAN, AND CORNELIUS O'LEARY, *Belfast: Approach to Crisis. A Study of Belfast Politics, 1613–1970*. London: Macmillan, 1973.

CANNING, PAUL, *British Policy towards Ireland, 1921–1941*. Oxford: Clarendon Press, 1985.

CARROLL, JOSEPH T., *Ireland in the War Years, 1939–1945*. Dublin: Gill and Macmillan, 1976.

CARTER, CAROLLE J., *The Shamrock and the Swastika*. Palo Alto, CA.: Pacific Books, 1977.

COLLINS, MARTIN (ED.),   *Ireland after Britain*. London: Pluto Press, 1985.

COOGAN, TIMOTHY PATRICK,   *Ireland since the Rising*. New York: Praeger, 1966.

CURRAN, JOSEPH M.,   "Ireland since 1916," *Éire-Ireland*, 1 (Autumn 1966), 14–28.

———,   "The Irish Free State," *University Review*, 5 (Spring 1968).

DARBY, JOHN,   *Conflict in Northern Ireland: The Development of a Polarized Community*. New York: Barnes & Noble Books, 1976.

DE PAOR, LIAM,   *Divided Ulster*. Harmondsworth, England: Penguin, 1970.

DWYER, T. RYLE,   *De Valera's Darkest Hour, In Search of National Independence, 1919–1932*. Dublin: Mercier Press, 1982.

———,   *De Valera's Finest Hour: In Search of National Independence, 1932–1959*. Dublin: Mercier Press, 1982.

EDWARDS, OWEN DUDLEY,   *The Sins of Our Fathers: Roots of Conflict in Northern Ireland*. Dublin: Gill and Macmillan, 1970.

FANNING, RONAN,   *Independent Ireland*. Dublin: Helicon, 1983.

FARRELL, BRIAN,   *Chairman or Chief: The Role of the Taoiseach in Irish Government*. Dublin: Gill and Macmillan, 1971.

———,   *Communication and Community in Ireland*. Dublin: Mercier Press, 1984.

FENNELL, DESMOND,   *Beyond Nationalism*. Dublin: Ward River Press, 1985.

FISK, ROBERT,   *In Time of War*. Philadelphia: University of Pennsylvania Press, 1983.

FITZGERALD, GARRET,   *Towards a New Ireland*. London: Charles Knight, 1972.

GARVIN, TOM,   *The Evolution of Irish Nationalist Politics*. New York: Holmes & Meier, 1981.

HACHEY, THOMAS E.,   "Irish Republicanism Yesterday and Today," in *Ethnicity and War*, ed. Winston Van Horne. Madison: University of Wisconsin System AESCC, 1984.

———,   "The Partition of Ireland and the Ulster Dilemma," in *The Problem of Partition: Peril to World Peace*, ed. Thomas E. Hachey. Skokie, IL.: Rand McNally, 1972.

HARKNESS, D. W.,   *The Restless Dominion: The Irish Free State and the British Commonwealth of Nations, 1921–1931*. Dublin: Gill and Macmillan, 1969.

———,   "Mr. de Valera's Dominion: Ireland's Relations with Britain and the Commonwealth, 1932–38," *Journal of Commonwealth Political Studies*, 8.3 (November 1970), 206–228.

HARRIS, ROSEMARY,   *Prejudice and Tolerance in Ulster: A Study of Neighbors and Strangers in a Border Community*. Manchester: Manchester University Press, 1972.

HESLINGA, M. W.,   *The Irish Border as a Cultural Divide*. Atlantic Highlands, N.J.: Humanities Press, 1962.

HODSON, H. V.,   "Éire and British Commonwealth," *Foreign Affairs*, 16 (1938), 525–36.

JOHNSON, D. S.,   "Northern Ireland as a Problem in the Economic War, 1932–38," *Irish Historical Studies*, 22 (1980).

KEATINGE, PATRICK,   *The Formulation of Irish Foreign Policy*. Dublin: Institute of Public Administration, 1973.

———,   *A Singular Stance: Irish Neutrality in the 1980s*. Dublin: Institute of Public Administration, 1984.

KENNEDY, KIERAN A., AND BRENDAN R. DOWLING,   *Economic Growth in Ireland: The Experience since 1947*. Dublin: Gill and Macmillan, 1975.

KENNEDY, LIAM,   *Two Ulsters: A Case for Repartition*. Belfast: Kennedy, 1986.

LAFFAN, MICHAEL,   *The Partition of Ireland, 1911–1925*. Dundalk: Dundalgen Press, 1983.

LEE, JOSEPH, AND GEARÓID Ó TUATHAIGH,   *The Age of de Valera*. Dublin: Ward River Press, 1982.

LONGFORD, EARL OF, AND O'NEILL, T. P.,   *Eamon de Valera*. London: Hutchinson, 1970.

MACEOIN, GARY,   "The Irish Republican Army," *Éire-Ireland*, 9 (Summer 1974), 5.

MACMANUS, FRANCIS (ED.),   *The Years of the Great Test, 1926–1939*. Cork: Mercier Press, 1967.

MAGEE, JOHN,   *Northern Ireland: Crisis and Conflict.* London: Routledge Kegan Paul, 1974.

MANNING, MAURICE,   *The Blueshirts.* Dublin: Gill and Macmillan, 1971.

MCCAFFREY, LAWRENCE J.,   *Ireland from Colony to Nation State.* Englewood Cliffs, NJ: Prentice-Hall, 1979.

————,   "The Roots of the Irish Troubles," *America,* January 31, 1976, pp. 69–70.

MCCRACKEN, J. L.,   *Representative Government in Ireland.* London: Oxford University Press, 1958.

MCGUIRE, MARIA,   *To Take Arms: My Years with the IRA Provisionals.* New York: Viking, 1973.

MCMAHON, DEIRDRE,   "A Transient Apparition: British Policy towards the de Valera Government, 1932–35," *Irish Historical Studies,* 22 (1981).

MOODY, T. W., AND J. C. BECKETT (EDS.),   *Ulster since 1800: A Social Survey.* London: British Broadcasting Company, 1957.

MURPHY, DERVLA,   *A Place Apart.* Old Greenwich, CT.: Devin-Adair Co., 1978.

MURPHY, JOHN A.,   *Ireland in the Twentieth Century.* Dublin: Gill and Macmillan, 1975.

————,   "The New IRA, 1925–1962," in *Secret Societies in Ireland,* ed. T. Desmond Williams. New York: Barnes & Noble Books, 1973.

NEESON, EOIN,   *The Civil War in Ireland.* Cork: Mercier Press, 1966.

NELSON, SARAH,   *Ulster's Uncertain Defenders.* Belfast: Appletree Press, 1984.

NOWLAN, KEVIN B., AND T. DESMOND WILLIAMS (EDS.),   *Ireland in the War Years and After, 1939–1951.* Dublin: Gill and Macmillan, 1969.

O'BRIEN, CONOR CRUISE,   *States of Ireland.* New York: Vintage Books, 1973.

O'CARROLL, J. P., AND JOHN A. MURPHY (EDS.),   *De Valera and His Times.* Cork: Cork University Press, 1983.

O'CONNOR, SEAN,   *A Troubled Sky: Reflections on the Irish Educational Scene, 1957–1968.* Dublin: Educational Research Centre, 1986.

O'MALLEY, PADRAIG,   *The Uncivil Wars: Ireland Today.* Boston: Houghton Mifflin, 1983.

PECK, JOHN,   *Dublin from Downing Street.* Dublin: Gill and Macmillan, 1978.

PHILLIPS, WALTER A.,   *The Revolution in Ireland, 1906–1923* (2nd ed.). London: Longmans, 1926.

POWER, PAUL F.,   "The Sunningdale Strategy and the Northern Majority Consent Doctrine in Anglo-Irish Relations," *Éire-Ireland,* 12 (Spring 1977), 35–67.

RAYMOND, RAYMOND JAMES,   "The Economics of Neutrality: The United States, Great Britain and Ireland's War Economy. 1937–45," Ph.D. diss., University of Kansas, 1980.

REED, DAVID,   *Ireland: The Key to the British Revolution.* London: Larkin Publications, 1984.

ROSE, RICHARD,   *Governing without Consensus: An Irish Perspective.* London: Faber and Faber, 1971.

SAVORY, DOUGLAS,   "The Irish Republic and Neutrality in 1941," *Contemporary Review,* 196 (1959), 164–166, 221–224.

SCHMITT, DAVID E.,   *The Irony of Irish Democracy.* Lexington, MA.: Heath, 1973.

SCHUNK, THOMAS,   "A Special Relationship: Britain, Éire and the Commonwealth, 1947–1949." Ph.D. diss., Marquette University, 1986.

SHEARMAN, HUGH,   *Anglo-Irish Relations.* London: Faber and Faber, 1948.

SHORE, BERNARD,   *The Emergency: Neutral Ireland, 1939–45.* Dublin: Gill and Macmillan, 1978.

SMIDDY, T. A.,   "The Position of the Irish Free State in the British Commonwealth of Nations," in *Harris Foundation Lectures,* Chicago, 1927.

SMYLLIE, R. M.,   "Unneutral Neutral Éire," *Foreign Affairs,* 24 (January 1946), 317–326.

TIERNEY, MARK,   *Modern Ireland since 1850.* Dublin: Gill and Macmillan, 1978.

VALIULIS, MARYANN GIALANELLA,   *Almost a Rebellion: The Irish Army Mutiny of 1924.* Cork: Tower Books, 1985.

WHITE, TERENCE DE VERE,   *Kevin O'Higgins.* Tralee, Ireland: Anvil Books, 1966.

WHYTE, JOHN,   *Church and State in Modern Ireland.* New York: Barnes & Noble Books, 1971.

WILLIAMS, T. DESMOND (ED.),   *The Irish Struggle, 1916–1926.* Toronto: University of Toronto Press, 1966.

YOUNGER, CARLTON,   *Ireland's Civil War.* London: Fontana Books, 1968.

Special Topics

THE RELIGIOUS DIMENSION OF IRISH CULTURE AND POLITICS

AKENSON, DONALD, *The Church of Ireland: Ecclesiastical Reform and Revolution, 1800–1885.* New Haven, CT.: Yale University Press, 1971.

BECKETT, J. C., *The Anglo-Irish Tradition.* Ithaca, N.Y.: Cornell University Press, 1976.

BELL, GEOFFREY, *The Protestants of Ulster.* London: Pluto Press, 1976.

BOWEN, DESMOND, *Paul Cardinal Cullen and the Making of Modern Irish Catholicism.* Dublin: Gill and Macmillan, 1983.

———, *The Protestant Crusade in Ireland, 1800–70.* Montreal: McGill–Queen's University Press, 1978.

CONNOLLY, S. J., *Priests and People in Pre-Famine Ireland, 1780–1845.* New York: St. Martin's Press, 1982.

CORISH, PATRICK, *The Irish Catholic Experience: A Historical Survey.* Wilmington, DE.: Michael Glazier, 1985.

HYNES, EUGENE, "The Great Hunger and Irish Catholicism," *Societas,* 8 (Spring 1978), 137–156.

KEENAN, DESMOND J., *The Catholic Church in Nineteenth Century Ireland.* New York: Barnes & Noble Books, 1983.

KERR, DONAL A., *Peel, Priest and Politics*. Oxford: Clarendon Press, 1982.

LARKIN, EMMET, *The Historical Dimensions of Irish Catholicism*. Washington, D.C.: Catholic University Press of America, 1984.

——, *The Making of the Roman Catholic Church in Ireland, 1850–1860*. Chapel Hill: University of North Carolina Press, 1980.

——, *The Consolidation of the Roman Catholic Church in Ireland, 1860–1870*. Chapel Hill: University of North Carolina Press, 1987.

——, *The Roman Catholic Church and the Modern Irish State, 1878–1886*. Philadelphia: American Philosophical Society, 1975.

——, *The Roman Catholic Church and the Plan of Campaign, 1886–1888*. Cork: Cork University Press, 1978.

——, *The Roman Catholic Church in Ireland and the Fall of Parnell, 1888–1891*. Chapel Hill: University of North Carolina Press, 1979.

McCAFFREY, LAWRENCE J., "Irish Nationalism and Irish Catholicism: A Study in Cultural Identity," *Church History*, 42 (December 1973), 1–11.

MILLER, DAVID W., *Church, State, and Nation in Ireland, 1898–1921*. Pittsburgh: University of Pittsburgh Press, 1973.

——, *Queen's Rebels: Ulster Loyalism in Historical Perspective*. New York: Barnes & Noble Books, 1978.

O'SHEA, JAMES, *Priest, Politics and Society in Post-Famine Ireland: A Study of County Tipperary, 1850–1891*. Atlantic Highlands, N.J.: Humanities Press, 1983.

STEWART, A. T. Q., *The Narrow Ground: Aspects of Ulster, 1609–1969*. London: Faber and Faber, 1977.

TITLEY, E. BRYAN, *Church, State and the Control of Schooling in Ireland*. Montreal: McGill–Queen's University Press, 1983.

WHYTE, JOHN, *Church and State in Modern Ireland*. New York: Barnes & Noble Books, 1971.

LAND

BEW, PAUL, *Land and the National Question in Ireland, 1858–82*. Dublin: Gill and Macmillan, 1978.

CASEY, DANIEL J., AND ROBERT E. RHODES (EDS.), *Views of the Irish Peasantry, 1800–1916*. Hamden, CT.: Archon Books, 1977.

CLARK, SAM, *Social Origins of the Irish Land War*. Princeton, N.J.: Princeton University Press, 1979.

——, AND JAMES S. DONNELLY, JR. (EDS.), *Irish Peasants, Violence and Political Unrest, 1780–1914*. Madison: University of Wisconsin Press, 1983.

CROTTY, R. D., *Irish Agricultural Production: Its Volume and Structure*. Cork: Cork University Press, 1966.

DONNELLY, JAMES S., JR., *The Land and People of Nineteenth Century Cork*. London: Routledge & Kegan Paul, 1975.

——, *Landlord and Tenant in Nineteenth Century Ireland*. Dublin: Gill and Macmillan, 1973.

GEARY, LAURENCE M., *The Plan of Campaign, 1886–1891*. Cork: Cork University Press, 1987.

O'NEILL, KEVIN, *Family and Farm in Pre-Famine Ireland*. Madison: University of Wisconsin Press, 1984.

POMFRET, JOHN, *The Struggle for Land in Ireland*. Princeton, N.J.: Princeton University Press, 1930.

Solow, Barbara Lewis, *The Land Question and the Irish Economy, 1870–1903.* Cambridge, MA.: Harvard University Press, 1971.

Steele, E. D., *Irish Land and British Politics: Tenant Right and Nationality, 1865–1870.* Cambridge, England: Cambridge University Press, 1974.

Townshend, Charles, *Political Violence in Ireland: Government and Resistance since 1848.* New York: Oxford University Press, 1983.

Vaughn, W. E., *Landlords and Tenants in Ireland, 1848–1904.* Dublin: Gill and Macmillan, 1984.

LITERATURE AND IRISH CULTURAL NATIONALISM

Brown, Malcolm, *The Politics of Irish Literature from Thomas Davis to W. B. Yeats.* Seattle: University of Washington Press, 1972.

Brown, Terence, *Ireland: A Social and Cultural History, 1922–79.* Ithaca, N.Y.: Cornell University Press, 1985.

Corkery, Daniel, *The Hidden Ireland.* Dublin: Gill and Son, 1967.

——, *Synge and Anglo-Irish Literature.* Cork: Cork University Press, 1955.

Comerford, R. V., *Charles Kickham (1828–82): A Study in Irish Nationalism and Literature.* Dublin: Wolfhound Press, 1979.

Dawe, Gerald, and Edna Longley (eds.), *Across a Roaring Hill: The Protestant Imagination in Modern Ireland.* Dover, N.H.: Blackstaff Press, 1985.

Deane, Seamus, Seamus Heaney, Richard Kearney, Declan Kiberd, and Tom Paulin, *Ireland's Field Day.* Notre Dame, IN.: University of Notre Dame Press, 1986.

Fallis, Richard, *The Irish Renaissance.* Syracuse, N.Y.: Syracuse University Press, 1977.

Flanagan, Thomas, *The Irish Novelists, 1800–1850.* New York: Columbia University Press, 1959.

Harmon, Maurice, "By Memory Inspired: Themes and Forces in Recent Irish Writing," *Éire-Ireland,* 8 (Summer 1973), 3–19.

Howarth, Herbert, *The Irish Writers: Literature and Nationalism, 1880–1940.* New York: Hill & Wang, 1959.

Hutchinson, John, *The Dynamics of Cultural Nationalism: The Gaelic Revival and the Creation of the Irish Nation State,* London: Allen and Unwein, 1987.

Kelleher, John, "Irish Literature Today," *Atlantic,* March 1945, pp. 70–76.

Kiely, Benedict, *Modern Irish Fiction.* Dublin: Golden Eagle Books, 1950.

Larkin, Emmet, "A Reconsideration: Daniel Corkery and His Ideas on Irish Cultural Nationalism," *Éire-Ireland,* 8 (Spring 1973), 42–51.

Lyons, F. S. L., *Culture and Anarchy in Ireland, 1890–1939.* Oxford: Clarendon Press, 1979.

Loftus, Richard J., *Nationalism in Modern Anglo-Irish Poetry.* Madison: University of Wisconsin Press, 1964.

Martin, Augustine, "Literature and Society," in *Ireland in the War Years and After, 1939–51,* ed. Kevin B. Nowlan and T. Desmond Williams. Dublin: Gill and Macmillan, 1969.

McCaffrey, Lawrence J., "Daniel Corkery and Irish Cultural Nationalism," *Éire-Ireland,* 8 (Spring 1973), 35–41.

——, "Trends in Post-revolutionary Irish Literature," *College English,* 18 (October 1956), 26–30.

O'CONNOR, FRANK, *A Short History of Irish Literature*. New York: Capricorn Books, 1967.

O'CONNOR, ULICK, *All the Olympians: A Biographical Portrait of the Irish Literary Renaissance*. New York: Atheneum, 1987.

Ó TUAMA, SEAN (ED.), *The Gaelic League Idea*. Cork: Cork University Press, 1972.

THOMPSON, WILLIAM IRWIN, *The Imagination of an Insurrection: Dublin, Easter 1916*. New York: Harper & Row, 1967.

THUENTE, MARY HELEN, *W. B. Yeats and Irish Folklore*. New York: Barnes & Noble Books, 1981.

THE AMERICAN DIMENSION

ADAMS, WILLIAM FORBES, *Ireland and Irish Emigration to the New World from 1815 to the Famine*. New York: Russell & Russell, 1967.

AKENSON, DONALD, *The United States and Ireland*. Cambridge, MA.: Harvard University Press, 1973.

BROWN, THOMAS N., *Irish-American Nationalism*. Philadelphia: Lippincott, 1966.

CARROLL, FRANCIS M., *American Opinion and the Irish Question, 1910–23*. New York: St. Martin's Press, 1978.

CLARK, DENNIS, *Hibernia America: The Irish and Regional Cultures*. New York: Greenwood Press, 1986.

COLEMAN, TERRY, *Going to America*. New York: Pantheon, 1972.

CRONIN, SEAN, *Washington's Irish Policy, 1916–1986: Independence, Partition, Neutrality*. Dublin: Anvil Books, 1986.

CUDDY, JOSEPH EDWARD, *Irish America and National Isolationism, 1914–1920*. New York: Arno Press, 1976.

D'ARCY, WILLIAM, *The Fenian Movement in the United States, 1858–1886*. Washington, D.C.: Catholic University of America Press, 1947.

DOYLE, DAVID, *Irish-Americans, Native Rights, and National Empires: The Structure, Divisions, and Attitudes of the Catholic Minority in the Age of Expansion, 1890–1901*. New York: Arno Press, 1976.

DRUDY, P. J. (ED.), *The Irish in America: Emigration, Assimilation and Impact*. New York: Cambridge University Press, 1985.

FUNCHION, MICHAEL, *Chicago's Irish Nationalists, 1881–1890*. New York: Arno Press, 1976.

GREELEY, ANDREW, *The Irish-Americans: The Rise to Money and Power*. New York: Harper & Row, 1981.

HERNON, JOSEPH M., JR., *Celts, Catholics, and Copperheads: Ireland Views the American Civil War*. Columbus: Ohio State University Press, 1968.

HOLLAND, JACK, *The American Connection: U.S. Guns, Money, and Influence in Northern Ireland*. New York: Viking, 1987.

JENKINS, BRIAN, *Fenians and Anglo-American Relations during Reconstruction*. Ithaca, N.Y.: Cornell University Press, 1969.

MCCAFFREY, LAWRENCE J., *The Irish Diaspora in America*. Washington, D.C.: Catholic University of America Press, 1984.

——— (ED.), *Irish Nationalism and the American Contribution*. New York: Arno Press, 1976.

———, ELLEN SKERRETT, MICHAEL FUNCHION, AND CHARLES FANNING, *The Irish in Chicago*. Champaign: University of Illinois Press, 1987.

MCMANAMIN, FRANCIS G., *The American Years of John Boyle O'Reilly, 1870–1890*. New York: Arno Press, 1976.

MILLER, KERBY A., *Emigrants and Exiles: Ireland and the Irish Exodus to North America.* New York: Oxford University Press, 1985.

O'GRADY, JOSEPH PATRICK, *Irish-Americans and Anglo-American Relations, 1880–1888.* New York: Arno Press, 1976.

RODCHECKO, JAMES PAUL, *Patrick Ford and His Search for America: A Case Study of Irish-American Journalism.* New York: Arno Press, 1976.

SCHRIER, ARNOLD, *Ireland and the American Emigration, 1850–1900.* Minneapolis: University of Minnesota Press, 1956.

SHANNON, WILLIAM V., *The American Irish.* New York: Macmillan, 1963.

———, "The Lasting Hurrah," *New York Times Magazine*, March 14, 1976.

TARPEY, MARIE VERONICA, *The Role of Joseph McGarrity in the Struggle for Irish Independence.* New York: Arno Press, 1976.

WARD, ALAN J., *Ireland and Anglo-American Relations, 1880–1921.* London: Weidenfeld and Nicolson, 1969.

WITTKE, CARL, *The Irish in America.* New York: Russell and Russell, 1970.

Selected Titles Relating to the Irish Experience Published Since 1987

GENERAL STUDIES AND HISTORICAL MONOGRAPHS

AKENSON, DONALD HARMON, *Small Differences: Irish Catholics and Irish Protestants, 1815–1922: An International Perspective*. Montreal: McGill-Queens University Press, 1988.

ARDAGH, JOHN, *Ireland and the Irish*. London: Hamish Hamilton, 1994.

BARTON, BRIAN, *Brookeborough: The Making of a Prime Minister*. Belfast: Institute of Irish Studies, Queens University of Belfast, 1989.

BOYCE, D. G., *The Irish Question and English Politics, 1868–1986*. London: Macmillan, 1988.

BOYCE, D. G., R. Eccleshall, and V. Geogheagan (EDS.), *Political Thought in Ireland since the Seventeenth Century*. London: Routledge, 1993.

BOYCE, D. GEORGE, *Nineteenth Century: The Search for Stability* (New Gill History of Ireland). Dublin: Gill and Macmillan, 1991.

BOYLE, JOHN W., *The Irish Labor Movement in the Nineteenth Century*. Washington, D.C.: Catholic University of America Press, 1988.

BOYLE, KEVIN, AND TOM HADDEN, *Northern Ireland: The Choice*. New York: Penguin Press, 1994.

BRADY, CIARAN (ED.), *Ideology and the Historians* (Historical Studies XVII). Gigginstown: Lilliput Press, 1992.

BROOKE, PETER, *Ulster Presbyterianism: The Historical Perspective, 1610–1970.* New York: St. Martin's Press, 1987.

BROWN, TERENCE, *The Whole Protestant Community: The Making of a Historical Myth.* Derry: Field Day Pamphlet 7, 1985.

BRUCE, STEVE, *The Edge of the Union: The Ulster Loyalist Political Vision.* Oxford: Oxford University Press, 1994.

———, *God Save Ulster: Politics and Paisleyism.* Oxford: Clarendon Press, 1986.

BURNS, ROBERT E., *Irish Parliamentary Politics in the Eighteenth Century* (Vol. I, 1714–1734, and Vol. II, 1734–1760). Washington, D.C.: Catholic University of America Press, 1989, 1990.

CANNY, NICHOLAS, *From Reformation to Restoration: Ireland, 1534–1660.* Dublin: Helicon Ltd., 1987.

CARLSON, JULIA (ED.), *Banned in Ireland: Censorship and the Irish Writer.* Athens: University of Georgia Press, 1990.

CLANCY, PATRICK, ET AL., *Ireland: A Sociological Profile.* Dublin: Institute of Public Administration, 1986.

CONNOLLY, S. J., *Religion, Law, and Power: The Making of Protestant Ireland, 1660–1760.* Oxford: Clarendon Press, 1992.

COOGAN, TIM PAT, *De Valera: Long Fellow, Long Shadow.* London: Hutchinson, 1993.

———, *Disillusioned Decades: Ireland, 1966–1987.* Dublin: Gill and Macmillan, 1987.

CULLEN, LOUIS, *The Hidden Ireland: Reassessment of a Concept.* Gigginstown: Lilliput Press, 1988.

CURTIN, NANCY J., *The United Irishmen: Popular Politics in Ulster and Dublin, 1791–1798.* Oxford: Clarendon Press, 1994.

DALY, MARY E., *Industrial Development and Irish National Identity, 1922–1939.* Syracuse, N.Y.: Syracuse University Press, 1992.

DAVIES, R. R., *Domination and Conquest: The Experience of Ireland, Scotland, and Wales, 1100–1300.* Cambridge: Cambridge University Press, 1990.

DAVIS, RICHARD, *Young Ireland Movement.* Dublin: Gill and Macmillan, 1988.

DICKSON, DAVID, *New Foundations: Ireland 1660–1800.* Dublin: Helicon; Longwood, 1987.

DICKSON, DAVID, ET AL. (EDS.), *The Gorgeous Mask: Dublin, 1650–1850.* Dublin: Trinity History Workshop, 1987.

ELLIOTT, MARIANNE, *Wolfe Tone: Prophet of Irish Independence.* New Haven, Conn.: Yale University Press, 1989.

ENGLISH, RICHARD, *Radicals and the Republic: Social Republicanism in the Irish Free State, 1925–1937.* Oxford: Oxford University Press, 1994.

ERIE, STEVEN P., *Rainbow's End: Irish-Americans and the Dilemma of Urban Machine Politics, 1840–1895.* Berkeley: University of California Press, 1988.

FARRELL, SEAN, *Patrick Pearse and the Politics of Redemption: The Mind of the Easter Rising, 1916.* Washington, D.C.: Catholic University of America Press, 1994.

FOSTER, R. F., *Modern Ireland, 1600–1972.* New York: Viking Press, 1988.

———, *Paddy and Mr. Punch: Connections in Irish and English History.* London: Penguin Press, 1993.

GARVIN, TOM, *Nationalist Revolutionaries in Ireland, 1858–1928.* Oxford: Clarendon Press, 1987.

HACHEY, THOMAS E., AND LAWRENCE J. MCCAFFREY (EDS.), *Perspectives on Irish Nationalism.* Lexington: University Press of Kentucky, 1989.

HARRIS, MARY, *The Catholic Church and the Foundation of the Northern Irish State.* Cork: Cork University Press, 1993.

HOPKINSON, MICHAEL,   *Green Against Green: The Irish Civil War.* Dublin: Gill and Macmillan, 1988.

JENKINS, BRIAN,   *Era of Emancipation: British Government of Ireland, 1812–1830.* Montreal: McGill-Queens University Press, 1988.

KEARNEY, RICHARD,   *Migrations: The Irish at Home and Abroad.* Belfast: Wolfhound Press, 1991.

KEE, ROBERT,   *The Laurel and the Ivy: The Story of Charles Stewart Parnell and Irish Nationalism.* New York: Viking Press, 1994.

KENNEDY, DENNIS,   *The Widening Gulf: Northern Attitudes to the Independent Irish State, 1919–1949.* Belfast: Blackstaff Press, 1988.

KENNEDY, KIERNAN A., THOMAS GIBLIN, AND DEIRDRE MCHUGH,   *The Economic Development of Ireland in the Twentieth Century.* London: Routledge, 1988.

KEOGH, DAIRE,   *The French Disease: The Catholic Church and Irish Radicalism, 1790–1800.* Dublin: Four Courts Press, 1993.

KEOGH, DERMOT,   *Ireland and Europe, 1919–1948.* Dublin: Gill and Macmillan, 1988.

KILROY, PHIL,   *Protestant Dissent and Controversy in Ireland, 1660–1714.* Cork: Cork University Press, 1994.

LARKIN, EMMET,   *The Consolidation of the Roman Catholic Church in Ireland, 1860–1870.* Chapel Hill: University of North Carolina Press, 1987.

———,   *The Roman Catholic Church and the Home Rule Movement in Ireland, 1870–1874.* Chapel Hill: University of North Carolina Press, 1990.

LEE, J. J.,   *Ireland, 1912–1985: Politics and Society.* Cambridge: Cambridge University Press, 1990.

LENNON, COLM,   *Sixteenth Century Ireland: The Incomplete Conquest.* Dublin: Gill and Macmillan, 1994.

LUDDY, MARIA, AND CLIONA MURPHY (EDS.),   *Women Surviving: Studies in Irish Women's History in the Nineteenth and Twentieth Centuries.* Dublin: Poolbeg Press, 1990.

MACDONAGH, OLIVER,   *The Emancipationist: Daniel O'Connell, 1830–1847.* London: Weidenfeld and Nicholson, 1989.

———,   *The Hereditary Bondsman: Daniel O'Connell, 1775–1830.* London: Weidenfeld and Nicholson, 1988.

MANSERGH, NICHOLAS,   *The Unresolved Question.* New Haven, Conn.: Yale University Press, 1990.

MCCAFFREY, LAWRENCE J.,   *The Irish Question: Two Centuries of Controversy.* Lexington: University Press of Kentucky, 1995.

———,   *Textures of Irish America.* Syracuse, N.Y.: Syracuse University Press, 1992.

MCGUIRE, [N. A.] (ED.),   *Kings in Conflict: The Revolutionary War in Ireland and Its Aftermath, 1689–1750* (Dufour Editions). Belfast: Blackstaff Press, 1990.

MITCHELL, ARTHUR,   *Revolutionary Government in Ireland: Dail Eireann, 1919–1922.* Dublin: Gill and Macmillan, 1995.

MURPHY, CLIONA,   *The Women's Suffrage Movement and Irish Society in the Early Twentieth Century.* Philadelphia: Temple University Press, 1989.

NI DHONNCHADHA, MAIRIN, AND THEO DORGAN (EDS.),   *Revising the Rising.* Derry: Field Day, 1991.

NOLAN, JANET A.   *Ourselves Alone: Women's Emigration from Ireland, 1885–1920.* Lexington: University Press of Kentucky, 1989.

O'BRIEN, CONOR CRUISE,   *Ancestral Voices: Religion and Nationalism in Ireland.* Dublin: Poolbeg Press, 1994.

O'CONNOR, EMMET,   *The Labour History of Ireland, 1824–1960.* Dublin: Gill and Macmillan, 1993.

O'GRADA, CORMAC,   *Ireland Before and After the Famine: Explorations in Economic History, 1800–1925.* Manchester: Manchester University Press, 1988.

O'HALPIN, EUNAN, *The Decline of the Union: British Government in Ireland, 1892–1920.* Syracuse, N.Y.: Syracuse University Press, 1987.

O'LEARY, BRENDAN, AND JOHN MCGARRY, *The Politics of Antagonism: Understanding Northern Ireland.* Atlantic Highlands, N.J.: Athlone Press, 1993.

O'MALLEY, PADRAIG, *Biting at the Grave: The Irish Hunger Strikers and the Politics of Despair.* Boston: Beacon Press, 1990.

RAFFERTY, OLIVER P., *Catholicism in Ulster: An Interpretive History.* Columbia: University of South Carolina Press, 1994.

RICHTER, MICHAEL, *Medieval Ireland: The Enduring Tradition.* New York: St. Martin's Press, 1988.

SALMON, TREVOR, *Unneutral Ireland.* Oxford: Clarendon Press, 1989.

SHANNON, CATHERINE B., *Arthur J. Balfour and Ireland, 1874–1922.* Washington, D.C.: Catholic University of America Press, 1988.

SILVERMAN, MARILYN, AND P. H. GULLIVER (EDS.), *Approaching the Past.* New York: Columbia University Press, 1992.

TRUXES, THOMAS M., *Irish-American Trade.* Cambridge: Cambridge University Press, 1988.

VAUGHAN, W. E. (ED.), *A New History of Ireland. Vol. V: Ireland Under the Union, 1801–1870.* Oxford: Clarendon Press, 1989.

WARD, ALAN J., *The Irish Constitutional Tradition: Responsible Government and Modern Ireland.* Washington, D.C.: Catholic University of America Press, 1994.

LITERATURE

BARTLETT, THOMAS, GEAROID O. TUATHAIGH, RIAINA O'DWYER, AND CHRIS CURRAN (EDS.), *Irish Studies: A General Introduction.* Dublin: Gill and Macmillan, 1988.

BOLGER, DERMOT (ED.), *The Vintage Book of Contemporary Irish Fiction.* New York: Vintage Books, 1994.

CAIRNS, DAVID, AND SHAUN RICHARDS, *Writing Ireland: Catholicism, Nationalism, and Culture.* Manchester: Manchester University Press, 1988.

CASEY, DANIEL J., AND RHODES, ROBERT E. (EDS.), *Modern Irish-American Fiction.* Syracuse, N.Y.: Syracuse University Press, 1989.

DEANE, SEAMUS (ED.), *The Field Day Anthology of Irish Writing* (3 vols.). New York: Norton, 1991.

FAIRHALL, JAMES, *Joyce and the Question of History.* Cambridge: Cambridge University Press, 1993.

FANNING, CHARLES, *The Irish Voice in America: Irish-American Fiction from the 1760s to the 1980s.* Lexington: University Press of Kentucky, 1990.

FOSTER, JOHN WILSON, *Colonial Consequences: Essays in Irish Literature and Culture.* Gigginstown: Lilliput Press, 1991.

HOLROYD, MICHAEL, *Bernard Shaw. Volume 1: The Search for Love.* London: Chatto and Windus, 1988.

————, *Bernard Shaw. Volume 3: The Lure of Fantasy, 1918–1950.* New York: Random House, 1991.

JEFFARES, A. NORMAN, *W. B. Yeats: A New Biography.* London: Hutchinson, 1988.

KENNEDY, BRIAN P., *Dreams and Responsibilities: The State of the Arts in Independent Ireland.* Dublin: The Arts Council of Ireland, 1992.

KRAUSE, DAVID (ED.), *The Letters of Sean O'Casey* (Vol. III). Washington, D.C.: Catholic University of America Press, 1989.

LLOYD, DAVID, *Anomalous States: Irish Writing and the Post-Colonial Movement.* Durham, N.C.: Duke University Press, 1993.

MOYNIHAN, JULIAN,   *Anglo-Irish: The Literary Imagination in a Hyphenated Culture.* Princeton: Princeton University Press, 1995.

O'DONNELL, SHAUN,   *Imagining Boston: A Literary Landscape.* Boston: Beacon Press, 1990.

SLOAN, BARRY,   *The Pioneers of Anglo-Irish Fiction, 1800–1850.* New York: Barnes and Noble, 1987.

STANSFIELD, PAUL SCOTT,   *Yeats and Politics in the 1930s.* New York: St. Martin's Press, 1988.

THUENTE, MARY HELEN,   *The Harp Re-Strung: The United Irishmen and the Rise of Irish Literary Nationalism.* Syracuse, N.Y.: Syracuse University Press, 1994.

Index

About the Authors

Thomas E. Hachey is currently dean of the College of Arts and Sciences and professor of Anglo-Irish history at Marquette University, Milwaukee, Wisconsin. The author and/or editor of seven books and several dozen articles on various aspects of British and Irish history, Hachey has spent summers and sabbaticals researching and teaching in Ireland and Britain. He is a past president of the American Conference for Irish Studies.

Joseph M. Hernon, Jr., recently retired as professor of Irish history at the University of Massachusetts, Amherst. The author of several books and fourteen articles, Professor Hernon is actively engaged in research and writing, and he returns frequently to Trinity College, Dublin, where he first began his career as a graduate student.

Lawrence J. McCaffrey is professor emeritus of history at Loyola University of Chicago. The author and/or editor of ten books and a long list of articles in American and Irish scholarly journals, Professor McCaffrey is also a past president of the American Conference for Irish Studies. He taught Irish history for a number of summers at the School of Irish Studies, Dublin, and at the Irish Studies Summer School, University College, Cork.

DATE DUE

JAN 6	
DEC 1 3 P.M.	
OCT 1 6 2006	
GAYLORD	PRINTED IN U.S.A.